Praise for Arlie Russell Hochschild's *Strangers in Their Own Land*

"Masterly." —Atul Gawande, *The New Yorker*

"Humble but important." —David Brooks, *The New York Times*

"*Strangers in Their Own Land* is extraordinary for its consistent empathy and the attention it pays to the emotional terrain of politics. It is billed as a book for this moment, but it will endure." —Gabriel Thompson, *Newsday*

"Hochschild moves beyond the truism that less affluent voters who support small government and tax cuts are voting against their own economic interest. . . . *Strangers* overturns redneck caricatures to reveal people whose dignity is too often dismissed." —Dotun Akintoye, *O, the Oprah Magazine*

"We are indebted to Hochschild for her patience, intelligence, and generosity of spirit." —Theo Anderson, *In These Times*

"Exemplary . . . It is the clearest narrative exposition yet of the social basis of the Trump backlash and of right-wing populism generally." —Robert Kuttner, *The American Prospect*

"Arlie Russell Hochschild's *Strangers in Their Own Land* will certainly be among the most timely of books in this moment of seeming near apocalypse. . . . Remarkable." —Sean McCann, *Los Angeles Review of Books*

"Hochschild is fascinated by how people make sense of their lives. . . . These attentive, detailed portraits . . . reveal a gulf between Hochschild's 'strangers in their own land' and a new elite." —Jedediah Purdy, *The New Republic*

"*Strangers in Their Own Land* . . . provides great perspective on how some voters feel alienated and disconnected." —Mitch Landrieu, mayor of New Orleans, *Politico*

"Hochschild comes to know people—and her own nation—better than they know themselves." —Heather Mallick, *The Toronto Star*

Arlie Russell Hochschild is the author of nine books, including *The Second Shift*, *The Time Bind*, *The Managed Heart*, *The Outsourced Self*, and a children's book, *Coleen the Question Girl*. Four of her books have been named as *New York Times* Notable Books of the Year. Her work has appeared in sixteen languages, and *Strangers in Their Own Land* has been translated into seven. Two plays have been based on her work. The winner of the Ulysses Medal as well as Guggenheim, Mellon, Fulbright, and Sloan grants, she lives in Berkeley, California, with her husband, the writer Adam Hochschild.

ALSO BY ARLIE RUSSELL HOCHSCHILD

STRANGERS
IN THEIR
OWN LAND

ANGER AND MOURNING ON THE AMERICAN RIGHT

Arlie Russell Hochschild

THE NEW PRESS

NEW YORK
LONDON

Requests for permission to reproduce selections from this book should be mailed to:
Permissions Department, The New Press, 120 Wall Street, 31st floor, New York, NY 10005.

First published in the United States by The New Press, New York, 2016
This paperback edition published by The New Press, 2018

Distributed by Two Rivers Distribution

ISBN 978-1-62097-225-0 (hc)
ISBN 978-1-62097-349-3 (pbk)
ISBN 978-1-62097-398-1 (e-book)
CIP data is available

The New Press publishes books that promote and enrich public discussion and understanding of
the issues vital to our democracy and to a more equitable world. These books are made possible
by the enthusiasm of our readers; the support of a committed group of donors, large and small;
the collaboration of our many partners in the independent media and the not-for-profit sector;
booksellers, who often hand-sell New Press books; librarians; and above all by our authors.

www.thenewpress.com

Composition by dix!
This book was set in Fairfield LH

Printed in the United States of America

2 4 6 8 10 9 7 5 3 1

For
Harold and Annette Areno

And for
Willie, Wilma, Marylee, Mike T., Clara, and the General

Contents

CONTENTS

Preface

When I began this research five years ago, I was becoming alarmed at the increasingly hostile split in our nation between two political camps. To many on the left, the Republican Party and Fox News seemed intent on dismantling much of the federal government, cutting help to the poor, and increasing the power and money of an already powerful and rich top 1 percent. To many on the right, that government itself was a power-amassing elite, creating bogus causes to increase its control and handing out easy money in return for loyal Democratic votes. Since that time both parties have split their seams and Donald Trump has burst onto the scene, quickening the pulse of American political life. I had some understanding of the liberal left camp, I thought, but what was happening on the right?

Most people who ask this question come at it from a political perspective. And while I have my views too, as a sociologist I had a keen interest in how life *feels* to people on the right—that is, in the emotion that underlies politics. To understand their emotions, I had to imagine myself into their shoes. Trying this, I came upon their "deep story," a narrative *as felt*.

The subject of politics was a big departure for me but my close-up approach was not. In a previous book, *The Second Shift*, I focused on the abiding question of how parents guard care and time for life at home when both work outside it. I found myself sitting on kitchen floors in the homes of working families, watching to see which parent a child called for, which parent answered the phone, the relative gratitude each partner felt to the other.

In search of a family-friendly workplace, I hung out in parking lots outside industrial plants and corporate headquarters to observe the hour when weary workers headed home (*The Time Bind*) and explored workers' fantasies of the vacations they'd go on, the guitar they would learn, "if only they had time." I conducted in-depth interviews with Filipina nannies (*Global Woman*) and, in a small village in Gujarat, India, interviewed commercial surrogate mothers who carry the genetic babies of Western clients (*The Outsourced Self*). All this work led me to believe strongly in paid parental leave for working parents of newborns and adoptive babies—a policy offered by all the world's major industrial nations except the United States. Now that most American children live in homes in which all adults work, the idea of paid parental leave seemed to me highly welcome, humane, overdue. But this ideal has come slam up against a new truth—many on the right oppose the very idea of government help for working families. In fact, apart from the military, they don't want much government at all. Other ideals—strengthening environmental protection, averting global warming, ending homelessness—face the same firmly closed door. If we want government help in achieving any of these goals, I realized, we need to understand those who see government more as problem than solution. And so it was that I began my journey to the heart of the American right.

Already in the late 1960s, sensing a split in American culture, my husband Adam and I set off to live for a month in Kings Kauai Garden Apartments—complete with jungle bird and beast sound effects piped into a common jungle decorated patio—in Santa Ana, California, to try to get to know members of the John Birch Society, an earlier right-wing precursor to the Tea Party. We attended meetings of the society and talked to as many people as we could. Many members we met had grown up in small towns in the Midwest and felt deeply disoriented in California's anomic suburbs, an unease they transformed into a belief that American society was at risk of being taken over by communists. Looking around, we could well understand why they felt "taken over"—in a few years, entire orange groves had disappeared into parking lots and shopping malls, a case of wildly unplanned urban sprawl. We too felt taken over by something, but it wasn't communism.

I have lived most of my life in the progressive camp but in recent years I began to want to better understand those on the right. How did they come to hold their views? Could we make common cause on some issues? These questions led me to drive, one day, from plant to plant in the bleak industrial outskirts of Lake Charles, Louisiana, with Sharon Galicia, a warm, petite, white single mother, a blond beauty, on her rounds selling medical insurance. Unfazed by a deafening buzz saw cutting vast sheets of steel, she bantered with workmen, their protective gear lifted to their brows, their arms folded. She was an appealing and persuasive fast-talker. ("What if you have an accident, can't pay bills or can't wait a month for your insurance to kick in? We insure you within twenty-four hours.") As they reached for a pen to sign up, Sharon talked to them about deer hunting, about the amount of alligator meat in boudin—a beloved spicy Louisiana sausage—and about the latest LSU Tigers game.

As her story unfolded while we drove between plants, Sharon recounted how her dad, a taciturn plant worker, had divorced her troubled mother, remarried, and moved into a trailer a thirty-minute drive away, all without telling her brother or her. I left alive with questions. What had happened to her father? How had the fate of his marriage affected her as a little girl, then as a wife and now as a single mother? What were the lives of the young men she talked to? Why was this bright, thoughtful, determined young woman—one who could have benefited from paid parental leave—an enthusiastic member of the Tea Party, to whom the idea was unthinkable?

I thanked Sharon directly, of course, for allowing me to follow her in her rounds, but later in my mind I thanked her again for her gift of trust and outreach. And after a while it occurred to me that the kind of connection she offered me was more precious than I'd first imagined. It built the scaffolding of an empathy bridge. We, on both sides, wrongly imagine that empathy with the "other" side brings an end to clearheaded analysis when, in truth, it's on the other side of that bridge that the most important analysis can begin.

The English language doesn't give us many words to describe the feeling of reaching out to someone from another world, and of *having that interest welcomed*. Something of its own kind, mutual, is created. What a gift. Gratitude, awe, appreciation; for me, all those words apply and I don't know which to use. But I think we need a special word, and should hold a place of honor for it, so as to restore what might be a missing key on the English-speaking world's cultural piano. Our polarization, and the increasing reality that we simply don't know each other, makes it too easy to settle for dislike and contempt.

I first experienced reaching out and being reached out to as the child of a Foreign Service officer. In my child's mind, I had been given a personal mission, parallel to my father's, to befriend the people of all the foreign countries my father's job took us to. I was instructed to reach out, I imagined, to people who spoke, dressed, walked, looked, and worshipped differently than we did. Had my father really asked me to do this? I don't think so. Why do it? I had no idea. That understanding came later. Curiously, I felt that same gratitude for connection when, many decades later, I drove from plant to plant with Sharon, and when I talked with the many others I've met in the course of researching this book. I felt I was in a foreign country again, only this time it was my own.

STRANGERS
IN THEIR
OWN LAND

PART ONE

The Great Paradox

1

Traveling to the Heart

Along the clay road, Mike's red truck cuts slowly between tall rows of sugarcane, sassy, silvery tassels waving in the October sun, extending across an alluvial plain as far as the eye can see. We are on the grounds of the Armelise Plantation, as it was once called. A few miles east lies the mighty Mississippi River, pressing the soils and waste of the Midwest southward, past New Orleans, into the Gulf of Mexico. "We used to walk barefoot between the rows," Mike says. A tall, kindly white man of sixty-four, Mike removes his sunglasses to study an area of the sugarcane, and comes to a near stop. He points his arm out the truck window to the far left, "My grandma would have lived over . . . *there*." Moving his arm rightward, he adds, "My great uncle Tain's carpentry shop was about . . . *there*." Nearby was the home of another great uncle Henry, a mechanic nicknamed "Pook." A man called "Pirogue" ran the blacksmith shop where Mike and a friend hunted scraps of metal that shone, through his boyhood eyes, "like gold." His grandfather Bill oversaw the cane fields. Miss Ernestine's, Mike continued, was to the side of . . . *that*. A slim black woman, hair in a white bandana, Mike recalls, "She loved to cook raccoon and opossum for her gumbo, and we brought her what we had from a day's hunt, and Choupique fish too. I can hear her calling out the window when her husband couldn't start their car, 'Something's *ailing* that car.'" Then Mike points to what he remembers of a dirt driveway to his own childhood home. "It was a shotgun house," he muses. "You could aim right through it. But it held the nine of us okay." The house had been renovated slave quarters on the Armelise Plantation and Mike's father had been a plumber who serviced homes on and off it. Looking out the window of the truck, it's clear that Mike and I see different things. Mike sees a busy, beloved, bygone world. I see a field of green.

We pull over, climb down, and walk into the nearest row. Mike cuts us a stalk, head and tails it, and whittles two sticks of the fibrous sugarcane. We chew it and suck the sweetness from it. Back in the truck, Mike continues his reverie about the tiny bygone settlement of Banderville, finally dismantled only in the 1970s. About three quarters had been black and a quarter white, and they had lived, as he recalls it, in close, unequal, harmony. Mike had passed his boyhood in an era of sugar, cotton, and mule-drawn plows and his adulthood in the era of oil. As a teenager earning money over the summer for college, he had laid wooden boards through mosquito-infested bayous to set up oil-drill platforms. As a grown, college-educated man, he had trained himself as an "estimator"—calculating the size, strength, and cost of materials needed to construct large platforms that held oil-drilling rigs in the Gulf, and to create the giant white spherical tanks that stored vast quantities of chemicals and oil. "When I was a kid, you stuck a thumb out by the side of the road, you got a ride. Or if you had a car, you gave a ride. If someone was hungry, you fed him. You had community. You know what's undercut all that?" He pauses. "Big government."

We climb back in his red truck, take a swig of water (he has brought plastic bottles for us both), and continue edging forward through the cane as our conversation shifts to politics. "Most folks around here are Cajun, Catholic, conservative," he explains, adding with gusto, "I'm for the Tea Party!"

I'd first seen Mike Schaff months earlier standing at the microphone at an environmental rally on the steps of the Louisiana state capital in Baton Rouge, his voice cracking with emotion. He had been a victim of one of the strangest, literally earth-shaking environmental disasters in the nation, one that robbed him of his home and community—a sinkhole that devoured hundred-foot-tall trees and turned forty acres of swamp upside down, as I shall describe. That raised a big question in my mind. The disaster had been caused by a lightly regulated drilling company. But as a Tea Party advocate, Mike had hailed government deregulation of all sorts, as well as drastic cuts in government spending—including that for environmental protection. How could he be both near tears to recall his lost home and also call for a world stripped of most government beyond the military and hurricane relief? I was puzzled. I sensed a wall between us.

Empathy Walls

You might say I'd come to Louisiana with an interest in walls. Not visible, physical walls such as those separating Catholics from Protestants in Belfast, Americans from Mexicans on the Texas border, or, once, residents of East and West Berlin. It was empathy walls that interested me. An empathy wall is an obstacle to deep understanding of another person, one that can make us feel indifferent or even hostile to those who hold different beliefs or whose childhood is rooted in different circumstances. In a period of political tumult, we grasp for quick certainties. We shoehorn new information into ways we already think. We settle for knowing our opposite numbers from the outside. But is it possible, without changing our beliefs, to know others from the inside, to see reality through their eyes, to understand the links between life, feeling, and politics; that is, to cross the empathy wall? I thought it was.

I'd asked Mike Schaff to show me where he'd grown up because I wanted to understand, if I could, how he saw the world. By way of introduction, I'd told him, "I'm from Berkeley, California, a sociologist, and I am trying to understand the deepening divide in our country. So I'm trying to get out of my political bubble and get to know people in yours." Mike nodded at the word "divide," then quipped, "Berkeley? So y'all must be *communist!*" He grinned as if to say, "We Cajuns can laugh, hope you can."

He wasn't making it hard. A tall, strongly built man in tan-rimmed glasses, he spoke succinctly, in a low near mumble, and was given both to soulful, sometimes self-deprecating, reflection and stalwart Facebook proclamations. Explaining his background, he said, "My mom was Cajun and my dad was German. We Cajuns call ourselves coon asses. So since I was half Cajun, and half German, my mom called me half-ass." We laughed. Mike was one of seven children his dad had raised on a plumber's wage. "We didn't know we were poor," he said, a refrain I would hear often among those I came to know on the far right, speaking of their own or their parents' childhoods. Mike had an engineer's eye, a sportsman's love of fish and game, and a naturalist's ear for the call of a tree frog. I didn't know any members of the Tea Party, not to really talk to, and he didn't know many people like me. "I'm pro-life, pro-gun, pro-freedom to live our own lives as we see fit so long as we don't hurt others. And I'm anti–big government," Mike said. "Our government is way too big, too greedy, too incompetent, too bought, and it's not ours anymore. We need to get back to our local communities, like we had at Armelise. Honestly, we'd be better off."

Not only have the country's two main political parties split further apart on such issues, but political feeling also runs deeper than it did in the past. In 1960, when a survey asked American adults whether it would "disturb" them if their child married a member of the other political party, no more than 5 percent of either party answered "yes." But in 2010, 33 percent of Democrats and 40 percent of Republicans answered "yes." In fact, *partyism,* as some call it, now beats race as the source of divisive prejudice.

When Americans moved in the past, they left in search of better jobs, cheaper housing, or milder weather. But according to *The Big Sort: Why the Clustering of Like-Minded Americans Is Tearing Us Apart* by Bill Bishop and Robert G. Cushing, when people move today, it is more often to live near others who share their views. People are segregating themselves into different emotionally toned enclaves—anger here, hopefulness and trust there. A group of libertarian Texans have bought land in the salt flats east of El Paso, named it Paulville, and reserved it for enthusiastic "freedom-loving" followers of Ron Paul. And the more that people confine themselves to like-minded company, the more extreme their views become. According to a 2014 Pew study of over 10,000 Americans, the most politically engaged on each side see those in the "other party" not just as wrong, but as "so misguided that they threaten the nation's well-being." Compared to the past, each side also increasingly gets its news from its own television channel—the right from Fox News, the left from MSNBC. And so the divide widens.

We live in what the *New Yorker* has called the "Tea Party era." Some 350,000 people are active members, but, according to another Pew poll, some 20 percent of Americans—45 million people—support it. And the divide cuts through a striking variety of issues. Ninety percent of Democrats believe in the human role in climate change, surveys find, compared with 59 percent of moderate Republicans, 38 percent of conservative Republicans, and only 29 percent of Tea Party advocates. In fact, politics is the single biggest factor determining views on climate change.

This split has widened because the right has moved right, not because the left has moved left. Republican presidents Eisenhower, Nixon, and Ford all supported the Equal Rights Amendment. In 1960, the GOP platform embraced "free collective bargaining" between management and labor. Republicans boasted of "extending the minimum wage to several million more workers" and "strengthening the unemployment insurance system and extension of its benefits." Under Dwight Eisenhower, top earners were taxed at 91 percent; in 2015, it was 40 percent. Planned Parenthood has come under serious attack from nearly all Republican presidential candidates running in 2016. Yet a founder of the organization was Peggy Goldwater, wife of the 1964 conservative Republican candidate for president Barry Goldwater. General Eisenhower called for massive investment in infrastructure, and now nearly all congressional Republicans see such a thing as frightening government overreach. Ronald Reagan raised the national debt and favored gun control, and now the Republican state legislature of Texas authorizes citizens to "open carry" loaded guns into churches and banks. Conservatives of yesterday seem moderate or liberal today.

The far right now calls for cuts in entire segments of the federal government—the Departments of Education, Energy, Commerce, and Interior, for example. In January 2015, fifty-eight House Republicans voted to abolish the Internal Revenue Service. Some Republican congressional candidates call for abolishing all public schools. In March 2015, the Republican-dominated U.S. Senate voted 51 to 49 in support of an amendment to a budget resolution to sell or give away all non-military federal lands other than national monuments and national parks. This would include forests, wildlife refuges, and wilderness areas. In 1970, not a single U.S. senator opposed the Clean Air Act. Joined by ninety-five Republican congressmen, Senator David Vitter of Louisiana, one of the most polluted states in the union, has called for the end of the Environmental Protection Agency.

And the Tea Party's turn away from government may signal a broader trend. During the depression of the 1930s, Americans turned to the federal government for aid in their economic recovery. But in response to the Great Recession of 2008, a majority of Americans turned away from it. As the political divide widens and opinions harden, the stakes have grown vastly higher. Neither ordinary citizens nor leaders are talking much "across the aisle," damaging the surprisingly delicate process of governance itself. The United States has been divided before, of course. During the Civil War, a difference in belief led to some 750,000 deaths. During the stormy 1960s, too, clashes arose over the war in Vietnam, civil rights, and women's rights. But in the end, a healthy democracy depends on a collective capacity to hash things out. And to get there, we need to figure out what's going on— especially on the more rapidly shifting and ever stronger right.

The Great Paradox

Inspired by Thomas Frank's book *What's the Matter with Kansas?*, I began my five-year journey to the heart of the American right carrying with me, as if it were a backpack, a great paradox. Back in 2004, when Frank's book appeared, there was a paradox underlying the right–left split. Since then the split has become a gulf.

Across the country, red states are poorer and have more teen mothers, more divorce, worse health, more obesity, more trauma-related deaths, more low-birth-weight babies, and lower school enrollment. On average, people in red states die five years earlier than people in blue states. Indeed, the gap in life expectancy between Louisiana (75.7) and Connecticut (80.8) is the same as that between the United States and Nicaragua. Red states suffer more in another highly important but little-known way, one that speaks to the very biological self-interest in health and life: industrial pollution.

Louisiana is an extreme example of this paradox. *The Measure of America*, a report of the Social Science Research Council, ranks every state in the United States on its "human development." Each rank is based on life expectancy, school enrollment, educational degree attainment, and median personal earnings. Out of the 50 states, Louisiana ranked 49th and in overall health ranked last. According to the 2015 National Report Card, Louisiana ranked 48th out of 50 in eighth-grade reading and 49th out of 50 in eighth-grade math. Only eight out of ten Louisianans have graduated from high school, and only 7 percent have graduate or professional degrees. According to the *Kids Count Data Book*, compiled by the Annie E. Casey Foundation, Louisiana ranked 49th out of 50 states for child well-being. And the problem transcends race; an average black in Maryland lives four years longer, earns twice as much, and is twice as likely to have a college degree as a black in Louisiana. And whites in Louisiana are worse off than whites in Maryland or anywhere else outside Mississippi. Louisiana has suffered many environmental problems too: there are nearly 400 miles of low, flat, subsiding coastline, and the state loses a football field–size patch of wetland every hour. It is threatened by rising sea levels and severe hurricanes, which the world's top scientists connect to climate change.

Given such an array of challenges, one might expect people to welcome federal help. In truth, a very large proportion of the yearly budgets of red states—in the case of Louisiana, 44 percent—do come from federal funds; $2,400 is given by the federal government per Louisianan per year.

But Mike Schaff doesn't welcome that federal money and doubts the science of climate change: "I'll worry about global warming in fifty years," he says. Mike loves his state, and he loves the outdoor life. But instead of looking to government, like others in the Tea Party he turns to the free market. Mike's mother had voted for the Louisiana Democrat Edwin Edwards because he was Cajun and for Jack Kennedy because he was Catholic; "Democrat" wasn't a bad word when he was going up. But it is now. Mike had long worked for a small business and advocates a free market for businesses of all sizes, and from this yet another paradox seemed to unfold. Many Tea Party advocates work in or run small businesses. Yet the politicians they support back laws that consolidate the monopoly power of the very largest companies that are poised to swallow up smaller ones. Small farmers voting with Monsanto? Corner drugstore owners voting with Walmart? The local bookstore owner voting with Amazon? If I were a small business owner, I would welcome lower company taxes, sure, but strengthening the monopolies that could force me out of business? I didn't get it.

Wrapped around these puzzles was a bigger one: how can a system both create pain and deflect blame for that pain? In 2008, reckless and woefully underregulated Wall Street investors led many to lose savings, homes, jobs, and hope. Yet, years later, under the banner of a "free market," many within the growing small-town right defend Wall Street against government "over-regulation." What could be going on?

Maybe the best way to find out, I thought, was to reverse the "Big Sort," to leave my blue neighborhood and state, enter a red state, and try to scale the empathy wall. My neighbors and friends on my side of the wall are more or less like me. They have BA degrees or more and read the *New York Times* daily. They eat organic food, recycle their garbage, and take BART (the public rail system) when they can. Most have grown up on one or the other coast. Some are churchgoers, but many call themselves "spiritual" and don't regularly go to church. Many work in public or nonprofit sector jobs, and are as puzzled by all this as I am. When I started out, I had no close friend who'd been born in the South, only one who worked in oil, and none in the Tea Party.

In his *New York Times* essay, "Who Turned My Blue State Red?" Alec MacGillis offers an intriguing answer to the Great Paradox. People in red states who need Medicaid and food stamps welcome them but don't vote, he argues, while those a little higher on the class ladder, white conservatives, don't need them and do vote—against public dollars for the poor.

This "two notches up" thesis gives us part of the answer, but not most. For one thing, as I was to discover, the affluent who vote against government services use them anyway. Virtually every Tea Party advocate I interviewed for this book has personally benefited from a major government service or has close family who have. Several had disabled elderly parents lacking private long-term care insurance, and had them declared indigent in order to enable them to receive Medicaid. Another man, whose wife suffered a severely disabling disease and whose care would have bankrupted him, lovingly divorced her to make her eligible for Medicaid. The able-bodied brother of a disapproving sister—both Tea Party—received SNAP benefits. The brother of another put in for unemployment during hunting season. Most said, "Since it's there, why not use it?" But many were ashamed and asked me to dissociate their identity from such an act, which I've done. But shame didn't stop those who disapproved of public services from using them.

MacGillis suggests that voters really act in their self-interest. But do they? The "two notches up" idea doesn't explain why red state voters who were not themselves billionaires opposed taxing billionaires, the money from which might help expand a local library, or add swings to a local park. The best way to test the MacGillis idea, I figured, is to pick out a problem that affluent voters in poor red states *do* have, and to show they don't want government help for that either. In other words, the two-notch-up voter may say, "Let's cut welfare to the poor because I'm not poor." Or, "Never mind improving public schools. My kid goes to a private one"—although no one I spoke to talked like this. But they do themselves face other problems the government could help with, which brings me to the keyhole issue in this book: environmental pollution. Through a close-up view of this issue, I reasoned, I could uncover the wider perspective that drove people's responses to it and to much else.

To begin with, I wanted to go to the geographic heart of the right—the South. Nearly all the recent growth of the right has occurred below the Mason-Dixon line, an area that, encompassing the original Confederate states, accounts for a third of the U.S. population. In the last two decades the South has also grown by 14 percent. Between 1952 and 2000, among high school–educated whites in the South, there has been a 20 percent increase in Republican voters, and among college-educated whites, the increase was higher still. In the nation as a whole, whites have moved right: between 1972 and 2014, the share of whites identifying as Democrats fell from 41 percent to 25 percent, while the share identifying as Republicans grew from 25 percent to 27. (The percent of whites claiming they are independent also grew during this time.) So if I wanted to understand the right, I would need to get to know the white South.

But where in the South should I go? In the 2012 election, in the nation as a whole, 39 percent of white voters voted for Barack Obama. In the South, 29 percent did. And in Louisiana, it was 14 percent—a smaller proportion than in the South as a whole. According to one 2011 poll, half of Louisianans support the Tea Party. Next to South Carolina, Louisiana also held the highest proportion of state representatives in the U.S. House of Representative's Tea Party Caucus.

As luck would have it, I had one contact in Louisiana—Sally Cappel, the mother-in-law of a former graduate student of mine. It was Sally who would introduce me to the white South and, through a friend, to the right within it. A Lake Charles–based artist, Sally was a progressive Democrat who in the 2016 primary favored Bernie Sanders. Sally's very dear friend and a world-traveling flight attendant from Opelousas, Louisiana, Shirley Slack was an enthusiast for the Tea Party and Donald Trump. Both women had joined sororities (although different ones) at Louisiana State University. Each had married, had three children, lived in homes walking distance apart in Lake Charles, and had keys to each other's houses. Each loved the other's children. Shirley knew Sally's parents and even consulted Sally's mother when the two got to "fussing too much." They exchanged birthday and Christmas gifts and jointly scoured the newspaper for notices of upcoming cultural events they had, when they were neighbors in Lake Charles, attended together. One day when I was staying as Shirley's overnight guest in Opelousas, I noticed a watercolor picture hanging on the guestroom wall, which Sally had painted as a gift for Shirley's eleven-year-old daughter, who aspired to become a ballerina. With one pointed toe on a pudgy, pastel cloud, the other lifted high, the ballerina's head was encircled by yellow star-like butterflies. It was a loving picture of a child's dream—one that came true. Both women followed the news on TV—Sally through MSNBC's Rachel Maddow, and Shirley via Fox News's Charles Krauthammer, and each talked these different reports over with a like-minded husband. The two women talk by phone two or three times a week, and their grown children keep in touch, partly across the same political divide. While this book is not about the personal lives of these two women, it couldn't have been written without them both, and I believe that their friendship models what our country itself needs to forge: the capacity to connect across difference.

To begin with, I read what other thinkers had to say about the rise of the right. At one extreme, some argued that a band of the very rich, wanting to guard their money, had hired "movement entrepreneurs" to create an "astro-turf grassroots following." In *The Billionaires' Tea Party*, for example, the Australian filmmaker Taki Oldham had found that home-grown "citizen groups" challenging climate change were funded by oil companies, and argued that populist anti-government rage was orchestrated by corporate strategy. Others argued that extremely rich people had stirred the movement to life, without arguing that grassroots support was fake. The *New Yorker* staff writer Jane Mayer describes the strategy of billionaire oil baron brothers Charles and David Koch to direct $889,000,000 to help right-wing candidates and causes in 2016 alone. "To bring about social change," Charles Koch says, "requires a strategy" that uses "vertically and horizontally integrated" planning "from idea creation to policy development to education to grassroots organizations to lobbying to litigation to political action." It was like a vast, sprawling company that owns the forest, the pulp mill, the publishing house, and pays authors to write slanted books. Such a political "company" could wield astonishing influence. Particularly in the years after *Citizens United v. Federal Election Commission*, the 2010 Supreme Court decision permitting unlimited anonymous corporate gifts to political advocacy groups, this influence is, indeed, at work. Just 158 rich families contributed nearly half of the $176 million given to candidates in the first phase of the presidential election of 2016—$138 million to Republicans and $20 million to Democrats. Through Americans for Prosperity, the Koch brothers have circulated a pledge in Congress to curb the authority of the EPA.

Armelise Plantation, where Mike Schaff was born, and Bayou Corne, where he lived and had hoped to die, were a few miles from a strip of the Mississippi now studded with petrochemical plants and popularly called, with good reason, "Cancer Alley." Was concern about this issue in Mike Schaff's interest? He thought so. No one was paying him to attend local meetings of the Tea Party, nor were they paying his neighbors, many of whom shared his views.

In *What's the Matter With Kansas?* Frank argues that people like Mike are being greatly misled. A rich man's "economic agenda" is paired with the "bait" of social issues. Through appeal to abortion bans, gun rights, and school prayer, Mike and his like-minded friends are persuaded to embrace economic policies that hurt them. As Frank writes, "*Vote* to stop abortion: *receive* a rollback in capital gains taxes. . . . *Vote* to get government off our backs; *receive* conglomeration and monopoly everywhere from media to meat packing. *Vote* to strike a blow against elitism, *receive* a social order in which wealth is more concentrated than ever before in our lifetimes." His beloved fellow Kansans, Frank argues, are being terribly misled.

So how does it work to be misled? Can we be smart, inquiring, well-informed, and still misled? Mike was highly intelligent, consulted a number of news sources—although his main source was Fox News—and he talked politics endlessly with family, neighbors, and friends. Like me, he also lived in an enclave of like-minded people. Mike didn't think the Koch-funded idea-machine was duping him. In fact, Mike wondered whether a Soros-funded machine was duping me. Purchased political influence is real, powerful, and at play, I think, but as an explanation for why any of us believe what we do, duping—and the presumption of gullibility—is too simple an idea.

Our home enclaves often reflect special cultures of governance tying politics to geography. This is the thesis of Colin Woodard's *American Nations*. Rural areas in the Midwest, the South, and Alaska lean right while large cities, New England, and the two coasts lean left, he notes. Bound by a tradition of small-town governance and oriented toward Europe, New Englanders tend to believe in good government for the "common good."

Appalachians and Texans tend to be freedom-loving government minimalists. Tracing their roots to a caste system, whites in Dixie states treasure local control and resist federal power—linked as that is to the defeat, 150 years ago, of the South by the North. Resistance to federal taxation, the historian Robin Einhorn notes, also originated in the South. Regional traditions are real, of course, but less immutable than Woodard suggests. And while the far right is strongest in the South, most of its members make up a demographic—white, middle to low income, older, married, Christian—that spans the whole nation.

Others point to the moral values of the right. In *The Righteous Mind*, for example, Jonathan Haidt argues, unlike Frank, that people are not misled but instead vote in their self-interest—one based on cultural values. While right and left both value caring and fairness, he notes, they place different priorities on obedience to authority (the right) and originality (the left), for example. Surely, this is true. But a person can hold a set of values calmly, or in a state of fury that brings a whole new party into being. What makes the difference between the two? Theda Skocpol and Vanessa Williamson rightly argue that it is a unique coalescence of circumstances—predisposing factors and precipitating ones. Primary among the latter were the Great Recession of 2008 and government efforts to forestall it, the presidency of Barack Obama, and Fox News.

While all these works greatly helped me, I found one thing missing in them all—a full understanding of emotion in politics. What, I wanted to know, do people *want to feel*, what do they think they *should or shouldn't* feel, and what *do they feel* about a range of issues? When we listen to a political leader, we don't simply hear words; we listen predisposed to want to feel certain things. Some broad emotional ideals are shared across the political spectrum but others are not. Some feel proud of a "Give me your tired, your poor, your huddled masses" Statue of Liberty America, while others yearn to feel proud of a Constitution-abiding, work-your-own-way-up America.

At play are "feeling rules," left ones and right ones. The right seeks release from liberal notions of what they *should feel*—happy for the gay newlywed, sad at the plight of the Syrian refugee, unresentful about paying taxes. The left sees prejudice. Such rules challenge the emotional core of right-wing belief. And it is to this core that a free-wheeling candidate such as the billionaire entrepreneur Donald Trump, Republican candidate for president in 2016, can appeal, saying, as he gazes upon throngs of supporters, "See all the *passion*."

We can approach that core, I came to see, through what I call a "deep story," a story that *feels as if* it were true. As though I were seeing through Alice's looking glass, the deep story was to lead me to focus on a site of long-simmering social conflict, one ignored by both the "Occupy Wall Street" left—who were looking to the 1 and the 99 percent within the private realm as a site of class conflict—and by the anti-government right, who think of differences of class and race as matters of personal character. The deep story was to take me to the shoulds and shouldn'ts of feeling, to the management of feeling, and to the core feelings stirred by charismatic leaders. And, as we shall see, everyone has a deep story.

Visits and Follow-Arounds

But first, the people. I originally based myself in Lake Charles, a town of 74,000 in southwest Louisiana, some thirty miles north of the Gulf of Mexico. Half were white, half black, many of Cajun ancestry. Three percent were foreign-born. Twenty-three percent of residents had a BA, and the median household income was $36,000 per year. Seated in Calcasieu Parish (Louisiana's French heritage led to the use of "parishes" instead of "counties"), Lake Charles hosts seventy-five festivals in the surrounding area, and its Mardi Gras Museum claims the largest collection of Mardi Gras costumes in the world. It attracts tourists to its three large casinos and workers to its rapidly expanding petrochemical industry.

Once there, I scouted out members of the far right in a number of ways. To begin with, Sally Cappel and Shirley Slack helped set up four focus groups, two made up of liberals, two of Tea Party advocates. Each group met in Sally's kitchen, and I followed up the Tea Party sessions with interviews of individual Tea Party advocates, sometimes interviewing their spouses and parents too. I say "interview" because I asked people to sign a sheet describing my purpose before we talked. But at the end of two or three hours, they often said it was very nice *visiting with you,* and in truth, these sessions often turned into a mix of interview and visit.

An accountant I met through a Tea Party focus group invited me to a series of monthly luncheon meetings of the Republican Women of Southwest Louisiana, playfully quipping, "Maybe we'll change your mind!" There I discovered a well-attended, highly-organized gathering of white, middle-aged, professional women, and a special table of teenagers in red T-shirts. At each luncheon I met new people at my table and made dates to follow up with them, often meeting their families and sometimes their neighbors. I was invited to visit two private Christian schools and to attend Baptist, Pentecostal, and Catholic church services and activities, including a 40s-Plus Pentecostal Gumbo Cook-Off. One woman at the Republican women's luncheon was a Pentecostal pastor's wife who introduced me to many in her church and invited me to join her and her friends in a game of Rook (a fifty-seven-card game of so-called "missionary poker," which provides evangelical players a happy alternative to card games associated with gambling). I met a man whose great uncle had been the Grand Wizard of the Ku Klux Klan (a reason his grandfather had moved to another town) and met a white member of the Tea Party and strong Baptist woman who had adopted an African American baby and a South American child.

I also followed the campaign trails of a Republican candidate for the U.S. Senate and his Tea Party rival, which took me to the Acadian Village Pig Roast in Lafayette, a rice festival and boat parade in New Iberia, a get-out-the-vote event in Crowley, and a union meet-and-greet in Rayne. At each whistle stop, I chatted with my neighbors. A marine biologist and environmental activist, Mike Tritico—a political independent and son of a furniture store owner—told me of right-wing friends who vehemently opposed his activism. A tall man of seventy with a teacherly manner and encyclopedic grasp of local industry, he was seen as a recluse by some (he lived in a disheveled cabin in the woods of Longville), as a saint by others, and as a thorn in their side by state regulatory officials. I asked if I could tag along with him and meet his adversaries. Mike was game.

Over five years, I accumulated 4,690 pages of transcripts based on interviews with a core of forty Tea Party advocates and twenty others from various walks of life—teachers, social workers, lawyers, and government officials—who enlarged my perspective on my core group. From within that core group, I selected a small number who illustrated particular patterns especially well. With their permission, I followed them around, asking to see where they were born, attended school and church, shopped, and had fun with them, and tried to get a feel for the influences on them. While all supported the Tea Party, they varied greatly among themselves. Some went to church three times a week, others not at all. Some had seven guns, others three, of which some were behind glass, others in a bedside drawer. They differed in how they saw poverty. One man said, "I asked the security guy at our local grocery store what sort of stuff gets stolen from the store. He said it was mainly rice, beans, and baby food. That tells you something." Others thought such reports were "exaggerated." They differed in their fears. One man told me he had bought a secondhand medical book at Goodwill in case the economy "crashed and burned" and he had to set his own broken arm. Another stocked provisions in case we "all have to be self-sufficient," and he had neighbors doing the same. Most were less alarmed. My core group differed in their suspicion of President Obama, too, and in their denigration of him. The Facebook page of one Tea Party advocate showed mug shots of President Obama, front and side, a name plate below his image, while another showed him in "public housing." Most were angry, afraid, some in mourning for real losses, but in their emotional complexion, too, they differed widely among themselves. (For more on my research, see Appendix A.)

I was definitely not in Berkeley, California. For one thing, the occasional turn of phrase was different: "As fast as a duck can eat a June bug. . . . Up to my ass in alligators. . . ." One man referred to unadorned—yep-nope—speech as "talking Yankee." Churches grand and humble studded the landscape, in some towns, one a block. Three aisles in Lake Charles's largest bookstore were dedicated to Bibles of different colors, shapes, and print sizes, and to leather-bound Bible study notebooks. Some restaurants advertised "Lenten Season Specials," appealing to the Catholic French Creole and Cajun residents. Certain absences also reminded me I was not at home: no *New York Times* at the newsstand, almost no organic produce in grocery stores or farmers' markets, no foreign films in movie houses, few small cars, fewer petite sizes in clothing stores, fewer pedestrians speaking foreign languages into cell phones—indeed, fewer pedestrians. There were fewer yellow Labradors and more pit bulls and bulldogs. Forget bicycle lanes, color-coded recycling bins, or solar panels on roofs. In some cafés, virtually everything on the menu was fried. There were no questions before meals about gluten-free entrees, and dinner generally began with prayer. Farther east from Lake Charles and along the strip of petrochemical companies lining the lower Mississippi, I saw quite a few signs for personal injury lawyers ("Just call Chuck"). In the absence of the talismans of my world and in the presence of theirs, I came to realize that the Tea Party was not so much an official political group as a culture, a way of seeing and feeling about a place and its people.

I compared the student activity groups registered at Louisiana State University in Baton Rouge (the alma mater of some I talked with) with those at the University of California, Berkeley, where I have long taught. At Louisiana State (a campus of some 30,000 had some 375 student groups), I found student chapters of the Oilfield Christian Fellowship, the Agribusiness Club, the Air Waste Management Association, the Society of Petrophysics and Well Log Analysts, and a War-gaming and Role Playing Society (WARS)—none of which had analogues at U.C. Berkeley. (A Sierra Student Coalition was formed in 2015–16.)

U.C. Berkeley (with 37,000 students and 1,000 student organizations) listed Amnesty International and the Anti-Trafficking Coalition, Building Sustainability at Cal, Environmental Science Student Association, Global Student Embassy at Berkeley (to promote grassroots environmental cooperation)—groups with no analogues at LSU. Mike Schaff had graduated from the University of Louisiana at Monroe and had joined the chess club, Circle K (Kiwanis), and a military fraternity called Scabbard and

Blade. With an enrollment of around 7,000, his university featured some 150 student groups. One group—Cupcakes for a Cause—raised money to help women veterans. Another group, the ULM Fishing Team, held monthly tournaments. At Northeastern Louisiana State, student clubs included College Republicans and Young Americans for Liberty but not College Democrats.

Driving around Lake Charles, I noticed "Don't Tread on Me" bumper stickers on the back of a few pickup trucks, showing a coiled rattlesnake with an extended tongue. The symbol, first created by a colonial Revolutionary War general in 1775, has been adopted nationally by the Tea Party. Although it came down in 2011, I saw an enormous "Where's the Birth Certificate?" sign on Interstate 49 between Lafayette and Opelousas, publicly questioning President Obama's birthplace. At the edge of a used-truck lot on Route 171 between Longville and DeRidder, an hour's drive north of Lake Charles, a placard on the side of a wooden hut ominously proclaimed it the "Obama Smokehouse."

Reminders of the racial divide were everywhere. In the Westlake cemetery, for example, a roadway divided the graves of whites and blacks. The grass around the whites' graves had been recently trimmed while that around the black graves had not. Another example was a granite statue of a young Confederate soldier in front of the old Calcasieu Parish Courthouse, above a plaque thanking those who "defended the South." No parallel sites commemorated slave heroes or victims of lynching. On my 2016 visit to Lake Charles, I noticed a small flag of the early confederacy—thirteen stars in the upper left, and red, white, and red bands to the right—at the base of this monument. Three of the five parishes of southwest Louisiana, not to mention the Jefferson Davis Bank and freeway, are named after Confederate officials of the Civil War, and the state has ninety Confederate monuments, some unveiled as recently as 2010. Only fifteen years ago, a cross was burned near a trailer in Longville, where one of my guides, Mike Tritico, and friends of his I came to know lived—the last known burned cross in the state. Six men were charged and sentenced by federal prosecutors. Race seemed everywhere in the physical surroundings, but almost nowhere in spontaneous direct talk.

A Keyhole Issue

I wanted to get up close. The best way to do that, I thought, was to come to know one group of people in one place, focusing on a single issue. This issue was not a case, as mentioned earlier, of well-to-do voters voting down government measures they themselves didn't need. Everyone I talked to wanted a clean environment. But in Louisiana, the Great Paradox was staring me in the face—great pollution and great resistance to regulating polluters. If I could truly enter the minds and hearts of people on the far right on the issue of the water they drink, the animals they hunt, the lakes they swim in, the streams they fish in, the air they breathe, I could get to know them up close. Through their views on this keyhole issue—how much, if at all, should government regulate industrial polluters?—I hoped to learn about the right's perspective on a wider range of issues. I could learn about how— emotionally speaking—politics works in us all.

As an oil state with a record of going light on regulation, Louisiana has suffered decades of severe environmental damage. During the time I was doing my research, the fracking boom also hit Lake Charles, and the town rapidly became the center of a stunning $84 billion planned investment in southwest Louisiana—one of the biggest investments in American industry. Lake Charles had become ground zero for production of American petrochemicals.

I brought industrial growth into view through interviews with public officials—the mayor of nearby Westlake and the head of the Southwest Louisiana Task Force for Growth and Opportunity (which had just been given the assignment of planning for the arrival of 18,000 workers to be housed in "man camps"; 13,000 of these workers were from out of state, including Filipino pipefitters).

While in Lake Charles, I stayed at Aunt Ruby's Bed and Breakfast. By the edge of the bathtub in my quarters, I discovered a moisturizing body wash, on the back side of which were listed in small print the ingredients: petroleum, ammonium laureth sulfate, sodium lauroamphoacetate, ammonium lauryl sulfate, lauric acid, sodium chloride, hydroxypropyltimonium chloride. The same ingredients, it occurred to me, could be found in the plastic in my sunglasses, my watch band, my computer, my moisturizer. Lake Charles produced the airplane fuel that brought me there and the gasoline I was getting around on, and much of this was produced by companies close by.

To prepare for my journey, I re-read Ayn Rand's *Atlas Shrugged*, a Tea Party bible lauded by the conservative radio pundit Rush Limbaugh and former Fox News television commentator Glenn Beck. Rand describes serving the needy as a "monstrous idea." Charity, she says, is bad. Greed is good. If Ayn Rand appealed to them, I imagined, they're probably pretty selfish, tough, cold people, and I prepared for the worst. But I was thankful to discover many warm, open people who were deeply charitable to those around them, including an older, white liberal stranger writing a book.

Given its liberal reputation, I worried about telling people I taught at U.C. Berkeley. I secretly hoped my Louisiana acquaintances would respectfully recall its seventy-two Nobel Laureates, its proud academic standing. But no. When I told one man that I lived in Berkeley, he immediately replied: "Oh, you got *hippies*." Another had seen a Fox News report of Berkeley students protesting fee hikes. They had linked themselves together with iron chains and stood before TV cameras on the edge of the roof of a campus building. If one fell, so would they all, which was, I guess, their point. "Did you say Berkeley students need an A *average* to get in?" someone asked me, incredulous. "The chain thing seems pretty stupid to me."

From across the table at a meeting of the Republican Women of Southwest Louisiana, Madonna Massey, a gospel singer, declared that she "*loved* Rush Limbaugh." In the past, I'd found Limbaugh harshly opinionated, and, incurious and offended, I'd routinely switched the dial. But now I told Madonna, "I'd love to talk about what you love about him." When we sat down a week later to sweet teas at a local Starbucks, I asked Madonna what she loved about Limbaugh. "His criticism of 'femi-nazis,' you know, feminists, women who want to be equal to men." I absorbed that for a moment. Then she asked what I thought, and after I answered, she remarked, "But you're nice . . ." From there, we went through Limbaugh's epithets ("commie libs," "environmental wackos"). Finally, we came to Madonna's basic feeling that Limbaugh was defending her against insults she felt liberals were lobbing at her: "Oh, liberals think that Bible-believing Southerners are ignorant, backward, rednecks, losers. They think we're racist, sexist, homophobic, and maybe fat." Her grandfather had struggled as a desperately poor Arkansas sharecropper. She was a gifted singer, beloved by a large congregation, a graduate of a two-year Bible college, and a caring mother of two. In this moment, I began to recognize the power of blue-state catcalls taunting red state residents. Limbaugh was a firewall against liberal insults thrown at her and her ancestors, she felt. Was the right-wing media making them up to stoke hatred, I wondered, or were there enough blue-state insults to go around? The next time I saw Madonna, she was interested to know if it had been hard for me to hear what she'd said. I told her it wasn't. "I do that too sometimes," she said, "try to get myself out of the way to see what another person feels."

As I walked with Mike Schaff through the sugarcane fields of the old Armelise Plantation, or sat with Madonna in the Living Way Pentecostal Church, I was discovering good people at the center of this Great Paradox. How could kindly Madonna oppose government help for the poor? How could a warm, bright, thoughtful man like Mike Schaff, a victim of corporate malfeasance and wanton destruction, aim so much of his fire at the federal government? How could a state that is one of the most vulnerable to volatile weather be a center of climate denial?

So, curious to find out, I began this journey into the heart of the right.

2

"One Thing Good"

There he is, seated on his wooden front porch overlooking a trim yard in suburban DeRidder, Louisiana, watching for my car. He rises from his chair, waving with one arm and steadying himself on his walker with the other. A large-chested, six-foot-three man with a gray crew cut and jet-blue eyes, Lee Sherman, age eighty-two, beams me a welcoming smile. A player for the Dallas Texans football team (later renamed the Kansas City Chiefs) for two years, an honoree in *Who's Who of American Motorsports*, a NASCAR racer who drove 200 miles an hour in a neck brace and fire suit, and the proud purchaser of a waterski boat once owned by TV's Wonder Woman, Lee shakes my hand, apologizing, "I'm sorry to be on this thing," he points to his walker, "and not take you through the house properly." He doesn't feel like his old self, he says, but accepts his feeble legs good-naturedly. Given his dangerous work at Pittsburgh Plate Glass, he is happy to be alive. "All my co-workers from back then are dead; most died young," he tells me as he slowly leads me through a tidy home toward the dining room table on which he has set coffee cups, coffee, cookies, and a large photograph album.

Driving north from Lake Charles through southwest Louisiana to DeRidder, I had passed a miscellany of gas stations, Family Dollar stores, payday loan offices, diners—where once lush, green rice fields grew, sometimes striated by wet canals where farmers cultivated crayfish—flat on all sides to the horizon. Some 17 miles west of DeRidder, on land bordering Texas, lay a vast pine wilderness, once a no-man's-land where the legendary outlaws

Bonnie and Clyde robbed and roamed. To the north lay soy, sugarcane, and bean fields, oil derricks nodding in the far distance. Southeast of De-Ridder by 130 miles sat Baton Rouge, the capital of Louisiana. Along the great Mississippi, between it and New Orleans, stand majestic plantation manor houses surrounded by gracious skirts of green lawn where once lived the richest families in America. Now tourist sites, they are overshadowed by giant neighboring petrochemical plants, such as Shintech, ExxonMobil, and Monsanto.

Lee has also become an ardent environmentalist due to things he had suffered, seen, and been ordered to do as a pipefitter in a petrochemical plant. Calcasieu Parish, in which he had worked for fifteen years at the Lake Charles–based Pittsburgh Plate Glass company, is among the 2 percent of American counties with the highest toxic emissions per capita. According to the American Cancer Society, Louisiana has the second highest incidence of cancer for men and the fifth highest male death rate from cancer in the nation.

But Lee has recently volunteered to post lawns signs for Tea Party congressman John Fleming, who earned a score of 91 on the right-wing FreedomWorks scorecard and favors cutting the Environmental Protection Agency, weakening the Clean Air Act, and drilling on the outer continental shelf, as well as opposing the regulation of greenhouse gases and favoring less regulation of Wall Street. Lee is a regular at meetings of the DeRidder Tea Party, wearing his red, white, and blue party T-shirt featuring an eagle sharpening its talons. So why was Lee the environmentalist eager to plant lawn signs for a politician calling for cuts in the EPA? If I could answer this question, maybe I could unlock the door to the Great Paradox.

Maybe I could also find the key to Lee's own journey from left to right. For years, back when he worked in a naval shipyard outside Seattle, Washington, he had campaigned for Senator Scoop Jackson, a Cold War–era liberal Democrat who championed civil rights and human rights. Brought up by a working single mother who fought in the shipyards for equal pay for equal work, Lee describes himself as "an ERA baby." When he came south for work in the 1960s, however, he turned Republican, and after 2009 he joined the Tea Party.

We seat ourselves, pour our coffee, and I ask him to tell me about his childhood. Lee speaks slowly, deliberately, as if for posterity.

"I was a dare-devil kid, one of seven boys. At around age seven, I roped down a bunch of poplar tree branches, tied myself to them, and released them so I could *fly*," Lee recalls with a laugh. "I flew pretty high"—he describes a broad arc with his arm—"and landed in a prickly blackberry thicket. It hurt. But my mom didn't come get me because she wanted me to learn a lesson. I didn't, though," he added. Lee drove cars long before he had a license, and at age twelve stole, flew, and safely landed a neighbor's biplane.

Even at a younger age, Lee was an active child. "When I was about five, I got pneumonia and had to stay in bed for three months. My great grandma (a Native American who lived on a Crow reservation in Montana) sat *on* me, not *with* me, so I wouldn't get up. That's how she kept me still so I could learn to crochet."

As a young man, Lee trained as a coppersmith in the U.S. naval shipyards outside Seattle, where his dad worked as an electrician. When traveling south for work in 1965, Lee was hired by Pittsburgh Plate Glass as a maintenance pipefitter and soon earned a workroom reputation as a mechanical genius. "He can make nuts and bolts and rods and pipes and estimate lengths to the millimeter without having to measure or re-measure them," Mike Tritico, the environmental activist, told me, when he put the two of us in touch. And on weekends Lee raced cars, one of his plant supervisors always asking on Monday how Saturday's race had gone.

Lee was fearless and careful, a good fit for his dangerous job at PPG—fitting and repairing pipes carrying lethal chemicals such as ethylene dichloride (EDC), mercury, lead, chromium, polycyclic aromatic hydrocarbons (PAHs), and dioxins. Mysteriously, these same chemicals had found their way into a nearby waterway called Bayou d'Inde—a bayou on which a Cajun family, the Arenos, had lived for many generations, and greatly suffered, and whose extraordinary connection to Lee we will learn.

At one point, Lee narrowly escaped death, he tells me, taking a careful, long sip of coffee. One day while he was working, cold chlorine was accidentally exposed to 1,000 degree heat, which instantly transformed the liquid to gas. Sixteen workers were in the plant at the time. Noting that the company was short of protective gear, Lee's boss instructed him to leave. "Thirty minutes after I left," Lee says, "the plant blew up. Five of the fifteen men I left behind were killed." The next afternoon, Lee's boss asked him to help search for the bodies of the five dead workers. Two were found, three were not. Acid had so decomposed the body of one of the three victims that his remains came out in pieces in the sewer that drained into Bayou d'Inde. "If someone hadn't found him," Lee says, turning his head to look out his dining room window, "that body would have ended up floating into Bayou d'Inde."

In the 1960s, safety was at a minimum at PPG. "During safety meetings," Lee tells me, "the supervisor just gave us paperwork to fill out. Working with the chemicals, we wore no protective facial masks. You learned how to hold your nose and breathe through your mouth."

"The company didn't much warn us about dangers," Lee says, adding in a softer voice, "My coworkers did. They'd say, 'You can't stand in that stuff. Get out of it.' I wouldn't be alive today, if it weren't for my co-workers."

The pipes Lee worked on carried oxygen, hydrogen, and chlorine, and when a pipe sprung a leak, he explains, "I was the guy to fix it."

"Did you use your bare hands?" I ask.

"Oh, yeah, yeah."

Eventually the general foreman issued badges to the workers to record any overexposure to dangerous chemicals, Lee says, "but the foreman made fun of them. It's supposed to take two or three months before the gauge registers you've reached the limit. My badge did in three days. The foreman thought I'd stuck it inside a pipe!" Such was the scene in the late 1960s at the PPG plant in Lake Charles, Louisiana.

Accidents happened. One day, Lee was standing in a room, leaning over a large pipe to check a filter, when an operator in a distant control room mistakenly turned a knob, sending hot, almond-smelling, liquid chlorinated hydrocarbons coursing through the pipe, accidentally drenching him. "It was *hot* and I got completely soaked," Lee tells me. "I jumped into the safety shower and had the respirator in my mouth, so I wasn't overcome. But the chemical was burning pretty bad. It really gets you worst underneath your arms, in between your legs, up your bottom." Despite the shower, he said, "The chemical ate off my shoes. It ate off my pants. It ate my shirt. My undershorts were gone. Only some elastic from my socks and my undershorts remained. It burned my clothes clean off me."

Lee's supervisor told him to go home and buy another pair of shoes, socks, undershorts, Levis, and work shirt—and to bring in the receipts, to be reimbursed. A few days later, he brought his receipts into his supervisor's office. The bill was about $40.00. But his supervisor noted about the incinerated clothes that he had already put some wear into them. "You got about 80 percent use of the shoes and about 50 percent use of the pants," he told Lee. "In the end, taking into account discounts for previous wear," Lee notes wryly, "My supervisor gave me a check for eight dollars. I never cashed it."

Lee's work at PPG was a source of personal pride, but he clearly did not feel particularly loyal to the company. Still, he did as he was told. And one day after his acid bath, he was told to take on another ominous job. It was to be done twice a day, usually after dusk, and always in secret. In order to do this job, Lee had to wield an eight-foot-long "tar buggy," propelled forward on four wheels. Loaded on this buggy was an enormous steel tank that held "heavy bottoms"—highly viscous tar residue of chlorinated hydrocarbon that had sunk to the bottom of kitchen-sized steel vessels. A layer of asbestos surrounded the tank, to retain heat generated by a heater beneath the buggy. Copper coils were wound around its base. The hotter the tar, the less likely it was to solidify before it was dumped. Inside was toxic waste.

Working overtime evenings, under cover of dark, his respirator on, Lee would tow the tar buggy down a path that led toward the Calcasieu Ship Channel in one direction and toward Bayou d'Inde in another.

Lee would look around "to make sure no one saw me" and check if the wind was blowing away from him, so as to avoid fumes blowing into his face. He backed the tar buggy up to the marsh. Then, he said, "I'd bend down and open the faucet." Under the pressure of compressed air, the toxins would spurt out "twenty or thirty feet" into the gooey marsh. Lee waited until the buggy was drained of the illegal toxic waste.

"No one ever saw me," Lee says.

The Bird

Lee helps himself to a cookie, eats it slowly, and lingers over an event that occurred one day while he was alone on the bank with his secret. "While I was dumping the heavy bottoms in the canal, I saw a bird fly into the fumes and fall instantly into the water. It was like he'd been shot. I put two shovels out into the mud, so I could walk on them into the marsh without sinking too far down. I walked out and picked up the bird. Its wings and body didn't move. It looked dead, but its heart was still beating. I grew up on a farm, and I know about birds. I walked back on the shovels to the bank with the bird. I held its head in my right hand and its wings and body in my left hand. I blew into its beak and worked it up and down. Then it started breathing again. Its eyes opened. But the rest of its body still didn't move. I put it on the hood of my truck, which was warm. Then I left the bird to go check my tar buggy. But when I got back, the bird was gone. It had flown away. So that was one thing good."

During the afternoon, Lee circles back to the story of the bird, alternating between it and the story of the tar buggy. "I knew what I did was wrong," he repeats. "Toxins are a killer. And I'm very sorry I did it. My mama would not have wanted me to do it. I never told anybody this before, but I knew how *not* to get *caught*." It was as if Lee had performed the company's crime and assumed the company's guilt as his own.

But, like the bird, Lee himself became a victim. He grew ill from his exposure to the chemicals. After Lee's hydrocarbon burn, "My feet felt like clubs, and I couldn't bend my legs and rise up, so the company doctor ordered me put on medical leave. I kept visiting the company doctor to see if I was ready to come back, but he kept saying I shouldn't come back until I could do a deep knee bend." Lee took a medical leave of eight months and then returned to work. But not for long.

After fifteen years of working at PPG, Lee was summoned to an office and found himself facing a seven-member termination committee. "They didn't want to pay my medical disability," Lee explains. "So they fired me for absenteeism! They said I hadn't worked enough hours! They didn't count my overtime. They didn't discount time I took off for my Army Reserve duty. So that's what I got fired for—absenteeism. They handed me my pink slip. Two security guards escorted me to the parking lot." Lee slaps the table as if, decades later, he has just gotten fired again.

The Fish Kill and the Showdown

Seven years later, Lee would meet an astonished member of that termination committee once again. There had been an enormous fish kill in Bayou d'Inde, the bayou downstream from the spot where Lee had dumped the toxic waste and rescued the overcome bird, a bayou on which the Areno family lived. A Calcasieu Advisory Task Force met to discuss the surrounding waterways, to describe them as "impaired," and to consider issuing a seafood advisory warning people to limit their consumption of local fish.

Local waterways had long been contaminated from many sources. But in 1987, the state at last issued a seafood advisory for Bayou d'Inde, the Calcasieu Ship Channel, and the estuary to the Gulf of Mexico. The warning was shocking, the first in memory, and it called for limits "due to low levels of chemical contamination." No more than two meals with fish a month, it said. No swimming, water sports, or contact with bottom sediments. It was a very belated attempt by the state of Louisiana to warn the public of toxins in local waters.

Instantly fishermen became alarmed. Would they be able to sell their fish? Would residents limit what they ate? Were they now being asked to look at fish not with relish for a scrumptious gumbo, jambalaya, or all-you-can-eat fish fry, but as dubious carriers of toxic chemicals? The carefully cultivated notion of harmony between oil and fishing—all this was thrown into question, and not just in Louisiana; one-third of all seafood consumed across the nation came from the Gulf of Mexico, and two-thirds of that from Louisiana itself.

Many livelihoods were at stake. From net to plate—fishermen, grocery stores, trucking companies, and restaurant workers—all were furious at the government officials who had declared the seafood advisory. The government was a job killer, and many jobs were at stake:

Shrimp provided 15,000 jobs,
oysters 4,000 jobs,
crab 3,000 jobs, and
crawfish provided 1,800 jobs, including
1,000 crawfish farmers and the 800 commercial fishermen who catch wild crawfish.

By 1987 several things had transpired that would affect the fishermen's response to the edict. For one thing, PPG was not alone. Other industries had been polluting so much that Louisiana had become the number-one hazardous waste producer in the nation. For another thing, the U.S. Congress had established the Environmental Protection Agency (1970), the Clean Air Act (1970), and the Clean Water Act (1972). In addition, many small grassroots environmental groups had sprung up throughout the state, led by homemakers, teachers, farmers, and others appalled to discover backyard toxic waste, illness, and disease. Around the time of the advisory, local activists were rising up against toxic dumping around Lake Charles and nearby Willow Springs, Sulphur, Mossville, and elsewhere, part of the "front-porch"—or "kitchen-sink"—politics of the 1970s and 1980s.

Peggy Frankland, a lively woman now in her early seventies, the daughter of farmers, and a former homecoming queen in eastern Texas who now lives on a pecan farm in Sulphur not far from PPG, describes the scene at the time of the seafood advisory: "We tore up my station wagon and my friend's husband's copy machine. We talked in churches, schools, met with Boy Scout leaders and officials in Lake Charles, Baton Rouge, and Washington,

D.C. People said we weren't Christian but animists who worshiped the Earth instead of God. We were called 'zealots' and 'country goats.' We tried to meet state legislators, who ignored us as silly housewives." As Frankland tells the story in her book *Women Pioneers of the Louisiana Environmental Movement*, "companies were treating our land and rivers like toilets, and we were standing up to it."

As Frankland, a Democrat, noted, "We could say, 'Hey, there's a *federal law* about clean water. You've contaminated our water. How're you going to clean it up?'" But most of Frankland's activists are now Tea Party Republicans and, like Lee Sherman himself, are averse to an overbearing federal government, and even to much of the EPA. There it was: the Great Paradox through a keyhole.

In the meantime, the Louisiana Department of Health and Hospitals posted warning signs about fishing and swimming, signs promptly riddled with bullets or stolen. This, then, was the context when a member of the PPG termination committee had a surprise encounter with Lee Sherman.

As Lee continues his story, we each take another cookie. Burton Coliseum, the largest public meeting place in Lake Charles at the time, was filled "with about a thousand angry fishermen and others in the fish industry." Lee continues, "When the meeting was called to order, it was standing room only. I could hear murmuring in the crowd. Oh, they were ready to kill the government."

A row of company officials, including two from Pittsburgh Plate Glass, company lawyers, and state officials, all sat behind a table on a stage in front of the crowd. A state official stood to explain the reason for the seafood advisory: the fish had been contaminated. Citizens had to be informed. What had caused it? The officials from PPG seated on stage feigned ignorance. The meeting went on for twenty or thirty minutes, catcalls to the government officials rising from the crowd.

Then, to everyone's astonishment, uninvited, Lee Sherman—long since fired by Pittsburgh Plate Glass—climbed on stage. With his back to the officials, he faced the angry fishermen, lifted a large cardboard sign, and slowly walked from one side of the stage to the other, so all could read it: "I'M THE ONE WHO DUMPED IT IN THE BAYOU."

The entire coliseum went silent.

Officials tried to get Lee to leave the stage. But a fisherman called out, "We want to hear him."

"I talked for thirty-six minutes," Lee recalls. "Someone said, 'Sherman, you gotta sit down, it's so-and-so's turn to talk!' But another guy said, 'No, I want to hear him!' I told them I had followed my boss's orders. I told them the chemicals had made me sick. I told them I'd been fired for absenteeism. The only thing I didn't tell them was that sitting behind the front table on stage was a member of the PPG Termination Committee that had fired me. He had even once placed bets on my weekend NASCAR races. That was the best part—the PPG guys had both hands over the backs of their heads."

Now the fishermen knew the fish were truly contaminated. Soon after the meeting, the fishermen filed a civil lawsuit against PPG and won an out-of-court settlement that gave a mere $12,000 to each.

Another Realm, Another Vindication

Lee had worked at hard, unpleasant, dangerous jobs. He had loyally followed company orders to contaminate an estuary. He'd done his company's moral dirty work, taken its guilt as his own, and then been betrayed and discarded himself, as a form of waste. The most heroic act of Lee's life had been to reveal to the world a company's dirty secret, and to tell a thousand fishermen furious at the government that companies like PPG were to blame.

Yet over the course of his lifetime, Lee Sherman had moved from the left to the right. When he lived as a young man in Washington State, he said proudly, "I ran the campaign of the first woman to run for Congress in the state." But when Lee moved from Seattle to Dallas for work in the 1950s, he shifted from conservative Democrat to Republican, and after 2009, to the Tea Party. So while his central life experience had been betrayal at the hands of industry, he now felt—as his politics reflected—most betrayed by the federal government. He believed that PPG and many other local petro-chemical companies at the time had done wrong, and that cleaning the mess up was right. He thought industry wouldn't "do the right thing" by itself. But in the role of counterweight, he rejected the federal government. Indeed, Lee embraced candidates who wanted to remove nearly all the guardrails on industry and cut the EPA. The Occupational Safety and Health Administration had vastly improved life for workmen such as Lee Sherman—and he appreciated those reforms—but he felt the job was largely done.

In the life of one man, Lee Sherman, I saw reflected both sides of the Great Paradox—the need for help and a principled refusal of it. As a victim of toxic exposure himself, a participant in polluting public waters, hating pollution, now proudly declaring himself as an environmentalist, why was he throwing in his lot with the anti-environmental Tea Party? Not because the Koch brothers were paying him to, at least directly. Lee was putting up Tea Party lawn signs for free. Still, his source of news was limited to Fox News and videos and blogs exchanged by right-wing friends, which placed him in an echo chamber of doubt about the EPA, the federal government, the president, and taxes.

Indeed, Tea Party adherents seemed to arrive at their dislike of the federal government via three routes—through their religious faith (the government curtailed the church, they felt), through hatred of taxes (which they saw as too high and too progressive), and through its impact on their loss of honor, as we shall see. Lee's biggest beef was taxes. They went to the wrong people—especially welfare beneficiaries who "lazed around days and partied at night" and government workers in cushy jobs. He knew liberal Democrats wanted him to care more about welfare recipients, but he didn't want their PC rules telling him who to feel sorry for. He had his own more local—and personal—way of showing sympathy for the poor. Every Christmas, through Beau-Care, a Beauregard Parish nonprofit community agency, he and his wife, "Miss Bobby," chose seven envelopes off a Christmas tree and provided a present for the child named on the enclosed card. ("The card tells you a child's shoe size. If the size is too big, we know the shoe is actually going to an adult and we don't give. But my wife spends money we don't have on the kids.")

Indeed, Lee and Miss Bobby were living on Social Security and finding it a very tight squeeze. Two events further soured him on the IRS. In one, he got a part-time job to earn a little extra money, but worked more hours than federal rules allowed, got caught, and had to wait a year to get back on Social Security. Only help from their Mormon church and from Mike Tritico, himself poor, saw Lee through that year. More enraging was a second event. "I made a date with a clerk in the local IRS office to collect a tax refund of a certain amount, and nothing about that meeting did I like," Lee explains. "The gal wore a see-through blouse, to distract me. Then she asked me for every possible receipt, tallied the amount up wrong, and gave me less than I had coming. She cheated me. I needed that money, but I never cashed that check."

"I'm a stubborn man," Lee explains, "and if you cross me, I don't ever forget it." He wanted to feel vindicated, just as he'd felt against PPG's accusations of absenteeism when a member of the Termination Committee appeared at the seafood advisory meeting in the Burton Coliseum. He'd also found vindication, he felt, against that government clerk, all IRS clerks, and indeed the source of all taxes—the government. He'd gotten even. He'd done another Burton Coliseum. He'd joined the Tea Party.

Lee had been mad when PPG fired him, two guards marching him out to the parking lot. "I have a gun," he tells me, "and I didn't think of hurting people, certainly not my co-workers, but the place, yes. I was *that* mad." But at the same time, the workplace had been where he'd experienced his finest hour, had shown his great skill, his bravery, his endurance, his manhood. And when he added it all up, he was more mad at the government. PPG gave him money. The government was taking it away.

Three and a half hours after sitting down with Lee at his dining room table, the cookies are gone. As I take my leave, Lee gets back up on his walker and slowly sees me to his front porch, which stands adjacent to a four-door garage (the garage is bigger than the house) in which sit three race cars in various stages of repair. Leaning along one wall is a stack of thirty plastic lawn signs Lee plans to plant in local lawns for John Fleming, Tea Party candidate for the U.S. Congress.

As we part, Lee flashes me a bright smile, invites me back—we haven't yet looked at his photo album—and waves a cheery good-bye. After those secret sessions at dusk emptying the tar buggy into the public waters of the estuary, the toxic waste had moved downstream into Bayou d'Inde where I'd heard a couple had long lived. Were they part of the paradox too? I thought I should meet them.

3

The Rememberers

I am seated on a soft living room couch in the home of Harold Areno, a gentle Cajun pipefitter who is carefully holding before me, from his adjacent chair, a large photo album. He draws his hand back and forth over the plastic covers on the black and white photos. He turns the pages slowly, searching for one. Seventy-seven and a former deacon in the Lighthouse Tabernacle Pentecostal Church, he's dressed in a plaid shirt and jeans. He speaks in a slow baritone, his eyes on the page, often concluding a line of thought with a light chuckle as if to say, "It's all right."

He points. There it is. His mother, father, himself, and nine siblings standing in two rows, squinting into the sun on the bank of Bayou d'Inde. It is 1950. Harold names his brothers and sisters. He tells how his mother used to catch gar by coaxing the fish to the side of the boat with bait, patting their sides, then lifting them by the gills into the boat. He turns to the next page of his album slowly. Now a photo of his father and his siblings, all born and raised just across Bayou d'Inde, a term meaning "bayou of the Indians." Now, in different constellations, the family is picnicking, now clowning, now swimming, now dropping a watermelon off a boat to play with in the water and later eat.

But it's not just his family he wants me to see. As if introducing friendly neighbors, he points behind the family to something else. Standing proud in the water, behind the faces in the photograph, are commanding bald cypress trees, large triangular trunks rising from the water, once the glorious queens of the forested wetlands of southern Louisiana and still the official state tree. Green moss hangs from outstretched lower branches, tree after tree, like lace shawls in a dance hall. "They were so tall the sun hardly hit the marsh," Harold says in a quiet voice. Reaching 150 feet high, these trees can live 600 years, and some have been known to live 1,700 years. Harold's father built fishing boats out of cypress, some flat-bottomed dugout pirogues traditional to Cajun culture. He would bring logs to a nearby mill, saw them in his shop, and build them into boats, which he rented to fishermen. For $30 a month, he also tended a humpback bridge, which could be swung sideways by turning a wheel to make way for boat traffic, and otherwise he fished and farmed.

"Throw a Cajun in a swamp," Harold chuckles, his eyebrows lifting for emphasis, "and he can make a livin'."

But that was before.

From the edge of his yard, Harold points to the bayou's brackish water. Piercing its surface here and there are lifeless gray trunks, some bent over like defeated soldiers, as far as the eye can see. It's a tree graveyard. Harold's arm falls to his side, limp.

Bayou d'Inde winds a few miles from the spot where Lee Sherman had leaned over the tar buggy, opened the valve, and let the toxic waste spew out into public waters. From that spot, the waterway led in one direction toward the Arenos, and in the other it narrowed into the Calcasieu Ship Channel, widened into intertidal mudflats dotted with salt meadow cord grass, and poured ponderously south, thirty miles into the Gulf of Mexico, from which comes nearly half the seafood on the American dinner table. From the tar buggy dumpings in the PPG marsh, there was a very large "downstream." By following Lee's deeds to the Arenos, I hoped to discover a different vantage point on the Great Paradox.

Going on three generations, the Arenos have fished, caught game, and raised gardens on land around and beneath their immaculate tan wooden home with green shutters, neatly trimmed lawn, and driveway edged in lilies and hibiscus, a white truck in the driveway. Facing the water is a porch, along one side of which hangs an enormous American flag. The Arenos' home is one of only two on Bayou d'Inde Pass Road for about a mile. The house next door, once Harold's sister's, had long lain vacant. Other families, too, have moved out, leaving a long stretch of scrub pine between the narrow tar road and the bayou.

"We didn't know what we had until it was gone," Harold says. He had grown up on one side of the bayou and raised a family on the other, "within hollerin' distance" of his birthplace. But in addition to losing his youth, his trees, and many in his family, Harold has lost a way of life. "We had forty acres," he tells me, the photo album now resting closed in his lap. "On two of them we grew butter beans, corn, and vegetables. We could catch frogs at night and fish in the daytime—gar, bass." There were other fish too, he says: crocker, menhaden, stripped mullet, and red fish, which all had once fed the great snowy egrets, white and brown pelicans, gulls, herons, spoonbills, terns, and killdeer—birds that had once thrived in the bayou. "The frogs would sing and carry on all night long. You could drink the water then."

Harold and his nine siblings settled across the family's forty acres of land along the bayou. "We didn't go to the store but once a month to get sugar, vanilla, and such. We had chickens, hogs, cows, and a garden. We lived off the bayou. We ate bullfrogs for Sunday dinner, and catfish chowder any time. We'd add the sugar and vanilla to the cream from our cows to make our own ice cream."

"My mama was a French lady," Harold declares. "She spoke French, played *The Watermelon Man* on her accordion, and cooked three meals a day for twelve on a wooden stove. She was a big woman, about 220 pounds," Harold says. "She'd kill the chicken, put the meat in a pot of gumbo, and use the guts for bait on a line to catch catfish. We didn't waste nothing."

Like many in southwest Louisiana, the Arenos were descended from French Catholic Acadians—or Cajuns, as they came to be called. The British harshly expelled the Cajuns from New Brunswick, Canada, in 1765, in the wake of a victorious war against France. British ships deposited them in various coastal states. Eventually seven boatloads of Cajuns arrived in New Orleans Harbor, many of whom then migrated to the swamplands of southwest Louisiana, mingling with and partly displacing the Atakapa Indians.

His parents had little schooling, as Harold recounts, because French was banned from schools, and French speakers were discouraged from attending. Harold himself only got through the eighth grade.

Like Harold, Annette Areno remembers the bayou from before. A beautiful woman in her seventies, she has golden-gray ringlets drawn high on her head. She wears glasses, a pink blouse, and long floral-patterned skirt. A warm, spirited woman, she speaks in a soft, deliberate way. She listens to Harold's stories, supplementing and amending them, carrying the seriousness of them in her tone of voice, but freely offering her own observations and thoughts about the bayou, comparing it to her grandfather's farm where she grew up in Kinder, Louisiana. She has recently won a lifetime achievement award as custodian at nearby Sam Houston High School. "I clean up after teenagers," she says with a playful roll of her eyes.

"I remember sitting under the cypress for shade in the heat of the summer. The moss hanging on it was green then. Frogs could breathe and they could find all kinds of minnows. Then industry came in. It began to stink so bad you had to leave the windows down on hot nights. It killed the cypress and grass from here clear out to the Gulf. And you still can't eat the fish or drink the water."

Harold adds, "Floating bits of rubber would clog the water pump on your motorboat. We were downstream from Firestone."

The Arenos' forty-six-year-old son, Derwin, arrives at the door. A lively, brown-haired pipefitter—like his dad—who works at a nearby petrochemical plant, he is dropping by on his day off with takeout from Popeye's—chicken, rice and beans, coleslaw, sweet rolls. Annette makes coffee and puts out lunch for all of us, apologizing for not cooking herself.

After prayer, Derwin joins in on what seems like a well-worn family conversation. "I was born in 1962, and growing up here, all I ever remember seeing was dead cypress trees and a stinky, nasty smell from the water. Now wherever I go, I can *smell* whether the water and air are good or bad. It's like a special instinct. The water here is clearer today on the surface, but you don't want to stir the mud on the bottom. And these days, at night, the winds from the east smell of something burning, always at night."

"I haven't heard a bullfrog in this bayou for years," Harold adds, "I heard one holler about three years ago, from inside one of them drains, but he didn't holler long. I don't know if someone caught him or if he died." Harold describes how during a "fish kill" the fish flopped about on the surface of the water and on the banks "trying to breathe."

Then he turns to turtles, and I gradually realize we are going through a terrible inventory. "We noticed the eyes of the turtles had turned white. They would sit still on a log and never jump off to catch and eat something. They'd gone blind and starved to death." Harold and Annette alternate speaking of various marine creatures with intimacy and resolute calm, as if to lay each to its proper rest.

"My dad found his cows, tipped over, lying down," Harold continues. "They had drunk the water. And the chickens. First, they'd walk around, their wings hung down. Then they'd lie down dead. And his herd of goats and sheep, all dead." He gives a mirthless baritone chuckle that seems to say, "What can you do?"

I feel as if I've come upon the scene of a slow-motion crime. Lee Sherman's tar buggy was only one part of it. Other companies and the state government were another. Continuing with a flash of indignation, Harold says, "My nephew used to raise hogs. And you know a hog can stand almost anything. Because of the bad water, my nephew had to cook the slop he fed them. But the hogs got out of the pen and went to drink the bayou water and died. The health unit came down on my *nephew* for not keeping his hogs away from the bad water, but they *didn't do nothing about the bad water.*"

In their braided tale—Harold's, Annette's, and Derwin's—I feel both resignation and defiance. As they talk they glance toward the window at the bayou beyond, downward toward their plates, and occasionally to me to see how I am absorbing their words. There is no insisting on response, only a shaking of heads as if to say, "All this should never have happened." They have been kept waiting for years for word on a lawsuit, a wait that has nearly worn them down and spent their anger.

But there is more. Animals and fish are not all they have lost. I brace myself.

Shifting in his chair and coughing slightly, Harold continues, "My brother-in-law J.D. was the first. He came down with a brain tumor and died at forty-seven. Then my sister next door, Lillie Mae, had breast cancer that went into her bones. My mom died of lung and bladder cancer. And others up the bayou: Edna Mae and Lambert both died with cancer. Julia and Wendell, live two miles from here, they got it. My sister grew up here but moved over to Houston River and she's fighting cancer. And my other brother-in-law, he had prostate cancer that went in the bone." (Both Annette and Harold are cancer survivors.)

"The only one that didn't get cancer was my daddy," Harold says, "and he never worked in the plants. Everybody else—all us kids and our spouses that lived on these forty acres—come down with cancer."

In Harold's immediate family, all those who got cancer, except for Annette and Harold, died of it. No one in earlier generations—like that of Harold's grandfather—suffered from or died of cancer. And, as Pentecostals, no one in the family smoked or drank liquor.

At a loss for words, I ask obtusely, "So is the water cleaner now?"

"Oh no," Derwin says. "After a hard rain, the bayou rises and pollution from the plants gets mixed in with it, and you can smell something bad. Nowadays there's talk of cleaning it up, but I don't know how they can."

The three turn to talk of how one gauges the safety of fish these days, and very different philosophies emerge. Harold won't eat fish out of Bayou d'Inde—that in itself spells danger. "On TV they try to play down any danger," he cautions. "After the BP [British Petroleum] spill, they said the shrimp were fine to eat. But is anybody checking them? I don't think so. I wouldn't eat them."

Then to his parents' amazement, Derwin tells how he judges safety by the look, smell, and digestibility of a fish. "I don't worry if the shrimp smells good and tastes good and feels good after you eat them." Harold cautions, "But still, they could be dangerous. We used to eat fish all the time, but only every now and again now, and never from this bayou. As for fishing, I do catch and release."

"I caught and cooked me some of them reds," Derwin continues, "because them redfish *migrate to here* all the way from the Gulf. Just because they're here now doesn't mean they *spawned* and grew up here. The reds don't stay here like gar. So a while back I figured, well, I'm okay. I took them, I cleaned them. I tried smelling them before cooking them to see if I could maybe smell any kind of little funny smell that didn't smell like normal fish. They seemed like they was kind of normal. But I didn't have any of that gar way down by the Gulf to compare them to. I cooked them on the pit, barbequed them, and then I ate them. I was trying to pinpoint any kind of funny taste but I was like, 'man, it tasted good.' I ate them."

Annette looks at her son with loving concern. To Derwin, the criterion is the fish's breeding habitat; redfish are safe, gar is not. Harold agrees with Annette: "No fish from the bayou is safe." But if he were to eat it, Harold adds, he'd eat the safe *part* of the fish. "I asked the man from Fish and Game where he took the flesh from the fish when he tested it. He told me, 'I take the fat tissue of that fish and I also take the dark part of the flesh. Your chemicals lie in the *fat* tissue and in the *dark part* of that fish.' So then I said, 'I'm glad I talked to you. If I eat that fish I ain't going to eat the belly or the dark part.'"

Why this story?

The Napkin Map

A while back, Mike Tritico, the marine biologist and longtime friend of the Arenos, had drawn me a map on a napkin. In the middle was a dot, representing the Arenos' home on Bayou d'Inde. A mile and a half east of it was Pittsburgh Plate Glass (PPG), where Lee Sherman and Harold Areno had both worked. I was later to travel by boat with Harold and Mike around the Lake Charles estuary to the very bank where Lee had secretly dumped the tar buggy of toxic waste into public water. Tall, broom-like silver green cord grass grew along the bank, hiding Lee's terrible secret through its very appearance of normality.

Now owned by another company and renamed Axiall, PPG is a chlorinated hydrocarbon manufacturing facility. Four miles east of the Arenos' home stand the Conoco docks—the site of a 1994 leak of over 1.5 million tons of ethylene dichloride (EDC), one of the largest chemical spills in North America. Four miles north from the Arenos' home is Entergy's coal-fired, electricity-generating Nelson Station. Two miles to the north is Willows Springs, a black settlement on which in 1982 a hazardous waste management firm, Brown and Ferris International, dumped waste in open landfills, sickening the local citizens. Also to the north is Sasol, the mighty South Africa–based energy and chemical company, now building the first U.S. gas-to-liquids plant and the largest new industrial facility expansion in the United States. Beyond that, three hundred miles to the southeast, in the Gulf of Mexico, the Deep Water Horizon oil rig had exploded in 2010 in the worst marine oil spill in world history. Bayou d'Inde was at the epicenter, I realized, of an entire petrochemical empire—and of the Great Paradox.

Most of what polluted the bayou sank to the bottom of it—mercury, heavy metals, ethylene dichloride (EDC), and chlorinated dioxins. So at first the danger lay mainly there. But when the U.S. Army Corps of Engineers twice dredged the nearby ship channel to ease the passage of commercial ships, "they scooped the toxic sludge from the bottom and pasted it on the banks right and left, without marking where they put it," Harold tells me. So now the Arenos can't trust the banks either. That was a decision of the U.S. Army Corps of Engineers, the federal government, I noted.

What about stricter regulation of the polluters? I ask, wondering if the Arenos had voted for political candidates who pushed for cleaning the mess up or, like Lee Sherman, had not.

"Stricter regulation would be good," Harold replies. "We're not against industry," Annette clarifies. "We were happy when industry came. It brought jobs. We were glad for Harold to get one. But for decades now, they've done nothing to clean up the bayou or compensate us to move."

Like other friends and family, the Arenos are Republican and had voted in the presidential election of 2012 for Mitt Romney. "He's a big business guy, of course," Harold explains. "If he were here he'd be having friendly visits with the CEOs of the companies around here. He wouldn't be cleaning up the mess."

But Harold and Annette speak with a mildness of manner, a flatness of voice, that makes me sense I am inquiring into an area of life in which they'd mostly given up interest. "We vote for candidates that put the Bible where it belongs," Harold adds. "We try to be right-living, clean-living people, and we'd like our leaders to live that way and believe in that, too." Before settling on Romney in the 2012 election, they had favored the former senator from Pennsylvania, Rick Santorum. The Arenos disapprove of "greedy corporations" stepping on the little guy. "Oil interests tried to suppress the development of the electric car," Annette adds. Agreeing, Harold says: "Republicans stand for big business. They won't help us with the problems we've got here."

But Republicans put God and family on their side and "we like that. The Scripture says Jesus wants us to be about his Father's business," Annette says. Their faith had guided them through a painful loss of family, friends, neighbors, frogs, turtles, and trees. They felt God had blessed them with this courage to face their ordeals, and they thanked Him for that. "I don't know what people do if they don't know Him," Annette adds. For the Arenos, religious faith has moved into the very cultural space in which politics might have played a vital, independent role. Politics hadn't helped, they felt, and the Bible surely had.

For governor of Louisiana, the Arenos had twice voted for Bobby Jindal on grounds of faith and family values. Jindal wasn't for cleaning up the environment, however. In remarks to the Heritage Foundation, the conservative think tank, he had said that emissions regulations and environmental protections were a way President Obama was "holding our economy hostage to their radical ideas." In 2014 Jindal had also given $1.6 billion to industry as "incentives" to invest in Louisiana—$394 per citizen of Louisiana— while simultaneously cutting about the same amount out of the state budget and laying off 30,000 public sector workers—among them nurses, nurse's aides, medical technicians, public school teachers, and safety inspectors.

People on the right seemed to be strongly moved by three concerns— taxes, faith, and honor. Lee Sherman was eager to lower his taxes, the Arenos to protect their Christian faith. Added to these basic motives were certain personal wishes: Lee, who had borne the guilt of polluting public waters and been cheated by a dishonest official at a tax office, wanted to feel vindicated.

The tax office was corrupt, and taxes themselves were connected to dishonesty, he felt. One didn't know where they went or for what. The Arenos shared Lee's concern, but added another personal wish. Given their extended ordeal and the importance of God and the church in getting through it, they felt a powerful drive to place themselves in spiritually guided hands. For both Lee and the Arenos, at issue in politics was trust. It was hard enough to trust people close at hand, and very hard to trust those far away; to locally rooted people, Washington, D.C., felt very far away. Like everyone I was to talk with, both also felt like victims of a frightening loss—or was it theft?—of their cultural home, their place in the world, and their honor.

The politicians who most won their trust offered no help on cleaning the place up. And those who offered help, well, who were they? What were they pushing? That was the dilemma. Both Lee and the Arenos had voted for Republican congressman David Vitter, who voted in 2011 to eliminate the entire Environmental Protection Agency. He also voted against a National Endowment for the Oceans, which would protect oceans, coastal areas, and Great Lakes ecosystems. He battled the EPA on its report of a relationship of formaldehyde exposure to cancer, and won a score of 0 on the League of Conservation Voters scorecard.

As for threats to coastal Louisiana from climate change, no one they voted for thought it was real. Republican governor Jindal had called climate change a "Trojan horse" from which would emerge a new horde of government regulators. Lee Sherman thought the idea of climate change was "a bunch of hooey." It was a big state idea. It evoked *liberal* fear, not *conservative* suspicion and bravado. But Harold and Annette and Mike Tritico bent over their Bibles, from time to time in the Arenos' living room, to study the book of Revelation, chapter 11, verse 18. There it was written that God would bring ruin to those who ruin the earth. In the book of Mark, chapter 13, verse 19, they also found "For there will be greater anguish in those days than at any time since God created the world. And it will never be so great again." Through these passages, the three brought their faith to bear on the issue of climate change and, given his training in marine biology, Mike brought science to it. Together they worked out that climate change was, indeed, a man-made disaster-in-waiting that called for strong countermeasures. In the climate of opinion around them, they were brave to do so. But their concern raised the question: how could repairs be made? On that, the Bible gave them clearer answers than politics did.

The Rememberers

"They don't even want 'No Fishing or Swimming' signs up around here," Derwin observes. "Some time ago signs was put up, but someone took 'em down. Who did that? I don't know. But it seems like whoever they were, they don't want people to know—or if they knew, they don't want [them] to remember—that it's polluted around here. On TV you see these ads for Shell Oil with beautiful egrets flying across a green marsh, music playing. You wonder what they're trying to make us forget," he says. We are on to dessert and coffee and there is a nodding of heads around the table.

The Arenos didn't simply remember the good old days of a clean Bayou d'Inde. They remembered *against* the great forgetting of industry and state government. This larger institutional forgetting altered the private act of mourning. And not just that. It altered the Arenos' very identity. They had not left Bayou d'Inde. They were stayers. They didn't want to leave, and even if they had wanted to, they couldn't afford to. The polluting companies had given them no money to enable them to move. And the value of their house had now fallen, for who would want to live on Bayou d'Inde Pass Road, even in a home as beautifully kept up as theirs? The Arenos had become stay-at-home migrants. They had stayed. The environment had left.

The Greek word "nostalgia" derives from the root *nostros,* meaning "return home," and *algia,* meaning "longing." Doctors in seventeenth-century Europe considered nostalgia an illness, like the flu, mainly suffered by displaced migrant servants, soldiers, and job seekers, and curable through opium, leeches, or, for the affluent, a journey to the Swiss Alps. Throughout time, such feeling has been widely acknowledged. The Portuguese have the term *saudade.* The Russians have *toska.* The Czechs have *litost.* Others too name the feeling: for Romanians, it's *dor,* for Germans, it's *heimweh.* The

Welsh have *hiraeth*, the Spanish *mal de corazon*. Many who have suffered from this illness of heart have been forced to leave a beloved home that is itself still there. But Harold and Annette Areno live at home in an environment no longer there.

I meet other rememberers too. One man recalls forests of towering bald cypress, clear-cut in the 1920s. Plaques issued by the U.S. Forest Service now memorialize these trees in the Atchafalaya National Heritage Area. Some federal worker must have come up with the bright idea to call these venerable trees "Louisiana Purchase Trees"—trees alive during the 1803 Louisiana Purchase. Other trees were named for being alive during the 1812 inauguration of Louisiana as a state. Those who cared about the state could now care about the trees. They were state ancestors. Paul Ringo, a member of a nonprofit environmental group called Riverkeepers, didn't need such an idea to keep memory alive. Living in a cabin off the grid on the edge of the Sabine River, whose waters were inked by an upstream paper mill, Paul hears the nightly gurgle and roar of the Sabine. He tracks pollutants in it and escorts bands of "prayer warriors" who pray over the river. In truth, he himself is such a warrior. He holds sacred the memory of the Atakapa Indians, who once inhabited the river basin, and has helped discouraged descendants in negotiations with the state. "The Sabine River is a public river," Paul Ringo told me on a visit I paid him, "But if you can't drink in the river, and you can't swim in the river, or fish in the river, or baptize your young in the river, then it's not your river. It's the paper mill's river." Like the Arenos, Paul Ringo is a rememberer.

But such thinking is not much shared around town on two accounts. First, new business was coming to town, bringing with it a euphoric celebration of new jobs, new money, and new products. Talk was of "economic progress," and nostalgia would get in its way. "Don't you believe in economic progress?" people could ask. Also, as a cause, environmental protection had fallen into the hands, people felt, of left-leaning government expansionists and do-nothing local officials.

With one avenue of nostalgia blocked, the State Tourist Bureau has busily promoted another through Lake Charles's seventy-five annual festivals, fairs, and special events: Mardi Gras, a gala event second only to that in New Orleans, Cajun-Zydeco Music, and Lake Charles Contraband Days—two weeks of joyous celebration of the pirates of old. Then there is the Crawfish Festival in Breaux Bridge, the Frog Festival in Rayne, and the Giant Omelet Celebration in Abbeville. They put fun into memory.

Many workers in the petrochemical plants were conservative Republicans and avid hunters and fishers who felt caught in a terrible bind. They loved their magnificent wilderness. They remembered it from childhood. They knew it and respected it as sportsmen. But their jobs were in industries that polluted—often legally—this same wilderness. They had children to take care of and felt wary of supporting any environmental movement or federal government action that might jeopardize them. The general talk around town was that the choice was between the environment and jobs. On Fox News, in the local paper, in talk with friends, that was the refrain: too much nostalgia for croaking frogs and clean rivers might seem like just that—too much nostalgia. The basic feeling around town was that one shouldn't get too hung up on the environment, feel too nostalgic for cleaner times, or be too retro; that wasn't what residents were "supposed to feel." That's because a fracking boom was on, and many new industries were on their way to Lake Charles to process the natural gas it freed from the cracked earth.

So ironically, strangely, embarrassingly, the memory of Southern environmental glory fell, in part, to respectful clerks in federal offices and to northern environmentalists. With their memorial plaques, the federally financed U.S. Forest Service was inviting residents to remember the history of their own ancient trees. The New York–based Riverkeepers Alliance, started by Washington, D.C.–born environmentalist Robert F. Kennedy Jr., reminded a local citizenry what could be lost if citizens didn't watch out. The Arenos welcomed these northern environmentalists as natural allies in their own difficult struggle, as did Mike Schaff, who had faced a great loss of his own.

The Arenos were rememberers facing a strange "structural amnesia," as the British anthropologist Sir Edward Evan Evans-Pritchard called it when studying something utterly different. Evans-Pritchard had been researching a pastoral people of the Sudan called the Nuer, who had a remarkable memory for some things and completely forgot about others. Men and women both remembered eleven generations of male ancestors, for example, but largely forgot their female counterparts. There was, the anthropologist sensed, a structure to what they remembered and forgot that was based on the power of the Nuer's dominant institution—the kin system. Dominant within that system were men. So memory, Evans-Pritchard reasoned, was an indirect expression of power.

The Arenos faced structural amnesia about something else and linked to a different source of power: the Louisiana Chemical Association, the Society of the Plastics Industry, the Vinyl Institute, Shell Oil, PPG Industries, and their leaders in government. Spokesmen for this source of power drew the popular imagination to the exciting economic future. The Arenos felt that their silent bayou, their buried kin, their dead trees were forgotten, like the female half of the Nuer.

Coming Down on the Little Guy

Harold adds an important idea to that of Evans-Pritchard. "The state always seems to come down on the *little* guy," he notes. "Take this bayou. If your motorboat leaks a little gas into the water, the warden'll write you up. But if *companies* leak thousands of gallons of it and kill all the life here? The state lets them go. If you shoot an endangered brown pelican, they'll put you in jail. But if a company kills the brown pelican by poisoning the fish he eats? They let it go. I think they *overregulate* the *bottom* because it's *harder* to regulate the *top*." It isn't just that the power structure rigs collective memory. It rigs the enforcement of rules too. The higher up the ladder of power, the more likely one was to get off; the lower down, the less likely. Environmental regulation was like that.

If the power elite want to forget about pollution, and if they impose structural amnesia on a community, you need an omnipotent mind to remember how things once were. You needed, the Arenos felt, God. He remembers how it was. He knows what was lost. If the federal government was committed to a multicultural America that dimmed the position of the Christian church, it was getting in the way of that church, diminishing the importance of God, and it was God who had enabled them to survive their terrible ordeal.

To Derwin—who, having brought lunch to his parents, is packing up to go—the solution to Bayou d'Inde lies far beyond power, politics, or science. A devoted believer in the rapture, as are his parents, Derwin describes the approach of the "End Times." Quoting from the book of Revelation, he says, "The earth will burn with fervent heat." Fire purifies, so the planet will be purified 1,000 years from now, and until then, the devil is on the rampage, Derwin says. In the Garden of Eden, "there wasn't anything hurting your environment. We'll probably never see the bayou like God made it in the beginning until He fixes it himself. And that will happen pretty shortly, so it don't matter how much man destroys."

Harold and Annette look forward to the rapture too, but they want man to repair the earth *before* it comes. They've already waited long enough and nearly despair of politics. A commission to study the pollution, "partnering" with industry, had been meeting occasionally for decades. Newcomers to Lake Charles were not privy to this history of pollution, and the Tourist Bureau had no interest in reviving the memory of it. Buried with the memory of the damage, too, was a general appreciation of the extraordinary fortitude that had been called upon in Harold and Annette Areno over so many years. At least the Lord remembered what they'd endured and remembered the courage it took to endure it.

As I take leave of the Arenos, I ask them about the lawsuit they have filed against the polluters of Bayou d'Inde. Fifty-three plaintiffs, residents on the bayou and workers in nearby companies, had sued twenty-two companies. "We're still waiting," Harold answers. Nothing could fully make up for the loss of trees, birds, and fish from their beloved bayou, but the Arenos are hoping mightily that the lawsuit will at least provide money to move, for despite their attachment to the place, their distrust of the water, the banks, the air makes them feel like refugees in their own home. If they win the suit, it will be a moral victory, a remembered fact. A lawyer who worked in the firm that filed their suit (the lead lawyer had passed away) tells me with a sigh that it is common corporate strategy, with the cooperation of the state agencies, to string these lawsuits out for so long that plaintiffs die before money is due. Still, much time has passed.

Among the plaintiffs in this suit, I am astonished to learn, is a man I have already met—Lee Sherman. Lee and the Arenos had played different roles in the pollution of Bayou d'Inde, but each recognized the other as a victim. They'd become good friends. In 2012, all three were watching speeches by Republican presidential candidate Mitt Romney. He wouldn't help the country clean up dirty rivers, they thought, but as an opponent to the right to abortion, he was for "saving all those babies"—and that seemed to them the more important moral issue on which they would be ultimately judged.

Harold walks me to my car. I get in, open my window, and fasten my seat belt. "We're on this earth for a limited amount of time," he says, leaning on the edge of the window. "But if we get our souls saved, we go to Heaven, and Heaven is for eternity. We'll never have to worry about the environment from then on. That's the most important thing. I'm thinking *long-term.*"

4

The Candidates

Under a big tent in the restored Acadian Village outside Lafayette, Louisiana, the accordion is leading the fiddle, guitar, and washboard in a catchy, fast-paced Zydeco-Cajun swamp-pop tune. Middle-aged women in jerseys, Bermuda shorts, and sneakers draw partners up from their picnic tables to the dance floor. Men in cowboy hats with curled brims two-step, and a few teenage girls with swinging ponytails move in well-practiced jitterbugs with mothers or grandmothers. Two cooks in tall white hats briefly join in. Picnickers in the mainly white crowd chuckle as a toddler is led to the bandstand with a tiny washboard hung on his neck and distractedly runs a stick over it. Elsewhere, children scamper between festive face-painting, balloon vendors, and snow-cone stands. Dishes of pork, beans, rice, and gumbo are lined up on a long table to the side of the tent, and an enormous basket of cracklins passes from table to table.

It is a balmy Saturday an hour's drive east from Bayou d'Inde. I've come to the Boustany Boucherie, a public pig roast and campaign whistle stop for the Republican U.S. congressman Charles Boustany. In this 2012 election, he is running in a tight race against fellow U.S. congressman and Tea Party caucus member Jeff Landry. Until recently Landry had represented District 3, while Boustany represented District 7. After the 2010 census reflected a loss of population—each seat has to represent roughly the same number of people—Louisiana lost one seat, and like musical chairs, the two men criss-cross the same territory, event after event, competing for the one remaining seat.

The pig roast is held in a park commemorating the mid-nineteenth-century life of Acadian settlers—later called Cajuns—in southwest Louisiana. Within the village green are simple restored wood houses with mud walls and tin roofs. Clustered around a pond and majestic Evangeline oaks are a blacksmith shop, a spinning and weaving house, and a small Catholic church whose wooden sign reads "La Chapelle du Nouvel Espoir 1850" (Chapel of New Hope). An old, rusted harrowing machine and plow stand motionless in the nearby grass, and a wooden shed shelters a twenty-seven-foot dugout canoe such as Harold Areno's father built for fishermen on Bayou d'Inde.

How, I wonder as I sit down at a picnic table, do politicians such as Boustany and Landry deal with Bayou d'Inde or other places like it on Mike Tritico's napkin map? Do they remember what happened? Would they help such people as Lee Sherman or Harold and Annette Areno? If they call for smaller federal government, how do they propose to fix the problems that form part of the Great Paradox that has brought me to Louisiana? I ask myself, again, how people in a poor state with the worst health in the nation can look askance at a federal government that provides 44 percent of its state budget, and how such a polluted state can take a dim view of government regulation of polluters. A political campaign has a central place in the cultural life of a people. It tells citizens what issues powerful people think are worth hearing about.

I was backing into the picture I wanted to see by noticing what wasn't in it. It was like trying to understand a photograph by studying the negative. I found myself focusing not on what people remembered, focused on, and said, but on what they forgot, disregarded, and did not say. I was backing into the deep story, as I am calling it, and noticing what, in human consciousness, it crowded out.

My developing focus on silence was not a reward for some brave climb over the empathy wall. I was still way over on my side of it, saying to myself, if the Louisiana environment is in such a mess, I hope these politicians talk about cleaning it up. If not, why not? Something commonsensical was beginning to seem mysterious. Many of the Tea Party people I met seemed to me warm, intelligent, generous—not like people out of the frightening pages of Ayn Rand. They have community, and church, and goodwill toward those they know. Many, like Lee Sherman and Harold and Annette Areno, care deeply about the environment. But for each of them, there was something else, I was coming to realize, that was even more important. Taxes, church? That seemed part of it. But were these the whole story? Congressman Boustany was a mainstream Republican popular with his constituency, with a reputation for honesty, a trained surgeon but a regular guy, pro-oil. He was a man who could get money from Washington but also make jabs at the "Washington elite." He could both complain about Washington being too out of touch and put you in touch with it. The Boucherie door prize was a symbol of the federal government—a congressional club cookbook with a homemade Christmas ornament made by Mrs. Boustany, wrapped in a small American flag (which by some fluke I won). People blamed their woes on Washington, but prized attachment to it too. Jeff Landry was a Tea Party Republican, which, according to one 2011 poll, had won the sympathy of nearly half of Louisiana voters. So I was curious what differences between the two men would emerge.

After a while the band stops. Dancers sit down. Congressman Boustany, bespectacled and balding, rises to the podium and begins: "We've been through hurricanes together. We've been through a moratorium on oil drilling that hurt jobs. We've been through a financial and economic crisis." Louisiana needs "conservative leadership you can trust." In a later radio interview, he boasts that he defeated a bill to tax oil and gas companies that would have raised $60 billion, opposed a moratorium on drilling after the BP disaster, and voted for the Keystone pipeline.

At a rice-and-beans supper at a union hall in Rayne a few days later, his rival, Congressman Landry, a former sugarcane field worker and policeman with a heavy Cajun drawl, makes a remarkably similar speech, only adding periodically, "If it ain't good for y'all, I ain't voting for it."

"You can take a high school graduate—and I know some people that didn't even finish high school," Landry says, "work that tail off in the oil and gas industry—and make better money than most people make anywhere else in this country." He continues: "I'm tired of the government being in my business. . . . When I was struggling and we needed help, I never went straight to the government. You know where I went? I went into my church. I went into my community. I mean, who built the hospitals in this country? You go back and look. Our Lady of Lourdes—that ain't the government, O.K.? All those Baptist hospitals up in the Midwest? And the Catholic hospitals on the East Coast? That wasn't the government; that was people helping people. The answers to [our] problems are right here in places just like Rayne."

But questions from the floor in this mainly older crowd focus on how to get more and better federal government services. "Why haven't the over-sixty-five received a cost-of-living raise on their Social Security check?" one man asks. (Landry's answer is to retire later.) Another asks about Medicare. Another elderly woman complains that she has to pay $28 to hire a cab to get to the doctor. "Why isn't there free van transport for seniors?" To these questions, Landry has no answers.

A few days after a union hall meet-and-greet in Crowley, Congressman Landry speaks at a boat parade in New Iberia. Some in the crowd are munching on devil hot dogs—chili sauce, mustard, and sugar—along with fried chicken and double chocolate whiskey caramel brownies. "We have to take our country back from a government that has ignored our Constitution, dismissed our conservative values, and spent our tax dollars like drunken sailors. Of course, that's unfair to the sailors," Landry declares to a nodding crowd.

About a third of the gathering are black, and there seem to be quite a few multiracial picnic groupings of families and friends, some there more for the food and music, I am told by two white attendants, than the politics. One black woman confides: "Oh, I'm voting for Obama. We have really *poor* people here. My twenty-one-year-old grandson says he's going to vote Republican, but I don't know if he means it or he's just trying to raise my blood pressure."

In all the speeches, between the Pledge of Allegiance at the beginning and invitations to gumbo cook-offs at the end, I am again struck by what both candidates avoid saying—that the state ranks 49th out of 50 on an index of human development, that Louisiana is the second poorest state, that 44 percent of its budget comes from the federal government—the Great Paradox.

At the same time, the rivals both express and promote a culture that has produced the Great Paradox. They disdain "insider Washington" while trying to pry as much money from it for Louisiana as they can. The two men verge on—but refrain from—competing for how many government agencies they would strip away, as other prominent Southern Republicans have done. In the 2012 presidential race, Texas Governor Rick Perry called for abolishing three federal departments, though during a nationally televised debate, he famously forgot the third one. (They were Commerce, Education, and Energy.) Republican Ron Paul called for eliminating the Internal Revenue Service, FEMA (Federal Emergency Management Agency), and the Department of Health and Human Services. As mentioned, Congressman David Vitter called for axing the EPA.

On my keyhole issue, the story was this: the seat of District 3, the parish of Calcasieu, which the two were competing to represent, is one of the most polluted counties in the nation—the district includes companies on Mike Tritico's napkin map, as well as the half-remembered, half-forgotten tragedy of Bayou d'Inde. (In 2015, of the nine main waterways in the parish, the EPA listed eight as "impaired" and the ninth as "unassessed.") In 2015, Lafayette Parish also had a hundred facilities with current violations of the law and eighty-nine with "formal enforcement actions in the last five years," according to the EPA.

Most of those I interviewed voted for Boustany, who won. But all along the campaign trail, I heard not a word about Boustany's vote to roll back regulation of Wall Street, a measure that would strengthen monopolies and hurt small business people, many of whom were Tea Party members. I heard nothing about federal and state subsidies to oil companies, lowered corporate taxes, the role of oil in the erosion of the Louisiana coast, or unclean waters. Their voting records told where they stood. Boustany voted to cut funds for the Environmental Protection Agency, to block fuel-efficiency standards for cars, to ban federal fracking safeguards, to halt Clean Air Act protections for smog, soot, and mercury pollution, and to gut the core of the Clean Water Act—the federal "floor" of water quality standards that states must meet. He voted to redefine "healthy air," basing the definition of it on the *feasibility* and *cost* to polluting industries, and not on human health. Representative Landry did the same. On the League of Conservation Voters' scorecard of members of Congress, both Boustany and Landry had earned a lifetime score of 6 out of a total possible 100. Louisiana produced 31 pounds of toxic release per person to air, water, and land in 2012. By comparison, the United States as a whole produced 11 pounds per capita. Neither candidate said a word about all this.

Silence on the environment extended to the minor candidates in this race as well. At a "Meet You at the Polls" gathering of several hundred citizens in Crowley, a libertarian vowed to "get the government out of the way" so Louisiana can "plant hemp in rice fields." A Democrat began, "I don't agree with everything the Democratic Party or the president say," before declaring himself pro-life, pro-marriage, pro-gun, and pro-oil. Only one candidate came out for "protecting our coast," in part because it would "protect our energy industry."

At a Landry union hall campaign stop, three dozen retired plant workers sit around wooden picnic tables eating a rice-and-bean dinner from paper plates. When it comes up, they speak of the Democratic Party as a tattered memory from a distant past. One man says that he'd been waiting until his father died before he voted Republican, a comment greeted with knowing laughter around the table. Another man adds, "The only Democrat left in my family is my wife, and she's voting for Landry." More laughter. A former so-called blue dog democratic state, since 1970 Louisiana has voted Republican in seven out of ten presidential elections. And in such older white crowds, this shift rightward seems bound to continue. As one man explains, "A lot of us have done okay, but we don't want to lose what we've got, see it given away." When I ask him what he saw as being "given away," it was not public waters given to dumpers, or clean air given to smoke stacks. It was not health or years of life. It was not lost public sector jobs. What he felt was being given away was tax money to non-working, non-deserving people—and not just tax money, but honor too. If that tax money could come back to citizens—as a sort of "raise" in the midst of a three-decade-long national economic lull, why not?

As with Mike Schaff, Lee Sherman, and the Arenos, conversations moved toward this rift between deserving taxpayers and undeserving tax money takers, those in a class below them. Repeatedly, I was to find, this rift was an emotional flashpoint, especially for men who worked in oil and other predominantly male jobs in the private sector. But it was a guy thing to hunt and fish, too, and these days if the ducks they shot ate fish from Bayou d'Inde, it took some of the fun out of hunting. Still, if it is between animals and people, the man at the Landry union hall table concludes, people matter more: "These days, American men are an endangered species too."

The General, the Psychological Program, and "Just Enough Talk of Jobs"

Meanwhile, a potential candidate for governor of Louisiana has broken the silence on the environment held all along this campaign trail. He's dressed in army fatigues and stands six feet five inches tall when he gets up from a Baton Rouge hotel breakfast table to greet me. We adjourn to a conference room where he sits, takes off a military cap bearing three large stars, and lays it on the table. A much decorated lieutenant general in the U.S. Army, in September of 2005 General Russel Honoré led the Joint Task Force and a thousand National Guardsmen to rescue stranded residents of New Orleans overwhelmed by the floodwaters and chaos of Hurricane Katrina. Taking up that job after it was famously bungled by FEMA chief Michael Brown, a Bush contributor and Oklahoma lawyer with an interest in horses, Honoré became known as a "Category 5 General" (a term used to describe storms). He reminded guardsmen to point their guns down, because "we're on a rescue mission, damn it." Beloved to thousands of rescued Katrina flood victims, the General became a statewide legend.

Born the youngest of twelve children in Point Coupee Parish, northwest of Baton Rouge, the General is by origin black Creole, though people affectionately call him the "Ragin' Cajun" for his wide strides, forceful manner, and authoritative bass voice. The mayor of New Orleans called him "a John Wayne kind of dude." But this is a serious underestimation. For the expressions that cross Honoré's long face, with its aquiline nose and thin salt-and-pepper mustache, alternate between compassion, humor, thoughtfulness, and indignation. He's an empathy wall leaper.

"I have nothing against oil and gas making money in Louisiana," the General begins matter-of-factly. "But the oil companies need to clean up after themselves, and they haven't. They need to fix what they break, and they haven't. And pretty much theirs is the only voice we hear."

"Why," I ask Honoré, "don't citizens ask politicians to clean up their environment?" The General pauses: "All the people in Louisiana hear is jobs, jobs, jobs. And there's just enough to it, that people slip into believing it's the whole story. Really they're captives of a psychological program."

Honoré has called for cleanup of polluted rivers and abandoned oil wells, and for monitoring devices inside industrial plants, similar to those in airplane cockpits, to tell what has caused a disaster. In recent years, the General has also led what he calls "The Green Army"—a consortium of small environmental groups. "I wasn't aware of the extent of our problem until I looked out the window of the helicopter that took me to New Orleans after Katrina," the General says. "The landscape was littered for miles with debris. I remember commenting to the pilot, 'The storm must have caused that mess,' and hearing back, 'No, those are abandoned oil derricks from years back.'"

After an hour, Honoré offers to drive me in his truck along River Road, which parallels the Mississippi River between Baton Rouge and New Orleans, a span now popularly known as Cancer Alley. "You see the river?" The General points his arm out the window at the Mississippi. I am reminded of Mark Twain's *Life on the Mississippi*, and looking at the map I had been charmed by the names of the towns along it: Convent, Saint Gabriel, Saint

Rose, Saint James. I knew that here over half of the nation's grain and a fifth of its other exports floated to the Gulf and out to the world.

"You know what you're looking at?" Honoré asked. I thought I did. "That's not the Mississippi's water. That's Monsanto water. Exxon water. Shell Oil water. It's a public waterway, but that's private water. Industry owns the Mississippi now. There's hardly a public dock along it."

The great river has long been polluted, it turns out. "Back in the 1950s," one man told me, "a steam boat left New Orleans propelled by freshly painted red paddles. By the time it had arrived upriver in Natchez, the red paint had vanished."

Riding in the General's truck, as in Mike Schaff's truck, through the sugar plantation, I become aware of what I can't see. With Schaff, it was history. With the General, it was pollution. Indeed, most of the pollution in Louisiana is invisible to the naked eye. We drive through Gonzales, a small town situated along Cancer Alley that is promoted by the Louisiana Visitor's Bureau as the Jambalaya Capital of the World. Gonzales is the site of spring-time festivals in which cooks stir enormous pots filled with 700 pounds of rice. Nearby is "a fisherman's haven," heralded by LouisianaTravel.com, near places "great for hiking and wildlife watching." The site offers a "Cajun Pride Swamp Tour" too. Gonzales seems to be a one-town ongoing party—above ground.

But the Jambalaya Capital is sadly located on one the most polluted industrial strips in the world. A hundred and fifty facilities line the two sides of the Mississippi, an eighty-five-mile strip, each plant surrounded by chain-link fences, some with entrances whose signs proudly announce the small number of work days missed due to accidents. Many plants were built on former cotton and sugarcane plantations. Other towns along River Road—Plaquemine, St. Gabriel, Geismar, Donaldsonville—lie in parishes that in 2013 ranked in the top 3 percent of U.S. counties in reported toxic releases, according to the EPA. Louisiana is the nation's sixth leading state in generating hazardous waste, and it is third in the nation for the amount of hazardous waste it imports from other states. "We *import* hazardous waste from *Arkansas*," the General continues, eyes wide as if in disbelief, "because they've got *stricter* regulations than we do." Throughout the state, there are many injection wells drilled deep underground and surrounded by casing into which hazardous waste is pumped, and worrisome studies had occasionally appeared in the press about them.

"Louisiana has a lot of oil," the General continues. "And a lot of people think that's a blessing. And if done well, it could be. But it's not done well." Companies, he points out, have drilled over 220,000 wells, found 600 producing oil fields, and built 8,000 miles of pipelines and canals in this state. Over 25,000 miles of underwater pipelines connect offshore drilling platforms to onshore refineries in Louisiana and Texas. But the companies put the state government in their pockets, the General points out, and people pay the price.

He pulls his truck alongside an embankment bordering the Mississippi on the campus of Southern University, a formerly all-black college, his alma mater. We get out and walk across the grass to gaze at the river. He points to an island far across the way. "You see the tip of that island? They call that Free Nigger Point, because if a man could swim across the river to it, he could reach the Underground Railroad and he was free. Many couldn't swim and drowned. But today, if he gulped the water, he'd get sick and die gradually of pollution."

"The Spill Makes Us Sad, the Moratorium Makes Us Mad"

Combining what I could not hear in the speeches of Congressmen Boustany and Landry with what I could not see out the window of the General's truck, I began to understand how easy it would be to forget or ignore the problems with Louisiana's environment. But what if a disaster were so spectacular, so visible for miles, so long lasting, so publicized, and so far into the arena of "never before" that you couldn't ignore it? What would my Tea Party friends say?

Of course, just such a spectacular event *did* occur in 2010—the BP oil rig Deepwater Horizon exploded in the Gulf of Mexico off the coast of

Louisiana. President Obama called it "the worst environmental disaster America has ever faced." The blowout killed eleven workers and injured seventeen. It ruptured an oil pipe 10,000 feet below the surface of the water, from which oil gushed into the Gulf continuously for three months. The spill released the equivalent of one Exxon Valdez–sized oil spill every three to four days—for 87 days.

Highly trained engineers were helpless. Anxious experts testified on television. Louisiana's 397-mile Gulf coast was critical, they said, to the life cycle of over 90 percent of all fish and 98 percent of all commercial species in the entire Gulf of Mexico. Eyeless shrimp and infant dolphins washed ashore, and oil balls appeared along an estimated 650 miles of coastline. Pelicans died. Crab traps were soiled and shrimp harvests were decimated. Oil leaked onto oyster plots. After the blowout, carcasses of 6,000 birds, 600 sea turtles, over a hundred bottlenose dolphins, and other marine mammals, including whales, washed ashore. Later studies discovered that embryos of fish, especially tuna, that had been exposed to BP oil showed distorted body shapes, hearts, and eyes.

More bad news followed. Some 90,000 fishermen had lost their livelihood and were offered jobs to clean up the spilled oil, using their own boats, in the Vessels of Opportunity program. However, their protective gear was inadequate against the oil and the dispersant Corexit, and some developed skin lesions, blurred vision, breathing difficulties, and headaches.

In response, President Obama ordered a six-month moratorium on deep-sea drilling until safeguards could be put in place, reasoning that it was better to have one disaster than two or more. No one knew for sure why the accident had occurred. At that time, the blowout preventer BP had used had never before been used at a depth of 10,000 feet. Even the robots used to explore the site of the blowout had never before been used, so no one knew if they would work. Thirty-two other rigs were still drilling in the Gulf using similar technology at such depths. BP itself did not object to the moratorium. Altogether, it seemed to many a wise step.

But months later, a team of Louisiana State University researchers asked some 2,000 residents of the devastated coast, "Do you favor or oppose a moratorium that would halt offshore drilling until new safety requirements are met?" Half opposed it, and only a third favored it. When asked, "Have your views about other environmental issues such as global warming or protecting wildlife changed as a result of the oil spill?" seven out of ten answered "no." The rest—interestingly, the less educated and female—said "yes." The inland Louisianans I spoke with, like Congressmen Boustany and Landry, were also adamantly opposed to Obama's moratorium.

Why? Loss of drilling revenue was one thing. But federal government "over-regulation" was another. "It's not in the company's *own interest* to have a spill or an accident. They try hard," one woman told me. "So if there's a spill, it's probably the best the company could do." Another recalled all the everyday things we use that are made from oil. One man even declared that "what caused the spill was *over*regulation. If the government hadn't been looking over BP's shoulder, it would have regulated itself, and the spill wouldn't have happened."

One woman summed it up: "The spill makes us sad, but the moratorium makes us *mad*." The governor and senators of the state called for an end to the moratorium. In partial response, President Obama ended it a month early, but that earned him no points with those I spoke with. "What did Obama know up there in Washington?" they asked. In the speeches of the two congressmen a few years later, not a word was said about the spill.

Maybe, I thought, the coastal Louisianans who opposed the ban were expressing loyalty to the oil industry and private sector, and falling into a historic refrain against the federal government. But given their vulnerability to loss and contamination, maybe they were managing strong feelings of anxiety, fear, and anger about what they already knew. Maybe they were saying to themselves, "We can't afford to worry about this. We need to set thoughts of it aside, manage our anxiety and not acknowledge that we're doing so."

With this in mind, I returned to the Great Paradox. From my initial perspective, Louisiana, like other red states, was coping with a great number of challenges. Perhaps for better-off people of the far right, problems such as poverty, poor schools, and medical care didn't come up because such problems didn't hit them directly. Pollution hit better-off people too. But they seemed braced to tough it out. As for blame, it seemed as if Dad had left a dreadful mess, and you blamed Mom because Mom's used to absorbing blame for what goes wrong and trying to fix it, and she's still there. At least it seemed like that at first.

Freedom to, Freedom from, Freedom for Whom?

So how did Louisianans look at government regulation of *any* sort? I thought an answer to that might help me understand the coastal Louisianans who were sad at the spill but mad at the government. Maybe it was government regulations in general they resented. At first glance, Louisiana's own policies seemed flamboyantly opposed to the very idea of regulation. With regard to alcohol, Louisiana is one of the most permissive states in the nation. You can pull into a drive-through frozen daiquiri stand and buy daiquiris in "go-cups"—the only legal proviso being that the plastic lid is pressed on and the straw is not yet inserted. At a Caribbean Hut in Lake Charles, a satisfied customer reported ordering a 32-ounce Long Island Iced Tea with a few extra shots, a piece of Scotch tape placed over the straw hole—so it was "sealed"—and drove on. And only in 2004 did it become illegal to drive with unsealed containers. There is even a late July "Defend the Daiquiri Festival" held in New Orleans—supported, naturally, by an alcohol lobbying group.

An unlicensed vendor can sell handguns, shotguns, rifles, or assault weapons, and large-capacity magazines. A person can buy any number of guns and, except for handguns, need not register them, or report a theft of one, or hesitate to take them into parking lots and state parks. Louisiana also has a "Stand Your Ground" law, permitting a frightened homeowner to shoot first. A person can walk into a bar on Bourbon Street in New Orleans with a loaded gun.

Indeed, a gun vendor in Louisiana can keep no records, perform no background checks, and sell guns to an array of customers forbidden in other states: those with violent and firearms-related misdemeanors, people on terror watch lists or "no fly" lists, abusers of drugs or alcohol, juvenile offenders, and criminals with a history of serious mental illness or domestic violence. In 2010, the governor passed a law that permitted concealed handguns in churches, synagogues, and mosques. The next year, Louisiana had the highest rate of death by gunfire in the country, nearly double the national average.

Still, many I talked to were ardent believers in the right to bear arms. Mike Schaff had four guns. "A 22 rifle, a 22 pistol that I got when Daddy died, a .40 Smith & Wesson Automatic, and a 12 gauge shotgun. These killed varmint or deer," he explained, while "the Smith & Wesson's for self-defense." He went on to describe his first wife's rifle and another long Kentucky rifle, a "show gun" he had assembled from a kit. But he now had four, which he described as "nothing for the South. Most have seven or eight guns." He didn't have a conceal and carry permit, he added, but said he would get it eventually if "things got worse."

Looked at more closely, an overall pattern in state regulation emerges, and the Great Paradox becomes more complicated than it first seemed. Liquor, guns, motorcycle helmets (legislation had gone back and forth on that)—mainly white masculine pursuits—are fairly unregulated. But for women and black men, regulation is greater. Within given parameters, federal law gives women the right to decide whether or not to abort a fetus. But the state of Louisiana has imposed restrictions on clinics offering the procedure, which, if upheld in the U.S. Supreme Court, would prevent all but one clinic, in New Orleans, from offering women access to it. Any adult in the state can also be jailed for transporting a teenager out of state for the purposes of an abortion if the teen has not informed her parents.

Young black males are regulated too. Jefferson Davis Parish passed a bill banning the wearing of pants in public that revealed "skin beneath their waists or their underwear," and newspaper accounts featured images, taken from the back, of two black teenage boys exposing large portions of their undershorts. The parish imposed a $50 fine for a first offense and $100 for a second. A town ordinance in Ville Platte (in which 54 percent of the population is black) requires residents to wear "something reflective" and visible from all directions on an outer garment when walking after dark.

Next to the death sentence, prisons are the ultimate instrument of regulation. The United States incarcerates a higher proportion of its population than does any nation in the world outside the Seychelles Islands—more than Russia or Cuba. Louisiana incarcerates the highest proportion of its population of all the states in the union, and those inmates are disproportionately black. It also houses Angola, the nation's largest maximum security prison, in which rules are notoriously harsh. The prison is the site of the longest-standing case of solitary confinement in the nation—a black man, Albert Woodfox, who had been locked up for twenty-three out of every twenty-four hours a day for forty-three years before finally being released on February 19, 2016. So while the state boasts a reputation of an almost cowboy-style "don't-fence-me-in" freedom, that is probably not how a female rape victim who wants an abortion, or a young black boy in Jefferson Davis Parish, or Albert Woodfox see the matter.

Yet when people spoke indignantly of regulation, it was not abortion clinics and prisons that came to mind, but rather what the government was telling them to buy in stores. At a meeting of the Republican Women of Southwest Louisiana, across-the-table talk of regulation focused on the promotion of fluorescent or LED light bulbs: "The government has no right to regulate the light bulbs we buy," one woman declared. "I made my husband change all my light bulbs *back* to the *old* ones." Others complained of all the "forced" salads on the menus in fast food restaurants now. "I don't need the government telling me what to eat," one woman complained. "You remember that apron that says 'If the cook ain't fat, I ain't eatin' it?'" one woman asked to a round of happy laughter. Others were irritated by a local ban on driving on sidewalks, or on having more than one RV in your yard, and still others by child-protection devices. One woman recalled an age without child-proof lids on medicine bottles or car seat belts. "We let them throw lawn darts, smoked alongside them," she said. "And *they survived.* Now it's like your kid needs a helmet, knee pads, and elbow pads to go down the kiddy slide." Laughter rippled around the table.

Self-Service Regulation

One Cub Scout den mother named Louise, a warm-hearted bookkeeper and mother of three, lives near a petrochemical plant. She believes the plants should be regulated—"We regulate everything else, why not them?"—but had observed events that made her wonder how carefully they actually were. So she kept an informal vigil over nearby plants. "You can go months without a scare," she explains. "Then sometimes you'll hear noises or the windows rattle. You half hold your breath. We'll call: 'Dad, you all right?' [her father-in-law worked in a plant], and he'll say, 'Yeah, everything's fine.' If something happens at Firestone, I'm going to burn up my son-in-law's phone [use the phone a lot] calling everyone who knows somebody at the plant." Other times, she says, "You come over the bridge at night, and see haze hanging in the air. We have humid, heavy air in Lake Charles. It's like someone throwing covers over you, and then a smell, and you wonder, what's getting trapped?" She continues, "My house is less than three miles from Citgo, as the crow flies. We had a release today, but they said it didn't leave the confines of their property." With a laugh she adds, "So me and my neighbor, we go, 'Oh, thank goodness, just to the fence.'"

Another woman watched the color of industrial flares rising from nearby plant smoke stacks. "If it's a strange color, I'll call up a relative or friend: 'Why is it blue today?' Or 'Why is it red?' Or if you hear something or smell something, you turn on the radio or TV, and see if there's anything crawling across the screen telling you what's just happened. Around the plants, pollution is personal."

"Is the state doing all it can to assure safety?" I asked one man I sat next to at the Boat Parade in New Iberia. "I don't know. Sometimes they don't tell us the truth about what's going on because they don't want to alarm us," he replied. "And, of course, we don't want to be alarmed."

In 2013 an explosion took place at the Axiall plant—the old PPG with a new name and management—the second in thirteen months. It sent massive, dark clouds churning upward over Lake Charles, Westlake, and eastern Sulphur, carrying hydrochloric acid, ethylene dichloride, and vinyl chloride.

Drivers caught the event on their cell phones and posted pictures and videos of the clouded sky on YouTube and Facebook. Twenty-seven people—most of them drivers caught on the I-10 freeway—were treated in local emergency rooms for trouble breathing. The freeway was closed for three hours, and a "Shelter in Place" command was ordered for the nearby population. But the Louisiana Department of Environmental Quality reported that its detection equipment showed N.D.—"non-detect." Citizens were left to reconcile the fact that their iPhones and computer screens were saying, "plain, obvious, terrible," and the state was saying, "Didn't see it. Can't tell.".

The General is turning his truck around and we are returning back up River Road, along Cancer Alley to Baton Rouge. I ask him to respond to a question I often heard, "If companies want to avoid accidents themselves, why do we need the government?" He answered, "Less regulated industries have more accidents and more regulated industries have fewer; regulation works." Then with a wry smile, he continues, "But here we have 'self-regulation.' The federal EPA passes the buck to the state Department of Environmental Quality. The state passes the buck to the oil companies. They regulate themselves. It's like me driving this truck 100 miles an hour down River Road. I call up the Highway Patrol and say, 'Officer, excuse me. I'm speeding right now.'"

In all the talk at the gatherings for Congressmen Boustany and Landry and around the table at the Republican Women of Southwest Louisiana, I heard a great deal about freedom in the sense of freedom *to*—to talk on your cellphone as you drove a car, to pick up a drive-in daiquiri with a straw on the side, to walk about with a loaded gun. But there was almost no talk about *freedom from* such things as gun violence, car accidents, or toxic pollution. General Honoré was no nervous nelly, but he was mindful of the vulnerable communities around the "self-regulated" plants. "Part of the psychological program is that people think they're free when they're not," he said. "A *company* may be free to pollute, but that means the *people* aren't free to swim."

How did the psychological program work? Maybe I was missing the most obvious answer: jobs. Oil brought jobs. Jobs brought money. Money brought a better life—school, home, health, a piece of the American Dream. Maybe it was not so much that the people sitting with me in the audiences of the campaign rallies hated the federal government but that they loved the private sector, especially the queen of it in Louisiana: oil. Maybe I'd been so busy listening to the "unsung tune" about cleaning up pollution that I wasn't hearing the loud and clear song about jobs. After all, Jeff Landry had held up a sign in Congress during a speech by President Obama: "Oil = Jobs." And maybe government regulations were killing them.

General Honoré had told me that talk was of jobs, jobs, jobs, and there was "just enough in it" that people believed it. He'd told me that the "psychological program" involved the belief that there was a terrible choice *between* jobs and clean water or air. But how many jobs depended on oil? And was it either-or? Before I understood government, maybe I had to understand the private sector. Maybe there were tough choices I didn't see.

5

The "Least Resistant Personality"

Before me is Dr. Paul Templet, a PhD in chemical physics, recently retired from teaching at Louisiana State University, and for four years head of the Louisiana Department of Environmental Quality, during which time pollution of all kinds dropped in half. Templet knows jobs, environment, and trade-offs, and we're seated around a table with coffee and cake to talk about this in a friend's home in Baton Rouge. His manner is friendly, energetic, purposeful. He wears a mustache, goatee, and dark-tinted glasses and doesn't look his seventy-three years. He is wearing a rust-colored T-shirt and khaki pants and lifts his coffee cup to his mouth in a thoughtful manner, as if respecting the importance of the topic at hand more than the coffee. A Cajun born in Port Allen, Louisiana, as a teenager he had unloaded sandbags from railroad cars at Dow Chemical.

In the speeches of Congressmen Boustany and Landry, Senator Vitter, and Governor Jindal, a certain logic unfolded. These were leaders my Tea Party friends gladly voted into office, and so I wanted to understand this logic, see if it made any sense to me, and figure out why it made sense to them.

The logic was this. The more oil, the more jobs. The more jobs, the more prosperity, and the less need for government aid. And the less the people depend on government —local, state, or federal—the better off they will be. So to attract more oil jobs, the state has to offer financial "incentives" to oil companies to get them to come. That incentive money will have to be drawn from the state budget, which may lead to the firing of public sector workers, which, painful as it might seem, reduces reliance on government and lowers taxes. It is a red state logic. But the paradox is that it goes with being a poor state with a lot of problems.

So to begin with, I ask Paul, "How many Louisiana jobs are in oil and petrochemical plants?" "Today, less than 10 percent," he answers. I am shocked. For all the talk of jobs, this seems below the level that would justify General Honoré's remark that there was "just enough to" all the talk about jobs, that people felt threatened by the word "environmental" and gave an exasperated sigh at "regulation." But later when I check his figures I discover that the highest estimate—offered by the Louisiana Mid-Continent Oil and Gas Association—was 15 percent of all jobs in the state. The lowest—from the U.S. Bureau of Labor Statistics—was 3.3 percent. (This included all jobs in oil and gas extraction, support activities for mining, petroleum, and coal products manufacturing, and pipeline transportation in 2014.)

After all the talk by Congressmen Boustany and Landry and others, why so few? The industry is highly automated. To *build* a petrochemical plant, you need many construction workers for a temporary period, and then their job is over. To *run* a petrochemical plant, you need a small number of highly trained engineers, chemists, and operators to keep watch over panels of gauges and to know what to do when there's trouble. Then you need a few repairmen such as Lee Sherman.

But a fracking boom was on, and maybe that meant more jobs coming in. According to the 2014 Sasol-sponsored Southwest Louisiana Regional Impact Study, some 18,000 jobs, a small proportion of them permanent, would open up by 2018. But seven out of ten of these jobs would be filled, the report said, by workers from outside southwest Louisiana. Many companies would recruit professionals from around the world. Construction workers building the "man camps"—barracks within enclosed encampments—were Mexican, people said. The man camps would house 5,000 pipefitters, an undisclosed number of them Filipinos on temporary visas. Filipino workers have worked for over a decade on oil platforms in the Gulf.

Meanwhile, most permanent jobs in the state—85 percent of them—

involved doing something else, such as teaching children, nursing the ill, building mobile homes, playground equipment, and yachts, repairing aircraft, being stagehands for films being made in what some were calling the "Hollywood South," conducting tours through plantation manor homes, catching fish, and farming.

Perhaps oil jobs took priority, in official thinking, because oil brought in more state revenue. But severance taxes—fees paid when oil or gas is taken out of the ground—from oil contributed only 14 percent of the state's budget revenue, down from 42 percent in 1982. It was the largest single source of revenue, though, and this was the rationale behind Governor Bobby Jindal's plan to lure more oil and petrochemical business to Louisiana. (Oil companies also gave him a million dollars in campaign money, as my Tea Party interviewees were well aware. Critics also argued that the oil companies would come anyway since the oil, the pipe lines, the petrochemical plants, the port, the whole setup was already there.)

To offer an "incentive," Jindal lowered corporate income taxes so that state revenue from such companies fell from $703 million in 2008 to $290 million in 2012. He lowered oil severance taxes so that the state received over $1 billion in 2008 but less than $886 million in 2012. It also lost another $2.4 billion between 2000 and 2014 because some oil companies were exempted from oil severance taxes altogether. (With approval from the state, new businesses are eligible to avoid paying local property taxes on new building and equipment costs.) Indeed, according to the Louisiana Economic Development and Tax Foundation, Louisiana offers "the lowest business taxes in the entire country for new manufacturing projects." And for three years it was impossible to tell whether the oil companies paid anything at all to the state since the job of auditing oil company payments was handed over to the Office of Mineral Resources, which has close ties with the industry and which, between 2010 and 2013, performed no audits at all. So apart from providing 15 percent of jobs in Louisiana, oil was providing less and less financial benefit to the state. Oil was costing more to lure to the state and, once there, giving less to it. Meanwhile, to pay for this, public workers were fired and the state debt—$83 billion in 2012, much of it in unfunded public pension liabilities—remained.

Dr. Templet and I are on a second round of coffee and a second layer of revelations. "Oil brought in some jobs," Templet says, "but it causes other jobs to disappear or simply inhibits other sectors—such as the seafood industry and tourism—from growing." Oil rig explosions such as the 2010 BP Deepwater Horizon blowout severely hurt the seafood and tourism industries—oyster fishermen, deep sea fisherman, wholesalers, restaurateurs, and hotel workers were impacted. No one wants to eat oil-tainted shrimp or vacation on beaches strewn with tar balls. Despite the implication of the annual Morgan City Louisiana Shrimp and Petroleum Festival, oil and seafood do not go well together. Oil cut jobs in another way too. The "incentive" money Jindal gave oil went hand in hand with the cuts to 30,000 public sector jobs—nurses, medical technicians, teachers.

One defense of oil jobs was that they were highly paid, and that salaries would "trickle down" through consumption that increased jobs and wages of other workers. But did it? "Not much," Templet says. That's because oil wages don't trickle down; they leak out. As he explained, "Most of the plants are owned by foreign companies. Sasol is based in Johannesburg. Royal Dutch Shell is based in The Hague. BP is based in London. Citgo is a wholly owned subsidiary of Petróleos de Venezuela. Magnolia LNG is based in Perth, Australia. Phillips 66, spun off from ConocoPhillips in 2012, is based in the United States but not in Lake Charles. So most top executives in these companies are not building luxury homes and swimming pools in Lake Charles, Sulphur, or Westlake. Stockholders aren't spending their dollars there either, but rather where they live, in Greenwich, Connecticut, say, or Mill Valley, California."

The income of temporary Filipino pipefitters and Mexican green-card holders doesn't "trickle down" either, since most dutifully send money back to needy families abroad. Indeed, some local citizens complained that imported Filipino workers don't spend their money in local stores. Summing it up, Templet calculates that Louisiana "leaks" about a third of the gross state product, the sum of the value of all goods and services produced by the state.

Thinking again of the Great Paradox, I ask Templet whether the appearance of oil in Louisiana reduces the state's poverty. "No," he answers, "Louisiana was poor before oil came, and we're poor today—the second poorest in the U.S." In 1979, 19 percent of Louisianans lived below the poverty line; in 2014, it was 18 percent. In addition, ill-schooled poor people of any race find it hard to get the kind of highly skilled permanent jobs oil brings in. And oil hadn't improved the schools—they are financed by local property taxes, which are higher in rich areas and lower in poor ones.

Still, 15 percent of the people did get good jobs. Two-thirds of their salaries didn't leak out. This was good news. But what was the whole picture? Perhaps oil in Louisiana represented a strategy for economic growth conservatives pulled for—what sociologists Caroline Hanley and Michael T. Douglass call a "low road" strategy. Union bans, lower wages, corporate tax rebates, and loose implementation of environmental regulations are used as lures to get industry that *exists somewhere else* to move to one's own state. Fifty years ago, such a strategy brought the New England textile industry to the South, and these days it is bringing Mercedes from New Jersey to Georgia, Toyota from California to Texas, and Nissan from California to Tennessee. Louisiana brought jobs into the state, not by nurturing new business in the state, but by poaching jobs in another state. The "high road" strategy, as the researchers describe it, is to *stimulate new jobs* by creating an attractive public sector, as California did in Silicon Valley and Washington State did in Seattle. Perhaps, it occurred to me, the first strategy for economic development was backed by one party (the Tea Party, Louisiana model), and the second strategy by another party (the Democratic, California model).

Templet and I are on our third round of coffee and cake, and I want to return to a central idea in General Honoré's "psychological program"—one that taps into understandable right-wing anxiety about good jobs—that in America, you must *choose between* jobs or a clean environment. Many Louisianans I spoke with told me that, either by intent or in effect, environmental regulations kill jobs. This was the idea behind talk of "environmental wackos." But Templet refers me to a 1992 study by the MIT political scientist Stephen Meyer, who rated the fifty states according to the strictness of their environmental protection. Meyer then matched regulatory strictness to economic growth over a twenty-year period and found that the tougher the regulation, the more jobs were available in the economy. A 2016 survey of the world's major economies also found that strict environmental policies improved, rather than handicapped, competitiveness in the international market. If this was the growing consensus among Organisation for Economic Cooperation and Development (OECD) economists, I wondered why my Tea Party friends weren't hearing about it.

Perhaps because of two final parts of Templet's picture: a growing dominance of oil and its show of generous company largesse. As companies squeeze favors out of the state, he argued, the more urgent its citizens' needs for good schools and hospitals, the less the poor are able to use what opportunities exist, and the more atrophied become other sectors of the economy—which further concentrates power in the hands of oil.

Ironically, companies often privately give back to the community in gestures of goodwill. To do this they use the incentive money the cash-strapped state government has given them to lure them into the state in the first place. Dow Chemical gives to the Audubon Nature Institute. Shell Oil Company supports the National Fish and Wildlife Foundation. Pittsburgh Plate Glass pays for a "Naturelab–Classroom in the Woods" near Lake Charles. Sasol funds a project to record the history of Mossville, a black community its expansion displaced. The Louisiana Chemical Association gives to the Louisiana Tumor Registry. The people of Louisiana are now grateful—here Templet pauses for a moment of sad irony—"not just for jobs, but for gifts."

The Red and Blue of Pollution

On my drive back to Lake Charles, I considered a discouraging idea. Maybe Louisiana was an oddball oil state, atypical of other red states across the nation. Maybe it just told a story of oil. Was it leading me away from the heart of the right? I had imagined the South to be the center of the right, and Louisiana a center of the South. But was Louisiana an outlier, or was it an example of a nationwide story?

When I got home, I discovered an answer—a startling 2012 study by sociologist Arthur O'Connor that showed that residents of red states suffer higher rates of industrial pollution than do residents of blue states. Voters in the twenty-two states that voted Republican in the five presidential elections between 1992 and 2008—and who generally call for *less* government regulation of business—lived in *more* polluted environments. Residents in the twenty-two Democratic states that generally favor stricter regulation, he found, live in cleaner environments. This would be discouraging news for my Tea Party friends.

My Berkeley-based research assistant, Rebecca Elliott, and I asked one further question: was it just red *states* that were correlated to higher rates of pollution, or the *counties* of red-leaning individuals within any given state? We looked at the relationship between political views and pollution. For one we went to publicly available data on the EPA website. There we found scores for each county in the nation reflecting risk of exposure to pollution (Risk-Screening Environmental Indicators, or RSEI scores). These measure the amount of chemical release, the degree of its toxicity, and the size of the exposed population. It is the best measure we have of citizen exposure to pollution. This we linked with a second source of information—individual opinions recorded in the well-established General Social Survey. We were studying the link between what people *believed* about the environment and politics, and their actual *risk* of exposure to pollution linked to the county they lived in.

If, in 2010, you lived in a county with a *higher* exposure to toxic pollution, we discovered, you are *more* likely to believe that Americans "worry too much" about the environment and to believe that the United States is doing "more than enough" about it. You are also more likely to describe yourself as a strong Republican. There it was again, the Great Paradox, only now it applied to my keyhole issue: environmental pollution across the entire nation. Far from being an oddball state, Louisiana told a nationwide story. (See Appendix B.)

The "Least Resistant Personality"

I thought back to the Areno home on Bayou d'Inde. Why did PPG and other companies decide to build there and not somewhere else? Proximity to oil certainly came first. But were there other factors too? The poorer the state, research found, the less regulated it was likely to be. So were poor people in poor states less likely to worry about out-of-state profit "leakage" or state handouts to industry? Or were they understandably just hoping for a job and preparing to endure?

Certainly no Louisianan I talked to liked pollution. But what if some people are more prepared than others to put up with things they didn't like? After I'd returned home from my visit to Baton Rouge, I discovered an illuminating report on how industries deal with the fact that people don't want them to move in next door. It was written by J. Stephen Powell of the Los Angeles–based consulting firm Cerrell Associates, Inc., and was entitled "Political Difficulties Facing Waste-to-Energy Conversion Plant Siting." The fifty-seven-page report was proprietary and eventually leaked—by whom, I couldn't find out. It was produced in a different time (1984) and place (Los Angeles) but is as relevant today as it was then. The California Waste Management Board paid Cerrell Associates $500,000 to define communities that would not resist "locally undesirable land use" (LULU): "Undesirable" is what the Arenos felt about Pittsburgh Plate Glass in Bayou d'Inde.

The plant that the Waste Management Board wanted to set up would be hard to live near. The facility being considered would smell and sometimes be noisy. "Waste-to-Energy facilities also pose a potential health risk in terms of air pollution," Powell wrote. "Emissions from a plant may include varying amounts of nitrogen oxides, carbon monoxide, sulfur dioxide, hydrocarbons, and particulate matter and other matter for which health standards have not yet been established." Company trucks could cause traffic congestion. The plant would reduce property values and provide relatively few jobs, he also pointed out.

So how can such a company get a community to accept it? The plant manager's best course of action, Powell concluded, would not be to try to change the minds of residents predisposed to resist. It would be to find a citizenry unlikely to resist.

Based on interviews and questionnaires, Powell drew up a list of characteristics of the "least resistant personality profile":

- Longtime residents of small towns in the South or Midwest
- High school educated only
- Catholic
- Uninvolved in social issues, and without a culture of activism
- Involved in mining, farming, ranching (what Cerrell called "nature exploitative occupations")
- Conservative
- Republican
- Advocates of the free market

When the big oil companies first came to Louisiana in the 1940s, 40 percent of adults in Louisiana had no more than a fifth-grade education, and its citizens were the least likely in the nation to move out of state. From the seventies on, most people had become Republican advocates of the free market and minimal government. Most of the people I met fit some or all of the criteria—they were long-time residents, high school educated (half were), conservative, and Republican. That description fit the Arenos and largely fit Lee Sherman. Those who resisted the oil industry fit a very different profile—young, college educated, urban, liberal, strongly interested in social issues, and believers in good government. Was the "least resistant personality" one susceptible to what General Honoré had called the "psychological program"—the talk of "jobs, jobs, jobs" that had "just enough to it?" Or was that too easy an idea, an idea from my side of the empathy wall?

I'd taken measure of the talk and silences of public life in the heartland of the right. I'd seen what my Tea Party friends were putting up with. But the empathy wall was higher than I'd imagined. I could see what *they* couldn't see, but not—as Yogi Berra might say—what *I* couldn't see. I still felt blind to what *they* saw and honored. I needed to do something else, to enter the *social terrain* that surrounded and influenced them. Included in that were industry, state government, the church, and the press. How did these basic institutions influence their feelings about life? I thought I would start with industry, which is what brought me across the I-10 bridge from Lake Charles to an open door at the office of Mayor Bob Hardey in Westlake City Hall.

PART TWO

The Social Terrain

6

Industry: "The Buckle in America's Energy Belt"

Seated in the Westlake mayor's office with Bob Hardey, I am watching a video of a groundbreaking ceremony honoring the expansion of Sasol, the South Africa–based petrochemical giant six miles northeast of the Arenos' home in Bayou d'Inde. At sixty, Hardey is a vital, athletic, balding man, boyish in manner, eyes fixed on the video with irrepressible delight. On screen, two hundred dignitaries in suits and ties sit facing the microphone. On a 3,034-acre site, Sasol is investing $21 billion in an energy complex that will be the single largest foreign direct-investment manufacturing project in U.S. history. It is part of an even larger planned multi-company investment totaling $84 billion spread over sixty-six industrial projects in southwest Louisiana over the next five years. A "Qatar on the Bayou," the *Wall Street Journal* called it. It will call for "losing 26 public roads, buying out 883 public property lots." And in their place will rise "new cities of fertilizer plants, boron manufacturers, methanol terminals, polymer plants, ammonia factories and paper-finishing facilities."

Mayor Hardey is the seventh speaker. "I didn't have a thing written down," he recalls, "but I thought I should look like I did." An instrumentation foreman at Phillips 66 before running for mayor of Westlake, Hardey hasn't given many public speeches, he says. "So I just got up there with my iPad. It had a picture of my wife, so I looked at her." He passes me his iPad to show me the image of his seated, dark-haired, smiling wife.

His iPad facing him, part shield, part support, Bob tells the dignitaries that Westlake has been home to four generations of Hardeys. A road there bears his family name. He, his father, his son have worked in local plants, as he hopes his grandson will. But things here will have to change, he adds. "My son and his wife have dreamed a long time about building their own home. At last in 2015 they were in the middle of building it here in West-lake, near my wife and me. I was helping my son put in his plumbing. Then he told me Sasol needed his land. It wanted him to sell and move. I got up from my plumbing and said, 'Son, I'll help you put in plumbing in your *next* house.'"

The audience was rapt.

Westlake is a sprawling gray expanse of smokestacks rising from immense steel-girded fortresses, with a row of enormous, round, white, flat-topped storage tanks, which, illuminated at night, looks like a strangely beautiful great emerald city. But there is often a chemical odor. "They say, 'Ah, West-lake, y'all got that smell,'" Hardey continues in his speech. "I say, 'Man, that *smells like rice and gravy.*'" The audience laughs knowingly, and applauds more loudly than for other speakers.

I was meeting with Mayor Hardey to try to see the Great Paradox from his point of view. The people I was getting to know would have strongly resisted Dr. Templet's analysis that the oil industry suppressed other lines of work, drew a third of revenue out, left pollution, and did nothing to resolve the many problems saddling the state. I was trying to enter the state of mind in which criticisms of the overreliance on oil or the harmful side effects of fracking would seem misdirected, in which other things loomed more important. Among my Tea Party friends, the mention of Sasol was often ac-companied by the word "billion," as in a $7 billion investment for the ethane cracker, a $14 billion investment for the gas-to-liquids plant. It conveyed the idea of power, importance, and prosperity.

Did this enormous investment overturn Templet's dim picture of jobs in fossil fuels, I wondered, or illustrate it? Maybe the new fracking-spurred gold rush helped explain why people were dying to relieve themselves of the federal government. Who needed it with such opportunity at hand? My visit to Hardey would be a first step in exploring the *institutional context* conducive to the worldview of Mike Schaff, Lee Sherman, and others of the right.

Westlake and Lake Charles had recently become ground zero in a surprising new gold rush for natural gas. The gas could be sucked from the ground, piped to plants, processed into various chemical feed stocks, and piped out to still other plants, which manufactured such things as Frisbees, plastic hair brushes, garden hoses, steering wheels, computer cases, Bubble Yum, bed liners, medical gowns, jet fuel, wasp spray, grocery bags, and Hershey bars.

After we talk, Mayor Hardey drives me around Westlake to give me a sense of what the Sasol expansion will mean. It's a two-mile-square town surrounded by land zoned "heavy industrial" and indeed inhabited by industry. It has a weekly newspaper, one high school, one middle school, two elementary schools, four banks, and eighteen churches. We pass a Family Dollar Store, auto repair shops, a rib-eye-and-burger bar, and the Isle of Capri Casino Hotel. Such signs of a town's life hardly seem "heavy industrial," but that doesn't mean they won't be soon. Hardey can already envision which buildings will come down, and which others will go up.

"See that Assembly of God church? Sasol bought it for $2,500,000, will tear it down, and build over it. They paid $4,000,000 for First Baptist. It's as if money is no matter. They need to enlarge the road to haul in heavy equipment."

"See that?" Hardey is pointing out the window. "That's a Methodist church. The deacon overbid, wanted a million three hundred. Sasol backed away from the table. Now the state may declare eminent domain and give it to Sasol, which will tear it down. The congregation may not get a penny. A member of the Board of Trustees is waiting in my office now," Hardey said. "He wants me to push Sasol to pay them to move. We'll see."

We pass a cemetery. On one side of a bisecting roadway, the lawn is freshly cut. Hardey has just mowed it himself. (On the other side, payment came from a different source. The dead were black and the lawn less recently cut.) After he retired from Phillips 66, Bob kept a part-time job cutting public lawns. It had stuck with him when his sister said, "You're mayor now, Bob, but stay who you are." Cutting lawns has kept him a regular guy, connected to the place he deeply loves. His two daughters and son all lived within blocks of him in Westlake in large, shrub-lined suburban homes. His brother had lived nearby but had recently taken Sasol money and moved. Hardey had helped to build his parents' nearby home too. In their eighties now, they were planning to remain as Sasol moved in, zoning land heavy industrial around them.

Hardey has embraced the changes, and shares with me his vision of a new Westlake, one 25 to 30 percent larger in population. "See that park? I'd like to double it. And that golf course? We could put in tasteful housing for executives and professionals coming in."

But some of his grand vision glosses over possible problems now troubling local residents. He slows down his SUV to point out the window to an acre of grass. "See that? We could plant a screen of trees right there, and put up a 'man camp' behind it."

"A man camp?" I ask.

"We're expecting 5,000 temporary construction workers and 500 permanent technical workers. The construction workers will stay in man camps," he explains matter-of-factly. According to the local *American Press*, industry would have openings for new welders, scaffolding workers, pipefitters, operators, iron workers, insulators, instrumentation techs, and electricians. R.B. Smith, vice president of workforce development at the Southwest Louisiana Economic Development Alliance, urged potential local workers to "invest in yourselves" and train in a trade. But others said that local applicants weren't coming forward because they'd learned that companies wouldn't hire them without "experience"—apprenticeships, which the companies themselves weren't offering. Instead, the *American Press* said, "Construction and workforce developers are targeting international locals in Ireland, which has an unemployment rate of 14.6 percent, and the Philippines to fill service industry and construction jobs." So behind a strip of trees is where the man camps housing foreign workers would stand.

Residents don't want the man camps near them, Hardey says. What if the imported workers included rapists or burglars? they'd asked the mayor. "I don't want to tell them, but they're already living near a few registered sex offenders in nearby trailer parks; they just don't know it."

Hardey describes another dilemma more on his mind. "The previous mayor handed me a deficit budget. So Westlake is broke. Meanwhile Sasol hasn't given me a dime. We're right in the middle of their expansion, but mostly, they don't actually need our land, except for some heavy-haul throughways. But we could use some money, like to build the man camp here in Westlake, or executive housing on the golf course. I've been petting Sasol's dog. I'm waiting to see if they'll come through. If they don't, I have a trick in my bag."

Hardey stops his SUV, chuckling, and points to a nondescript strip of weeds. "See that 300-foot strip? That piece of land belongs to me. Sasol can't build over it or under it, and they need it. So that's the trick in my bag. I don't want to have to call my lawyer and pull it out. But I can. I'd like to use it to improve this town."

There is a history of discovery and invention behind the fracking boom. Rich alluvial soil has opened the way for the growth of cotton, rice, and sugarcane—like that Mike Schaff had shown me on the former Armelise Plantation. But in a sodden rice field in 1901, a farmer discovered oil. In the 1920s and 1930s, technology was adapted to drilling along the marshy Louisiana coast, then in the 1940s, along the outer continental shelf. Along the way an enormous warren of pipelines was laid belowground, aboveground, and underwater. Then, from 2003 on, new technology enabled the horizontal fracturing of shale rock. Drill bits can now bore down 1,000 to 5,000 feet into the earth and turn sideways. Water, salt, and chemicals—the exact composition remains proprietary information—can be pressure-pumped through the pipes to crack open shale rock, and other pumps suck out the natural gas that is released.

Seen as an environmental curse to many, the fracking boom brought money and pride to Mayor Hardey and most others I talked to. Stuck in the

South, the poorest region in the nation, Louisiana now seemed perched to become the proud center of an industrial renaissance, a shiny new buckle in the nation's energy belt. Louisiana wouldn't come last; it would come first. And that would bring a welcome end to the Great Paradox.

On the Brink of the Boom

The fracking boom was big. People I talked to followed it proudly. Leading economists were forecasting for Louisiana one of the highest growth rates in the country—a five-year growth rate for 2014–2018 of 4.7 percent. New jobs would be highly paid. Salaries for permanent workers would hover around $80,000 plus benefits. As a carpenter in Louisiana you can earn about $33,000; as a truck driver, $46,000; and as an elementary school teacher, $34,000. Maybe you needed training to get a job as a plant operator, but you didn't need a college degree.

And it wasn't just jobs. Fracking could strengthen American foreign policy. Instead of importing oil from unstable or authoritarian countries like Saudi Arabia and Uzbekistan, the United States could extract natural gas from its own soil. It could even *export* natural gas through a widened Panama Canal to energy-hungry Japan, or to a Russia-dependent Ukraine. Indeed, the two biggest oil refineries in southwest Louisiana (Citgo and Phillips 66), which usually *imported* oil from Mexico and Venezuela, were reconfigured to *export* it.

But in all the euphoria, missing was any public mention of the new sources of pollution that were to be added to the old. In my hour and a half with Mayor Hardey, that topic didn't arise. Hadn't Lake Charles been through an investment rush before, and hadn't it resulted in the pollution of Bayou d'Inde? Similar hosannas had gone up in 1966, when Pittsburgh Plate Glass first moved upstream from Bayou d'Inde. In 1966, the *American Press* had written of how investments "stagger the imagination." An editorial described how chemicals PPG produced would help rubber resist abrasion, add color to rubber, and make ink pigment that wouldn't show through the back side of a newspaper. The wonders of new investments, products, and jobs had all felt to the citizenry of the 1960s—including Harold and Annette Areno—as exciting as they did to Mayor Hardey now.

"The Sasol plant alone is expected to emit 85 times the state's 'threshold' rate of benzene each year," Dennis Berman wrote in the *Wall Street Journal*. "It will also produce massive streams of carbon dioxide and treated water."

"I don't want to wear a gas mask to go to bed at night," one pipefitter declared at one four-and-a-half-hour public hearing regarding the Sasol expansion.

Sasol also sought and received permission to use public water—thirteen million gallons a day of relatively clean water from the Sabine River. This it would use, pollute, and dump back in the Calcasieu River. In addition, the state granted Sasol permission to emit an estimated 10,000,000 tons of new greenhouse gases every year. No effort at carbon capture was proposed, and now that the door was open, more companies were submitting similar proposals, anticipating similar approval. "How about the issue of water use?" I ask Hardey. "The companies are in compliance," he answers, and indeed they were. The state had okayed it.

Meanwhile, the city government of Lake Charles launched its own Ozone Advance Program, which focused exclusively on what private citizens could do. They could drive shorter routes in their cars or walk. They could quit idling their car engines. They could mow their lawns less often. The plan called for a "school flag program"—green for good, yellow for moderate, red for high-ozone—to let "the community know that . . . if you have somebody that has difficulty breathing, today's not a good day to be outside."

As I was trying to climb this slippery empathy wall, a subversive thought occurred to me: do we need all the new plastic the American Chemical Association is promising us? Weren't we entering into a strange cycle? Many people I was talking to carried around plastic water bottles, partly for convenience, partly out of distrust of local waters. And with cheap natural gas at hand, the American Chemical Association said it could triple the amount of feedstock needed to make plastic. But if we triple our plastics, more petrochemical companies will pollute more public waters, which will lead more people to pay for more plastic bottles filled with ever more scarce clean water. We'll throw away more plastic bottles, buy more, and further expand the market for plastic, the production of which pollutes water. But I was straying from my goal, getting into the spirit of things.

Two Roads to Prosperity: Huey Long Versus Bobby Jindal

The heady excitement of the fracking boom hides some deeply important—and little discussed—political choices, of course. In the last Louisiana oil boom, from 1928 to 1932, in the midst of the Great Depression, Louisiana governor Huey Long, the progressive demagogue—the Kingfish, as he was called—declared "every man a king," taxed oil companies, using that money to put a "chicken in every pot," give out free textbooks to schoolchildren, create evening literacy courses for adults, and build roads, bridges, hospitals, and schools. Long curbed homelessness and poverty. Before succumbing to the lure of oil money himself, Long embraced the ideal of an activist government that lifted the poor and added to the common good.

By contrast, from 2007 to 2015, as mentioned, Governor Bobby Jindal drew $1.6 billion *from* schools and hospitals to give *to* companies as "incentives." This strategy put some chickens in some pots, of course, and indirectly took them away from others. Like nearly everyone I talk to, Mayor Hardey twice voted for Governor Jindal, as did his family. And were he alive today, very few Louisianans would vote for Huey Long.

When I ask Hardey about his political orientation—he was a moderate Republican—he immediately answers, "I've had enough of *poor me*." As he explains, "I don't like the government paying unwed mothers to have a lot of kids, and I don't go for affirmative action. I met this one black guy who complained he couldn't get a job. Come to find out he'd been to *private* school. I went to a local public school like everyone else I know. No one should be getting a job to fill some mandated racial quota or getting state money not to work." Jindal had reduced state money for "poor me's." With the jobs coming in now, we "ought to close the unemployment office," Hardey declares. "You can get a $15 to $18 [an hour] job flagging" (i.e., holding traffic flags around construction sites).

The second of five children, Hardey had learned to stand his ground among friendly competitors for parental attention. And it was rare that he pleaded "poor me." He had become a beloved and effective defender of his community. But it was industry itself, he felt, that had permitted him to access his own potential, and to become the man he was.

"In grade school and high school," he tells me solemnly, "I wasn't anything. I couldn't comprehend things." Might he have had an undiagnosed learning disability? I ask. "No," he replies simply. "I just couldn't comprehend. And I wasn't an athlete, either. There was nothing I was good at." But he continues, "When I got to the plant, starting in the maintenance department, I discovered I could do things. They promoted me from there. When I retired I was an instrumentation foreman overseeing a lot of operators, and had a salary of $180,000." Phillips 66 had done for Hardey what college or the army did for others: helped him discover his native intelligence, feel honored, provide handsomely for his family without leaving his ancestral home—achieve the American Dream.

Why couldn't blacks and legal immigrants do the same? he thought. As a young man in the 1970s, seeking work in the plants, Hardey had been told, "We had to fill our quotas for blacks." Was this truly the case, I wondered, or was this what company recruiters told white job seekers they turned down? He was not a racist, Hardey told me, but he favored no special breaks for blacks or foreigners. In a racially separated world, it's possible to have racial disadvantage without racial prejudice. Whites can turn for help to white neighbors with good connections in the plant. Blacks turn to black neighbors without them. Maybe, Hardey thought. But that seemed a problem you could fix without the federal government horning in. Hardey had worked his own way up *despite* federal intervention, as he saw it.

Others I talked to felt the same, only more strongly. Government-sponsored "redistribution"? No! Hardey's family members had all prospered. But in other families, some struck it rich, others got drunk and divorced and ended up poor. The family was a chancy redistribution system all its own, it seemed. After the 2008 crash, too, some got rich, others got poor. And you didn't want the government playing favorites *on top of that.*

It felt better to stick to the free market, to industry, to a company like Phillips 66 or Sasol.

And Governor Jindal's $1.6 billion incentive to lure industry to the state? "Good idea," Hardey says. Sure, these were the richest companies in the world, and Louisiana was a poor state. "But you needed to sweeten the deal to get companies to come to Louisiana *instead of Texas*," he explains. "Now my grandson will have a good job *here!*" Maybe from a national point of view, it didn't matter if Sasol located in Houston or Lake Charles, but for Bob Hardey and his son and his grandson, it mattered greatly.

As for pollution, the mayor thought it was a problem from the past. "We used to vent bad stuff," he says, "but the EPA restricts flares now." As for cancer, he thinks it is mainly genetic. "My dad's worked in and lived near the plants all his life, and I have too, and so have my brothers and son, and none of us have had cancer. But the best man at my wedding worked in and lived around the plants just like we did. And he got cancer. His brother died of it. His cousin got it. It's genes." But he adds, "I'll tell you where they do have a problem, that's *east* of here, between Baton Rouge and New Orleans. There, it's the chemicals."

Do We Need Good Schools and Nice Parks?

How could Westlake or Lake Charles prepare to attract new workers to the area? A 347-page Regional Impact Study, largely funded by Sasol, asked this question. "Family recruitment may present a challenge," it noted neutrally, "due to the general perception of South Louisiana as portrayed in the media." The town needed to "improve the quality of life" in order to recruit professional chemists, engineers, and physicists from elsewhere.

To do this, they had to become highly desirable places to live, with state-of-the-art public schools, innovative art and music programs, magnificent parks, freshly paved sidewalks, clean lakes to swim in, and exciting museums open regular hours. Lake Charles had a beautiful historic district, but city officials had recently approved a large cell tower in the midst of it. As for public water, a 2014 early summer "swim at your own risk" advisory issued by the Louisiana Office of Public Health warned residents of such things as sewage overflow and polluted storm water runoff in local rivers, lakes, and marshes, and advised them not to put their hands in local water if they had open wounds.

The governor, as mentioned, had cut money for schools, parks, and pollution control. By 2015, under Governor Jindal, funds for the state's twenty-eight public colleges and universities had been drastically cut. Louisiana has long stood 46th out of 50 states in per-student spending on public education. According to the Louisiana Commission on Higher Education, since 2008 the governor has eliminated $800 million from the higher education budget, leading to cuts of academic programs and the loss of 854 faculty and 4,734 other employees. Students were thrown into turmoil. Many faculty were looking to relocate. The possibility of recruiting the best minds in the nation ground to a quick halt. Only after public outcry did the governor restore some funds to public education—and cut public health and environmental protection instead.

As for poor public schools, the study suggested "re-drawing attendance zones to accommodate growth in enrollment," and added, matter-of-factly, that the state should "explore options and ramifications of ending the De-segregation Order." Now a privately funded report was telling the town Sasol was moving into that its public sector was down on its heels. Your first-rate integrated schools? Where are your un-cracked sidewalks? Your clean lakes? To attract outside talent for the private sector, it turned out, you needed a thriving public sector, for which the two-term, Tea Party–supported governor had drastically cut funds.

Mayor Hardey was trying hard to get money from Sasol so he could welcome the newcomers to a more beautiful and upgraded Westlake. But Sasol turned out to be a tough bargainer. Sasol needed water for industrial purposes and wanted Westlake to dig a new well. But it would only pay 25 percent of the cost with the state of Louisiana paying the other 75 percent. For the repaving of heavy-haul roadways—on which Sasol was virtually the only heavy hauler—the state, parish, and town (with a grant) paid 90 percent, Sasol, 10 percent. While the Regional Impact Study called for a state-of-the-art public sector in Westlake and Lake Charles, Governor Jindal had cut state funds to the bone. Mayor Hardey had to struggle with the unwelcome thought that Westlake was a "poor me."

Strange Events

Meanwhile, missing from the speeches at the groundbreaking ceremony and from the memories of nearly everyone I spoke to was an event that took place near these very grounds: one of the largest chemical leaks in American history. The leak was discovered in 1994 in a forty-year-old, mile-long underground pipeline connecting Condea Vista to the Conoco docks, which were a few miles from the Arenos' home on Bayou d'Inde. The pipe carried ethylene dichloride (EDC) and was used to store it as well. EDC is known for its capacity to penetrate dense clay and much else. A slow leak had gone undetected for decades. By the time it was discovered, eighteen to forty-six million pounds of EDC had sunk through the southern Louisiana blackjack clay, and scientists feared it was heading for the Chicot Aquifer, the sole source of drinking water for the 700,000 people of southwest Louisiana.

In 1994, Condea Vista hired cleanup workers to remove as much EDC as they could, some 1.6 million pounds of it. But the cleanup crews were given inadequate protective gear. "The guys were out there in their galoshes and blue jeans digging with shovels, and putting in sump pumps," one man told me, "no respirators." No one warned them about the effect of EDC on breathing, on cardiac arrhythmia, or on fertility. Many cleanup workers fell ill. "The men had a hard time breathing," an involved lawyer recounted. "But Condea Vista management told them their illnesses derived from other causes."

Finally five hundred cleanup workers sued Condea Vista. Attending public hearings on this was a tiny group of environmental activists, among whom was the ever ebullient Lee Sherman—Lee's wife, Miss Bobby, was the group's secretary treasurer—as well as Mike Tritico and Harold and Annette Areno.

Strange things began to happen. Files went missing from the lawyer's office. A new man joined the group, became its leader, and then started disrupting meetings with accusations of wrongdoing until, confused and discouraged, the tiny group disbanded, never to meet again. It wasn't until 2008 that people learned the cause of these strange events. And even after it became known, the tarnished memory of Condea Vista had faded. The new owner of the plant—one having nothing to do with the scandal—was Sasol.

As Mayor Hardey drives us back to Town Hall, I am beginning to understand more about the context of the right. As the Cerrell report had suggested, companies may try to avoid challenge by moving to communities that tend to be conservative, Republican, Catholic, high school educated, and not activist. In the case of Westlake, one of those very people had become a public-spirited mayor. The plants had allowed Bob Hardey to discover his high intelligence and capacity for leadership, his dignity, in ways his schools had failed to do. The plants allowed him to gather his entire family around him and, on a generous supervisor's salary, keep them in high comfort. Wherever the top brass of Sasol and other incoming plants lived, Bob Hardey's large, loving family, his church, his neighbors were all right there in Westlake.

Hardey didn't see how the federal government had helped him; if anything its affirmative action policies had almost gotten in his way. But industry had been hard on Hardey too. "Four generations of Hardeys have lived in Westlake. And now with Sasol expanding," he tells me, "a lot of my family is forced to move. My brother has already moved. My son and his wife were finished building their dream house, and now they're moving out."

His voice softens. "We have a family cemetery in the middle of the Sasol expansion. It's shaped like a triangle, and the land all around it is zoned 'heavy industrial' now. So our family cemetery will be surrounded by Sasol on all sides. But the company has promised to give us access. My grandmother is buried there, eighty-six when she died. And a nine-month-old baby girl we lost is there too. I want to be buried in that cemetery."

7

The State: Governing the Market 4,000 Feet Below

The community of some 350 residents had long gloried in what they called a "piece of heaven." The neat, modest homes faced Crawfish Stew Street on one side and a canal on the other, leading to the bayou and extraordinary vistas of wide-winged water birds swooping gracefully from water to tupelo and cypress. Nearly everyone had a boat, knew the good fishing spots, got on with their neighbors, and enjoyed a good crawfish boil. Mike Schaff had said of his Bayou Corne neighbors, we're nearly all "Cajun, Catholic, and conservative, predisposed to the Tea Party." But among them, Mike Schaff was the most ardent—he had joined the Tea Party, gone to meetings, spoken out. Raised in a shotgun house in the sugarcane field we had driven through together, and a lifelong employee in oil, Mike wished to feel himself in a nearly wholly private world, one as far as he could get from government taxes and regulation. But what would happen, I wondered, if a community of people such as Mike suffered a sudden catastrophe that, beyond any doubt, could have been prevented by respect for government regulation? What was his understanding about the state? Could I see why he felt as he did? These questions had led me to Mike Schaff and the Bayou Corne Sinkhole.

Because just that catastrophe occurred in August of 2012. First, neighbors noticed tiny clusters of bubbles on the surface of the water. Had a gas pipe traversing the bottom of the bayou sprung a leak? A man from the local gas company checked and declared the pipes fine. At the same time, Mike recalls, "We smelled oil, strong." Then he and his neighbors were startled by the shaking and rumbling of an earthquake. Since earthquakes had never before occurred in this part of Louisiana, one woman imagined a "garbage truck had dropped a dumpster." A single mother of two living in a mobile home a mile from Bayou Corne thought her washing machine was on, then remembered it had been broken for months. A man was eating dinner from his TV dinner tray when it began to shake. As Mike recalls, "I was walking in the house when I felt like I was either having a stroke or drunk, ten seconds; my balance went all to hell." A while later, he noticed a jagged crack zigzag across the concrete underneath his living room carpet. Lawns began to sag and tilt in strange directions.

Not far from Mike's home, the earth under the bayou was beginning to tear open. As if a plug was pulled in a bathtub, a hollow "mouth" of a crack in the bottom of the bayou began sucking down brush and pine from the surface of the earth. Majestic, century-old cypress trees crashed down in slow motion and were dragged sideways into the bubbling water, drawn down into the gaping mouth of a sinkhole. Down went bush, grassland, and even a boat. An oily sheen had appeared on the surface of the water, and to prevent its spread, two cleanup workers were called in to cast booms around the oil not far from the sinkhole. To do this, the two men tied their boat to a tree, standing in it to do their work. But the tree began to tilt and drift. The workers were rescued in time but their boat disappeared into the sinkhole.

In the following days and weeks, polluted mud was thrown back up onto the surface of the water in a weird and terrible exchange of pristine swamp forest for oily sludge. Oil oozed to the surface of the water, and natural gas emanated here and there from land and water. "During a rain, the puddles would shine and bubble, like you'd dropped Alka Seltzer tablets in them," Mike says. The sinkhole grew. First it took the area of a house lot, then a football field. By 2015, the sinkhole stretched over thirty-seven acres. Then the gassy sludge had also infiltrated the aquifer, threatening the drinking water.

Residents noticed that the main road into the community began to sink and feared it would cave in. Levees along the bayou, originally built to contain rising waters in times of flood, had also begun to sink, threatening to extend the sludge beyond their boundaries.

The Cause and the Blame

The culprit in this strange accident was a Houston-based drilling company, Texas Brine. As its name suggests, Texas Brine drilled for intensely concentrated salt, which it sold to manufacturers of chlorine, and which is also useful in fracking. It drilled down 5,600 feet beneath the bayou into an enormous underground geological formation called a salt dome—unseen and fairly common in the Gulf. In a highly risky maneuver—disregarding the advice of their own consulting engineer, and with the okay of a government official also aware of the danger—Texas Brine drilled underneath Bayou Corne. On the books were regulations that were disregarded by both company and state.

The drill accidentally pierced a side wall of a teardrop-shaped cavern inside the Napoleonville Dome. (The Napoleonville Dome is an underground block of salt, three miles wide and a mile deep, sheathed by a layer of oil and natural gas. It is well known to people in the area, but not much outside it, and private companies drill deep inside the salt to hollow out pockets, large and small, some shaped like straight posts, others like mushrooms or cones. Inside them, companies store chemicals.)

When the drill pierced the side of one cavern inside the dome, a catastrophe slowly unfolded. Weakened, one wall of the cavern crumpled under the pressure of the surrounding shale. Water was sucked down, drawing trees and brush with it. Oil from around the dome oozed up. The earth shook. In places its surface tilted and sank.

The disaster drew public attention to a vast underground world—previously unknown to me—and raised important questions about how a free-market economy in a highly regulation-averse culture was handling toxic chemicals in some 126 salt domes in Louisiana—plus more offshore—stored from 3,000 to 18,000 feet beneath the surface of the earth.

In the Napoleonville salt dome, a lively commerce was going on. Petrochemical companies *own* fifty-three caverns and some seven more companies *rent* space in them. These are valuable, large storage depots for the many chemicals used in oil drilling, fracking, and plastic manufacturing. Texas Brine rents six caverns. Dow and Union Carbide owns others into which they have pumped fifty million gallons of ethylene dichloride (EDC). While it surprised me to learn how far down into the earth free enterprise went, such underground storage systems have long been accepted practice in the Gulf region; the National Petroleum Reserves have themselves long been stored in a similar way.

Still, I wondered, if one company could drill one hole in one cavern and cause a sinkhole that made methane gas bubble in rain puddles, what else could happen, with earthquakes now in motion, and other EDC-filled caverns nearby—all in a culture in which the very idea of regulation has fallen into very low esteem?

My keyhole issue had taken me 4,000 feet down into the earth. And following it down the hole was the Great Paradox: the Tea Party feared, disdained, and wanted to diminish the federal government. But they also wanted a clean and safe environment—one without earthquakes sending toxins into aquifers or worse. But here was the rub: didn't America need a culture of respect for the safeguarding of such concerns? Don't we need government workers—ones with no skin in the game—to do the safeguarding? How did my good, bright, and caring friend Mike Schaff and others put these two desires together?

The Minimal State

Dapper in a blue shirt and khaki pants, Governor Bobby Jindal steps down from his helicopter and strides rapidly toward a cluster of waiting officials and restless refugees from the Bayou Corne Sinkhole, as it is now named. Many residents, seven months on, are still homeless, doubling up with relatives, living in trailers, motels, and campers. One couple had celebrated Thanksgiving in a twenty-four-hour Laundromat because they had nowhere else to go. Burly security men with close-shorn hair and dark glasses fan out around the governor. Hand outstretched, Jindal walks rapidly forward to greet officials and listens, head tilted, hands on hips, to their words. He moves toward a podium set in a green field not far from the sinkhole.

The earth had opened ominously on August 3, 2012. Four months later, on December 16, 2012, a resident posted on his Facebook page:

Where Are You Bobby Jindal?????

You were elected to be the leader of our State. . . . Bayou Corne/ Grand Bayou . . . was declared a State of Emergency by your office on August 3rd [2012]. . . . There are mini earthquakes, methane, benzene and hydrogen sulfide being released into the community. This community has been through hell and back and is still living a nightmare. In my opinion and many others you have . . . done absolutely nothing helpful to this community.

Seven months after the disaster, on March 19, 2013, Governor Jindal visits the sinkhole for the very first time. He has helicoptered in from Baton Rouge, forty miles away—"it's only a five-minute ride," one disgruntled resident tells me—to address the gathering.

With a line of white-shirted officials behind him and a thin scattering of distressed residents, arms folded, facing him, Governor Jindal speaks rapidly and emphatically from a fact-studded script. The very pace of his talk conveys mastery, urgency, busyness, and, perhaps, avoidance. The state is doing all it can to help, he tells the gathering. He's appointing an independent Blue Ribbon Commission. He's on the case.

The governor finishes his prepared remarks and calls on local officials to speak, before finally opening himself to restless residents for questions. One resident asks the governor why he waited seven months to come the short distance. Noting that the governor announced his visit only at 9:00 A.M. of the morning he was to arrive at 2:00 P.M. the same afternoon, another asks why, after the seven-month delay, such short notice? Why was the meeting also set for two o'clock on a weekday when most people would be at work? Had the governor *seen* the sinkhole?

By now, the homes of 350 residents were part of a "sacrifice zone," as officials called it. A geologist hired by Texas Brine had earlier explained to shocked residents that "nobody in the world has ever faced a situation like this." Was a nearby cavern, still being drilled into, also in danger of collapse? When would the gas, the earthquakes stop? The Blue Ribbon Commission is looking into it, the governor says.

A Two-Beer Levee Job

To drive to Mike Schaff's home, I turn right on Gumbo Street, left on Jambalaya, pass Sauce Piquant Lane, and park on Crawfish Street, opposite a two-story yellow wooden home. The street is deserted, the grass high. Planted around his yard are fruit trees—satsuma orange, grapefruit, mango, and fig—but the fruit hangs unpicked.

"I'm sorry about the grass," Mike says as he greets me wearing an orange-and-red striped T-shirt, jeans, and boots. With the sweep of a muscular arm, he points to an unpruned rose arbor, "Just haven't kept the place up." Mike has set out coffee, cream, sugar, and a jar of peaches to take when I leave.

"This has been the longest six months of my life. To tell you the truth, I'm depressed," he says. "Five years ago I moved here from Baton Rouge to live with my new wife," he says, pouring us coffee. But "with the methane gas emissions all around us now, it's not safe. So my wife has moved back to Alexandria and commutes to her job from there. I see her on weekends. The grandkids don't come, either, because what if someone lit a match? The house could blow up."

Mike sleeps uneasily. He has placed a gas monitor in his garage and checks it from time to time. "The company drilled a hole in my garage to see if there was gas under it. There was: 20 percent higher than normal." He avoids lighting matches. He lives day to day among his cardboard boxes, keeping watch over his neighbor's property and a wary eye on wandering feral cats.

The governor had issued an evacuation order for all residents of Bayou Corne, but Mike could not bring himself to leave. "I'm here to guard the place against a break-in—there've been quite a few—and to keep the other stayers company." After a long pause, he adds, "Actually, I don't want to leave."

"Excuse this," he says, pointing to a jagged crack in the cement to the side of a rolled-up carpet. "The earthquake caused that. We never had earthquakes before the sinkhole, or methane gas rising from our lawns."

After coffee, Mike walks me to the edge of his backyard, speaking in the present tense as if his life is ongoing: "This is where we have neighbors in for crawfish boils." Visible across the canal, and up and down it, are other patios with grills, yoo-hooing distance across. But now, he tells me, "It's no longer Janet and Jerry. It's no longer Tommy. It's no longer Nicky and his wife. It's no longer Mr. Jim." He points around. "It's Texas Brine, Texas Brine, Texas Brine, and Texas Brine. It'll be eighty-eight weeks this Monday," he continues. "As of now there's me, Tommy, Victor, and Brenda, and that's it." Texas Brine has been negotiating prices to buy neighbors out.

It had been a close-knit community with a shared devotion to fishing, hunting, wildlife, and conservative politics. Married five years to his beautiful new wife—Mike's third marriage, his wife's second—this is the last situation he'd imagined being in. "We're a close community here." He gestures around as if to introduce me to invisible friends. "We have our own Mardi Gras, parties at Miss Eddie's Birdhouse." The husband of a neighbor, a bird-lover, had built a structure to shelter birds, considered noisy by neighbors. After he died, his widow converted it into a party house with a Jacuzzi and strobe lights. "We help each other rebuild levees during floods. You got the two-beer levee job, or the four-beer one." He laughs. "We love it here."

Other Bayou Corne refugees I would interview said the same. One man named Nick showed more photos of children parading around the neighborhood in decorated bikes, neighbors in decorated golf carts, and boat trailers for the Mardi Gras Bayou Corne Hookers Parade, celebrants dancing in the street—some years to the music of a live band. "We used to have fishing tournaments. The winner was the one with the heaviest catch, and we ended up holding a fish fry."

Even if government helped people—and he didn't think it did much— government should never, Mike felt, erode the spirit of a community. He had grown up in a dense circle of aunts, uncles, cousins, and grandparents, all within walking distance from each other on the Armelise Plantation. Now in his sixties, Mike felt happy to live in a community as close and cooperative as the one he had known as a boy.

For a man who could lose himself for hours in the garage assembling a two-seater Zenith 701 airplane from a kit, and who described himself as "to myself," such a community brought cheer. The sociability of Bayou Corne brought him out of himself. It wasn't the simple absence of government Mike wanted, it was the feeling of being inside a warm, cooperative group. He thought the government replaced that.

His was also a love of place. Just as Mayor Hardey loved Westlake, Mike Schaff loved Bayou Corne. Just as Sasol was expanding onto Hardey family land, so Texas Brine had taken over Mike's home. But there was a difference. Hardey's family had been handsomely paid, his own home was unharmed, and he didn't mind industry as a neighbor. But Mike's home was in visible ruin and the community he loved was scattered to the wind—to Mississippi, Texas, and other parts of Louisiana.

Mike disappears into his boat garage and backs his boat out into the canal. I climb in. The boat sputters to life and putts out of the canal into the wider bayou. Swerving around dark stumps of dead cypress trees, we duck under strips of low-hanging Spanish moss, which look like fuzzy tatters of an old fur coat hang from cypress, tupelo gum trees, and swamp maples. We duck again to putt under a low bridge, then speed into a widening vista. "Around here you pull up bass, catfish, white perch, crawfish, and sac-a-lait—at least we used to. Now? They're swimming in a methane bath."

At a distance, we see a red, white, black, and yellow sign nailed to the gray trunk of a tupelo: "DANGER, KEEP OUT, HIGHLY FLAMMABLE GAS." The reflection of the warning wobbles in the rippling water. Mike points to small concentric circles of bubbles, scuttling outward like small bugs. "Methane."

Rumor, Panic, Blame

After the sinkhole, talk turned to blame, which ricocheted wildly from one thing to another. First Texas Brine blamed Mother Nature. Earthquakes were natural in this area, officials said, which wasn't true. Then it blamed and sued Occidental Chemical Company, the company from which it rented space in the Napoleonville salt dome. Then Texas Brine's insurance company blamed Texas Brine and refused to pay insurance. Then Texas Brine sued the insurance company. The legal wrangling expanded. Only 1,600 feet from the cave-in, Crosstec Energy Services rented an adjacent underground vault in the dome, filled with the equivalent of 940,000 barrels of butane gas. Wishing to continue business as usual, Crosstec sued Texas Brine on grounds that the cave-in had *prevented them from expanding* and led to the loss of storage contracts it could have made with companies wanting to rent. In 2015, Texas Brine sued yet another company, Oxy Petroleum, for $100 million for weakening the cavern wall by drilling too close to the cavern's edge back in 1986 and so causing the disaster in 2012. And so it went.

Meanwhile, still doubled up with family in spare rooms, trailers, and motels, shell-shocked refugees commuted to work from temporary quarters, turning to each other by e-mail and to the Internet and television news for updates. Anxious rumors flew. Would the stored gas ignite, causing a firestorm? Would earthquakes break the walls of other caverns containing dangerous chemicals? One alarmed writer for the Denver-based website Examiner.com feared an explosion "with the force of more than 100 H-bombs like the ones in Hiroshima and Nagasaki." Others called for calm and reason. Apparently wanting a break from the anxious talk, one man who'd stayed in his Bayou Corne home wrote on Facebook: "Took a break from painting patio furniture and caught eight of these li'l beauties [photo of fish] right from my pier in about an hour."

Some contributors to a website called *The Sinkhole Bugle* blamed both the company and the government but aimed their deepest anger at the government. Dennis Landry, owner of Cajun Cabins of Bayou Corne, pointed out, correctly, that the state Department of Natural Resources "knew for months" that the Texas Brine well had integrity problems and didn't tell local authorities. "I'm very upset about it. . . . I feel like I've been betrayed by the Louisiana Department of Natural Resources." One man even described Texas Brine as the "fall guy."

Moral Dirty Work

It was becoming easier to understand why energy refugees were so furious at the state government. First of all, it turned out that the secretary of the Louisiana Department of Natural Resources from 2004 to 2014, Scott Angelle, had known of the weak cavern wall but had given Texas Brine a permit to drill anyway. He had been transferred soon after the event to a different job and was now, to Mike's horror, running for governor. (Angelle later lost.)

Indeed, the caverns had been casually regulated. Similar accidents had occurred in the past and been forgotten—or remembered but discounted—like the structural amnesia the Arenos had encountered. Energy companies had understated the value of these caverns and their contents and had been undertaxed, it was discovered. The problem was not that the state government was too big, too intrusive, too controlling; it seemed to me that the state government had barely been present at all.

Beyond this, there were different expectations of business and government. Companies made money and were beholden to stockholders; it was understandable if they tried to "cover their ass," people told me. But the government was *paid* to protect people, so one could expect much more of them. Still, victims felt surprisingly hurt by Texas Brine, belying hope of a more personal touch. "After the sinkhole, company officials didn't come around to ask how we were doing. And after they reimbursed us, they gave us a month to get out," one aggrieved refugee told me, "When an ill eighty-three-year-old man asked Texas Brine for more time to get out they said, 'Okay, an extra week.'" Texas Brine didn't care. They were all about money. Mike himself expressed mixed feelings toward Texas Brine. He offered a bag of Satsuma mandarins to the Texas Brine manager at the beginning of one community meeting, quipping, "These don't have razors in them." Later he told me, "I laughed but the manager didn't." Victims were mad that Texas Brine "didn't have a heart," but not contemptuous. On the other hand, state officials were seen as tepid followers of corrupt higher-ups, whose envied new SUVs were seen as "paid for by my taxes."

Overall, just how well did Louisiana state officials do in protecting its citizens? An eye-opening 2003 report from the inspector general of the EPA offered an answer. Charged with evaluating implementation of federal policies by each state within the nation's six regions, the report ranked Louisiana lowest of all in Region 6. Companies had not been required to submit reports. Louisiana's database on hazardous waste facilities was filled with errors. The Louisiana Department of Environmental Quality (a title missing the word "protection") did not know if many companies were or were not "in compliance." Delays allowed sixteen facilities to discharge material into Louisiana waters without permits. The agency had failed to inspect many plants. Even when it found companies out of compliance, it had neglected to levy penalties or, if they were levied, to collect them. The inspector general concluded that he was "unable to fully assure the public that Louisiana was operating programs in a way that effectively protects human health and the environment."

Why such low marks? Three reasons, the inspector general concluded: natural disasters, low funds, and "a culture in which the state agency is expected to protect industry." As for lack of resources, funding for environmental protection had been cut in 2012 from a previous 3.5 percent of total yearly state funds to 2.2 percent. An alert auditor had also discovered that the state had accidentally "given back" about $13 million to oil and gas companies that it should have retained in taxes. As for the pro-industry "culture," permitting was indeed relatively easy. According to the state's own website, 89,787 permits to deposit waste or do anything that affected the environment were submitted between 1967 and July 2015. Of these, only sixty—or .07 percent—were denied.

Some state reports also reflected odd science. Comparing rates of pollution in different areas, detection levels were sometimes set high in the one and low in the other. In a 2005 study of the Calcasieu Estuary, Louisiana state scientists inexplicably concluded that it would be dangerous for children aged six to seventeen to swim in estuary waters, but not dangerous for "children six and under." Such reports were also nearly unreadable. One typical report read: "Analyses reported as non-detects were analyzed using method detection limits that were higher than the comparison values used as screening tools."

Sometimes the state simply lowered standards of protection. In an astonishing example of this, the Louisiana State Department of Health and Human Science offered advice to officials in other state agencies on what to tell the public about which fish are safe to eat. Issued in February 2012, and still online as of May 5, 2016, the report was written by one set of state officials for another. After a chilling description of a "cancer slope factor," the report continues, in a matter-of-fact tone, to advise the recreational fisherman on how to prepare a contaminated fish to eat: "Trimming the fat and skin on finfish, and removing the hepatopancreas from crabs, will reduce the amount of contaminants in the fish and shellfish," the document reads. Baking, broiling, and grilling are good, it said, because "the fat drains away from the fish and shellfish." Discard "juices which contain the fat . . . to further reduce exposure," it says. "Some contamination, like mercury and other heavy metals, however, are pervasive in the edible fish tissue," the report continues, in scientific deadpan prose, "and remain in the fish and shellfish even after cooking."

The report was shocking but it also made a certain grim sense. If the companies won't pay to clean up the waters they pollute, and if the state won't make them, and if poverty is ever with us—some people need to fish

Remove all skin

Cut away all
the fat along
the back

Cut away a V-shaped
wedge to remove the
dark fatty tissue along
the entire length of the fillet

Slice off the
belly fat

Protocol for Issuing Public Health Advisories for
Chemical Contaminants in Recreationally Caught Fish and Shellfish

for their dinner—well then, trim, grill, and eat mercury-soaked fish. At least the authors of the protocol were honest in what was a terrible answer to the Great Paradox. "You got a problem? Get used to it."

Mike Schaff had heard nothing of this advice, but when I describe it, he shakes his head. "There it is again, more bad government. Why raise salaries? Take Steve Schultz, who heads our Department of Natural Resources. When he first went to work for me and other Louisiana taxpayers, he started at $30,000, probably bought himself a mobile home or efficiency apartment his family could fit in. Then he got raises and moved to some fancy subdivision. Say we increase the budget for environmental protection. His salary rises from $150,000 to $190,000. The more money we give him, the more reason he has to be a yes man to Jindal and oil. To me, a public servant who doesn't make very much is more likely to be dedicated to what he's doing."

Mike's idea of dedication was modeled on the church. On another visit, Mike had driven me in his red truck to the Catholic grade school he'd attended across the street from the Catholic church where he had been confirmed and next to a graveyard where his parents and maternal grandparents lay buried. He recalled the nuns instructing him to clap the blackboard erasers on the sidewalk (God would reward him if he did). But he remarked in passing, "The nuns were great teachers and lived very modestly. *I think all public servants ought to be like those nuns.*" They wouldn't need much tax money. But he realized that the incentives to enter public service would be almost nil, making it hard to attract the best people, and on yet another visit, he confessed, "I could never live like they do."

Thinking over the Bayou Corne disaster, I was still puzzled. Mike embraced a free-market world because he wanted to preserve community. But did a total free-market world and local community go together? And in essence, wasn't Louisiana *already like* a society based on a near pure free market? Governor Jindal advocated the free market and small government—Mike had voted for him on those very grounds. He had cut public services, lowered funds for environmental protection, and installed pro-industry "protectors." The state hadn't functioned to protect the residents of Bayou Corne at all and, in the minds of some, had even absorbed the main blame for the sinkhole, just as Lee had absorbed the blame for PPG's pollution of Bayou d'Inde.

Having explored all the places the Great Paradox had taken me—from the 4,000-feet-deep storage vaults in the Napoleonville salt dome to the advice of state officials to recreational fishermen on how to prepare mercury-laced fish—I thought I was looking at an open-and-shut case for *good* government. But my new friend saw in this advice on how to prepare a contaminated fish an open-and-shut case for *less* government.

I had criticisms of the federal government myself—over-surveillance, the declaration of war in Iraq, letting off Wall Street speculators behind the 2008 crash, for example. But my criticisms were based on a faith in the idea of good government.

Mike lands his boat at his dock and we return to his dining room table. He has told me that we don't need Social Security or Medicare. "Take Social Security. If you and I hadn't had to pay into it," he told me, "we could have invested that money ourselves—even given the 2008 downturn—you and I would be *millionaires* by now."

We didn't need the Federal Department of Education, he thought (that could go to each state) or the Department of the Interior (we could privatize most public land). But hadn't Texas Brine just treated the public waters of Bayou Corne *as if* the company privately owned them? Did Mike want more of that? I was feeling stuck way over on my side of the empathy wall. So I turned my question around.

"What has the federal government done for you that you feel *grateful* for?" He pauses.

"Hurricane relief." He pauses again.

"The I-10 . . ." (a federally funded freeway). Another long pause.

"Okay, unemployment insurance." He had once been briefly on it.

I suggest the Food and Drug Administration inspectors who check the safety of our food.

"Yeah, that too."

"What about the post office that delivered the parts of that Zenith 701 you assembled and flew over Bayou Corne Sinkhole to take a video you put on YouTube?"

"That came through FedEx."

The military in which he enlisted in ROTC?

"Yeah, okay." Another pause.

And so it went. We don't need this, we don't need that. Other interviews went the same way, with the same long pauses.

How about the 44 percent of the state budget that comes from Washington, D.C.? Mike searches his mind. "Most of that goes for Medicaid. And at least half of the recipients, maybe more, aren't looking for work."

"Do you know any?" I ask.

"Oh sure," he answers. "And I don't blame them. Most people I know use available government programs, since they paid for part of them. If the programs are there, why not use them?" On another visit Mike recounted a near accident and rescue; he was taking his new bride and her two daughters on a boat ride when a powerful storm came up, his motor quit, and the boat rocked heavily. "First the girls screamed with delight. Then they got quiet. We almost capsized. Luckily the Coast Guard saw us and towed us to shore. I was glad to see him," Mike said, adding, "He did check if we had safety vests which I guess is okay."

What image of the government was at play? Was it a nosy big brother (the Coast Guard had checked for safety vests)? Was it a remote-controlling big brother (a federal instead of state Department of Education)? A bad parent playing favorites (affirmative action)? An insistent beggar at the door (taxes)? It was all of these, but something else too. Just as Berkeley hippies of the 1960s felt proud to be "above consumerism," to demonstrate their higher ideals of love and world harmony—even though they often depended on the parental money they were "above"—so too Mike Schaff and other Tea Party advocates seemed to be saying, "I'm above the government and all its services" to show the world their higher ideals, even though they used a host of them. For everything else it is, the government also functions as a curious status-marking machine. The less you depend on it, the higher your status. As the sociologist Thorstein Veblen long ago observed, our distance from necessity tends to confer honor.

I count all the reasons Mike disdained government. It displaced community. It took away individual freedom. It didn't protect the citizenry. Its officials didn't live like nuns. And the *federal* government was a more powerful, distant, untrustworthy version of the *state* government. Beyond that, Mike was surrounded by a local culture of endurance and adaptation; if fish have mercury, cut around the dark meat and eat the white. It was this culture of adaptation that Mike himself would later challenge, as we shall see.

But something else animated Mike's dislike for the government, something I was to discover wherever I went. Sometimes talk of it was angry, front and central; sometimes it was quietly alluded to. But over their heads, the federal government was taking money from the workers and giving it to the idle. It was taking from people of good character and giving to people of bad character. No mention was made of social class and enormous care was given to speak delicately and indirectly of blacks, although fear-tinged talk of Muslims was blunt. If the flashpoint between these groups had a location, it might be in the local welfare offices that gave federal money to beneficiaries—Louisiana Head Start, Louisiana Family Independence

Temporary Assistance Program, Medicaid, the national School Lunch and Breakfast Program, the Special Supplemental Nutrition Program for Women, Infants, and Children. Liberals were telling Americans to "feel sorry" for recipients, but those were coastal urban liberals trying to impose their feeling rules on older Southern and Midwestern Christian whites. And they seemed to be on the other side. So I wondered: did some of the malaise I was seeing derive from a class conflict, appearing where one least expected it (in the realm of government) and between groups (the middle/blue-collar class and the poor) that liberals weren't focusing on? Was this a major source of resentment fueling the fire of the right? And in that fight, did the entire federal government seem to them on the wrong—betraying—side? Maybe *this* was the main reason Mike was later to tell me, in reference to the 2016 presidential election and only half jokingly, that he could never bring himself to vote for the menshevik (Hillary Clinton) or the bolshevik (Bernie Sanders).

As I leave, Mike hands me the jar of peaches that had been on the table when I arrived. I drive back up Crawfish Street, past tilting yards, onto the potentially sinking only exit route, and wonder what news of Bayou Corne, federal regulations, handouts, and much else he received from church or from his favorite television channel—Fox News.

8

The Pulpit and the Press:
"The Topic Doesn't Come Up"

In the first ten minutes after meeting Madonna Massey for coffee at the Lake Charles Starbucks, I notice how many people seem happy to see her.

"Hi Madonna, you look beautiful today."

"Well thank you, Mr. Gaudet, you're looking well yourself."

"Hi Madonna, beautiful singing the other night."

"Thank you, Joey. How's your daughter doing?"

She wears a flowing floral skirt, and a mass of blond curls cascades to one side of her lacy jacket. She has an easy, friendly manner, a lilting laugh, and a wide smile that seems to cast a circle of warmth around her.

I had first met Madonna at a gathering of the Republican Women of Southwest Louisiana, where she told me she was a great devotee of the conservative radio talk show host Rush Limbaugh. "Oh, I follow the Rush doctrine," she'd said. "Especially what he says about femi-nazis." Imagining she'd be interesting to talk to, I'd asked if we could meet for coffee.

Upholding the right-leaning culture that surrounded me now was a so-cial terrain. I had explored industry and the state. But what of the church and the press? Mike Schaff had defended his beloved community against the encroachment of government. Did others feel the same about the church? Were my new Louisiana friends defending an honored *sphere*? Or,

independent of that, did the church promote *personal values* that might resolve the paradox I was exploring?

Nearly everyone I met in Louisiana goes to church. Harold and Annette
Areno attend the Lighthouse Tabernacle Pentecostal church. Harold Areno's
niece, Janice, meets Sundays with a small band of non-denominational
Christian worshippers awaiting divine guidance before choosing their next
pastor. Lee Sherman, who had pushed the tar buggy to the water's edge near
Bayou d'Inde, attends a Mormon church. Bob Hardey, the mayor of Westlake, attends a Catholic church. Mike Tritico quit one church, tried another,
and now conducts Bible study with the Arenos or on his own in his disbev-
eled cabin in Longville, and he attends a nearby Baptist church sing-along
for the lively accordion gospel music. Yet another Lake Charles survivor of
a desperate childhood would tell me that Sunday was her "favorite day." A
black Baptist minister in Crowley gently cautions a devoted all-black following against patronizing payday lenders. As a twice-divorced Catholic, Mike
Schaff declines Sunday services but, from his twenties on, has attended a
yearly Jesuit retreat, where he keeps two days of total silence, occasionally
sneaking a quick iPhone text. Some go to church twice a week, and meet
for Bible study too. People speak of children not as "going to church" but as
being *churched*. And this is said with the same pride as others might say
"highly educated" or "well mannered." Church in Louisiana—usually Baptist, Catholic, Methodist, or Pentecostal—is a pillar of social life.

In Donaldsonville, population 7,000—the nearest big town to the home
Mike Schaff was born in—Churchfinder.com reports eleven Baptist
churches, four Methodist, four Catholic, and one described as "spirit-filled."
To the west some 108 miles, Lake Charles, with its population of 70,000,
has 100 churches—mostly Baptist and "spirit-filled" (57) but also Pentecostal (12) and Catholic (13). That's a church for every 700 people. Some buildings hold a thousand worshippers, others a few dozen. By comparison, my
hometown of Berkeley, California, a city of 117,000, has 82 churches—one
for every 1,423 residents. Berkeley has eight synagogues, Lake Charles has
one, and Donaldsonville, none.

Around Lake Charles, God seemed in the air everywhere. Prayers were said before private meals and usually in public meetings before the flag salute. Church was in childhoods. "I went to church twice a week when I was a boy, and every day during revival," Harold Areno recalled of his youth in Bayou d'Inde. It was in business. At the Lake Charles Chamber of Commerce banquet at the Golden Nugget Casino, for example, Board Chairman Glen Bertrand found himself in a decidedly secular setting. But speaking of the great $84 billion investment in the region, he said, "I hope that we recognize our economic successes as a blessing from above."

Church as Emotional World

At 7:05 on a Thursday evening, Glenn Massey, Madonna's husband, is walking the aisles of Living Way Pentecostal Church, chatting with congregants, waiting for men to get off their shifts at the plants. I am sitting in the front row on the right, next to Madonna. It is where she usually sits, with her mother in the row behind; both are accomplished gospel singers. Outside, parishioners are parking their SUVs, tucking in shirts, combing hair, and walking from the parking lot toward an extended hand or the hugging arms of greeters in the foyer of the church. "Good to see you. . . . Glad you could make it."

By 7:15 P.M., some 700 worshippers are settled in their seats. As Pastor Glenn Massey speaks, gentle piano music runs beneath his words about how the Lord "smoked my spirit." His eyes are closed. His arms rise. His hands swivel and wave in gestures of drawing closer to God. After Pastor Glenn's words, his speaking in tongues (in direct communication with God, Pentecostals believe), parishioners come forward to assistant pastors who are ready to receive them. One woman bows in a posture of despair. Another flutters her hands as if freeing them of something dreadful. Dressed in military fatigues, a man stalks slowly back and forth below the edge of the dais, as if to protect the troubled worshippers or to calm an inner anxiety of his own. Every human emotion is on display.

Facing the worshippers, assistant ministers lay hands on a head, a shoulder, an arm, firmly, for a period of time, with a gentle shake as if to loosen a spirit. Others in the congregation come forward to lay hands on a person's back or arm, and still others lay hands upon those who have laid hands. Human layer upon layer, forming a momentary still life of human connection. At the end of the service, Pastor Glenn asks everyone who needs to forgive or be forgiven to come forward. Over half the congregation comes forward. When a certain time has passed, there is sighing, sometimes weeping, pats, and release. Plant workers slowly rise, shake hands, hug, chat briefly, and return to their pickup trucks and SUVs to head home.

Living Way focuses on human healing. The needs it fills seem like those met in less religious cultures by psychotherapy and meditation, as well as by family and friendship. Other churches, such as Trinity Baptist, a megachurch in Lake Charles, add a focus on help for the less fortunate. Parishioners have organized a food drive for Abraham's Tent, a local food pantry and soup kitchen.

Bulletin boards in other church hallways feature photos of groups of smiling African children lined up in their Sunday best in front of foreign church mission stations. Trinity Baptist has ministries in Ecuador, Africa, Peru, and Honduras, where they send two dozen doctors, nurses, and dentists each year and host vacation Bible School for children. A group from Trinity goes door to door sharing the gospel in Zimbabwe. Through her church, one woman organized a "one touch pillow" campaign, sending hundreds of soft pillows to American soldiers in Iraq and Afghanistan. "They are young, away from home, scared," she told me. "But when a soldier's head touches this pillow, he knows he's in touch with God." Still other churches organize bands of "prayer warriors" who gather to pray on behalf of those in trouble.

Baptist, Pentecostal, Catholic, and all the churches I visit also meet needs beyond the spiritual, in a way that avoids the indignity that my Tea Party friends link with things public. Trinity Baptist Church provides a large fitness center with stationary bicycles and muscle-strengthening machines. The mother-in-law of a Lake Charles congregant lost fifty pounds in the church fitness center. Her two children, when younger, loved to coast down a giant slide that began on one floor and descended to a recreation room on the floor below, where they discovered a brightly colored soft-sculpted octopus, whale, shark, alligator-piloted airplane, and giant sea gull. For older children at Trinity Baptist, a snack bar and social lounge were open on Sundays and a church camp during summers. It held "celebrate recovery" meetings for former addicts, sponsored its own sports teams for eighth through twelfth graders, and had golf tournaments for the older set. Churches typically ask parishioners to tithe—to give 10 percent of their income. For many this is a large sum, but it is considered an honor to give it. They *pay* taxes, but they *give* at church.

The Trinity giant slide reminded me of the imaginatively designed Dolores Park in the Mission neighborhood of San Francisco and the public programs offered by the San Francisco Recreation and Parks Department. On my side of the empathy wall, "public" services and programs were an almost entirely positive thing. I thought of the San Francisco's Girls' Choir and the teen musical theater that performs *Fiddler on the Roof*, for which middle school students get free acting and voice coaching. San Francisco provides funds for local artists to paint murals on forgotten underpasses. There are exercise classes: acro-yoga, hooping, handstands, partner flip. The city sports leagues include softball, basketball, and tennis. Then there are cooking, hiking, poetry slamming, square dancing, and lakeside summer camps you have to sign up for very early. The lessons and camp cost something, but the city offers needs-sensitive scholarships. City-sponsored volunteers clean off graffiti, maintain hiking trails, plant trees, and become children's walk guides in the botanical garden. Mobile Rec takes a mobile rock-climbing wall around the city. Greenagers is a program for ninth and tenth graders to improve green spaces. Such programs are open to people of all races and creeds, filling the same cultural space, it occurs to me, filled by the church programs I was discovering in Lake Charles.

Silicon Valley's Google, Facebook, and Twitter, like many companies around the country, offer on-site services that bring workers inside their commercial doors. Google offers its employees breakfast, lunch, and dinner, including on weekends, as well as on-site fitness centers, massages, napping pods, medical care, and car detailing. This offers a much desired private sector social world—one partly based on a different worship: work.

Church as Moral World

Madonna Massey recently moved to Lake Charles from Mississippi, so she is unfamiliar with the Arenos' ordeal at Bayou d'Inde or the lawsuit in which they were hoping for victory. She'd heard about the Bayou Corne Sinkhole and shakes her head at that. Madonna has read articles in the local *American Press* about "structural problems" in the I-10 bridge. "It spooks me out," she says. "Something about that bridge I don't like." But she'd read nothing in the paper nor heard anything on Fox News about a spill of EDC that was approaching the foundations of the I-10 bridge.

"I am so for capitalism and free enterprise," Madonna tells me as we sip our sweet teas at a cafeteria. "I hate the word 'regulate.' I don't want the size of my Coke bottle or type of lightbulb regulated. The American Dream is not due to socialism or the EPA. Sure, I want clean air and water," Madonna adds, "but I trust our system to assure it." Government workers do that, the thought streaks through my head. Still, in Madonna's worldview, it seems that one has the police to protect one's property, Rush Limbaugh to protect one's pride, and God to take care of the rest.

"Environmentalists want to stop the American Dream to protect the endangered toad," she says, "but if I had to choose between the American Dream and a toad, hey, I'll take the American Dream." Others I spoke to also pose the same either-or scenario—the very one Paul Templet had challenged.

Madonna was born in the non-dream town of Lake Providence, Louisiana, which *Time* magazine named as the poorest town in America. And she has since prospered beyond her wildest dreams. She is helping her husband build a much-beloved megachurch. A gifted gospel singer and mother of two, she has produced highly popular CDs with innumerable iTunes downloads, lives in a lovely house, and drives a white Mercedes.

Church had helped bring Madonna the American Dream, as it had for a good number in the congregation, it seemed. But there were rich churches and poor churches. About 10 to 15 percent of the congregation at Living Way is black, Madonna was happy to say, but Lake Charles is half black, so the numbers suggest, if not inequality, at least separation. With almost no exceptions, Lake Charles's mainly white churches are richer, and its mainly black churches are poorer. So if government were removed from the picture, and the church made a substitute for it, I wondered, wouldn't the churched world remain a highly unequal one? This isn't an issue Madonna engages. With God's help, she believes, everyone can rise as she has, one person at a time, if one truly and completely allows God to strengthen one's resolve.

The religious community appreciates the outdoors, I learn, but what do they have to say about keeping it clean? In a description on his church website, Pastor Jeffrey Ralston of First Pentecostal Church in Lake Charles notes: "I grew up in the country. My brother and I rode horses for miles and fished every day." Associate Pastor Jerod Grissom describes his hobbies as: "hunting . . . fishing in and around Louisiana, frogging." But there is no mention of the health of the habitats for these fish, game, and frogs. On the websites of ten major churches in Lake Charles, I found no mention of activities concerned with the polluted environment around them.

The National Association of Evangelicals is a voice for its 30,000,000 members, who make up a quarter of the American electorate, and a leading organization of the religious right with a political voice. This is true too of the Christian Coalition, which supported some 36 senators and 243 members of the House of Representatives, half of whom received a score of 10 percent or lower on the environmental scorecard of the League of Conservation Voters.

In a startling 2006 PBS television show called *Is God Green?* Bill Moyers tried to interview top leaders of the evangelical churches—including the Reverends Pat Robertson and Jerry Falwell and the Christian activist Ralph Reed. All of them referred Moyers to their shared spokesman, Dr. Calvin Beisner, an adjunct fellow at the Acton Institute for the Study of Religion and Liberty, based in Grand Rapids, Michigan. Beisner, in turn, cited Genesis chapter 1, verse 28: "Then God blessed them, and God said to them, 'Be fruitful and multiply, fill the earth and subdue it. Have dominion over the fish of the sea, over the birds of the air, and over every living thing that moves on the earth.'"

Dr. Beisner said the Bible also sanctioned mountaintop removal, presumably by coal companies. "If you are going to mine for precious metals, for fossil fuels, for anything else, you don't do that with a feather brush," Beisner tells Moyers. "I think the Scriptures actually tell us about the wonderful things that we can do with metals. We're told of gold and silver and other such things. Those things require mining, and 'force' is simply a scientific term for the application of energy to physical objects to bring about change. . . . My simple point about Genesis 1:28 [is] that we cannot escape the force involved in the Hebrew word for 'subdue.'" The Acton Institute was founded to "teach on (and) to favor a free market perspective," its website says, and it is financially supported by various corporations, including ExxonMobil.

But within the evangelical church, a small number of green voices are rising, calling for care of the environment—"creation care." In 2006, some eighty-six religious leaders signed a statement entitled "Climate Change: An Evangelical Call to Action." A West Virginia–based coalition opposed to coal blasting established a group called "Christians for Mountains." So in the nation at large, a debate about the environment has begun, especially among the young.

But I saw no hint of such a debate in my encounters with evangelical believers. Word from the Lake Charles pulpits seemed to focus more on a person's *moral strength to endure* than on the will to change the circumstances that called on that strength. The service offered a collective, supportive arena, it seemed, within which it was safe to feel helpless, sad, or lost. As in an hour of therapy, the individual drew strength from support in order to endure what had to be endured. The church had given comfort to Harold and Annette Areno. Another grief-stricken parishioner, the mother of an ill child living in the highly polluted town of Mossville, told me, "I don't know how I could have gotten through this without my church." As for altering the pollution, poverty, ill health, and other things that had to be endured, for many that lay beyond the doors of the church.

Like the Arenos and others, Madonna believes in the rapture. According to the Bible, "The earth will groan," she tells me, "and earthquakes, tornadoes, floods, rain, blizzards, strife will occur, and the earth *is* groaning." Drawing from the books of Revelation and Daniel, Madonna believes that within the next thousand years, gravity will release the feet of believers as they ascend to Heaven, while non-believers will remain on an earth that will become "as Hell" (Revelation 20:4–20; Daniel 9:23–27). After the rapture, the world will end for a time before Christ creates it anew and begins a new thousand-year period of peace, Madonna explains.

So what should we do about the groaning earth? I ask Madonna. "I want my ten great-grandchildren to have a great planet," she replies, "but the earth may just not be here." She poses a question I myself wondered about. "The BP oil spill in the Gulf of Mexico? I don't know; some would say, 'Let it go.'" Then she adds, "I'm giving you my Bible answers. I'm not well educated." Madonna attended two years of Bible College in Mississippi and explains, "This is not what you'd learn at your university, but mine is a true belief." This belief offered her a graphic image of the creation of the earth in seven days. It put the age of the earth at six thousand years. The City of Heaven, she told me, was a cube 1,500 miles square, divided into 12 bejeweled stories, each 120 miles high with gates, the largest one of pearls.

Across the nation, many share these beliefs with Madonna. According to a 2010 Pew Research Center report, 41 percent of all Americans believe the Second Coming "probably" or "definitely" will happen by the year 2050. Images of the rapture that believers have posted on the Internet suggest a growing gulf between those who rise to Heaven and those who stay on earth. In one image, svelte, well-dressed adults rise to a blue sky. Perhaps the rapture speaks to shared and understandable anxieties about an earthly economy, it occurs to me. For many congregants, well-paid, union-protected jobs through which a man could support a stay-at-home wife are gone for all but a small elite. Given automation and corporate offshoring, real wages of high school–educated American men have fallen 40 percent since 1970. For the whole bottom 90 percent of workers, average wages have flattened since 1980. Many older white men are in despair. Indeed, such men suffer a higher than average death rate due to alcohol, drugs, and even suicide. Although life expectancy for nearly every other group is rising, between

1990 and 2008 the life expectancy of older white men without high school diplomas has been shortened by three years—and truly, it seems, by despair. In their tough secular lives, life may well feel like "end times."

But word from the pulpit also seems to turn concern away from social problems in Louisiana—poverty, poor schools, pollution-related illness— away from government help, and away from the Great Paradox.

Media as Anxiety Producer

We are still drinking sweet teas at the cafeteria, and Madonna pokes at her cell phone to show me her Twitter feed, which reflects the list of sources of information she relies on: the Republican National Committee, Jeb Bush, Michael Reagan, Michelle Malkin, the *National Review*, the *Drudge Report*, Donald Trump. Then it continues with motivational quotes, Fox News, Debbie Phelps (the mother of Olympic swimmer Michael Phelps), and various Christian leaders. Madonna's car radio is tuned to Rush Limbaugh, her "brave heart."

As a powerful influence over the views of the people I came to know, Fox News stands next to industry, state government, church, and the regular media as an extra pillar of political culture all its own. Madonna tunes into Fox on the radio, television, and Internet. Up in Longville, where few subscribe to cable, Mike Tritico told me he could tell who was watching Fox News by the tilt of rooftop aerials. "It's nearly all Fox," he said. Fox gives Madonna and others the news. It suggests what the issues are. It tells her what to feel afraid, angry, and anxious about.

To some, Fox is family. One woman, a great reader who is highly attuned to world news, tells me she listens to Fox throughout the day. When she turns the ignition in her SUV, Fox News comes on. When she sits at her computer in her study at home, she tunes in to Fox via a small television to the right of her monitor. At the end of the day, sitting in a soft chair next to her husband, before a large screen, she watches the five o'clock news on Fox. "Fox is like family to me," she explains. "Bill O'Reilly is like a steady, reliable dad. Sean Hannity is like a difficult uncle who rises to anger too quickly.

Megyn Kelly is like a smart sister. Then there's Greta Van Susteren. And Juan Williams, who came over from NPR, which was too left for him, the adoptee. They're all different, just like in a family."

Fox offers news and opinions on matters of politics, of course, but it often strikes a note of alarm on issues—diseases, stock market plunges—with little direct bearing on politics. All news programs address our emotional alarm systems, of course. But with talk of a "terror mosque" at Ground Zero, of the "left's secret immigration plan" to wipe traditional America off the face of the earth, of Obama's supposed release of the ISIS leader Abu Bakr al-Baghdadi, of his supposed masterminding the massacre at Fort Hood, Fox News stokes fear. And the fear seems to reflect that of the audience it most serves—white middle- and working-class people. During the series of police killings of young black men, Fox reporters tended to defend white police officers and criticize black rioters. It defended the right to own guns and restrict voter registration, and it continually derided the federal government. While many claimed to listen to various stations—one car repair man listened to Brigham Young University radio on Sirius XM—in the evenings they watched Fox, and it was often Fox News that was digested along with dinner.

Sitting amidst his boxes near the sinkhole, Mike Schaff watches Bill O'Reilly and the rest of the Fox family for his main news, but routinely channel surfs to CNN, MSNBC, and CBS, with a special curiosity about how liberal commentators like Rachel Maddow describe Southern white conservatives. "A lot of liberal commentators look down on people like me. We can't say the 'N' word. We wouldn't want to; it's demeaning. So why do liberal commentators feel so free to use the 'R' word [redneck]?"

None of the people I talked to one-on-one, off-and-on, over five years used the extreme language I heard on Fox. George Russell, a Fox commentator, spoke of the "green energy tyranny." Business anchor Eric Bolling referred to the EPA as "job terrorists" who are "strangling America." Fox News Business Network commentator Lou Dobbs commented in 2011 that "as it's being run now, [the EPA] could be part of the apparat of the Soviet Union." One woman's favorite commentator, Charles Krauthammer, compared the rise in

EPA air quality standards to an "enemy attack" on America. Fox offers no less news on the environment than did CNN or CNBC, but its oratory was inflammatory. Yet the words *tyranny, apparat, terrorist,* and *strangler* did not come up in my talks with Tea Party embracers in Louisiana.

We all intuitively filter the news ourselves. One well-read, enthusiastic member of the Tea Party relied mainly on Fox News to watch and the *Drudge Report* to read online. But she sometimes dipped into the liberal media, occasionally purchasing the Sunday *New York Times* "just for the arts section." The rest of the *Times,* she said, "I throw away. It's too liberal to read." She was a devotee of Fox News, but, employed as a flight attendant, she sometimes found herself in foreign cities, flipping channels on the TV in her hotel: BBC, CNN, MSNBC. "CNN is not objective at all," she complains. "I turn it on for news and what I get is opinion."

"How can you tell straight news from opinion?" I ask. "By their *tone of voice,*" she explains. "Take Christiane Amanpour. She'll be kneeling by a sick African child, or a bedraggled Indian, looking into the camera, and her voice is saying, 'Something's *wrong*. We have to *fix* it.' Or worse, *we caused* the problem. She's using that child to say, '*Do* something, America.' But that child's problems aren't our fault." The Tea Party listener felt Christiane Amanpour was implicitly scolding her. She was imposing liberal feeling rules about whom to feel sorry for. The woman didn't want to be told she should feel sorry for, or responsible for, the fate of the child. Amanpour was overstepping her role as commentator by suggesting how to feel. The woman had her feeling guard up. "*No,*" she told herself in so many words, "That's *PC*. That's what liberals want listeners like me to feel. I don't like it. And what's more, I don't want to be told I'm a bad person if I don't feel sorry for that child." The social terrain around her—industry, government, church, media—lifted focus away from such a child's needs and from her own detachment from them. Again, I was backing into her deep story by exploring what it shut out. But all deep stories do that, and we all have deep stories.

Secret News

Long after Lee Sherman had polluted Bayou d'Inde, had fallen ill, and had been fired for "absenteeism" from his job, around the time he held up the "I'M THE ONE . . ." sign before a stadium of a thousand angry fishermen, he had joined a small environmental group called RESTORE. In 1994, a forty-year-old pipeline between Condea Vista and the Conoco docks was discovered to have sprung a leak—slow and over many years—of EDC into the soil. Ill-protected cleanup workers had become sick. Five hundred of them had sued the company and, in 1997, with modest recompense, won their case.

This was when the strange things had begun to happen. As Lee Sherman recalls: "We met in the den of Miss Bobby's and my house, some eight of us. The Arenos were there, and Mike Tritico. But a schoolteacher and his wife joined later. At first they seemed helpful. But little things happened. One day he and I were asked to buy some things for the group. He wrote down and held the list and on it were two GPSs. We got home with those, and people asked why we'd gotten them. He made it seem like I had bought them for *myself* with the *group's* money. I didn't say anything but I didn't like it." Another day, Lee recounted, "that man came early and asked to use Miss Bobby's computer. That was the computer she used for the group's bookkeeping." Having left the room momentarily, Miss Bobby noticed the man quickly changing the page on the computer screen. Later she discovered that he had downloaded spyware that copied her e-mail onto his computer. At the next meeting, Miss Bobby confronted the man, and after an acrimonious parting, the group fell apart, never to reassemble. No one knew the man's intent or why things in this tiny environmental group had gone so awry.

Ten years later, news of something called the "Lake Charles Project" surfaced. Wanting to stop troublemakers from helping workers bring more such lawsuits, Condea Vista had secretly hired a team to spy on RESTORE. Peter Markey, then manager of the Condea Vista's supply-chain operations, admitted in sworn deposition that for a quarter of a million dollars, the company had hired spies to infiltrate RESTORE. The spies were Special Forces retirees who worked for a Maryland-based security firm.

One investor in the security firm discovered company officials burning papers and became suspicious of wrongdoing. He took the unburned portion home and discovered among them files from the "Lake Charles Project."

What was that?

When asked during his deposition what the group was hired to do, Markey replied, "It was a surveillance operation . . ."

Attorney Perry Sanders asked, "What was being surveilled?"

"Environmental groups," Markey answered.

Attorney Sanders: "When you say they were being surveilled, what do you mean by that?"

Markey: "People go to the meetings and that type of thing."

Attorney Sanders: "What sort of people would go to meetings, you talking about like undercover operatives?"

Markey: "Yeah . . ."

Attorney Sanders: "Who knew about it?"

Markey: "The president. Probably the chief counsel."

The spies had collected tax records, listened in on phone calls, and photographed the Lake Charles home of Mike Tritico's mother, where he stayed.

When in 2008 news of the Lake Charles Project got out, it was through an investigative report by journalist James Ridgeway published in the left-leaning *Mother Jones* magazine, which none of my right-leaning friends in Louisiana had ever heard of. The local NBC affiliate television station KPLC broadcasted four programs, each a few minutes long, in the summer of 2008, in a series that began with "Condea Vista Hired Spies." But the archives of the main newspaper in the area, the Lake Charles–based *American Press*, contain no mention of it. The New Orleans–based *Times-Picayune* reported on a lawsuit filed by Greenpeace in 2011, which mentioned the 2008 exposé in passing. But by 2011, when I began interviewing people in town, no one remembered the spy case. The environmental group had broken up and Condea Vista was now called Sasol.

As I reviewed the social terrain of the right-leaning people I had come to know—the companies, the state government, the church, Fox News—I reflected on my keyhole issue. Everyone I was talking to was enduring a great deal of pollution and despite the silence from companies, politicians, and state officials, nearly everyone clearly knew it. To some, such as Lee Sherman and Harold and Annette Areno, exposure had become the defining experience of their lives. To others, it was a passing matter. While many, like Madonna Massey, spoke of their love of capitalism, the dominant industry in their economy presented a decidedly mixed story. Oil was highly automated and accounted for some 15 percent of jobs—and even some of those were going to foreign workers at lower pay. The state had made huge cuts to local jobs and social services in order to bring in companies and, instead of money trickling down, a third of it was leaking out. To some degree, the community had become the site of local production without being the site of local producers. They were victims without a language of victimhood.

I felt like I was working slowly backward toward an answer to the Great Paradox, daily crossing and re-crossing the empathy wall as I tried to stay focused on the viewpoints of my new friends. I started with problems (which was one side of the paradox). Many locals resisted this focus. Didn't I see how beautiful Louisiana was? Had I attended the Lake Charles Mardi Gras? Why such a gloomy focus? But I wasn't making these problems up. They were there—pollution, health, schooling, poverty.

Moving backward, if one admits a problem, one is obliged to admit to a desire to fix it. But who might fix the problem of pollution? Companies weren't volunteering. With regard to social support, churches lacked the mission and the money. Surprisingly, everyone agreed that if things were to be fixed, the federal government had to get involved. But if the federal government got involved, right-wing flags went up. It was too big, too incompetent, too mal-intentioned.

So maybe it was back to structural amnesia: Why the big fuss? What was the big problem? Didn't other things matter more—ISIS, immigration, undeserving government beneficiaries? Who had led them to expect all they felt entitled to expect—the over half of Louisianans who were beneficiaries, as Mike Schaff pointed out; the "fun-at-night gals" on the dole Lee Sherman envisioned; the "poor dears" Bob Hardey saw around town? Sure, some people cheat the government, I thought, and that's wrong. But it is a very long leap between annoyance at cheaters and hatred of nearly all federal government. Why that leap? The best path to the root answer, I thought, was through their deep story.

PART THREE

The Deep Story and the People in It

9

The Deep Story

Behind all I was learning about bayou and factory childhoods and the larger context—industry, state, church, regular media, Fox News—of the lives of those I had come to know lay, I realized, a deep story.

A deep story is a *feels-as-if* story—it's the story feelings tell, in the language of symbols. It removes judgment. It removes fact. It tells us how things feel. Such a story permits those on both sides of the political spectrum to stand back and explore the *subjective prism* through which the party on the other side sees the world. And I don't believe we understand anyone's politics, right or left, without it. For we all have a deep story.

There are many kinds of deep story, of course. Lovers come to know each other's childhood in order to understand how it feels to be the other person; they learn a personal deep story. Foreign leaders and diplomats try to understand national deep stories in order to relate more effectively to world leaders. They gather international deep stories. The deep story here, that of the Tea Party, focuses on relationships between social groups within our national borders. I constructed this deep story to represent—in metaphorical form—the hopes, fears, pride, shame, resentment, and anxiety in the lives of those I talked with. Then I tried it out on my Tea Party friends to see if they thought it fit their experience. They did.

Like a play, it unfolds in scenes.

Waiting in Line

You are patiently standing in a long line leading up a hill, as in a pilgrimage. You are situated in the middle of this line, along with others who are also white, older, Christian, and predominantly male, some with college degrees, some not.

Just over the brow of the hill is the American Dream, the goal of everyone waiting in line. Many in the back of the line are people of color—poor, young and old, mainly without college degrees. It's scary to look back; there are so many behind you, and in principle you wish them well. Still, you've waited a long time, worked hard, and the line is barely moving. You deserve to move forward a little faster. You're patient but weary. You focus ahead, especially on those at the very top of the hill.

The American Dream is a dream of progress—the idea that you're better off than your forebears just as they superseded their parents before you—and extends beyond money and stuff. You've suffered long hours, layoffs, and exposure to dangerous chemicals at work, and received reduced pensions. You have shown moral character through trial by fire, and the American Dream of prosperity and security is a reward for all of this, showing who you have been and are—a badge of honor.

The source of the American Dream is on the other side of the hill, hidden. Has the economy come to a strange standstill? Is my company doing okay? Will I get a raise this year? Are there good jobs for us all? Or just a few? Will we be waiting in line forever? It's so hard to see over the brow of the hill.

The sun is hot and the line unmoving. In fact, is it moving backward? You haven't gotten a raise in years, and there is no talk of one. Actually, if you are short a high school diploma, or even a BA, your income has dropped over the last twenty years. That has happened to your buddies too; in fact, some of them have stopped looking for good jobs, because they figure for guys like them, good jobs aren't out there.

You've taken the bad news in stride because you're a positive person. You're not a complainer. You count your blessings. You wish you could help your family and church more, because that's where your heart is. You'd like them to feel grateful to you for being so giving to them. But this line isn't moving. And after all your intense effort, all your sacrifice, you're beginning to feel stuck.

You think of things to feel proud of—your Christian morality, for one. You've always stood up for clean-living, monogamous, heterosexual marriage. That hasn't been easy. You've been through a separation yourself, a near—or actual—divorce. Liberals are saying your ideas are outmoded, sexist, homophobic, but it's not clear what *their* values are. And given a climate of secular tolerance, you remember better times, when as a child you said morning prayer and the flag salute—before "under God" became optional—in public school.

The Line Cutters

Look! You see people *cutting in line ahead of you!* You're following the rules. They aren't. As they cut in, it feels like you are being moved back. How can they just do that? Who are they? Some are black. Through affirmative action plans, pushed by the federal government, they are being given preference for places in colleges and universities, apprenticeships, jobs, welfare payments, and free lunches, and they hold a certain secret place in people's minds, as we see below. Women, immigrants, refugees, public sector workers—where will it end? Your money is running through a liberal sympathy sieve you don't control or agree with. These are opportunities you'd have loved to have had in your day—and either you should have had them when you were young or the young shouldn't be getting them now. It's not fair.

And President Obama: how did *he* rise so high? The biracial son of a low-income single mother becomes president of the most powerful country in the world; you didn't see that coming. And if he's there, what kind of a slouch does his rise make you feel like, you who are supposed to be so much more privileged? Or did Obama get there *fairly?* How did he get into an expensive place like *Columbia* University? How did Michelle Obama get enough money to go to *Princeton?* And then *Harvard* Law School, with a father who was a city water plant employee? You've never seen anything like it, not up close. The federal government must have given them money. And Michelle *should feel* grateful for all she has but sometimes she seems mad. She has no right to feel mad.

Women: Another group is cutting ahead of you in line, if you are a man: women demanding the right to the men's jobs. Your dad didn't have to compete with women for scarce positions at the office. Also jumping in line ahead of you are overpaid public sector employees—and a majority of them are women and minorities. It also seems to you that they work shorter hours in more secure and overpaid jobs, enjoying larger pensions than yours. That assistant administrator at the Department of Regulation has cushy hours, a fat pension awaiting her, lifetime tenure—and she's probably sitting at her screen doing online shopping. What has she done to deserve perks that you don't enjoy?

Immigrants: And now Filipinos, Mexicans, Arabs, Indians, and Chinese on special visas or green cards are ahead of you in line. Or maybe they snuck in. You've seen Mexican-looking men building the man camps that are to house Sasol's Filipino pipefitters. You see the Mexicans work hard—and you admire that—but they work for less, and lower white American pay.

Refugees: Four million Syrian refugees are fleeing war and chaos, thousands a day, appearing in boats on the shores of Greece. President Obama accepted 10,000 of them, two-thirds women and children, to settle in the United States. But word has it that 90 percent of the refugees are young men, possibly ISIS terrorists, poised to get in line ahead of you and get their hands on your tax money. And what about you? You've suffered floods, oil spills, and chemical leaks. There are days when you feel like a refugee yourself.

The brown pelican: Unbelievably, standing ahead of you in line is a brown pelican, fluttering its long, oil-drenched wings. The Louisiana state bird, pictured on the state flag, nests in mangrove trees on ribbons of sand along the coast. The brown pelican was at one time nearly wiped out by chemical pollution, but in 2009 it was removed from the endangered species list—a year before the 2010 BP oil spill. To keep surviving, it now needs clean fish to eat, clean water to dive in, oil-free marshes, and protection from coastal erosion. That's why it's in line ahead of you. But really, it's just an animal and you're a human being.

Blacks, women, immigrants, refugees, brown pelicans—all have cut ahead of you in line. But it's people like *you* who have made this country great. You feel uneasy. It has to be said: the line cutters irritate you. They are violating rules of fairness. You resent them, and you feel it's right that you do. So do your friends. Fox commentators reflect your feelings, for your deep story is also the Fox News deep story.

You're a compassionate person. But now you've been asked to extend your sympathy to all the people who have cut in front of you. So you have your guard up against requests for sympathy. People complain: Racism. Discrimination. Sexism. You've heard stories of oppressed blacks, dominated women, weary immigrants, closeted gays, desperate refugees, but at some point, you say to yourself, you have to close the borders to human sympathy— especially if there are some among them who might bring you harm. You've suffered a good deal yourself, but you aren't complaining about it.

Betrayal

Then you become suspicious. If people are cutting in line ahead of you, someone must be *helping* them. Who? A man is monitoring the line, walking up and down it, ensuring that the line is orderly and that access to the Dream is fair. His name is President Barack Hussein Obama. But— hey—you see him *waving* to the line cutters. He's helping them. He feels extra sympathy for them that he doesn't feel for you. He's on *their* side. He's telling you that these line cutters *deserve* special treatment, that they've had a harder time than you've had. You don't live near the line cutters or have close friends in most categories of the line cutters, but from what you can see or hear on Fox News, the real story doesn't correspond to his story about the line cutters, which celebrates so many black people, women, and immigrants. The supervisor wants you to sympathize with the line cutters, but you don't want to. It's not fair. In fact, the president and his wife are line cutters themselves.

You feel betrayed. The president is *their* president, not *your* president. Now you have your guard way up. Watch out for lies. Presidents and other officials often wear a small pin showing the American flag—a flag pin. Did you see what a *small* flag pin he is wearing today? Maybe that means he's not proud of America. So the great pride you feel in being an American cannot be conveyed through him. As a source of honor, being an American is more important to you than ever, given the slowness of this line to the American Dream, and given disrespectful talk about whites and men and Bible-believing Christians.

Obama's story seems "fishy." You're not a paranoid type, but it seems to you that either the federal government funded Obama's education or, even worse, secret strings were pulled. A friend of yours asks you whether or not you noticed that Obama took off his wristwatch for Ramadan. (She is referring to a custom of removing jewelry during the Muslim holy month.) "He was brought up on the Koran," a neighbor says.

You may not yet have the biggest house, but you can certainly be proud of being American. And anyone who criticizes America—well, they're criticizing you. If you can no longer feel pride in the United States through its president, you'll have to feel American in some new way—by banding with others who feel as strangers in their own land.

Intermission

Meanwhile, for the white, Christian, older, right-leaning Louisianans I came to know, the deep story was a response to a real squeeze. On the one hand, the national ideal and promise at the brow of the hill was the American Dream—which is to say *progress*. On the other hand, it had become *hard to progress*.

As an ideal, the American Dream proposed a right way of feeling. You should feel hopeful, energetic, focused, mobilized. Progress—its core idea—didn't go with feeling confused or mournful. And as an ideal, the American Dream did not seem to guide people in what to feel when they had attained some of their goals but not others—a state inspiring a more cautious impulse to protect what you already have.

Progress had also become harder—more chancy and more restricted to a small elite. The Great Recession of 2008 in which people lost homes, savings, and jobs had come and gone, but it had shaken people up. Meanwhile, for the bottom 90 percent of Americans, the Dream Machine—invisible over the brow of the hill—had stopped due to automation, off-shoring, and the growing power of multinationals vis-à-vis their workforces. At the same time, for that 90 percent, competition between white men and everyone else had increased—for jobs, for recognition, and for government funds. The year when the Dream stopped working for the 90 percent was 1950. If you were born before 1950, on average, the older you got, the more your income rose. If you were born after 1950, it did not. In fact, as economist Phillip Longman argues, they are the first generation in American history to experience the kind of lifetime downward mobility "in which at every stage of adult life, they have less income and less net wealth than people their age ten years before." Some become so discouraged they stop looking for work; since the 1960s, the share of men ages twenty-five to fifty-four no longer in the workforce has tripled.

This stalled American Dream hits many on the right at a particularly vulnerable season of life—in their fifties, sixties, and seventies. It is a time during which people often check their bucket list, take stock, and are sometimes forced to give up certain dreams of youth. It's a season of life in which a person says to him- or herself, "So this is it." As one man told me, "I thought one day I'd meet the girl of my dreams. I haven't and now I don't see her coming into my life." Another man had hoped to start his own swamp tour company but wasn't able to get it off the ground. Yet another had hoped to travel to rodeo shows around the South, but got sick. Who could one blame for such disappointments? Oneself, of course. But that only increases your intense focus on your place in line.

Age also meant age discrimination. Older men now in their sixties were the first to experience the diminishing American Dream, either by virtue of their lack of up-to-date training or because of company reluctance to pay age-related higher wages. But where were those federally funded training centers? And who can explain why it's so hard to get a good job?

A sixty-three-year-old man I met in Lake Charles, whom I will call Bill Beatifo, had a full crop of gray hair and a cherubic smile. As I came to know his story, I came to deeply appreciate his brave refusal to be discouraged.

His passion was sales. "I cut my teeth in cold calling," he said. "Sold trucks through Ryder truck rentals, Kirby vacuum cleaners, Amish sheds, short-term health insurance, you name it. For sixteen years I had done really well as a salesman and sales manager." Then a watershed moment came in 1992. "I was asked to fire some people under me. Then they got me. I'd been making $60,000. They said we've got to cut you to $40,000, but you can make up the $20,000 in commissions. But that $20,000 was really a cut. So I quit. They were cutting the older employees because we were more highly paid. I felt betrayed, especially by a co-worker who knew what was about to happen but didn't tell me."

Then he tried to replace the job he had lost:

"I called . . .

"E-mailed . . .

"Called . . .

"E-mailed . . .

"Waited . . .

"I almost never heard back. They can tell how old you are from your resume." The longer Bill was locked out of jobs in sales, the harder it became. He went on unemployment. "I was a ninety-nine-weeker," he said in a mirthless laugh, referring to maximum unemployment insurance. "It was almost too long; you don't actually look for work every day." He applied for a full-time job stocking grocery shelves but realized that, at his age, eight hours on his feet was too much.

Bill found a part-time job as a bookkeeper at a nearby truck garage for ten dollars an hour—the same wage he had earned summers as a college student in a union-protected factory job forty years earlier. He had applied for a job as a part-time guard at a gated community, which he didn't get. He also spent more time with what had long been a sideline: selling non-FDA-approved magnetic shoe inserts that "get rid of aches and pains," and he had bought stocks in a company that was "about to produce" a medical device he hoped to sell to hospitals. He sold Organo Gold coffee (non-government-certified "organic") to friends and acquaintances, which his daughter feared was a scam (you have to buy it before you sell it). But Bill wasn't the type to give up. He could endure pain. "I'm a capitalist," he said. "When they get the medical device out of production and into the market, my wife and I will be millionaires." As with other men I spoke with, the repeated term "millionaire" floated around conversations like a ghost.

Meanwhile, if men like Bill were being squeezed by automation, outsourcing, and the rising power of multinationals, they were also being squeezed by greater competition from other groups for an ever-scarcer supply of cultural honor. As we shall see, the 1960s and 1970s had opened cultural doors previously closed to blacks and women, even as immigrants and refugees seemed to be sailing past the Statue of Liberty into a diminishing supply of good jobs.

And the federal government was helping this happen. After Clinton's 1990s claim to "end welfare as we know it," rates of financial aid to the poor fell. But in response to the Great Recession, after 2008, welfare rose—mainly through Medicaid and SNAP—although these rates have peaked and are falling. (On this, see Appendix C.) Given trends in the economy and a more open cultural door, news of more "government giveaways" rang alarm bells. That was the squeeze.

Not all white middle- and working-class men in this squeeze moved right, of course. But many self-starters, men who'd done well for what they'd been given, those in evangelical churches in right-leaning rural and Southern enclaves, those who had emotionally endured—and the women who were like them or depended on them—were inclining right.

Catcalls

"Crazy redneck." "White trash." "Ignorant Southern Bible-thumper." You realize that's *you* they're talking about. You hear these terms on the radio, on television, read them on blogs. The gall. You're offended. You're angry. And you really hate the endless parade of complainers encouraged by a 1960s culture that seems to have settled over the land.

On top of that, Hollywood films and popular television either ignore people like you or feature them—as in *Buckwild*—in unflattering ways. "Two missing front teeth, all raggedy, that's how they show us," one man complained. The stock image of the early twentieth century, the "Negro" minstrel, a rural simpleton, the journalist Barbara Ehrenreich notes, has now been upgraded, whitened, and continued in such television programs as *Duck Dynasty* and *Here Comes Honey Boo Boo.* "Working class whites are now regularly portrayed as moronic, while blacks are often hyper-articulate, street smart . . . and rich."

You are a stranger in your own land. You do not recognize yourself in how others see you. It is a struggle to feel seen and honored. And to feel honored you have to feel—and feel seen as—moving forward. But through no fault of your own, and in ways that are hidden, you are slipping backward.

You turn to your workplace for respect—but wages are flat and jobs insecure. So you look to other sources of honor. You get no extra points for your race. You look to gender, but if you're a man, you get no extra points for that either. If you are straight you are proud to be a married, heterosexual male, but that pride is now seen as a potential sign of homophobia—a source of dishonor. Regional honor? Not that either. You are often disparaged for the place you call home. As for the church, many look down on it, and the proportion of Americans outside any denomination has risen. You are old, but in America, attention is trained on the young. People like you—white, Christian, working and middle class—suffer this sense of fading honor demographically too, as this very group has declined in numbers.

You have the impulse to call out, "I'm part of a minority *too!*" But you have criticized just such appeals for sympathy when others have made them on similar grounds. You feel stuck between a strong desire to be recognized for who you really are and all you've really done, and dread at joining the parade of "poor me's." You want to rise up against these downward forces. There is a political movement made up of people such as yourself who share your deep story. It's called the Tea Party.

Checking Back with My Friends

I return to my new Louisiana friends and acquaintances to check whether the deep story resonates with them. When I relate the story to him, Mike Schaff writes in an e-mail, "*I live your analogy.* We pay hundreds of millions of dollars in hard-earned taxes for these bureaucrats at the Department of Environmental Quality and the EPA to do their job and they do nothing of the sort. To add insult to injury, these slackers jump the line to retire before the workers who pay their salaries can. When the tax payer finally gets to retire, he sees the bureaucrats in Washington have raided the fund. And the rest of us are waiting in line."

When I relate it to Lee Sherman, he tells me, "You've read my mind." Janice Areno tells me, "You have it right, but you've left out the fact that the people being cut in on are *paying taxes* that *go to* the people cutting in line!" Another comments, "You didn't finish the story. After a while, the people who were waiting have had it and they get in their *own* line." And yet another adds, "That's it, but the American Dream is more than having money. It's feeling proud to be an American, and to say 'under God' when you salute the flag, and feel *good* about that. And it's about living in a society that believes in clean, normal family life. But if you add that, then yes, this's my story."

In his interviews with Tea Party members in New York, Jersey City, Newark, and elsewhere in New Jersey, the sociologist Nils Kumkar found spontaneous mention of the idea of annoyance at others cutting in line. In their interviews with Tea Party advocates in Massachusetts, Virginia, and Arizona and in their 2011 examination of nearly a thousand Tea Party websites, the sociologists Theda Skocpol and Vanessa Williamson also reported attitudes toward blacks, immigrants, public sector workers, and others parallel to those I found here.

Many spoke of sympathy fatigue. "Liberals want us to feel sympathy for blacks, women, the poor, and of course I do up to a point," one kindly restaurant proprietor explained. "I hear stories and they break my heart. But then sometimes, I don't know if I'm being had. I get men applying for a job. I give them a job and they don't show up. Is it just to put on their record that they applied and can continue on unemployment insurance? A woman came up to me at Wendy's saying she had two children and was looking to pay for a hotel because she was homeless. I asked her where her children were. 'Oh they're with mama.' Well, then aren't you living with mama? A man from the Red Cross came asking for food for Sunday dinner for the homeless. I gave it to him because it's food. But I don't even want to go over there to see. Maybe they're not trying to be independent. I don't want to change my mind about giving the food. I want to give." But he wanted to do it on the understanding his recipients were trying to better themselves, a requirement he worried liberals left out.

Behind the Deep Story: Race

The deep story of the right, the *feels-as-if* story, corresponds to a real structural squeeze. People want to achieve the American Dream, but for a mixture of reasons feel they are being held back, and this leads people of the right to feel frustrated, angry, and betrayed by the government. Race is an essential part of this story.

Curiously, the people of the right I came to know spoke freely about Mexicans (4 percent of Louisianans were Hispanic in 2011) and Muslims (who accounted for 1 percent) but were generally silent about blacks, who, at 26 percent, were the state's largest minority. When the topic of blacks did arise, many explained that they felt accused by "the North" of being racist—which, by their own definition, they clearly were not. They defined as racist a person who used the "N" word or who "hates" blacks. Mike Schaff did neither. Born on the Armelise sugarcane plantation, grandson of the overseer, he describes himself as a "former bigot . . . I used to use the 'N' word, and a lot of black kids I played with did too. But I stopped that back in 1968. I remember yelling from the stands of my college football stadium in 1968, rooting for our best player. 'Run! Nigger! Run!' And the next year in 1969 I was yelling, 'Run! Joe! Run!' I haven't used the word since. I look forward to a day when color just won't matter at all. I think we're halfway there."

As I and others use the term, however, racism refers to the belief in a natural hierarchy that places blacks at the bottom, and the tendency of whites to judge their own worth by distance from that bottom. By that definition, many Americans, north and south, are racist. And racism appears not simply in personal attitudes but in structural arrangements—as when polluting industries move closer to black neighborhoods than to white.

Among the older right-wing whites I came to know, blacks entered their lives, not as neighbors and colleagues, but through the television screen and newspaper where they appeared in disparate images. In one image, blacks were rich mega-stars of music, film, and sports—Beyoncé, Jamie Foxx, Michael Jordan, Serena Williams. Pro basketball legend LeBron James, they knew, earned $90 million from endorsements of commercial products alone. So what could be the problem? In a second image, blacks were a disproportionate part of the criminal class, and of its glorification in raunchy rap lyrics about guns, "hos," and "bitches." And in a third image, blacks were living on welfare. (But see Appendix C.) Missing from the image of blacks in most of the minds of those I came to know was a man or woman standing patiently in line next to them waiting for a well-deserved reward.

Behind the Deep Story: Gender

Gender, too, lay behind the disorientation, fear, and resentment evoked by the deep story. All the women I talked to worked, used to work, or were about to return to work. But their political feelings seemed based on their role as wives and mothers—and they wanted to be wives to high-earning men and to enjoy the luxury, as one woman put it, of being a homemaker. According to national polls, more men than women are Republican, or Tea

Party, and more men (12 percent in 2012) are members or supporters of the Tea Party than women (9 percent). And even within these conservative groups, women are more likely than men to appreciate the government's role in helping the disadvantaged, in making contraception available, in equal pay for equal work. It was this range of issues—especially the need for parental leave—that had led me, as I note in the preface, on this journey in the first place. The women I spoke to seemed to sense that if we chop away large parts of the government, women stand to lose far more than men, for women outnumber men as government workers and as beneficiaries.

I also noticed a curious gender gap *within* the right. When the conversation got around, as it inevitably did, to nonworking people getting "handouts" paid for by workers further back "in line," a gender divide emerged. When I asked one couple what proportion of people on welfare were gaming the system, the woman estimated 30 percent while her husband estimated 80 percent. There, inside the Tea Party, was the gender gap. Despite this difference, women and men of the right voted in similar ways, and more than gender—those affirmative action women cutting ahead in line—they jointly focused on race and class.

Behind the Deep Story: Class, the Federal Government, and Free Market as Proxy Allies

One can see the experience of being "cut in on" by one group after another as an expression of class conflict. This is perhaps a curious term to use. Certainly it is a term avoided by the right, and it is applied elsewhere by the left. But throughout American history such conflicts have appeared in different theaters of life, with different actors and different moral vocabularies in play. Each called for deep feelings about fairness. In the industrial nineteenth century, the classic form of class conflict took place on the factory floor, between owner and worker, and the issue was one of fair recompense for work. In 1892, a general strike took place in New Orleans. Railroad conductors struck against management for the ten-hour day, overtime pay, and the right to unionize. Other unions joined in sympathy, white workers standing with blacks despite attempts to divide them. The Chicago garment workers' strike in 1910 against a management cut in the piece rate, or the 1934 West Coast Longshore strike—all these took place between managers and workers, in a workplace, over pay, hours, or working conditions.

Today, although many such strikes continue—the Walmart strike of 2012, for example—many industrial work sites have been moved offshore to Mexico, China, Vietnam, and elsewhere. Other forms of social conflict have arisen in different theaters. One theater animates the politics of the left. It focuses on conflict in the private sector between the very richest 1 percent and the rest of America. Occupy Wall Street has such a focus. It is not between owner and worker over a higher wage or shorter hours of work. It is between haves and have-nots, the ever-more-wealthy 1 percent and the other 99 percent of Americans. What feels unfair to Occupy activists is not simply unfair recompense for work (the multi-million dollar bonuses to hedge fund managers alongside the $8.25 hourly rate for Walmart clerks) but the absence of tax policies that could help restore America as a middle-class society.

For the right today, the main theater of conflict is neither the factory floor nor an Occupy protest. The theater of conflict—at the heart of the deep story—is the local welfare office and the mailbox where undeserved disability checks and SNAP stamps arrive. Government checks for the listless and idle—this seems most unfair. If unfairness in Occupy is expressed in the moral vocabulary of a "fair share" of resources and a properly proportioned society, unfairness in the right's deep story is found in the language of "makers" and "takers." For the left, the flashpoint is up the class ladder (between the very top and the rest); for the right, it is down between the middle class and the poor. For the left, the flashpoint is centered in the private sector; for the right, in the public sector. Ironically, both call for an honest day's pay for an honest day's work.

Left and right also seemed to ally with different sectors of society. It is almost as if those I talked with thought about the government and the market in the same way others think of separate nations. Just as various nations back different sides in a foreign war, fighting each other on a "proxy" battlefront, in the same way those I spoke with seemed to talk about the federal government and the free market. The free market was the unwavering ally of the good citizens waiting in line for the American Dream. The federal government was on the side of those unjustly "cutting in."

Feeling betrayed by the federal government and turning wholeheartedly to the free market, the right is faced with realities the deep story makes it hard to see or focus on. Giant companies have grown vastly larger, more automated, more global, and more powerful. For them, productivity is increasingly based on cheap labor in offshore plants abroad, imported cheap foreign labor, and automation, and less on American labor. The more powerful they've become, the less resistance they have encountered from unions and government. Thus, they have felt more free to allocate more profits to top executives and stockholders, and less to workers. But this is the "wrong" theater to look in for the conflict that absorbs the right—except when a company like Texas Brine causes a sinkhole like the one in Bayou Corne.

And this may explain why much of the right isn't bothered by something else—the unaligned interests between big and small business. Many members of the Tea Party run or work in a small business—oil company suppliers, trailer parks, restaurants, small banks, and shops. Small businesses are vulnerable to the growth of big monopolies. What is transpiring today, Robert Reich argues in *Saving Capitalism*, is that big monopolies support policies that help them compete against smaller businesses by rewriting property bankruptcy and contract laws that favor big business over small. Under recently revised bankruptcy laws, the billionaire Donald Trump can freely declare bankruptcy while insulating himself from risks to investment, while smaller businesses cannot. The choice is not, Reich argues, between a governed and an ungoverned market, but between a market governed by laws favoring monopolistic companies and one governed by those favoring small business. Ironically, the economic sector that stands to suffer most from big monopolies is small business, many of which are run by those who favor the Tea Party. It might not be too much to say that the embrace of the 1 percent by mom-and-pop store owners is a bit like the natural seed–using small farmers' embrace of Monsanto, the corner grocery store's embrace of

Walmart, the local bookstore owner's embrace of Amazon. Under the same banner of the "free market," the big are free to dominate the small.

But it is very hard to criticize an ally, and the right sees the free market as its ally against the powerful alliance of the federal government and the takers. Even Lee Sherman, who had greatly suffered at the hands of Pittsburg Plate Glass, owned stock in it and exclaimed proudly to me, when I asked him how he felt about getting fired, "I was pissed and stunned but, hey, I didn't lose everything. I had $5,000 in stocks!"

In the undeclared class war, expressed through the weary, aggravating, and ultimately enraging wait for the American Dream, those I came to know developed a visceral hate for the ally of the "enemy" cutters in line—the federal government. They hated other people for needing it. They rejected their own need of it—even to help clean up the pollution in their backyard.

But that kind of extraordinary determination takes a certain kind of person—a deep story self.

10

The Team Player: Loyalty Above All

"You can tell I'm a Republican," Janice Areno says as she invites me to sit down in her office. Elephants fill three shelves of a wall opposite her desk. One is blue-and-white porcelain, a second is gold, a third is red, white, and blue and stands near a young child's drawing of a yellow one. One is shaped into a teapot. Another holds an American flag. There are large elephants and small, wooden and glass. There are elephants standing and elephants trotting. Next to her awards for outstanding service to her community and photos of relatives, the elephants had been gathered, over the years, from bake sales, luncheon raffles, and Republican conventions. "I see an elephant, I feel proud of this country."

I am seated across from Janice (pronounced Jan-EECE) in her spacious office where she has long worked as an accountant for Lacassane, a land management company in Lake Charles. She is the daughter of Harold Areno's oldest brother, and she herself grew up not far from Bayou d'Inde. She is a short woman with a purposeful handshake and a lively face who dresses in a no-nonsense gray pantsuit and practical shoes. She wears neither jewelry nor make-up; in this way, she "dresses Pentecostal," as she puts it. But with her somewhat mannish outfit and close-cropped brown-gray hair, she explains, "In some ways, I don't dress Pentecostal." Her manner is direct, forceful, usually good-humored. Across the desk, during our first of many meetings, she punches out a series of well-articulated opinions on a wide range of issues, and then comments humorously, aside, "You get me talking about all the *burrs under my saddle*." Then she quips, "Maybe I'll visit you in Berkeley and you can introduce me to naked hippies."

A blizzard of papers covers her large wooden desk. "Tax season," she explains. "I do returns for the cleaning lady and the computer guy, and I just finished taxes for the daughter of a co-worker." She's also been calling around to everyone she knows to donate food and furniture to a friend's relative, a soldier who had just returned from a second tour in Iraq to discover that his wife had abandoned their three small children. The oldest was feeding the younger ones remnants of stale cereal. Janice had joined her church's compassionate effort to rally around the man.

We joke. On a later visit to Lake Charles, I bring her a San Francisco 49ers cap; she is an ardent Dallas Cowboys fan. She tells me she'll wear it deer hunting, but can't promise to root for the 49ers. In truth, her home team is the right wing of the elephant, the Republican Party. Her loyalty to it defines her world.

Sixty-one and single, she is devoted to a large extended family and notes proudly, "I raised my sister's kids like my own." One nephew, now grown, lives in a trailer on her property and is helping her construct rooms in her large new home to accommodate one sister, maybe two, and anyone else it works out with. At Lacassane, Janice is usually the last to leave the office at night. As corporate secretary and senior accountant, she oversees the management of 21,000 acres of land, long ago part of a rice and soybean plantation. Throughout the years, the land has also been leased for hunting and oil and gas exploration. Lacassane also runs a large hunting lodge, licenses underground pipeline rights of way, and manages timber.

I ask Janice if we could visit her former school, church, and home in Sulphur, just west of Lake Charles. We leave her office, walk into the parking lot, and climb into her silver SUV. Fishing rods rattle in the back, along with a three-pound bag of pecans "crushed but not shelled" that she plans to give away to friends. Sulphur is an industrial town of 20,000 built in the 1870s. Out of the car window I see signs of many other lines of work in Louisiana: Richard's Boudin and Seafood Market, Sulphur Pawn and Discount Center,

Bebop's Ice House, lumber yards, barber shops, Family Dollar stores, Walgreens, J.C. Penney, PayDay Loans of Sulphur, and EZ Cash.

As we head for her old school, she begins to describe her childhood. "I was born in the middle of the pack, fourth of six. My dad was the oldest of ten, and my mom was the youngest of seven, and everyone married and had kids. On Daddy's side alone I have forty-six cousins, and on my mom's side it's about the same. One of my mother's brothers had eleven." Like many of those I talked to, Janice describes her childhood as "poor but happy." "My mother was a homemaker, but, boy, she cooked up a storm morning and night and washed for eight in a washhouse."

"I worked hard all my life. I started at age eight and never stopped," Janice begins. In the course of her work life, she had learned to tough things out, to endure. Endurance wasn't just a moral value; it was a practice. It was work of an emotional sort. Not claiming to be a victim, accommodating the downside of loose regulations out of a loyalty to free enterprise—this was a tacit form of heroism, hidden to incurious liberals. Sometimes you had to endure bad news, Janice felt, for a higher good, such as jobs in oil.

I was discovering three distinct expressions of this endurance self in different people around Lake Charles—the Team Loyalist, the Worshipper, and the Cowboy, as I came to see them. Each kind of person expresses the value of endurance and expresses a capacity for it. Each attaches an aspect of self to this heroism. The Team Loyalist accomplishes a team goal, supporting the Republican Party. The Worshipper sacrifices a strong wish. The Cowboy affirms a fearless self. Janice was a Team Loyalist.

Janice has not left her love of rural life behind. "I learned to handle a shotgun when I was six, picking off cottonmouth and copperhead snakes from a boat," she tells me. "Now I hunt deer, duck, and boar in season, and I fish on weekends. My daddy used to say if you shoot 'em, you clean 'em and eat 'em. Until I was forty, all my brothers and sisters did that. Now I take the meat to be ground into sausage."

We pass Janice's elementary school, named after the German scientist Herman Frasch, who developed a method of mining sulfur. Her high school's official emblem was a miner's hardhat, crossed pick, and shovel; its school colors were blue and gold. Janice had been in the Honor Society and 4-H, and she was a leader on the debate team, following that up with a BA from nearby McNeese State University and a career in accounting. Her father had not been so lucky, she told me. As the oldest of ten, he was forced to quit school early to help his father raise a garden to feed a family of twelve.

We stop in front of Janice's church, get out, pop the trunk, and carry in boxes of cups, plates, and hand wipes. These are to be used at a church supper to raise money for our troops in Iraq and Afghanistan. "People have stopped giving money for our boys, but they're *still* over there," she said. "We still have to care." We get back in her SUV and drive on.

Janice's talk of family focuses mainly on her father. "He had a third-grade education and supported a family of eight. He could do a lot of things, like mend a hole in fishing net like no one you ever saw," she says. At nineteen he learned pipefitting, joined the local union, and worked for more than thirty years at Cities Service (now Citgo). "He was never on disability or unemployment," she says proudly. "He could never have supported us all without the opportunity to work at the refinery." After he retired, her parents traveled in their camper and her dad worked construction. "I'm glad they got the chance to travel before he died."

The SUV slows down, and we pass a modest building that hardly stands out from the homes across a hedge on each side. This was where, as a small girl, Janice belonged to a full gospel church (which refers to speaking in tongues, prophecy, and gifts of healing) and attended Sunday morning, Sunday night, and Wednesday night—"no missing." Her grandfather had been a founding board member of this now relocated church, her dad had been treasurer. Now Janice was chairman of its board.

Diligence, Industry, Party

It was in church that Janice first learned the honor of work, she says. "As a twelve-year-old girl, I swept out the whole church by myself after Sunday and Wednesday services, and later mowed the lawn. I cleaned out the bathrooms, the boys and the girls, in back of the church. My parents would drop me off and pick me up later." She kept that job as she grew older, but added another job at a Tastee Freez stand. After high school, "I put myself through McNeese working forty hours a week as a telephone operator. I worked 1:30 to 10:00 P.M. and 3:00 to 11:00 P.M. and 4:00 P.M. to 12:00 A.M. It was hard to work long hours and get up to go to school the next morning, hurrying to get your studying in between. I only had one weekend a month off, no summers. It was rough." After that, she got a job in the company she works for still.

Janice is stoutly proud that, like her dad, she never "took a dime from the government. . . . For five years at the telephone company and forty-three years here . . . I never one time ever drew an unemployment check or got any government assistance," she says, adding, "I did get a small student loan when I was going to college—back then the government didn't just give it to you—and I paid every nickel of it back."

Getting little or nothing from the federal government was an oft-expressed source of honor. And taking money from it was—or should be, Janice felt—a source of shame. The sharpest "burr under my saddle," Janice declares, is "people who take government money and don't work."

"I know guys who work construction who quit so they can draw unemployment to hunt in season." It was the same with disability payments, she said: "A friend's daughter has a husband who works long enough to get hurt and puts in for disability. My own cousins, uncles, and brothers have done it. Sometimes there weren't jobs; then it's great to have welfare," she allows. "But when there *are* jobs, why couldn't they mow a church yard, or fold clothes at a care center, or clean out the school bathrooms? We pay them to do nothing—first through TANF [Temporary Assistance for Needy Families] and now through SSI [Supplementary Security Income, for elderly or disabled]. That's not right. They should *do something* to help." (On this, see Appendix C.)

Work had been a passport out of fear, poverty, and humiliation for her father and others a generation back. But Janice doesn't base her own sense of honor or that of others just on money. She doesn't base it on how gifted she is in her work, or whether her job makes for a better world—at least, none of this comes up. If people work as *hard* as she does, it *is* a better world.

Her feeling about work is part of a larger moral code that shapes her feelings about those ahead and behind her in line for the American Dream. "Hard" is the important idea. More than aptitude, reward, or consequence, *hard* work confers honor. It comes with clean living and being churched. Those getting ahead of her in line don't share these beliefs, she feels. Liberals—those associated with the social movements that brought in the line cutters—share a looser, less defined moral code, she feels. Liberals *don't give personal morality itself its full due*, probably because they aren't churched. Janice opposes abortion except under certain circumstances, but imagines there are "fifty million abortions a year, probably all Democrats." (She pauses for a moment of dark humor: "Maybe I should rethink that position.") With Supreme Court approval of gay marriage, with federal welfare for the idle, with fewer Americans "churched," with the PC amnesia concerning the heroism of the young boys who died for the South (however misguided the Confederate cause), her piece of America seems like a small, brave holdout against a national tide. The American Dream itself has become strange, un-Bibled, hyper-materialized, and lacking in honor. Even as she stands patiently in line, she is being made to feel a stranger in her own land. The only holdout for the better aspects of the past is the Republican Party.

If you have a job, you should apply yourself to it, even if you face a little risk, Janice feels. "Two of my brothers are pipe welders, and the guys they work with would stop work for small stuff," she complains. "On one job, the guys were welding aluminum. It helps to counteract the fumes you inhale if you drink milk, so the company brings them ten o'clock milk. It's in the union contract. If the company didn't bring them their milk at ten o'clock, thirty guys would wobble the job [stop working]. Now is that stupid or what? It wouldn't have killed them, one day. They could have brought their own milk." Janice's was a company perspective. For a period, she volunteered for the Lake Area Industry Alliance, visiting schools to explain the benefits of industry to students who might be getting another story from home or from the liberal media.

Work has a disciplinary function. "If there aren't jobs around, well, get people working on the highways, using wheelbarrows and shovels instead of all the dump trucks," she says. "When people got home at night, they'd be tired and wouldn't be out drinking or doing drugs."

Janice had even cooked up an imaginative scheme to bring jobs back to America: "America needs to dig up every rock and every headstone" of American veterans of World War II buried in France—which "hasn't been a good friend to us"—she declares, and "bring them back to American land, and let American workers mow the lawns around them with American lawnmowers."

If we can't substitute wheelbarrows for dump trucks, or import cemeteries to bring morality to the idle, her thoughts turn to war. "I'm not advocating war so people can work," she adds hastily, "but there's a positive side to the war—manufacturing missiles, Humvees, sewing uniforms—it's work."

Not everything in Sulphur concerns work, she tells me. We are coming up on an enormous fairgrounds, part of Sulphur's newly built arena and events center, with a 14,000 square foot ballroom for Mardi Gras and a rodeo arena for the Silver Spurs Rodeo "barrel contests" (where riders steer horses around barrels) and steer-roping contests. "On rodeo days, parents don't just drop their kids off and pick 'em up later," Janice says. "These are *family* events."

Janice understands the fix the idle are in; welfare gives them more than an available job would. "You can get an $8-an-hour job and maybe clear $250 a week," she says. "With welfare what it is, it's not worth it to get a real job." However, she and others like her speak of seeing with "my own eyes" parents driving up in Lexus cars to drop their children at a government-supported Head Start program. The government is trying to get her to feel sorry for people like that, Janice feels. She's not having it. Get a job.

Looking away from the wheel for a moment, Janice stares at me with eyes wide, preparing for my shock. "Some people think I'm too *hard-nosed*," she declares, "but I think if people refuse to work, we should let them starve. Let them be homeless." That 44 percent of the Louisiana budget that came from the federal government, much of it for welfare to the poor, she would just as soon give back. Giving money in return for nothing? That broke her moral rule: reward for work. So for her, there was no paradox in Louisiana coming in 49th in the human development index and 50th in overall health and right-wing resistance to the idea of federal government aid. They could have whatever rank they wanted, if they didn't work.

We stop at a drive-through Burger King to buy two Whopper Juniors, sit down to eat them with some large sweet teas, then head to Janice's dream house. Having grown up blocks away from Citgo, Janice has bought a plot of land in north Sulphur so as to be far away from the plants—a retirement "barn," as she calls it. She is constructing it, room by room, with the help of her nephew, who is planning to live there too, with his family. As we drive along, a call comes in on Janice's cell phone with a deafening clang; her nephew is checking in about a plumbing fixture.

With my questions about the Great Paradox, I am myself another burr under Janice's saddle, but I ask her my ultimate question: what about *children* born poor? Is she so indignant about idle parents that she won't reach out to the child? Does she oppose Head Start or subsidized lunch? "I would hope that the child would say, 'I'm going to work hard and get me an education and good job and get myself out of this environment,'" Janice answers. Beyond that, her solution is to get children "churched" and to limit the fertility of poor women. "Some people say I'm too hard-nosed," she says again, "but after one or two children, I'd have her tubes tied." Wouldn't that be the federal government acting as Big Brother? I prod. No, she answers. "She could decline to have her tubes tied and decline federal money."

Underlying Janice's reasoning is her idea about inequality itself. Some people may just be destined to remain at the end of the line for the American Dream. That's why she opposes redistribution of tax money from rich to poor. The fix wouldn't last. "Ten percent of the people have 90 percent of the money, okay?" she says. "But if you even it out, in a year—even in six months—10 percent of the people would still have 90 percent of the money.

A lot of people who win the Power Ball $247 million jackpots are bankrupt a decade later. They can't ward off beggars and cheats and don't know how to invest. We each have to find our own niche and learn to be happy where we are."

Not only does the federal government give too much, it does too much and owns too much, she feels. "We only need it to handle military and diplomatic matters and to build roads and dredge waterways," she says. As for government ownership of public lands, "We should hold on to the Grand Canyon, part of Yellowstone, a few others, but sell the rest of the national parks for development and jobs." The government also controls too much— guns, for example. Without imagining her view would surprise me, Janice argues that handing out guns is the best way to create democracy in the Middle East. "If everybody had a gun and ammunition, they could solve their own differences. There are dictators because the dictators have all the guns and people have none. So they can't stand up for themselves. If the government takes our guns away, the same thing will happen here," she predicts darkly. Others echoed her sentiment. When Obama first took office, rumors spread that he would take away people's guns, and stores around DeRidder, Lee Sherman told me, sold out of ammunition. Another man told me that a minister even led his congregation to Walmart to stock up.

The number of federal workers also seems to her "plumb out of whack." She doesn't venture a guess, but many I interviewed estimated that a third to a half of all U.S. workers were employed by the federal government—a common estimate was 40 percent. (Not knowing the figures myself, I looked them up. In 2013, 1.9 percent of American workers were civilian federal employees, and that percentage has declined over the last ten years. For more, see Appendix C.)

Many government workers waste taxpayer money doing useless work, she feels. Here Fox News offered her a rich supply of "can't top this" examples. First, there was Solyndra, a solar company that wasted a $535 million federal loan. Then an EPA worker was caught watching four hours of pornography films on a government computer, one called *Sadism Is Beautiful*. Then there was the National Endowment of the Arts–funded painting in which the artist Chris Ofili attached cow dung to the figure of the Virgin Mary. "That stuff disgusts me."

We had returned to her SUV and were heading back, fishing gear still rattling in the back. "Okay, we're a free country," she says, "but not *that* free. Maybe you can make a picture of Christ out of cow manure if you want to. You can make one of Mohammed out of cow manure if you want to. Or you can make one of Buddha out of manure if you want to. But don't let *my* tax dollars pay you the money to do it. You go out there and shovel that manure on your own." To Janice, the "other team" was behind the failed Solyndra, the EPA's *Sadism Is Beautiful* man, the manure artist. Not her team. No way.

Faces in Line

It is not just the moral laxity of the Democrats that galls Janice, but the imposition of such laxity *on her*. She is badgered for sympathy, she feels, and made to feel bad if she doesn't grant it. Take sexual orientation and gender identity. "If you're gay, go be gay. Just don't impose it on me," she says. When I suggest that gay people aren't imposing a gay lifestyle on her or others, she counters: "Oh yes they are," and cites the example of Chaz Bono, the child of pop singers Sonny and Cher, who was born a girl but later changed sex to become male. Janice had followed the story closely: "He was the cutest little girl on the show when I was growing up. When Cher's son said it would have been easier to grow up, if she/he had not experienced prejudice, I think Chaz was forcing his way of living *on me*. He wants the whole world to change so it will be easier for him to grow up. So I say, 'Go be a man if you want to. Go be gay if you want to.' I don't mind somebody being gay if they want to be gay. Just be a regular person, go to work, mow the lawn, fish. You don't have to be shouting it from the mountaintops. Don't make *me* change and don't call *me* a bigot if I don't. That's how we're portrayed. Cher Bono said on the Jay Leno program that the 'Tea Party are f——g nuts,' and that's the consensus in liberal Hollywood."

I return to an issue closer to her home: industrial pollution in Bayou d'Inde, where her uncle, Harold Areno, and his wife, Annette, live. "My grandfather homesteaded those forty acres before anybody even knew what a refinery was," she muses. "It's all killed now. It makes me not want to live in Bayou d'Inde and makes me sad." Industry had brought four toxic waste landfills to Sulphur, one only a block from her present home. But "they make what we need—plastic soda bottles, rubber-soled shoes, toothpaste. We *need* toothpaste."

Being a Team Player meant braving problems. To do so, Janice did a kind of work she didn't even count as work: the emotional work of accommodating such things as nearby toxic waste landfills, which in her heart of hearts she never would choose to live with. Sometimes Team Players had to suck it up and just cope.

The Rubberized Horse

Janice and I stop off at her aunt's house to meet her nephew Dicky. Janice's sister is along too. Janice had earlier told me a shocking story about a relative with a horse, and I wanted to talk with him directly, to hear the story again from him. I sat with Dicky, Janice, Janice's sister, and her aunt around a small kitchen table to hear a well-worn story that still evoked sadness and surprise.

Now retired from AT&T and working as a substitute teacher, Dicky had been a young boy in the 1950s. "I was riding my palomino horse, Ted," he recalls. "Normally Ted cleared ditches five feet across just fine. But this time the horse fell back into the water and sank down. He tried to climb up but couldn't. We tried to pull his reins, but couldn't get him up. Finally my uncle hauled him out with a tractor. But when Ted finally scrambled back out, he was coated all over with a strange film. I hosed him off but that only hardened the film on him. It was like a terrible glued-on wet suit. It was like rubber. The vet tried but couldn't save him, and Ted died two days later." The ditch was downstream from a Firestone polymers plant.

Dicky was heartbroken at the time, and it still shows as he tells the story. But Janice recalls the episode slightly differently. It saddens her too, but she doesn't allow her sadness to interfere with her loyalty to industry. She shakes her head as if to say, we sure did put up with a lot of things back then, but let's not linger on too much bad news, the way environmentalists do. As a child, she recalled hearing a great roar and seeing the nighttime sky turn orange. It was an accidental explosion at Cities Service (now Citgo). "We all thought the world had come to an end," she says. But that was then, she thought. Today "industry is in compliance with state-issued permits," and she sees no problems.

We leave Dicky and Janice's sister and drive on. After a while, Janice turns the SUV off the pavement onto a dirt road that winds between two large ponds. We are coming up to the "barn," her dream retirement home, built on forty acres of former lumber company land, six miles from the Sasol expansion. "I've stocked my left pond with catfish, and I'm digging the pond on the right now. We love to fish," she says proudly. She parks before an enormous building, covered by a long, flat, tin roof. The house isn't finished yet, but a rock garden in the front is already surrounding a small water fountain, a tiny peacock figurine, and two elephant statues, black and white, one with trunk upheld. Two deck chairs overlook the scene. "My sisters put that together," she remarks, chuckling.

Although single and childless, Janice has built a six-bedroom, four-bath estate with a large common family kitchen–living room where the whole clan can gather. The refrigerator is stocked with sodas. This "barn" can house her two sisters—Joyce, who is recovering from hip surgery and is ready to move in, and maybe Judy, who lives in Texas, should she become widowed. Her nephew Kelly, helping to build the place, has his trailer on the premises and has just brought in a basket of fresh eggs along with a report that one chicken has died. One day Kelly might build a place by the fishpond for himself and his daughter, Mattie—of whom he has half-time custody and whom everyone adores. In back of the barn is an RV shed, a potting shed ("Joyce loves plants"), a chicken coop, a yard for two goats, and a paddock for twelve horses. "And we have dogs," Janice adds. All along the back side of the barn is an enormous "rodeo arena" where Mattie, when she's older, can practice ropes and barrels. "I wasn't interested in a fancy place," Janice explains, "just serviceable, where we could all come." Weekends, you can see her atop her riding mower, cutting grass on eight of her forty acres.

As I walk around Janice's American Dream house, I began to understand how the deep story makes sense to her. She had made it out of the structural squeeze—aiming high on one side, facing a flat wage, uncertainty, competitors, and government aid on the other. Maybe her salary hadn't advanced in leaps and bounds, but she'd gotten to the head of the line. And man, oh man, that had been *hard*. You couldn't be some wilting violet. Along the way, it hadn't been so easy enduring surprise explosions, noisy machinery, and strange odors. To live with it, Janice managed anxiety nearly hidden to her, anxiety that now felt like second nature; it kept her steady and brave. It kept her focused on the good news of Citgo for her dad, Lacassane for herself, the "buckle in the energy belt," the free market. She felt *loyal* to capitalism as it worked through the petrochemical plants of Sulphur, Louisiana, the system that produced the miracle of her father's wage and her own. She wanted others to want to feel loyal to it. Wasn't it obvious? What else, besides family and church, was there worth feeling loyal to?

Such devotion wasn't respected, she felt. Indeed, she had to *defend* that devotion from a liberal perspective, which she associated with a morally lax, secular, coastal-based culture. It was one thing for certain categories of people to cut in line, but it was another to have false notions of the good and the true gain popularity and edge out her truer ones. Instead of the country agreeing with her community on the natural rightness of heterosexual marriage as the center of family life, she was now obliged to defend herself against the idea that these views were sexist, homophobic, old-fashioned, and backward. She also needed to defend her notion of the line itself. She didn't want to appear to critics as hard-hearted regarding the poor, immigrants, Syrian refugees. They simply shouldn't be ahead of her in line.

Not only her values, but even the kind of self she proudly exhibited—an endurance self—seemed to need defending, because it too seemed to be going out of fashion along with all the blue-collar jobs. "They used to brag on my dad at the plant that he was so reliable and steady." Janice tells me proudly. But what did that count for anymore? Like her father and uncle, Harold Areno, Janice feels proud to have a rooted self, a self based in a busy, dense, stable community of relatives, co-parishioners, and friends. A newer *cosmopolitan* self, one that seemed uprooted, loosely attached to an immediate community, prepared to know a lot of people just a little bit, a mobile, even migratory self—this seemed to be coming into vogue. Such a self took pride in exposure to a diverse set of moral codes, but did a person with that kind of self end up thinking "anything goes"? It was frightening. It was wrong. And Janice was having none of it.

She was doing yet more emotional work *disregarding* the downside of life in the buckle of America's energy belt. She was focused on the upside. Industry was a loyal friend to her, and she to it. As for pollution, "A company has a job to do; it's making things people want and need. Just like people have to go to the bathroom, plants do too. You *can't* just say, 'don't do it.'" But while she sided with Citgo, with Sasol, with Monsanto and other companies in the state, Janice felt obliged to set aside problems she knew existed but had decided to accept.

After I'd known her for several years, Janice told me that her sister, Joyce, a warm-hearted woman, was planning to move in with her in her new home. Joyce had worked for Olin Chemical as a shipping supervisor checking train cars that had been filled with phosgene (used in making pesticides and, at room temperature, a poisonous gas) without a facial mask. She began to suffer from a debilitating autoimmune disease, had to cut her hours, and struggled to get better with prednisone and naturopathy. Janice herself also suffered from an ailment that she says "is probably related to growing up near the plants." She was thinking of getting her blood checked. But she wasn't letting herself get "all anxious" about it.

Janice is already hosting monthly cookouts for the Areno clan. "We had sixty-seven people for a Good Friday cookout," she says proudly. "We have big cookouts at least once a month, twenty-five if you barely mention it, more if you spread the word. If we've got enough food, you eat; if the pots are bare, you didn't get here in time."

Even as pine forests have given way to vast industrial compounds and voters of the South have shifted right, Janice Areno is carrying forward the best she can from her roots—a loving family, ropes and barrels, catfish fishing, deer hunting, and "y'all come" cookouts—with the fruits of a BA and forbearance. She credits her team—her party and the industry she feels it represents—with all her good fortune in life. She's a Team Loyalist. She originally moved to north Sulphur to escape the plants. But construction soon began on Sasol's new ethane cracker, only six miles away. "If Sasol has a major fire or explosion, we'd be subject to it," she says philosophically. And with the fracking boom, other new plants might be creeping closer in the future too. "But hey, you're subject to earthquakes in Berkeley, California. Things happen." In the meantime, anyone can stretch out in a deck chair in front of Janice's new home, by a small fountain, and see an object of great loyalty—pudgy, white foot midair, tusks and trunk aloft.

11

The Worshipper: Invisible Renunciation

"Sunday's my favorite day," Jackie Tabor tells me, as if offering me a key to her whole life. We have just driven home from Sunday services at Trinity Baptist on my third visit with her. Her husband, Heath, has parked the tan SUV in the carport beside their high-riding Arctic Cat all-terrain vehicle with its large, deeply grooved tires muddied by his recent hunting trip.

Jackie is a petite, svelte, youthful forty-five, with shoulder-length dark hair, gold stud earrings, a pink cotton top and flats; casual dress and intense light eyes. She walks me through the hallway of her spacious home, restraining her excitable German shepherd, calming other dogs as we pass a hamster cage in her children's playroom. We enter a high-vaulted living room, where three antlered buck heads stare ahead from above a large stone fireplace. The drywall behind them? "Heath did all that and shot the bucks," she says, her eyes proudly wandering around. It seems a miracle to her that this could truly be hers.

Heath has grilled a tuna he's caught in the Gulf of Mexico and seasoned with piquant salsa. Jackie, Heath, their two children, and I sit down, pray, and enjoy the delicious fish. Heath describes the time he was out deep-sea fishing in the Gulf and, from a great distance, watched the fire of the 2010 BP Deepwater Horizon explosion. He had considered the possible effects of the oil and dispersant on his catch there, but figured it was minimal. Jackie rises from the table to fetch a children's sporting magazine that features their beaming ten-year-old son, Christian, hoisting high a large, dangling yellowfin tuna. The family loves fishing, hunting, and the outdoors, Jackie tells me.

After lunch, Jackie and I move to the living room, and the topic gravitates to her gratitude to Jesus. The Lord has given her all she treasures, she feels—a loving husband, two beautiful children, frisky dogs, and the chance to stay home with her children in a beautiful, all-paid-off home: the American Dream. Set in the affluent suburban development of The Courtyard on the outskirts of Lake Charles, with a double brick pillar entrance, hers is an earth-toned house bordered by azaleas and daisies. Weekday afternoons, the neighborhood is empty except for homemakers and an occasional black gardener edging hedges with an electric trimmer.

A successful contractor, Heath has built and repaired houses in the aftermaths of Hurricanes Katrina, Rita, Gustav, Ivan. If Louisianans measure time in storms, Heath measures it in ripped-off roofs, broken windows, flooded basements, and jobs to do, if only he could find enough good workmen for his crew around town.

"I Came from Nothing"

The very first words Jackie said to me when I first met her at a Tea Party focus group in Lake Charles were: "I came from *nothing!*" Growing up, there was so much she had wanted, and so little she could have—including loving attention. Along the way, she had learned a subtle lesson about managing strong wishes, and the counterintuitive effects of doing so. Sometimes it's wise to give up wanting something very badly, she felt. In His mysterious way, the Lord may ultimately grant your wish.

Like some others I spoke with in Louisiana, Jackie felt she had hold of an American Dream—but maybe just for now. Gesturing around her large living room, she says, "This could all vanish tomorrow!" She had worked hard. She had waited in line. She'd seen others "cut ahead," and this had galled her and estranged her from the government. Like Janice Areno, Jackie had developed a deep story self. She could accommodate the downside of the free market and sadly that included the bad news of industrial pollution, but she had her own way of doing so.

Jackie has brought me coffee and we are sitting alone in her living room to talk. She loves nature, she tells me. While Janice Areno, brought up close to nature, had focused on the fish she caught, the deer she shot, Jackie had spent her early years in Kansas City, had never fished, hunted, or even much got to the zoo. Ironically, when I brought up the topic of environmental pollution to Janice, she conceded that it existed and quickly moved on. But Jackie herself raised the topic and expressed her distress about it: "I saw a little boy swimming in Lake Charles last week. They should have warning signs up. What if that boy accidentally swallowed some water? He was diving. It's easy to do. It breaks my heart," she says. She feels the same about chemicals in the air and soil, and wishes, all things being equal, that for the health of her family they could move. So how, I wonder, did someone who so deeply appreciated nature, who did not avoid knowledge of injuries done to it, end up celebrating industry and the unrestrained consumption of all it produced? How did she, too, live the deep story?

Much of the answer began, as for us all, in childhood. On a snowy March day in 1990, Jackie was nineteen, jobless, homeless. She lay in the corner of the un-vacuumed living room floor in her older sister's apartment, beside her sister's dog. "I had no address. I'd found work at a Dallas hotel. I did well in a series of jobs, but I felt lost, kicked out, angry. My entire belongings fit in a suitcase. After my stepdad kicked me out, my sister was the only one I could turn to. She took me in. I'd been in her apartment six weeks, and I was treating her horribly," Jackie recalls. "I had two jobs, and when I wasn't working I was in my pajamas, smoking and drinking. While my sister was at work, I'd let the dishes pile in the sink, run up her phone bill, and let the house stay a mess. I lied. Every day I wrote a list, 'I will not lie. I will save my money. I will stop drinking.' I carried the list in my pocket everywhere I went. I meditated on it, then got halfway through the day, then quit. I felt dead. I was shattered, broken. I had come from nothing and I was heading for nothing."

Jackie had been born the fourth of five children to an Irish-Catholic homemaker and an abusive, alcoholic father who left when Jackie was eight. My mother "had to get on welfare to support us," she says. (She defends welfare for mothers in such situations, though she feels they are a small proportion of those on it.) "My mother got a job, then two, then three. We never took our problems to her. She had enough on her hands." Eventually, Jackie's mother moved to Louisiana and remarried. While their mother worked, the girls discovered their stepfather to be a "dirty-talking" sexual predator. But Jackie stood up to him. They quarreled, and her stepfather announced that if Jackie left home, she could never return. At nineteen, high school diploma and suitcase in hand, Jackie stepped out the front door of her home into what felt like an emotionally empty world. Later rescued by her sister, still lost, she underwent an experience that was to transform her life.

Her sister was at work. Out the window it was a "beautiful bluebird day," Jackie recalls, and lying on the floor with her sister's dog, Jackie had a moment of transformation. I looked up at the sky, and said, "If You really save people, Jesus, would you save me? I can't save myself." Then I got up off the floor. I had no idea what I was doing. I walked into the bathroom and looked in the mirror at a completely different girl. That was it."

"How did that different girl look?" I ask.

"Clean, beautiful. I believe that, for the first time, I saw in the mirror how He saw me. He showed me *who I am to Him*."

Everything—her marriage to Heath, her children, her living room with the graceful stone fireplace in a spacious house, all are testimony, she feels, to that magnified moment. After it, the smoking, drinking, lying all slowly ended. "Abraham Lincoln was a very good man. I revere Abe Lincoln," she muses. "But if Lincoln walked down the road, he wouldn't see me. Jesus would *see me*." Presidents? You can't see them and they don't see you. But Jesus is always there, she feels. And she had learned from Him how to trust to Him that good things would happen. Wishing too hard for things could even be counterproductive.

"I started to learn the Bible, and it said that 'those who *wait on* the Lord will mount up on wings like eagles. They will run and they won't grow weary.'" She pauses. "Those who wait. So that means when everything's right, things will happen. We don't necessarily have to *make* things happen."

Curiously, though, Jackie greatly admires her mother, who *did* make things happen. As an abandoned mother of five, on welfare, her mother had first found a low-paying job in a flower shop. "But you know how my mother got her first *good* job as a medical secretary? She applied for the job and stayed up night after night with library books teaching herself medical terms and jargon. Then she got dressed up, lied that she had a college education, and got the job. She did well, and ended up years later as an account executive in a large advertising agency." Jackie laughs with deep pride and delight; they don't teach that kind of gumption in college. Though highly enterprising herself, Jackie was following a different path, at least for now. Sometimes you have to manage your strong wishes; then something good happens—you win a protective husband, enjoy a paid-off house.

Reward for Renunciation

Having related this story, Jackie suddenly asks, "May I take you on an adventure?" We climb into her tan SUV, move her children's jackets and tennis shoes to the back seat, and drive past the double brick pillars of Courtland Place, past an empty field, out the main road, past strip malls, and into a modest housing development. She slows to a stop in front of a snug one-story townhouse in a pan-flat neighborhood of similar homes encircled by modest trim lawns. It was their first home, Jackie says. She and Heath had lived there for eight years when the children were small. Their neighbors were refinery operators, bartenders, machine repairmen, and cashiers from the three enormous casinos in Lake Charles. Many worked long hours, emptying the neighborhood of company. "We didn't get to know our neighbors, but the kids could ride their bikes," she says, pointing to a nearby cul-de-sac.

Jackie drives on for another ten minutes through other neighborhoods of brick homes hedged with modest shrubs until we arrive before a second home. "We built our second house in Pine Mist Estates and paid it off in three years," Jackie says. I snap a photo out the car window of an attractive red brick ranch house, with white trim and three mid-sized palm trees, their fronds gracefully arching over the front.

We'd seen two former houses. What was this adventure? I wonder.

Jackie goes on: "When we lived in Pine Mist Estates, I *always wanted* to live in Autumn Run," Jackie says. After we circle through another mid-scale development, there it is, a third house: the one she used to *dream about* when she lived in Pine Mist. It, too, is a one-story ranch house, set on a treeless corner lot, larger than the first but not as large as her present home. House 3 was bigger than house 2. But it was the house she didn't dare want.

Jackie had learned to be an obedient Christian wife, to subordinate her wishes to those of Heath. Having witnessed her mother's two disastrous marriages, she wanted a good marriage to Heath. And it seemed to her that the route to this was to act as Eve did to Adam; she would be as a "rib" to Heath, a helpmate. But this presented a conflict. "I wanted that house *so badly,*" she repeats, staring at the object of a once-powerful desire. "But I never breathed a word about wanting this house to Heath. We couldn't afford it. He was working so hard. I didn't want to pressure him. I was ashamed of wanting it when there was no way we could have it. He's never even known I wanted to live in Autumn Run *so bad.*"

"But look at it *now.* See the vinyl coming off the house right there?" A neighboring fence sagged—the lingering signs of the highly destructive Hurricane Rita. "Now the kids call it Autumn Run-down," she tells me. We have seen house 1 (the starter house), house 2 (a slightly larger house), and house 3 (her old dream house), and now we are headed back to house 4 (her own beautiful house). Jackie wants me to know something about her relationship to house 3, her old dream house. She had wanted it "too badly." "I *always dreamed* of living in Autumn Run," she says again. Jackie wants me to see this talisman of desire, this proof that it isn't wise to wish for something too hard. Her once-coveted house is nothing compared to the home she lives in now, which is "beyond my wildest dreams, the home paid off in three years, when I couldn't imagine less than thirty."

"I told my daughter, what if I had pushed to move to Autumn Run? We would have ended up there when this [our current house] is the house we're meant to be in. I told her that Bible passage about not necessarily having to make things happen."

Each house was as a step on a ladder to the American Dream. On one rung she had yearned too much for the next: that was the lesson. In a sense, Jackie's lesson ran counter to the deep story; one shouldn't wish too much for what seems like the next step toward the American Dream. That was grabbing. On the other hand, she had struggled hard emotionally not to grab for it. Our adventure was in coming to understand that lesson.

On our ride back to her home, Jackie gestures out the window. "See over there? That's Crestview." This is another housing development, where dream houses 5, 6, and 7 might be, she is pointing out. "This is where 'super-rich' people live." Then she adds, "I've never even driven there. I don't want to. I don't want to want a house there." It was hard enough wanting these other things she felt she couldn't have.

As we drive home, she reflects, "I was a poor little Irish girl. I was devastated that I didn't have a good home life, like everybody else did. I mean, some of my friends were rich kids who ended up going to lovely Ivy League colleges. In Chicago, we lived on the other side of Elliott Road. Everyone on our side of Elliott Road was poor. We looked nice, so you couldn't see that we didn't have anything." She so envied the girls on the other side of Elliott Road, with their happy families, their lovely homes. It had been a struggle to give up wanting what they effortlessly enjoyed. But with Jesus's help, she'd given it up. And her own beautiful house was His reward.

The reward for renunciation appeared to her in another way too. Although a born-again Christian, Jackie was reluctant at first to follow her husband into the Baptist Church, and even more reluctant to tithe 10 percent of their hard-earned wages to it. "And that's on top of the 33 percent taxes we pay the government," she notes. There was the house note to pay, the children's private Christian school tuition, hurricane and health insurance payments, car insurance, gas—and 10 percent on top of that. How could they swing it? Then more: Trinity had a fundraising campaign to renovate and expand the building, for which it was asking parishioners to consider committing an extra $3,000. At first Jackie thought, "We can't." Then thirty-seven, Heath was earning eighteen dollars an hour in his father's construction business, and his father shared a third of his profits with Heath as well. But Heath had signed a pledge to Trinity Baptist. And as a dutiful Christian wife, Jackie renounced her wish to pay off their debt.

If she renounced one wish, she'd discovered, a bigger one came true. As Hurricane Rita shredded homes, upended trees, and smashed houses, Heath got more work and earned more money. People living in fifth-wheel (towable) trailers got him to rebuild their homes. Heath was also asked to put in the drywall for Trinity's children's playroom and gym. "Even though we were tithing and giving the church $3,000, we paid off every loan," Jackie said.

In every job she has taken, Jackie explains, "I always end up the leader. I'm good at it." But on accepting Christ as her savior and joining Trinity, and becoming a Christian wife, she had renounced her wish to lead. "A wife is a helpmate to her husband. Eve was created to be a helper. I'm created to help Heath." By renouncing one desire, Jackie fulfilled another: she got to stay home with her children.

We have turned around now and are slowly driving back through this parade of neighborhoods to her home in The Courtyard, when the issue of environmental pollution comes up. "We live in a terribly polluted environment here," Jackie tells me. "My son's best friend, Patrick, recently died of a rare neuroblastoma at age nine. Nine—*that* young. His parents think some chemical around here caused it, but they can't prove it."

On the campaign trail, in the media, from the pulpit, and from industry I had observed a silence about pollution. It seemed like the kind of amnesia E.E. Evans-Pritchard had spoken of, the kind that had led the Areno family to remember the events on Bayou d'Inde in a spirit of defiance. This silence extends to Jackie's personal world as well. "Pollution? I don't talk about it much with friends," Jackie muses. "This whole town operates off of oil. So I could be talking to two moms whose husbands work in the plants. They think government regulation will hurt jobs, or stop new plants from coming in. You don't want to *remind* them of dangers. Or make them think you're *blaming them* for the work they do. It's too close to home." Again, the silence. Many plant workers were indeed caught in a bind—as enthusiastic members of the Calcasieu Rod and Gun Club and lovers of wildlife, they feel remorse about pollution, but as employees, they felt obliged to keep quiet about it. And so, out of deference, did Jackie and Heath. One consultant told me he saw "a notice in the men's room, 'Don't drink the water,' in Axiall [this being the former PPG]. . . . But you don't hear much talk about why that sign was there."

Jackie was a Worshipper. She had developed a worshipful attitude and a capacity for meaningful renunciation. Instead of overcoming her aversion to regulation, Jackie spoke of learning to live without it. In this way, she echoed Team Loyalists like Janice Areno. You accommodate. Clean air and water; those were good. She wanted them, just as she wanted a beautiful home. But sometimes you had to do without what you wanted. You couldn't have both the oil industry *and* clean lakes, she thought, and if you had to choose, you had to choose oil. "Oil's been pretty darned good to us," she said. "I don't want a smaller house. I don't want to drive a smaller car." An operator job in an oil plant is a passport to houses in Pine Mist. One of those rare engineering job gets you into Autumn Run, and a high management job gets you into Courtland. The Arctic Cat, the SUV, the house: all these, she felt, came indirectly from oil. For its part, the federal government got in the way of both oil and the good life.

As a Team Loyalist, Janice Areno had not allowed herself to feel too badly about pollution. Bayou d'Inde, the rubberized horse. As a loyalist to industry and the Republican Party, she defended herself against "too much" anxiety about pollution, the brown pelican, and human health. For her part, Jackie Tabor allowed herself to feel sad about these things. It was a terrible shame this had happened, she felt. But having permitted herself to feel sad about environmental damage, she renounced the desire to remediate it, because that would call for more dreaded government. Each had a different moment of emotional pause—Janice's was on the act of admitting to loss and grieving it. Jackie's important moment of emotional pause was upon the act of renouncing an important desire. A clean environment? Sadly, we can't have it.

"I'm named for Jacqueline Kennedy," she says, her face ready to receive my surprise. And she admires the Kennedys still. But today, she feels, as in the deep story, that "the government has gone rogue, corrupt, malicious, and ugly. It can't help anybody," she says. Like others, she feels that President Obama is not a real Christian and, neither through his upbringing nor in his loyalty, a true American. Her distrust has gone the full cascade: from president to the redistributive function of the federal government to nearly all government functions—including that of cleaning up the environment.

Along the way, Jackie goes out of her way to explain that she does not admire those who pay their taxes gratefully. She doesn't feel grateful for what the government does for her and doesn't believe others should either. In a lightly taunting way, she brings up the financier Warren Buffett. "He's rich. And he says he *wants* to pay higher taxes because that's fairer to poor people." (Buffett had said that he didn't think it fair that his secretary paid higher taxes than he did.) "Okay. Set the standard," Jackie taunts. "What's stopping you, buddy? Write that check if you don't think you pay enough taxes. Get on TV, the whole world will cover it, and be a hero from one end to the other. Knock yourself out. Why aren't you writing a check?" Jackie speaks with frustration. Buffett seemed to be asking for praise for being a good citizen in a system she no longer believes in. He was on offer as a role model for liberal gratitude for public schools, libraries, and parks. But those were liberal feeling rules, not hers.

"I'm not against stopping pollution, of course. I'm for regulating polluters," Jackie says, but she quickly amends what she said: "I *would be* all for it if the government didn't use pollution as an excuse to expand." And environmentalists are not to be trusted either. "They push the government to expand and have their own financial interest in solar and wind too."

What she holds separate from this betrayal and pursuit of self-interest are the Constitution and the American flag. On another visit, I come with Jackie to a performance at her son's small Christian school. Sitting near us in the audience are Jackie's kindly mother-in-law and her mother-in-law's mother. Her son Christian steps to the front of the assembled parents, asks them to stand, reads a passage from the Bible, asks them to be seated, and is followed by students who, one by one, do the same. As part of the performance, a video is shown and "America the Beautiful" is played. Looming high and majestic on the screen, backlit by a vivid sunset, the American flag waves. "Take a picture with your cellphone!" Jackie whispers, "of the *flag!*" The American government is a betrayer, she feels, but the American flag stays true.

Liberals seemed a problem for Jackie, because they believed different things and might get her children to believe them too. As we drive home from the performance, the children in the back of the SUV, she shakes her head recalling an incident: "My kids were watching a program called *Victorious* on the Disney Channel, which I thought would be fine," but the commentator started to talk about global warming. "We don't believe in global warming." That belief, too, seemed like an excuse for government expansion, part of the betrayal. "The commentator said that people that watch Fox News are idiots. It was a good thing I was watching TV with the kids and caught that. I thought, 'How long are my kids going to believe me over them?' A year? Six months?"

Jackie's impulse to clean up the environment had also been tempered by her faith: "I'm probably less an activist than I would be because of my faith today," she says. "As a kid, I wrote every president to tell him what I thought he needed to do. But now, I'm less involved. I do think a lot of activists are self-serving. You have to put up with things the way they are." She has a deep story self: she had fought her way out of a tough childhood, to the front of the line for the American Dream, a line in which she feared her family could lose its place. Meanwhile, as we drive past the American flag draped over a stone at the edge of her neighbor's yard, into the carport beside the Arctic Cat, with a small, sad shake of her head, Jackie says, "Pollution is the sacrifice we make for capitalism."

12

The Cowboy: Stoicism

A Vidalia onion sits within arm's reach of Brother Cappy's place at the dining room table, a warning—half joke and half serious—not to fight. Around the table some ten people are seated for Sunday dinner at the home of Brother Cappy and Sister Fay Brantley, two respected elders of the Pentecostal church in Longville, an hour's drive north from Lake Charles. Mike Tritico is their friend, and he has asked them if I could join. Everyone has come from either that church or the local Baptist one, and everyone knows about the onion. Debate between two men, regular luncheon guests and friendly adversaries, is about to begin. It is both poke-in-the-ribs home theater, a source of collective hilarity, and an airing of serious political difference. The onion is Cappy's standing joke, a way of saying, "Keep it civil, boys." Arguments could get heated over anything to do with the environment, regulation, and the government.

A fatherly man with half-moon eyes and thinning reddish hair, Brother Cappy is a well-liked retired telephone repairman. Before coming to their house, I had attended the Longville Pentecostal Church with the Brantleys. Brother Cappy had spoken at church, introducing the man who reported the attendance (thirty-eight parishioners) and the total collection ($42.45). His wife, Sister Fay, wearing a long, floral dress and pale-rimmed glasses, her gray hair swept into curls high on her head, had sung gospel tunes with zest in church and now warmly welcomes us into their cozy home. One by one, we pass the bird feeders and flower beds, climb the front steps onto the front porch, past the wooden swing where neighbors gather over coffee in the morning, and scatter a plump calico cat. The Brantley home is part of a larger family compound. "Our family all live right here," Sister Fay explains proudly. "Our daughter and family here [she points left], our son and family there [she points right]. My ninety-one-year-old mother lives behind us." They have with them the Brantleys' cousin who is in training to become a Pentecostal minister, and their son-in-law, an inspector at CertainTeed. "And Brother Cappy and Sister Fay have adopted *us*!" Mike Tritico adds brightly, referring to himself and another Sunday dinner regular, a retired repairman of railroad tracks and bridges. "So they've got a big family." Cappy and Mike had long been friends, and Cappy and another parishioner at the Pentecostal church had done a "faith healing" that cured Mike's back of terrible pain for twelve years, Mike said, which further deepened their bond. Beyond Sunday dinners, friends also gather most mornings to sit on the porch, drink coffee, gossip, and talk politics.

Three young women—the Brantleys' daughter, daughter-in-law, and granddaughter, a freshman at McNeese University—have stayed back from church to prepare steaming roast beef, gravy, potatoes, okra, green beans, corn bread, and sweetened ice tea. (They would catch the full gospel service later that evening.) They have set two tables—one for the women, smaller, in the kitchen, and one for the men, larger, in the dining room. The two sexes normally ate at separate tables, but Mike has asked the Brantleys if it would be okay for me to sit at the men's table, so I can listen in on the weekly debate between him and Donny McCorquodale.

And that's the man I'm eager to meet: a retired telephone company worker who hates regulators. Donny is a lanky, blond, fit man in his sixties, dressed in slacks and a blue shirt, slightly slouched in his chair, quiet. He is, Tritico tells me, the younger son of a highly religious mother, well known as a Baptist prayer warrior. When Donny was growing up, like some other devotees in Merryville, his mother was said to wear long dresses, have uncut hair, and occasionally switch young girls for immodesty. Perhaps rebelling against such strict rules, Donny grew up as the playground prankster and daredevil. Now on his second marriage, Donny is raising a young family, including two children, one an adopted boy from Honduras. Known for spontaneous acts of kindness, he once saw Tritico at a church yard sale eyeing a $25 wooden organ he could not afford. Donny handed money to the seller, hailed a handyman with a dolly, and paid him to deliver the organ to Tritico's cabin. Missing a key or two, and emitting an occasional hum, the organ sat for decades in Tritico's disheveled cabin, a reminder of Donny's good heart.

A former Democrat, Donny voted for Republican presidential candidate George W. Bush because "if Al Gore believes in climate change, he's too stupid to be president." Since then, he had moved to the right of the Republican Party.

A story about Donny had long circulated around Longville, and heads always shook in disbelief at the retelling. Like Cappy, Donny had long worked for the phone company, and both men drove repair trucks. One day as Cappy was driving his truck sixty miles an hour on the freeway, he heard a honk, glanced out his truck window, and was flabbergasted to see Donny driving his truck alongside him, as legend has it, also sixty miles an hour—in reverse. Donny was also known for secretly sticking pins in coworkers' Styrofoam coffee cups to make them dribble inexplicably. He has logged forests, worked the Alaska pipelines, handled electrical wires atop telephone poles—dangerous jobs. He also exceeds speed limits and hates environmentalists: "They talk pollution to death." If Janice Areno came to endurance through a loyalty to her team, the Republican Party, and Jackie Tabor by expressing a religious attitude of renunciation, Donny came to it through a celebration of daring. He is a Cowboy.

With loaded plates, everyone seats themselves and says prayers. Brother Cappy is seated at the head of the table; Donny and Mike Tritico sit to each side of him, across the table from each other. Both Donny and Mike are white, churchgoing residents of Longville, neighbors and friends on opposite sides of an issue. They both value honor and integrity. But there are key differences between them. Although mentally unstable, Mike's mother graduated from college, and Mike himself got three years into a medical degree and two years into a master's in marine biology before dropping out. Donny's parents are not college educated, but Donny headed into a forestry degree for a while before moving on.

The two men start to talk about the Lake Charles EDC leak discovered in 1994 in the pipe between Condea Vista and the Conoco docks, the largest toxic chemical spill in U.S. history. As I noted earlier, Condea Vista had hired five hundred cleanup workers to remove soil containing EDC from beneath the forty-year-old pipeline; part of the estimated total of between 19 million and 47 million pounds spilled. Workers were not given adequate protective gear, and by the late 1990s many had begun to have trouble breathing and had sued Condea Vista.

But the problem had not ended there. An underground plume of EDC had penetrated the clay and was slowly moving toward the pilings of the enormous I-10 bridge, which daily carries 50,000 vehicles between Lake Charles and Westlake. Madonna Massey had said the I-10 bridge was "spooky." Jackie Tabor avoided it. Others, too, spoke of it as "strange"— without mentioning the EDC leak.

Guests have risen, refilled their plates, and reseated themselves expectantly. And a debate between Donny McCorquodale and Mike Tritico over the EDC leak under the I-10 bridge begins.

The I-10 Bridge

"For the first time, the state highway department is talking about closing down the I-10 without building another bridge," Tritico begins. "They can't dig down to bedrock because of that spongy EDC-soaked clay. That tells you that *they* [the mayor of Lake Charles and city engineers] understand the danger. It's reasonable to be scared of the bridge and to wish there had been better oversight." Tritico is guided by the *precautionary principle*, the principle he returns to over and over in debates with Donny. "It's the principle doctors abide by: first do no harm." And to apply it to the I-10 you need good government, he feels.

"Don't jump on the company," Donny fires back. "They didn't *know* their pipe was leaking. They didn't realize that this was going to happen forty years back when they put the pipeline in."

Mike: "They can't say they *didn't know* in the 1970s what EDC would be doing to our clay today. Condea Vista and Conoco knew that EDC would ruin clay, because [the] industry conducted two different studies where they put the EDC into the local clay and it ruined it."

Donny: "They weren't convinced. Why would they believe these 'experts'? Just because some expert tells you X is true, doesn't mean X is true. You know, if you're making $1,000,000 a day on something and somebody wants you to stop it, you don't say that's the truth until you're *really convinced* it's the truth. I wouldn't have believed it."

Mike: "Companies contrive ignorance. They were saying: 'I'm going to believe what I want to believe even if you do give me scientific evidence.' They didn't react to information their own experts gave them."

Donny: "Experts can be wrong. You remember in 1963, when the seat belt law hit? I had a Pontiac that had a lap seat belt and I'd sit and wear it. The Chevys and Fords didn't have them. GMC trucks had a seat belt. So some people believed it was a good thing and others didn't. And later on, the regulators concluded that the lap belt wasn't the answer. *So we'd all agreed to a silly regulation.*"

Mike: "If Condea Vista and Conoco want to hide their heads in the sand and not admit that EDC could break up clay underneath the I-10, then later, when they're found responsible, they should have to pay."

Donny: "You can't always be ready to blame the company, like those lawyers are all set to do."

Mike: "But what if it is *their* fault and it's *your* bridge? Suppose you're in the car and the bridge collapses because the clay is spongy. Then suppose you die, okay? Your family will say 'wait a minute.' The company knew they were wrecking the clay."

Donny: "You want everything to be perfect, for companies to make no mistakes, and you—and we—can't live like that. If you aim for perfection, then you're being overly cautious, because we have to be able to take risks. That's how they split the atom—risk. That's how they made vaccines—risk.

They were daring. A lot of good things happen *because* people *dare* to take risks. With all these environmental regulations, we're being too cautious. We're avoiding bad instead of maximizing good.

"To live in civilization, you've got to take risks. There *will be* mistakes. You can't succeed by just always being perfect. People have to learn from their mistakes. We wouldn't have made the discoveries we have, live with the world of plastics we've got—car steering wheels, computers, the telephone wires I deal with—a lot of that's plastic. We wouldn't have built this country if we were all as risk-averse as you are. Do we want to go back to life in shacks reading by kerosene? Accidents happen. They used to spill kerosene. So what? Do you wish they hadn't ever used that?"

Mike: "No one's talking about going back to kerosene or never making mistakes."

Donny: "Regulation is like *cement*: you lay it down, and it hardens and stays there forever."

A ripple of laughter circulates around the circle. The women now seat themselves around the men's table.

Donny (continuing): "Once something is regulated it's hard to un-regulate it. And so, year after year at first—it's just a little at a time—but then after a while it's like it is now, hardened cement. *Everything* is regulated. We're all stuck in cement."

The conversation turns toward the over-regulation of playground fights. "Children have a natural desire to dominate and try to get what they want," Donny says. "It only stops when one guy is afraid his lip is going to get busted. That's the natural order. Regulation breaks that up. We don't see the harm overregulation can do."

Mike: "I'm not talking about regulating everything or avoiding all mistakes. I just don't want us to make *certain kinds* of mistakes—the kinds that spill chemicals into water and give people rare brain cancers and endometriosis, or that lead innocent people to drive on collapsing bridges and die, children too. Why let that happen if there's a known way to prevent it?"

Donny: "I think we all have to take our knocks, sadly. We all make our own independent decisions. With its overload of regulations, the government is almost living our lives for us. You're not you anymore; you're it."

Mike: "So if you're driving the car on the I-10, of your own free will, and you get hurt, is it *your* own fault that you get hurt?"

At this point, Donny's adopted daughter, a beautiful girl of sixteen, sits down in Donny's lap. He wraps his arms around her, continuing his debate. "I would say a lot of it is. I can't say what my kids would say."

A grandson goes around the table, guest by guest, politely asking each whether they want strawberries with their ice cream.

"You can get sick," Mike Tritico tells Donny. "I have been sick. And Mother Nature in Bayou d'Inde is sick. In fact, it has been made sick by people who think like you do. And it's hard to get to a place where people feel safe enough to live creative lives when the decisions of important leaders are based on bravado."

The room is quiet. The two are approaching a real showdown.

Mike continues: "So what if you're a guy like me, who tries to find out the cause and effect of the EDC spill, and the companies won't say, and the state government won't say. So through the Freedom of Information Act, you receive 3,000 pages, redacted, blacked out so that you still don't know the truth about the spill. Why should we have to settle for that? And how could it be my own fault that I got hurt or killed?"

Donny: "If risk is to be reduced at all, it should be done by regular people themselves. I've taken some risks, when I was a logger with Willie Baldwin, and we built log bridges, chained them together, and drove over the bridge with a big load of logs. That was a risk, and one guy did get hurt. You have to live with risk. But it's *real people—not the government*—that should be telling us what is or isn't too risky."

Mike: "But you need some people who make it their business to know more about very complicated things, so that all available information can be brought to bear on complex issues."

Donny: "But citizens can do the job. Some citizens complained about a smelly asphalt pit and it got closed."

Mike: "But what if the pit owners hadn't agreed to close it?"

Donny: "Then get a lawyer."

And so the debate continues. Everyone now returns with second helpings of strawberries and ice cream, the women handing around coffee. Tritico feels that Donny is an unwitting mouthpiece for the chemical *companies*. He embraces *their* right to take risks with *our* lives. And Donny, while conceding Mike's greater information on the matter, feels Tritico speaks for the *regulators*, who would turn society into a giant block of cement. Through the years, their dispute has continued on the Internet. Once, after Mike arranged for a professor to give a lecture in Lake Charles on global warming, the talk was reported in an online news article. Mike spotted a discrediting comment accusing the professor of propagating "lies." The comment was anonymous, but Tritico said, "Oh, that's probably Donny."

Sister Fay and the other women, now seated at one end of the men's table, turn the conversation to government welfare, out-of-wedlock births, addiction, and the reluctance to work for your living. Women on welfare have six or seven children, Fay notes. The consensus around the table is that the government could support one out-of-wedlock child but not the remaining "five or six," since the woman in question should have learned her lesson.

The debate between Mike and Donny echoes a larger finding from a 1997 study of four hundred workers in a Louisiana chemical plant that processed materials that were carcinogenic, mutagens, and flammable. Researchers John Baugher and J. Timmons Roberts of Brown University asked workers, "How often are you *exposed* to dangerous chemicals on the job?" and "Do you *worry* about exposure to these dangerous chemicals?" Worry about exposure, the researchers reported, was only loosely related to actual exposure. Hourly crafts workers—men such as Donny McCorquodale—worried less than you'd think they would, given their exposure. Managers and clerical workers worried more. For example, 50 percent of hourly crafts workers said they were "always or often" exposed to dangerous chemicals on the job, but only 40 percent said they worried about it; a higher proportion felt exposed than were worried.

Among managers and professionals, a smaller proportion (10 percent) said they were exposed, but a higher proportion (20 percent) said they worried about it. Relative to their actual exposure, workers worried less, and managers worried more. Women in the study were more likely to listen for warnings, take them seriously, and act with precaution than men were, and minorities did so more than whites. When asked about a long list of risks, white males stood out from all other groups as being less likely to see risk. Maybe Donny was more like the white male crafts worker, and Mike Tritico was more like the manager.

The two men also differed in what they thought ought to be done about exposure. They assigned *honor* differently. Exposed to danger in some of his jobs, Donny tended to stand brave against it and to honor bravery. Less exposed to danger, Tritico wanted to reduce the need for bravery. Donny said, in essence, "I'm strong. You're strong. Mother Nature is strong. We can take it." In this way, he resembled the Cowboy. Tritico valued the precautionary principle and said, in essence, "The real strength we need is to stand up to industry and the almighty dollar."

In the past, Mike had taken risks of a different sort himself. He had heard of a scientist who had testified at a public meeting, pointing out the dangers of a proposed dredging project. Angry workers felt his testimony would lose them work, and after the late-night meeting they ran his car off the road. Mike himself went to the same meeting hall weeks later to warn against the same project in the presence of the same glaring men. In the end, other men offered to escort him home. One could be brave without being a Cowboy.

What was life like in the plants themselves? I wondered. Were they governed by Donny's Cowboy perspective or Mike Tritico's precautionary principle? One safety inspector for Axiall—which had an enormous explosion in 2013 and again in 2014—had the job of trying to reduce the risk of accidents. The young man climbed towers and squeezed under machines to check pipes and valves and attach small red flags to pipes that needed replacing or valves tightening. Operators didn't like him coming around because each red flag meant extra work, he said. Some waved him away, "No, not today." Then he said, "They would gang up. I'd have to call their boss, and they hated that. So when they saw me, they'd say, 'Here comes Big Brother.' It was a stressful job."

On hearing this story, a man hired as a corporate industrial hygienist, tasked with sampling acid mist in the battery-charging area in a Ford battery plant, recounted this: "To set up the air monitors, I had to wear a respirator. Staff asked me to take it off since it might make workers who saw me with it on worry about the ill effect of the air on them. But they needn't have worried. Some of the guys started to taunt me, the corporate sissy who couldn't tough it out like they [did]. But when they laughed at me, I could see their teeth were visibly eroded by exposure to sulfuric acid mist."

Not all Cowboys are male, of course, and they hold many kinds of jobs. Among those I talked with, one was a state administrator, another an accountant, and several were homemakers. If the state of Louisiana itself had been seated at Brother Cappy and Sister Fay's dinner table, it might have taken Donny's side. For in Louisiana, as mentioned, it is legal to buy a frozen daiquiri with the lid snapped on, straw to the side, tape over the hole, at a drive-by shop. It's legal to gamble and to carry a loaded gun into a bar on Bourbon Street in New Orleans. In these ways, Louisiana is a Cowboy kind of state.

To Donny, the Cowboy expressed high moral virtue. Equating creativity with daring—the stuff of great explorers, inventors, generals, winners—Donny honored the capacity to take risk and face fear. He could take hard knocks like a man. He could endure. Janice Areno had accommodated environmental pollution through loyalty to job-providing industries and the party she identified with them. Jackie Tabor had accommodated it because it was "the sacrifice we make for capitalism." Donny accommodated out of respect for bravery. Each expressed a deep story self.

Like nearly everyone I spoke with, Donny was not one to think of himself as a victim. That was the language of the "poor me's" asking for government handouts. The very word "victim" didn't sit right. In fact, they were critical of liberal-sounding talk of victimhood. But I began to wonder whether the white, older conservatives in southwest Louisiana—Team Player,

Worshipper, Cowboy—were not themselves victims. They were braving the worst of an industrial system, the fruits of which liberals enjoyed from a distance in their highly regulated and cleaner blue states.

Further disagreements were later brought to the Sunday dinner table of Brother Cappy and Sister Fay. Accepting twenty thousand Syrian refugees, as President Obama proposed? No! comes the chorus around the table. Yes, says Mike Tritico. Who for president? Donald Trump! Donny says. No, says Mike. Issue by issue, so it goes.

Meanwhile, as we scrape the last delicious morsels from our dessert plates—no one had said no to the strawberries and Brother Cappy had never reached for the Vidalia onion—Tritico makes a last try to bait his adversarial friend.

"So Donny, how do you feel about crossing the I-10 bridge?"

"If my kids weren't with me," Donny answers, smiling. "I'd drive *fast*."

13

The Rebel: A Team Loyalist
with a New Cause

Handmade signs bob and lurch above the heads of the sparse crowd: "Clean Water for Baton Rouge," "Friends of Lake Peigneur," "Clean Water for Clean Seafood," "Oil Companies: Fix What You Broke." A rotund musician dressed in loose purple pants, a striped shirt, and a white fedora sits with his washboard, waiting to start his three-person Cajun band. A protestor walks about dressed as a large brown pelican. Organizers had tried to rouse interest, but in a city of 230,000, on this sunny Saturday, only about 150 have shown up.

It was at this rally on the front steps of the state house in Baton Rouge that I'd first met Mike Schaff. He was dressed in a bright yellow T-shirt with "Bayou Corne Sinkhole" printed on the front. With a protective arm, he had brought forward a victim to the microphone to speak before the gathering, but it was he who spoke with tears in his voice. "Five hundred and eighty-two days this woman has been out of her home," he told the crowd, and there were over "three hundred victims just like her." Since the disaster, Mike had been transformed into an activist. He didn't want others to go through the same ordeal. How, I wondered, did his new activism alter his feelings about the market-loving, government-hating Tea Party he so strongly embraced?

Mike had described himself as a "water baby. When I was about three, back when we lived on the Armelise Plantation, my daddy used to take me with him crawfishing. He's set the traps in a nearby swamp. Then he'd put me in a plastic tub and pull it along in the water as he waded through the water, emptying the traps. I loved it." Now as a sixty-four-year-old man, Mike had a modest home facing a canal issuing onto this glorious bayou that was the paradise he had yearned to retire to—a home on the water. Sitting alone at the kitchen table of his empty house a year and a half after the disaster, and some time after the rally, with cardboard boxes packed, the crack in his living room floor a reminder of recent earthquakes, a gas monitor in his garage, and a wary eye on feral cats, Mike had begun to write letters concerning key bills to members of the Louisiana legislature:

April 24, 2014

Friends, Supporters, and Distinguished Senators,

My name is Mike Schaff. . . . My desire was to live the rest of my days here and in my last will and testament to be able to turn over this precious jewel to my survivors. . . . Instead . . . the only legacy that I will be able to pass on are the countless tears that have been shed, the disrespect that we have been shown by both Texas Brine and our state officials themselves, and the cruel reality that despite hopes of a short-lived incident, the fact is that this tragedy can never truly be remedied . . .

Mike Schaff, Resident of Paradise
Stolen, Bayou Corne, Louisiana

He was speaking for Senate Bill 209, which would require companies to give victims the replacement value of lost homes within 180 days of an accident. The language of the bill was dry. Seated in the Louisiana legislature were many oil men—owners, past company employees, investors, and recipients of campaign donations—and the bill was tabled.

On another issue, Texas Brine had asked for permission from the state to flush toxic wastewater into the sinkhole it had caused, and Mike Schaff wrote the secretary of the Louisiana Department of Environmental Quality to object: "To Ms. Hatch, . . . Discarding polluted water back into the

Sinkhole is . . . akin to allowing BP to skim the oil from the Gulf of Mexico and dump it back into the Gulf."

And so it went, bill after bill, and speech after speech. For now he had become—still resisting the term—an environmental activist. By August of 2015 he had written fifty letters to state and federal officials. He had appeared in twenty local television interviews, fifteen print interviews, and five national and international television interviews. "This is the closest I've come to being a tree-hugger," he tells me with a rueful smile. After the sinkhole disaster, Mike had helped gather neighbors in a desperate circle of self-help. During that meeting, someone suggested inviting General Russel Honoré. Mike recalled imagining the General wouldn't come out for such a small group. But when the General responded immediately, something new emerged: the Green Army. As the General was to tell me in a separate interview, "As soon as I drove home from that first meeting, and thought about Mike, it occurred to me he would be great to work with, and we needed to start something big. The Green Army then became an umbrella organization for many small groups such as Baton Rouge Aquifer Protection, Restore Louisiana Now, and the Lower Mississippi Riverkeepers—one that could speak with the serious authority they would need to stand up to oil and the politicians who wanted to gut the EPA."

"A lot of people think the environment is a soft, feminine issue," the General mused. "We need Mikes." Don't be a Cowboy in enduring pollution, he seemed to say. Be a Cowboy fighting it.

But each time Mike rose before an audience to speak about Bayou Corne, he placed his hand over his mouth, delivered a few sentences in a cracked voice. "I've had a rough time because all the emotions rushed back over me as they have tended to do lately," he told me about a talk he gave to a Tea Party group. "The wound is still so fresh." Mike was brought up to admire Cowboys. "Southern men don't cry," he tells me, "and I haven't been much of a weeper." Still, he is disconcerted to discover himself choking up while speaking to the public about the disaster. "I pray one day I'll be able to speak with no tears, just anger," he tells me.

Before the sinkhole, Mike had worked all his life for oil, an ardent, conservative Republican and, since 2009, an unconflicted Tea Party loyalist. He was a "free-market man," he told me. But how free were people when companies were free to make methane gas bubble in your front yard? What was the Tea Party answer to that? This was the question before him.

Mike felt he had patiently "stood in line" too long for the American Dream. He had worked hard for a boss and company he liked, but like the 90 percent of Americans who saw no rise in income, Mike was caught in the long, dreary wait. He took offense at certain remarks rumored to have been made by a pro–Texas Brine wife of a retired Exxon engineer who lived in Bayou Corne: "She's one of thirty or forty owners of fancy-dancy homes on the other side of the highway," Mike remarked. And she "let slip that our housing was substandard. The home owners association on our side of the road allows trailers on house lots; on their side, they don't." He felt he'd done okay, but was vulnerable to nasty jibes like that. And more wealth felt within reach. Mike twice remarked on "millionaires" in the local area. One was the heavily bearded star of the reality television show *Duck Dynasty*, who combined conservative views with Cajun frontier skills. The other was a short, bearded man in T-shirt, blue jeans, and tennis shoes standing in the back row at a meeting of Sinkhole victims with Texas Brine, which I was attending with Mike. He introduced himself as "a poor" man, but the crowd tittered knowingly. No; he dressed poor, but he was rich. And there were others around like him, Mike said, with more money than him. From a shotgun home on the Armelise sugarcane plantation to a college education, a professional career, and a home on Bayou Corne, Mike had done well, but he didn't seem sure it was well enough.

Mike loves to fish, boat, and watch the outstretched wings of the egrets, white ibis, and roseate spoonbills. His e-mail handle is "Swampman." But through the years, he found little daylight time for any of this. "Hey, I haven't seen a month's vacation since I was twenty-two," he says ruefully. As an "estimator," he had calculated the size, strength, heat- and pressure-withstanding properties, and cost of materials needed to build enormous oil storage tanks and drilling platforms. He had been given only one week off a year for the first five years—sick time and vacation combined. For the next five, he was given two weeks off, and after ten years, three. For his entire working life, Mike had yearned for daylight leisure to spend in nature. So on the verge of retirement, he could hardly wait. Time with his new wife, time fishing and hunting, time with his grandchildren.

Then came the sinkhole.

After the last church service in Bayou Corne, in which the community sang "Amazing Grace" in French, his neighbors and friends scattered to camper-trucks, motels, and relatives' guestrooms, leaving Bayou Corne a ghost town encroached on by thirty-two acres of toxic sludge. All the fun times they'd had—at crawfish boils and fish-fries, at Miss Eddy's Birdhouse, the local Mardi Gras parade of Bayou Corne Hookers—all gone. Mike had tried to get the loss behind him. But three years later, he is still saying, "Bayou Corne will always be home."

In his new activism, Mike's long background in oil became a great asset. He knew the geology. He knew the economics. He knew the local lay of the land. He'd gained firsthand knowledge of dangerous chemicals. As a child he had crouched in the sugarcane field to watch the Piper Cub crop dusters fly low, their wheels nearly leafing through the tops of the cane stalks. After the pilot had sprayed DDT clouds and started to rise at the end of the row, Mike would pop up from the cane into the pesticide cloud to watch the plane turn for another pass. He knew about unawareness. But what was new for Mike was a close-up view of the politics—especially the attitude toward the environment expressed by Republican governor Bobby Jindal.

Closer to home, Mike found himself wedged uneasily between two groups. On matters of government and tax, he was 100 percent with the Louisiana Tea Party. Corrupt state officials had seemed to "cut in ahead" of him, as in the deep story. They were nothing like the self-abnegating nuns he thought public servants should resemble. He had low respect for most of the Louisiana regulatory officials and, in theory, little for their federal counterparts. But in one instance, when he doubted state officials who claimed to detect no oil in the Bayou Corne ground, Mike called for the more reliable "Feds" to double-check.

But now Mike's new environmental comrades were 99 percent liberals—

with their own different deep story, as I'll suggest later. "I'd be okay with 70–30," he says. He agreed with them that Louisiana "gave out drilling permits like candy." He agreed with them on fracking, and on getting industry to repair the coast their actions had destroyed. He agreed on alternative energy. Louisiana was 42nd out of 50 states on that one. He didn't agree with liberals on funding Head Start, Pell college grants, Obamacare, or Social Security. And that was fine. But in the back of his mind, Mike wanted to add the environment to the agenda of the Tea Party. How tough a sell would that be? He wanted to find out.

The Disaster Before the Sinkhole

Disasters could occur, get forgotten, and occur again. Like Harold and Annette Areno, Mike was now a rememberer. And the challenge he faced was how to make Bayou Corne the last accident of its kind, one everyone would remember.

In 1980, an even more disastrous drilling accident occurred in Lake Peigneur, about fifty miles west of Bayou Corne Sinkhole. Texaco had drilled a hole in the bottom of the lake and punctured an underlying salt dome. The resulting whirlpool had sucked down two drilling platforms, eleven barges, four flatbed trucks, a tugboat, acres of soil, trees, trucks, a parking lot, and an entire sixty-five-acre botanical garden. Miraculously, no one died. Days later, nine barges popped back up; two were never found. One man fishing in the lake that fateful day had tied his motorboat to a tree. But the tree itself began to move toward the vortex. Noticing it, the man quickly untied his boat from the moving tree and roared away at top speed.

But years later, a memory-softening documentary appeared about the Lake Peigneur disaster. Narrated in a laconic tone that placed these events in the distant past and focused on amusing ironies, the film—produced by the local Chamber of Commerce—seemed to relax the viewer. The narrator expressed gratitude that no humans died, of course. But he avoided blame of Texaco and focused instead on the small drill bit that seemed to have punctured the dome by itself. The film ends with an image of birds flying over the placid lake and a tourist bureau website inviting tourists to visit the site "where the accident happened." In fact, a video on the disaster has become an attraction in the Rip Van Winkle Gardens brochure: "Watch a salt mine swallow a lake at Rip Van Winkle Gardens on Jefferson Island, then tour Rip's Rookery, where roseate spoonbills nest every spring."

That was not the end. Only eight months after the Bayou Corne Sinkhole, the state issued a permit to a drill once again—in a massive new project in Lake Peigneur. It gave permission to the nation's largest distributor of natural gas, AGL Resources, to dredge the lake and drill three "waste wells" within which to deposit toxic waste. It granted permission to dig three additional wells to store natural gas, and another to drill for brine, all inside the salt dome underlying Lake Peigneur. "Thank God they decided the salt dome wasn't okay to store nuclear waste!" Mike declares.

Memory was short. The drilling company at Bayou Corne Sinkhole (2012) had forgotten the disaster of Lake Peigneur (1980). Now Lake Peigneur AGL Resources was forgetting—or overriding—both disasters. The Cowboys were running the regulatory agency. Save Lake Peigneur and the Louisiana Environmental Action Network (LEAN) jointly sued the state. A state judge put a stay on drilling, and at this writing, the matter rests there.

Alone at the dining table in his ruined home, Mike fired off a letter imploring a state senator to vote to ban, for a year, new permits to store hazardous waste and brine in underground cavities in salt domes, until stricter guidelines were developed. It was aimed at stopping drilling in Lake Peigneur. The bill did not pass.

Mike took on yet another big cause—the Louisiana Tea Party itself. Why couldn't they join a good fight? The coastal land of Louisiana had long been slowly sinking into the Gulf of Mexico. The state's coast provides 40 percent of the nation's wetlands, and its commercial fisheries provide a quarter to a third of the nation's seafood. Experts agree that a major cause of the land's subsidence is the extraction of oil and saltwater intrusion. Over the years, oil companies have dredged hundreds of canals and laid down pipeline through which oil drilled in the Gulf has been piped inland. Saltwater seeps in along the canals, killing grasses that once provided protection against Louisiana's frequent tropical storms. Since 1930, the state had already lost an area equal to the size of Delaware—an average football field every hour.

The National Oceanic and Atmospheric Administration (NOAA) faced an astonishing new task: de-listing coastal postal addresses. Gone is Yellow Cotton Bay, once a prime fishing settlement in Plaquemines Parish. Gone are Little Pass de Wharf and Skipback Bay. The church in Grand Bayou stands on stilts; a small cemetery is accessible only by boat. Thirty-one communities are now listed only in the historical record. Residents of Isle de Jean Charles are the first "climate refugees" to receive federal help moving to dry land.

In the aftermath of Hurricane Katrina, the state legislature set up the Southeast Flood Control Commission to come up with a plan for protecting Louisiana from floods. They concluded that the best course of action was to fill in the canals and repair the shore. Since this was a task the oil companies had in their contracts agreed to do, and had not done, in 2014 the commission did what had never been done: it sued the ninety-seven responsible oil companies. Governor Jindal quickly squashed the upstart commission. He removed members from it. He challenged its right to sue. In another unprecedented move, the legislature voted to nullify—*retroactively*—the lawsuit by withdrawing the authority to file it from those who had done so. A measure (SB 553) called for costs of repairs to be paid, not by the oil companies, but by the state's taxpayers.

Mike saw his chance. Still writing from his dining room table in Bayou Corne, he addressed fellow members of the New Orleans–based Louisiana Tea Party. Lower *taxes*! Surely, they would get behind this one, he thought, so he arranged to meet the group at the TJ Ribs steakhouse in Baton Rouge.

But, presented with the idea, the Tea Party faces went blank. The environment? That was a liberal cause. One man confused the Green Army with the Green Party. To Mike's astonishment, another member suggested moving the burden from the Louisiana taxpayer to the nation's taxpayers. "It was a total bust," he told me later. "I'd invited the General and I had to apologize to him for wasting his precious time."

Undaunted, Mike tried again with a different Tea Party gathering, this time in Ruston in north central Louisiana. Again, he asked General Honoré, and again the General spoke, this time wearing his American flag and eagle necktie. The issue was saltwater intrusion into their drinking water, and this time party members listened. "Why leave the issue of the environment to the left?" Mike argued. "It should be our issue too."

But how, I wondered, did that work—putting care for the environment together with the Tea Party call to defund—if not abolish—the EPA, along with other agencies of government? Mike's answer was the free market. "Follow the money," he said. "Make it in the financial interest of everyone to do the right thing. Texas Brine took risks, but it bought insurance. And that insurance company took out back-up insurance. It's in the *financial* interest of those insurance companies to make sure accidents don't happen. Let *them* be the regulators." Then he added, "The insurance companies need to be bonded [third-party guarantees promising to pay compensation if problems occur]. That will do it. All we need from the federal government are jails, courts, laws, and bonding. You regulate companies without federal regulators."

Interesting, I thought. But wait. Wasn't this exactly the setup that led to the sinkhole disaster in the first place? Texas Brine was insured by New York–based Liberty Insurance Company. Liberty was bonded, but it refused to pay and sued Texas Brine. Other companies insuring Texas Brine did the same, and it counter-sued them all. You had the courts, the laws, the jails, and bonding, and you had both an ecological and a legal mess. Besides, didn't rich companies hire many lawyers to come up against victims with one? I asked. "No," Mike countered. "It's rich oil companies up against rich insurance companies." Even so, don't you need another—federal—counterweight?

I thought back to Lee Sherman's life at PPG, to the rubberized horse, to the industrial explosion that made the young Janice Areno think the world was ending, to the Arenos' deceased relatives, dead animals, and missing frogs in Bayou d'Inde, to the events leading up to the seafood advisory. I thought of life before the EPA, and all this in a state that had so much natural magnificence to protect. Donny McCorquodale was right that some accidents were bound to happen, I thought. But without a national vision based on the common good, none of us could leave a natural heritage to our children, or, as the General said, be "free." A free market didn't make us a free people, I thought. But I had slipped way over to my side of the empathy wall again.

Mike agreed with a smidgen of this—a skeleton crew at the EPA, maybe. But the EPA was grabbing authority and tax money to take on a fictive mission, he felt—lessening the impact of global warming. This was just another excuse to expand, like governments do. As a whole, the federal government was eroding beloved communities such as those he loved. And if the federal government was anything like the Louisiana state government—which he thought it was—it wasn't worth believing in or paying taxes to. The "federal government" filled a mental space in Mike's mind—and the minds of all those on the right I came to know—associated with a financial sinkhole.

In fact, after the 2009 government bailout of failing banks, companies, and home owners, the federal government seemed to side with yet more line cutters. Now *debtors*, too, were cutting ahead of people and the federal government was inviting them to do so. This was a strange new expression of social conflict, undeclared, appearing on a new stage, with various groups undefined by class *per se*—blacks, immigrants, refugees—mixed in. And by proxy, the federal government was the enemy.

And on the personal side there was one more thing—the federal government wasn't on the side of men being manly. Liberals were certainly on the wrong side of that one. It wasn't easy being a man. It was an era of numerous subtle challenges to masculinity, it seemed. These days a woman didn't need a man for financial support, for procreation, even for the status of being married. And now with talk of transgender people, what, really, was a man? It was unsettling, wrong. At the core, to be a man you had to be willing to lose your life in battle, willing to use your strength to protect the weak. Who today was remembering all that? Marriage was truly between a man and a woman, Mike felt. Clarity about one's identity was a good thing, and the military had offered that clarity, he felt, even as it offered gifted men of modest backgrounds a pathway to honor. Meanwhile, the nearly all-male areas of life—the police, the fire department, parts of the U.S.

military, and the oil rigs—needed defending against this cultural erosion of manhood. The federal government, the EPA, stood up for the *biological* environment, but it was allowing—and it seemed at times it was causing—a *cultural* erosion. What seemed to my Tea Party friends to be dangerously polluted, unclean, and harmful was American culture. And against that pollution, the Tea Party stood firm.

Mike was a fighter but not a Cowboy, a man of religion but not a Worshipper, and a Team Loyalist but critical, in one big way, of his team. The team he wanted would dismantle much of the federal government that he blamed for many wrongs in America. He still saw the solution to many problems as non-governmental. But in his hour of need, faced with the Bayou Corne Sinkhole, he had called on the EPA to check the level of methane gas in his neighborhood. While Mike thought we needed policemen to protect the streets, he wasn't so sure about the EPA protecting the waterways. It could get too bossy. It could get too big.

At night after the evacuation of most of the Bayou Corne Sinkhole victims, he said, "I go out to look at the stars, and all the houses are dark." In the year before Mike moved, a scattering of other residents had also stayed on in their destroyed homes. One was a neighbor and dear friend, Nick, whose wife was facing her third bout with breast cancer. She was suffering from radiation treatments, and Nick felt it unwise to move her.

One evening Mike looked across Crawfish Stew Street and saw Nick standing on his lawn alone. He was smoking a cigarette, spirals of smoke drifting upward into the empty night. "He'd lost his house to the sinkhole. His wife was ill. Their dog was dying. But I sensed he was feeling bad about something new," Mike said. "So I walked across the street over to him. He's just gotten word that his son had pancreatic cancer."

Mike put his hand on Nick's shoulder, and the two men wept together for a long time.

PART FOUR

Going National

14

The Fires of History:
The 1860s and the 1960s

Stepping back in time, three streams of influence seemed present in the feelings of my Tea Party friends in Louisiana, one often spoken of and two, rarely. For one thing, the Tea Party movement is one in a long line of periodic heightened expressions "of a popular impulse endemic in American political culture," as the historian Richard Hofstadter has noted. Through the nineteenth and twentieth centuries, movements rose up against secularism, modernity, racial integration, and a culture of experts. But none before the Tea Party have so forcefully taken up the twin causes of reversing progressive reform and dismantling the federal government—a movement in response to the deep story. So within the long line of such movements, why this one? To answer that, we must look to two pivotal moments in history, I believe. One is the era of the 1860s, which has special meaning for the South. The second is the era of the 1960s, which resonates for the right wing across the nation.

The contemporary turn to the right in America has occurred mainly in the South, which is what drew me there. You don't have to be Southern to be Tea Party, of course, but the white South has been a center of it. What interests me about Southern history is the series of emotional grooves, as we might call them, carved into the minds and hearts of the people I came to know through the lives of their ancestors—many of whom were white farmers of small farms. It isn't the origin of certain ideas in history that I am curious about, as much as the way the past fixes patterns of class identification in our minds that we impose on the present. What might people be asked to want to feel? To believe they should feel? To actually feel? In broad, sketching strokes, what might be the impact of stories from grandparents, teachers, and history books on the ideas of those I've come to know?

The 1860s

The South had become "a section apart," in C. Vann Woodward's words, because of the plantation system. This system deeply affected well-to-do white planters and black slaves, of course. But it also left a deep imprint on another large group we often forget—poor white sharecroppers, small farmers, and tenant farmers, some of whom were the ancestors of those I came to know in Louisiana. In his classic *The Mind of the South*, W.J. Cash says that the plantation system "threw up walls [which] . . . enclosed the white man, walls he did not see." The poor white did not see himself "locked into a marginal life" but as "a potential planter or mill baron himself."

Within those walls, the cultural imagination focused intently on two groups—the dominant and dominated, very rich and very poor, free and bound, envied and pitied, with very little in between. Rich planters sipped foreign wine under crystal chandeliers, seated on European chairs, in white-pillared mansions. They saw themselves not as wicked oppressors but as generous benefactors, and poor whites took them as such. At the other extreme, poor whites saw the terrifying misery of the traumatized, short-lived slave. This set in their minds a picture of the best and worst fates in life. Compared to life in New England farming villages, there was much more wealth to envy above, and far more misery to gasp at below. Such a system suggested its own metaphoric line waiting for the American Dream—one with little room for the lucky ahead, and much room for the forgotten behind.

Between this top and bottom, Cash describes poor whites as living in unpainted houses with "sagging rail fences . . . and crazy barns which yet bulged with corn." However, as the plantation system grew, it became harder and harder to cope. Planters bought up the most desirable fertile plains, pressing poorer farmers onto the barren uplands. If poor white farmers tried to move to better land, they found that the planters had "seized the best lands there" even "beyond the Mississippi" in "Arkansas and Texas armed with plentiful capital and solid battalions of slaves." Poor whites were driven back "to the red hills and the sand lands and the pine barrens and the swamps—to all the marginal lands of the South." To plant cotton and sugarcane, plantation owners destroyed forests, which deprived "the farmer's table of the old abundant variety," reducing his diet to "cornpone and the flesh of razorback hogs." Since the planters relied on slave labor, and since they bought most of their hay, corn, beef, and wood from the North or Midwest, poor whites became surplus labor, left to live on what they themselves could produce. Marginalized and without demand for their labor, poor whites bore up under rude epithets—crackers, white trash, po buckra.

Transposing ancestral history onto our modern-day deep story, nineteenth-century poor whites stood very far back in line for the American Dream. There was no ethnic or gender parade of people "cutting in." The very idea of redistribution was anathema to the plantation system. And there was little by way of a government-supported public commons, the South being far poorer than the North in public libraries, parks, schools, universities.

Then came the Civil War, and the North devastated the South. Cities were burned, fields laid waste—some by the Confederate troops as they retreated. After the Civil War, the North replaced Southern state governments with its own hand-picked governors. The profit-seeking carpetbaggers came, it seemed to those I interviewed, as agents of the dominating North. Exploiters from the North, an angry, traumatized black population at home, and moral condemnation from all—this was the scene some described to me. When the 1960s began sending Freedom Riders and civil rights activists, pressing for new federal laws to dismantle Jim Crow, there they came again, it seemed, the moralizing North.

And again, Obamacare, global warming, gun control, abortion rights—did these issues, too, fall into the emotional grooves of history? Does it feel like another strike from the North, from Washington, that has put the brown pelican ahead of the Tea Partier waiting in line? I wondered. When I talked to Cappy Brantley in Longville about the 2016 presidential election, he commented with a gentle smile, "Hillary Clinton, Bernie Sanders—they're from the North."

A Different Costume

"From Baton Rouge to New Orleans, the great sugarcane plantations border both sides of the river all the way . . . standing so close together, for long distances," Mark Twain wrote in *Life on the Mississippi*, "that the broad river lying between the two rows, becomes a sort of spacious street." Along the seventy-mile strip, some four hundred graceful mansions, with two- or three-story white Grecian pillars, oak-canopied walkways, manicured gardens and ponds, are the ancient castles of America. They were built with profits from cotton.

The new cotton is oil, but the plantation culture continues. Indeed, a number of the white-pillared mansions of the great plantations have now been bought by oil and petrochemical companies. Dow Chemical bought four plantations—including the Australia Plantation and the Abner Jackson Plantation, and on the latter the company hosts conferences in its Big House. "We've always been a plantation state," Oliver Houck, a Tulane University law professor, observes. "What oil and gas did is replace the agricultural with an oil 'plantation culture.'" Like cotton, oil is a single commodity requiring huge investment and has, like cotton and sugar, come to dominate the economy.

The parallel between cotton and oil has its limits, of course. Cotton barons did not promise prosperity to poor farmers or slaves, as the oil industry has done to modern-day Louisianans. On the positive side, oil offers to restore lost honor. For if the plantation system brought shame to the South in the eyes of the nation, oil has brought pride. The hosannas of the Louisiana Chemical Association are expressed in the language of investment, profit, and jobs. But the new plantation seems to offer more—the Big House without the slave quarters.

Meanwhile, just as yeomen farmers were pressed back to make way for the sugar and cotton plantations, so too has oil partly crowded out the seafood industry and tourism, as Paul Templet noted. That also happened to a talkative man whom I discovered on one summer visit, a man sweating in his woolen Confederate cap and uniform as he worked as a period actor at the restored Oak Alley Plantation. This was the grandest of the majestic mansions along River Road, now a popular tourist attraction. He was stationed in a small tent behind the Big House. Displayed was a Civil War–era rifle, and on a hanger a Confederate uniform, cap, and knapsack. A friendly, blond man in his forties, he was paid to talk about the details of his make-believe life as a Confederate soldier of the 1860s, and he was doing a convincing job.

At the moment, there were no others in his tent. He invited me to sit down with him at a small table and talk. He set aside his prepared script to tell me, "Oil is the new cotton. I was born eight miles from here. My wife and I raise racehorses on an eight-acre farm. An oil company applied for permission to set up a tank farm half a football field away from our house" (an enormous storage facility that holds up to forty-six million barrels of crude oil). "And we couldn't stop it. No one could. We can't sell our house, either, because the value of it sank because now we're next to a tank farm."

Then the man looked around casually, as if to check if he could be overheard. "I'm here in my costume to represent a Confederate trooper. Confederates tried to get out from under the control of the federal government—to secede. But you can't secede from oil. And you can't secede from a mentality. You have to think your way into and out of that mentality. But they should get me in a different costume to talk about that."

Echoes from the 1960s and 1970s

A century later, another legacy was to fuel the right, not just in the South but across the nation. The 1960s and 1970s set off a series of social movements, which, to some degree, shuffled the order of those "waiting in line" and laid down a simmering fire of resentment which was to flame up years later as the Tea Party. During this era a long parade of the underprivileged came forward to talk of their mistreatment—blacks who had fled a Jim Crow South, underpaid Latino field workers, Japanese internment camp victims, ill-treated Native Americans, immigrants from all over. Then came the women's movement. Overburdened at home, restricted to clerical or teaching jobs in the workplace, unsafe from harassment, women renewed their claim to a place in line for the American Dream. Then gays and lesbians spoke out against their oppression. Environmentalists argued the cause of forest animals without forests. The endangered brown pelican, flapping its long, oily wings, had now taken its place in line.

As the 1960s transitioned to the 1970s, a movement focused on the social and legal system shifted into a movement focused on personal identity. Now to gain public sympathy it was enough to be Native American, or a woman, or gay. The patience of many on both left and right was tried. All these social movements left one group standing in line: the older, white male, especially if such a man worked in a field that didn't particularly help the planet. He was—or was soon becoming—a minority too.

If the civil rights movement and the women's movement had pointed the finger of blame at the entitled white male, maybe it was time for people to see white men as victims too, to be heard, honored, and put—or left— ahead in line. But this provided its members with a troubling contradiction: how do you join the identity politics parade and also bring it to a halt?

Perhaps the defining moment of the 1960s occurred in the South, which had remained the most conservative area of the country and the least prepared for the enormous changes that began in June of 1964: Freedom Summer. A thousand students, many from elite universities, traveled to Mississippi to register voters, teach black history, and help in what ways they could. (My husband, Adam, and I were among them.) Sixty civil rights workers were trained in voter registration in Plaquemine, Louisiana. Even though most black voter applicants were turned away, over a thousand got registered for the first time in their lives. Black students famously tried to integrate lunch counters, restaurants, hotels, housing, schools, and universities.

Especially for blacks, this was dangerous work. In the summer of 1964, three voter registration drive workers, one black and two white—James Chaney, Andrew Goodman, and Michael Schwerner—were murdered by the Ku Klux Klan in Philadelphia, Mississippi. This led to a national outcry and to the Civil Rights Act of 1964 and the Voting Rights Act of 1965. There were 1,062 arrests; 37 churches were burned or bombed, and the homes or businesses of 30 blacks were also bombed or burned. This was also the year the Mississippi Freedom Democratic Party delegation to the Democratic National Convention challenged the all-white regular delegation.

Where did this leave white, blue-collar Southern men, the most visible resisters to civil rights? In the shocked eyes of the nation, they lost moral standing. Many older males I spoke with were children or teenagers in the 1960s. Whatever their family's view or their own, however much sympathy they may have personally felt for blacks at the time, the public narrative was that the North had to come to the South, as it had with soldiers in the 1860s and during Reconstruction in the 1870s, to tell Southern whites to change their way of life. History was on the side of the civil rights movement. The nation honored its leaders. Southern whites bore the mark of shame, again, even though, as one man told me, "*We* didn't do those bad things."

Even though the federal government had been an instrument of racial segregation in the past, it now stood for racial equality. A slow drum roll began: in 1948, President Harry S. Truman integrated the armed services. In 1954, the Supreme Court, through *Brown v. Board of Education*, integrated schools. In 1957, President Dwight D. Eisenhower sent in federal troops and the National Guard to enforce federal law integrating schools in Little Rock, Arkansas. And that set the stage for more federal action in the decade to follow. In 1962, President John F. Kennedy sent five thousand federal troops to ensure the right of James Meredith to attend the University of Mississippi. President Lyndon B. Johnson signed the Civil Rights Act of 1964, the most sweeping civil rights law since Reconstruction. This was followed by an executive order for government contractors instituting affirmative action for minorities in employment. In 1968, Johnson banned discrimination in housing. And so it went—the federal government aiding a social movement of a people to take their rightful place in line for the American Dream.

The feminist movement followed the civil rights movement, picking up from earlier struggles for the right to vote, hold office, and own property in a one's own name. A series of legal decisions strengthening the equal protection clause of the Fourteenth Amendment were now applied in places of work that received any money from the federal government. Later, the movement for gay rights trod the same path through the 1970s.

Over time, new groups were added to older ones, and political and therapeutic cultures merged. Identity politics was born. Identities based on surviving cancer, rape, childhood sexual abuse, addiction to alcohol, drugs, sex work—these and more came to the media's attention. It became a race "for the crown of thorns," the critic Todd Gitlin, a former 1960s activist, lamented in his book, *The Twilight of Common Dreams: Why America Is Wracked by Culture Wars.* On the heels of these movements for social change, a certain culture of victimization had crept in. And where did that leave the older white male? As an ideal, fairness seemed to stop before it got to him.

Struggle for Honor

My Tea Party friends—and many now did feel like friends—responded to the fire of the 1960s by incorporating some parts of its message, and resisting others. One woman told me she loved Sarah Palin because she was a pro-life "feminist" who embraced "girl power" and "mama grizzlies." Another honored Martin Luther King Jr. as the model of level-headed leadership in contrast to the youthful urban hotheads who break store windows in rage at police brutality.

But they also had strong objections to some outcomes of the movements of the 1960s. If you have one drop of Native American blood, you qualify under some affirmative action guideline to get financial aid for college. But why does that put you ahead in line? they wondered. If a person said he or she was white, as a way of describing themselves in the manner of the Native American or black, they risked being seen as racist soldiers of the Aryan Nation. If they stood up to declare themselves proud to be male—unless they were part of a men's group trying to unlearn traditional ways—they risked being seen as male chauvinists. If they called for recognition for their lifetime of experience, their age, they risked seeming like old fools in a culture focused on youth.

Putting the 1860s and the 1960s together, white men of the South seemed to have lived through one long deep story of being shoved back in line. If in the nineteenth century the big planters had reduced the lot of the poor white farmer, twenty-first-century corporations had gone global, automated, moved plants to cheaper workers or moved cheaper workers in, and deftly remained out of sight over the brow of the hill. Some 280 of the most profitable American companies had dodged taxes on half of their profits, according to a 2011 study, but in the history-soaked deep story, you couldn't see that. You were left to imagine it, to feel you couldn't *do* anything about it. And to make matters worse, it was your sector, the free market, that was letting you down. Meanwhile, white wages leveled or sank and welfare expenditures rose.

The Honor Squeeze

So for older white men, the 1960s presented a delicate dilemma. On one hand, they did want to stand up, come forward, and express an identity like so many others had done. Why not us too? On the other hand, as members of the right, they had objected in principle to cutting in line, and disliked the overused word "victim." Still—and this was unsayable—they were beginning to *feel* like victims. Others had moved forward; they were the left behind. They disliked the word "suffer," but they *had* suffered from wage cuts, the dream trap, and the covert dishonor of being the one group everyone thought stood unfairly ahead of the line. Culturally speaking, the entire North had "cut in" and seemed to move the South to the back of the line, even as—and this was forgotten—federal dollars had steadily moved from North to South.

How, again, could the white male openly want to cut in line himself when he objected in principle to cutting in line? He was in conflict and responded to it by seeking honor in other ways. First, he would claim pride in work. But work had become less and less secure, and again, wages for the bottom 90 percent remained flat. Word was out that some workers at Toys "R" Us and Disneyland were being asked to train other workers destined to replace them for less pay. And the federal government was giving money to people who did no work, undercutting the honor accorded work itself. (But see Appendix C.)

If he couldn't take pride in work, the Tea Party man tried region and state, and there too he ran into difficulty. Most people I talked to loved the South, loved Louisiana, loved their town or bayou. But they were sadly aware of its low status. "Oh we're the flyover state," one Tea Party teacher told me. "We're seen as backward and poor," another complained. Like red-leaning Midwestern farmers who felt insulted to be called "hayseeds" or Appalachian coal miners who were seen as "hillbillies," as residents of their region, Southerners had taken an ill-deserved hit in the eyes of the nation.

If region and state couldn't serve as a basis for honor, surely strong family values could. Even when they couldn't manage to live up to their moral code—which favored lifelong, heterosexual, monogamous, pro-life marriage—they took pride in the code itself. It was not easy to live by such a code. One woman of the right had a gay brother who had been married, had a child, and abandoned both "just because of sex," and the episode had caused an upheaval in the family. In order to avoid the pain of divorce her own parents had caused her, one woman entered a covenant marriage. (Intended to strengthen the institution, covenant marriage was passed into law in Louisiana in 1997, and later in Arkansas and Arizona. It calls on the couple to sign an affidavit that they have undergone pre-marital counseling, and otherwise heightens the requirements for entry and exit from marriage.) She soon discovered her husband was gay, and while the couple later cooperated in raising their two children, she was glad she had tried to keep the marriage together "the way it should be." The fourteen-year-old daughter of another mother became pregnant and kept the baby. "I'm working full-time and she's got to finish school. Frankly it's been very hard." And it would have been easier for her young daughter, she feels, if she had had an abortion. But there was honor in keeping the baby and "doing the right thing"—an honor they felt to be invisible to liberals.

And church: many like Janice Areno spoke of the value of "being churched" and giving tithes. But some of the beliefs they learned in church—that the earth was made in seven days, that heaven was a giant cube, that Eve was born of Adam's rib, that evolution never occurred—were, if taken literally, seen in the eyes of a wider, more secular world as signs of a poor education.

But being Christian and taking Jesus as your savior was for Janice, Jackie, Madonna, and others a way of saying, "I commit myself to being a moral person. I daily try to be good, to help, to forgive, and in fact to *work hard at being good.*" "If I know a person is a Christian," one woman told me, "I know we have a lot in common. I'm more likely to *trust that he or she is a moral person* than I would a non-Christian."

Underlying all these other bases of honor—in work, region, state, family life, and church—was pride in the *self* of the deep story. The people I came to know had sacrificed a great deal and found honor in sacrifice. It had been hard for Janice Areno's father to drop out of school to help his dad raise a family of ten. Although nearly everyone I spoke to had two children, three at most and some none at all, a few honored their mothers or grandfathers for having raised very large families. It was a hard thing to do. They took pride in giving to local community—Mike Schaff's two-beer sandbagging against flood, Janice's friend's one-touch pillows for American troops, Jackie Tabor's work at Abraham's Tent.

What seemed like a problem to liberals—the fact that conservatives identify "up," with the 1 percent, the planter class—was actually a source of pride to the Tea Party people I came to know. It showed you were optimistic, hopeful, a trier. It wasn't a problem that you seldom looked behind you in line. Why would you want to blame a guy if he got all the way to the top? they wondered. That gaze forward, even when matters seemed hopeless, was a feature of the brave deep story self.

But such a self was less and less a source of honor, it seemed. Rising to the fore was another kind of self, a more upper-middle-class cosmopolitan self, with its more dispersed and looser friendship networks, its preparation to compete for entrance to big-name colleges and tough careers that might take a person far from home. Such cosmopolitan selves were directed to the task of cracking into the global elite. They made do with living farther away from their roots. They were ready to go when opportunity knocked. They took great pride in liberal causes—human rights, racial equality, and the fight against global warming. Many upper-middle-class liberals, white and black, didn't notice what, emotionally speaking, their kind of self was displacing. For along with blue-collar jobs, a blue-collar way of life was going out of fashion, and with it, the honor attached to a rooted self and pride in endurance—the deep story self. The liberal upper-middle class saw community as insularity and closed-mindedness rather than as a source of belonging and honor. And they didn't see that, given trends "behind the brow of the hill," their turn to be displaced might be next.

For the Tea Party around the country, the shifting moral qualifications for the American Dream had turned them into strangers in their own land, afraid, resentful, displaced, and dismissed by the very people who were, they felt, cutting in line. The undeclared class war transpiring on a different stage, with different actors, and evoking a different notion of fairness was leading those engaged in it to blame the "supplier" of the imposters—the federal government.

Syrian Refugees

With the arrival in 2015 of Syrian refugees to the United States, fleeing the flames of war at home, one more set of faces seemed to my Tea Party informants to be pulling ahead in line—and they were dangerous, besides. Lee Sherman saw the Syrians as potential members of ISIS. "Ninety percent of them are men, and I think we ought to put them in Guantánamo," he said. "But they aren't enemy combatants," I reminded him. "I know, but you can take the fences down, make it less like a prison," he replied. "If you let them into the U.S. they will have all our rights to things." Comparing the refugees to Southerners during the Civil War, Mike Schaff, himself a refugee from the Bayou Corne Sinkhole, said, "General Lee led brave Southerners who, though grossly outnumbered and woefully under-armed, refused to flee their country as refugees. They stayed, fought, and many died. Their wives and children, many raped and murdered, also stayed to care for their homes. After their defeat, again, they did not flee. They stayed to eventually reshape our government. The Syrians should stay, take a stand, and fight for what they believe in. If you flee, in my mind, you're a traitor unto yourself. This is harsh, I know, but sometimes we have to make tough choices." Jackie Tabor said, "We are protecting Muslims and persecuting Christians. Have you ever seen a Muslim charity event for people in need, or soup kitchen for the homeless? A Muslim Thanksgiving? Where is the Muslim name on the Declaration of Independence?" If Mike saw the Syrian refugees through the eyes of the 1860s, Jackie saw the official welcome offered them as more 1960s-style diversity, which threatened the core of the religious culture she held sacred.

As strangers in their own land, Lee, Mike, and Jackie wanted their homeland back, and the pledges of the Tea Party offered them that. It offered them financial freedom from taxes, and emotional freedom from the strictures of liberal philosophy and its rules of feeling. Liberals were asking them to feel compassion for the downtrodden in the back of the line, the "slaves" of society. They didn't want to; they felt downtrodden themselves and wanted only to look "up" to the elite. What was wrong with aspiring high? That was the bigger virtue, they thought. Liberals were asking them to direct their indignation at the ill-gotten gains of the overly rich, the "planters"; the right wanted to aim their indignation down at the poor slackers, some of whom were jumping the line.

One cultural contribution the South has made to the modern national right may be its persistent legacy of secession. In the nineteenth century, the secession was geographic: the South seceded from the North. Between 1860 and 1865, the eleven Confederate states established themselves as a separate territory and nation. The modern-day Tea Party enthusiasts I met sought a different separation—one between rich and poor. In their ideal world, government would not take from the rich to give to the poor. It would fund the military and the national guard, build interstate freeways, dredge harbors, and otherwise pretty much disappear.

So in the Tea Party idea, North and South would unite, but a new cleavage would open wide; the rich would divorce the poor—for so many of them were "cutting in line." In the 1970s, there was much talk of President Richard Nixon's "Southern strategy," which appealed to white fear of black rise, and drove whites from the Democratic Party to the Republican. But in the twenty-first century, a "Northern strategy" has unfolded, one in which conservatives of the North are following those of the South—in a movement of the rich and those identified with them, to lift off the burden of help for the underprivileged. Across the whole land, the idea is, handouts should stop. The richer around the nation will become free of the poorer. They will secede.

15

Strangers No Longer:
The Power of Promise

Normally when doing field research, a sociologist comes to a scene, then leaves it, and the scene itself remains unchanged. By my tenth visit with my core of white, middle-aged and older, Christian, married, blue- and white-collar Louisianans, I had discovered that virtually everyone I talked to embraced the same "feels-as-if" deep story. But by the end of my research there had been a profound change. With a Tea Party enthusiast, I drove to the rally at the Lakefront Airport in New Orleans of a rising Republican presidential candidate. Once back home, I checked in with my new friends and acquaintances to see how they felt about Donald J. Trump.

Looking back at my previous research, I see that the scene had been set for Trump's rise, like kindling before a match is lit. Three elements had come together. Since 1980, virtually all those I talked with felt on shaky economic ground, a fact that made them brace at the very idea of "redistribution." They also felt culturally marginalized: their views about abortion, gay marriage, gender roles, race, guns, and the Confederate flag all were held up to ridicule in the national media as backward. And they felt part of a demographic decline; "there are fewer and fewer white Christians like us," Madonna had told me. They'd begun to feel like a besieged minority. And to these feelings they added the cultural tendency—described by W.J. Cash in *The Mind of the South*, though shared in milder form outside the South—to identify "up" the social ladder with the planter, the oil magnate, and to feel detached from those further down the ladder.

All this was part of the "deep story." In that story, strangers step ahead of you in line, making you anxious, resentful, and afraid. A president allies with the line cutters, making you feel distrustful, betrayed. A person ahead of you in line insults you as an ignorant redneck, making you feel humiliated and mad. Economically, culturally, demographically, politically, you are suddenly a stranger in your own land. The whole context of Louisiana—its companies, its government, its church and media—reinforces that deep story. So this—the deep story—was in place before the match was struck.

The doors to the Lakefront Airport hangar in New Orleans open at 3:00 P.M. and the former reality television star and Republican candidate for president, Donald J. Trump, is scheduled for 6:00 P.M. and arrives some half an hour later. It is the day before the Louisiana presidential primary vote. Enthusiastic fans descend from buses that have carried them from far-flung parking lots to join those walking on foot to pass through security.

Red, white, and blue strobe lights slowly glide sideways and up, sideways and up, around the enormous space, as if to encircle the enchanted crowd with a feeling of ascendance. Milling about inside the hangar are two or three thousand fans in Trump hats, or wearing Trump shirts, holding and waving signs, "TRUMP; MAKE AMERICA GREAT AGAIN," or "SILENT MAJORITY STANDS WITH TRUMP." In front, an enormous American flag is draped against the wall.

Nearly everyone is white; apart from protestors, the only blacks I see are security guards or vendors hawking Trump T-shirts—$20 for one, $35 for two—on the lawn outside the hangar. People wear red, white, and blue caps. Men in beards and ponytails wave signs. A large, grizzled man in blue jeans and a checked shirt with long gray hair flowing down his back wanders about, an enormous American flag draped over one arm. Parents hold children on their shoulders. Another man in red and white striped pants stalks about in a tall hat. A young man wraps himself in an enormous American flag. Two men are wearing green shirts with the image of a $100 bill printed on them. Is this ironic or earnest? Or both? It is hard to tell. Throngs of two or three thousand mill about looking to the stage. Loud music is playing: the Rolling Stones' "You Can't Always Get What You Want."

The roving strobe light stops. Donald Trump climbs steps to the podium in front of the flag, turns, smiles, and waves to the excited crowd on all sides of him. A cheer breaks out: "Who Dat Say Dey Gonna Beat Dat Trump? Who Dat?" adapting a spectator chant for the New Orleans Saints football team. Trump thanks the crowd and begins by describing his ascent to power. "I started at 7 percent, and they thought I'd wipe out. Then I got 15 percent and then 25 . . ." His talk of "I" moves to "we." "We're on the rise. . . . America will be dominant, proud, rich. I am just the messenger."

People hoot and shout. They pump their signs frantically up and down, and wave them sideways.

"We're not going to let other countries rip us off!" Trump yells.

Cheers.

"We're not going to let it happen!"

Cheers.

"Our country is going to hell. But we're going to make it great again!"

Cheers.

"We're going to build a high wall and Mexico's going to pay for it!"

Cheers.

"We're going to build up our military!"

Roar.

"We're going to knock the hell out of ISIS!"

Another roar.

A wiry older man in a black suit with a red tie holds up a sign, "KKK FOR TRUMP," and flips it over to reveal, "TRUMP, DUKE FOR 2016." At first I think he is a protestor, but looking at his face more closely, surmise he's KKK. He flicks a security guard away with his arms but is finally escorted out.

Black Lives Matter protestors also appear, having marched in along with other protestors whose signs say things like: "THIS VET IS NOT 4 TRUMP"; "SMALL HANDS, SMALL HEART"; "NO TRUMP, NO KKK, NO FASCIST USA."

Seeing these, Trump orders security, pointing to a man, "Get that guy out. Get him *out*." Others in the crowd point to the dissenter. "*Out*."

"Why is this taking so long? I can't believe it's taking this long," Trump repeats, pointing to the protestor. Then, drowning out the protestors, the crowd erupts.

"U.S.A.!"

"U.S.A.!"

"U.S.A.!"

In later sites of protest, Trump himself initiates the U.S.A. chant. Dissent is one thing, the implication is, but being American is another.

After Trump's speech, the music resumes: Elton John's "Rocket Man."

Trump lingers to sign posters, hats, shirts, and boots. A small distressed boy with Trump-like moussed blond hair is handed to the candidate by proud parents to be photographed. A short woman in a red hat struggles frantically to see over the heads of taller fans, finally standing on a chair, her arms on the shoulders of a stranger who steadies her. I see a middle-aged man, arms uplifted, as in the rapture, saying to those around him and no one in particular, "To be in the *presence* of *such a* man!"

The next day, Donald Trump wins 41 percent of Louisiana's Republican primary vote, beating his evangelical rival, Ted Cruz.

In speeches to large, excited crowds, over the days to come, Trump tells his fans what he offers them. "I've been greedy. I'm a businessman . . . take, take, take. Now I'm going to be greedy for the United States" (wild cheers). He also draws a clear dividing line between Christians, to whom he promises the return of Christian public culture on one hand, and Muslims and protestors holding Black Lives Matter signs on the other. Some protestors he refers to as "bad, bad people. . . . They do nothing . . . you hear that weak voice out there? That's a protestor. . . . They aren't protestors. I call them disruptors." In other speeches Trump said, in reference to a protestor, "I'd like to punch him in the face" (February 23, 2016). "In the good old days they'd have ripped him out of that seat so fast" (February 27, 2016). "Knock the crap out of him, would you? Seriously . . . I promise you I will pay for the legal fees. I promise. I promise" (February 1, 2016). "Some are very violent. . . . Let's ruin . . . they're going to ruin . . . the rest of their lives . . . if they want to do this, let them have a big arrest mark. . . . Their lives are going to be ruined. . . . I'll press charges" (March 13, 2016).

Later Trump said of a man who tried to rush him on stage, "The man got taken down." Speculating on how he himself would have responded had the man reached him, Trump said, "I would have gone *bum, bum, bum*" (he imitates pummeling the man).

And on the issue of pollution that had so plagued the lives of the people of Louisiana? What would Donald Trump do about that? He's said of the EPA, "We're going to get rid of it in almost every form." (Cheers.)

Trump is an "emotions candidate." More than any other presidential candidate in decades, Trump focuses on eliciting and praising emotional responses from his fans rather than on detailed policy prescriptions. His speeches—evoking dominance, bravado, clarity, national pride, and personal uplift—inspire an emotional transformation. Then he *points to* that transformation. "We have passion," he told the Louisiana gathering. "We're not silent anymore; we're the loud, noisy majority." He derides his rivals in both parties for their inability to inspire enthusiasm. "They lack energy." Not only does Trump evoke emotion, he makes an object of it, presenting it back to his fans as a sign of collective success.

His supporters have been in mourning for a lost way of life. Many have become discouraged, others depressed. They yearn to feel pride but instead have felt shame. Their land no longer feels their own. Joined together with others like themselves, they now feel hopeful, joyous, elated. The man who expressed amazement, arms upheld—"to be in the presence of such a man!"—seemed in a state of rapture. As if magically lifted, *they are no longer strangers in their own land.*

"Collective effervescence," as the French sociologist Emile Durkheim called it in *The Elementary Forms of Religious Life,* is a state of emotional excitation felt by those who join with others they take to be fellow members of a moral or biological tribe. They gather to affirm their unity and, united, they feel secure and respected. While Durkheim was studying religious rites among indigenous tribes in Australia and elsewhere, much of what he observed could be applied to the rally at the Lakefront Airport, as well as many others like it. People gather around what Durkheim calls a "totem"—a symbol such as a cross or a flag. Leaders associate themselves with the totem and charismatic leaders can become totems themselves. The function of the totem is to *unify worshippers*. Seen through Durkheim's eyes, the real function of the excited gathering around Donald Trump is to unify all the white, evangelical enthusiasts who fear that those "cutting ahead in line" are about to become a terrible, strange, new America. The source of the awe and excitement isn't simply Trump himself; it is the unity of the great crowd of strangers gathered around him. If the rally itself could speak, it would say, "We are a majority!" Added to that is a potent promise—to be lifted up from bitterness, despair, depression. The "movement," as Trump has increasingly called his campaign, acts as a great antidepressant. Like other leaders promising rescue, Trump evokes a moral consciousness. But what he gives participants, emotionally speaking, is an ecstatic high.

The costumes, hats, signs, and symbols reaffirm this new sense of unity. To those who attend his rallies, the event itself symbolizes a larger rising tide. As the crowd exited the hangar, fans were saying to one another, "See how *many* of us there are." It felt to them that Trump had captured the flag.

One way of reinforcing this "high" of a united brother- and sisterhood of believers is to revile and expel members of out groups. In his speeches, Trump has spoken of "something within Islam which hates Christians," and of his intention to ban all Muslims from entering the country. He has spoken of expelling all undocumented people of Mexican origin. And only reluctantly and in truculent tones ("I repudiate, *okay?*") did he repudiate the notorious Louisiana KKK grand wizard, David Duke, thus signaling blacks as members of an out group. In nearly every rally, Trump points out a protestor, sometimes demonizing them and calling for their expulsion. (One protestor was even falsely depicted by his campaign as a member of ISIS.) Such scapegoating reinforces the joyous unity of the gathering. The act of casting out the "bad one" helps fans unite in a shared sense of being the "good ones," the majority, no longer strangers in their own land.

Emotionally speaking, something else very important was going on during the Trump rally. It is another way in which the match strikes dry kindling. Enhancing the elation at the Trump rally was a sense of release from the constrictions of politically correct speech and ideas. *"Let's get rid of PC,"* Trump calls out. He was throwing off not only a set of "politically correct" attitudes, but a set of *feeling rules*—that is, a set of ideas about the right way to feel regarding blacks, women, immigrants, gays—those alluded to in a sign held by a New Orleans woman protestor that said: "VOTE WITH YOUR HEART, NOT WITH YOUR HATE."

Those on the far right I came to know felt two things. First, they felt the deep story was true. Second, they felt that liberals were saying it was not true, and that they themselves were *not feeling the right feelings*. Blacks and women who were beneficiaries of affirmative action, immigrants, refugees, and public employees were not *really* stealing their place in line, liberals said. So *don't feel resentful*. Obama's help to these groups was not really a betrayal, liberals said. The success of those who cut ahead was not really at the expense of white men and their wives. In other words, the far right felt that the deep story was their *real* story and that there was a false PC cover-up *of* that story. They felt scorned. "People think we're not good people if we don't feel sorry for blacks and immigrants and Syrian refugees," one man told me. "But I am a good person and I *don't* feel sorry for them."

With the cover-up, as my new friends explained to me, came the need to manage the appearance of their real feelings and even, to some extent, the feelings themselves. They didn't have to do this with friends, neighbors, and family. But they realized that the rest of America did not agree. ("I know liberals want us to feel sorry for blacks. I know they think they are so idealistic and we aren't," one woman told me.) My friends on the right felt obliged to try to modify their feelings, and they didn't like having to do that; they felt under the watchful eye of the "PC police." In the realm of emotions, the right felt like they were being treated as the criminals, and the liberals had the guns.

So it was with joyous relief that many heard a Donald Trump who seemed to be wildly, omnipotently, magically free of all PC constraint. He generalized about all Muslims, all Mexicans, all women—including that all women menstruate, a fact Trump declared "disgusting." (He famously described Fox News newscaster Megyn Kelly as "bleeding from whatever.") Trump jovially imitated a disabled journalist by physically shaking his arm in imitation of palsy—all deeply derogatory actions in the eyes of Trump's detractors but liberating to those who had felt constrained to pretend sympathy. Trump allowed them both to feel like a good moral American and to feel superior to those they considered "other" or beneath them.

This giddy, validating release produced a kind of "high" that felt good. And of course people wanted to feel good. The desire to hold on to this elation became a matter of *emotional self-interest*. Many liberal analysts—myself included—have tended to focus on *economic interest*. It is a focus on this that had led me, following Thomas Frank's *What's the Matter with Kansas?*, to carry the Great Paradox like a suitcase on my journey through Louisiana. Why, I'd repeatedly asked, with so many problems, was there so much disdain for federal money to alleviate them? These were questions that spoke heavily to economic self-interest. And while economic self-interest is never entirely absent, what I discovered was the profound importance of emotional self-interest—a giddy release from the feeling of being a stranger in one's own land.

Having once experienced the elation—the "high"—of being part of a powerful, like-minded majority, released from politically correct rules of feeling, many wanted to *hold on to that elation*. To do this, they fended off challenge. They sought affirmation. One woman with whom I spent six hours talked about Trump continually, countering possible criticisms, leaving no interstitial moments when skepticism might emerge. It occurred to me that the reason for this shield of talk was to protect her elation.

When I returned for my final visit with my new friends on the right, I encountered a variety of responses to Donald Trump, about half for, half not. Janice Areno, the Team Loyalist, had become a stout Trump defender, as were others in her family and office. She remained undisturbed by the controversy he stirred, saying simply, "The country is going to hell in a handbasket and we need a strong leader to get back on track." A good number in the Sunday gatherings at Cappy and Fay's home in Longville found much to admire in Trump. For Donny McCorquodale, Trump could be the Cowboy in chief. As for Mike Schaff, the Tea Party sinkhole activist, his first choice was Texas senator Ted Cruz, despite the fact that Cruz had received a million dollars in campaign funding from oil and gas since 2011 and had described the EPA as "unbelievably abusive." For Mike the important things were small government, low taxes, guns, and the prohibition of abortion. But if Cruz lost the primary, Mike, like his wife and all but one of his six siblings, would vote for Donald Trump.

Not everyone planned to. Jackie Tabor, the Worshipper, said in an e-mail, "Trump scares me, which is too bad because he's obviously an amazing businessman, which would be pretty great considering the current state of the nation's finances." Harold and Annette Areno, the deeply committed Pentecostal couple living on Bayou d'Inde, recoiled at Trump's ridicule of a disabled man. Sharon Galicia, once president of Republican Women of Southwest Louisiana and an aspirant for a position in the state Republican Party, told me, "I think he's mean. But the plant workers I sell insurance to all think he's great." And if he becomes the Republican nominee, Trump has her reluctant vote too. One relocated refugee from Bayou Corne agreed, "I like what Trump says but I'm afraid of what he'd do," and was unsure how he would vote.

What many admired about Trump was his success as a businessman. He was a champion of private enterprise, they felt, and that fact had great appeal. During the depression of the 1930s, a number of Americans turned to a belief in socialism and communism, idealizing the central government and believing in leaders who represented their—elation-inspired—faith in it. During the current economic downturn, some on the far right have placed a parallel faith in capitalism.

Implicitly Trump promised to make men "great again" too, both fist-pounding, gun-toting guy-guys and high-flying entrepreneurs. To white, native-born, heterosexual men, he offered a solution to the dilemma they had long faced as the "left-behinds" of the 1960s and 1970s celebration o other identities. Trump was the identity politics candidate for white men. And he didn't actively oppose medical care for those in need. If he got elected, you could sign up for Trumpcare and feel manly too.

Around the world in the early twenty-first century, as the multinational companies that roam the globe become more powerful than the political states vying for their favor, it is the right wing that is on the move. Right-wing regimes—focused on national sentiment, strong central rule, and intolerance for minorities or dissent—have come to power in Russia, where President Putin has declared dissident voices as a sign of weakness and "Western influence"; in India, where the Bharatiya Janata Party (BJP) has declared India a "Hindu" nation; in Hungary, where anti-Soviet monuments are being replaced by anti-German ones; and in Poland, which is cracking down on a free press. It is becoming more vocal in France (the National Front), Germany (Alternative for Germany), and the United Kingdom (the Independence Party).

Versions of the deep story seem to have gone global.

16

"They Say There Are Beautiful Trees"

During the eight years Bobby Jindal was governor of Louisiana, he fired 30,000 state employees and furloughed many others. Social workers increased their caseloads. Child abuse victims were for the first time spending nights at government offices. Since 2007–2008, in the nation's second poorest state, Governor Jindal had cut funding for higher education by 44 percent. At the historically black Southern University, General Russel Honoré's alma mater, mold spread on building walls and rats scurried through dormitories. Most campus offices would operate two or three days a week. Given cuts to the state's judicial branch, in which eight out of ten of the accused rely on public defenders, lawyers had been laid off, and the accused languished in jails—sixty in New Orleans alone—their names on waiting lists with thousands of others, no lawyers to defend them. At the same time, the state faced a projected shortfall of $1.6 billion. Now even more cuts to the public budget were looming; Jindal's successor, Democratic governor John Bel Edwards, reluctantly announced in March of 2016 that in order to address the "historic fiscal crisis," the state would need nearly $3 billion— almost $650 per resident—just to keep up regular services during the next sixteen months. Jindal had cut corporate taxes as well as individual taxes and he had spent $1.6 billion in "incentives" to lure industry to the state, offering companies ten-year tax exemptions. Jindal had sold state-owned parking lots and farmland, potential sources of revenue. He put the state's hospitals in "business-friendly" hands for which costs proceeded to rise. He had gambled that oil prices would rise and that companies would reap taxable profits, and he had lost. The entire state of Louisiana had been placed into a sinkhole.

Nearly every Tea Party advocate I talked to had voted for Jindal twice, because he promised to enact their values. But after eight years of his governance, they hated the result. He had done what he promised—reduced taxes and cut the public sector—but he left the state in shambles. Still, Jindal already seemed forgotten. Speaking of Edwards trying to pick up the pieces, many echoed a comment by Mike Schaff: "Now we have a Democratic governor, and the first thing he does is raise taxes."

By 2016, Louisiana's financial sinkhole had exacerbated the Great Paradox. Their beloved Louisiana still ranked 49th out of 50 on general well-being and 44 percent of its state budget still came from the dreaded federal government. The state itself was a "poor me" who had to "cut in line" in front of other states—a situation worsened by Jindal's policies. But people weren't talking about Jindal or the unmoving Great Paradox. They knew it was there. They disliked it. But it wasn't on their minds. The deep story was.

"Victim" is the last word my Louisiana Tea Party friends would apply to themselves. They didn't want to be "poor me's." As Team Loyalists, Worshippers, and Cowboys, they are proud to endure the difficulties they face. But in the loss of their homes, their drinking water, and even their jobs in non-oil sectors of the economy, there is no other word for it: they are victims. Indeed, Louisianans are sacrificial lambs to the entire American industrial system. Left or right, we all happily use plastic combs, toothbrushes, cell phones, and cars, but we don't all pay for it with high pollution. As research for this book shows, red states pay for it more—partly through their own votes for easier regulation and partly through their exposure to a social terrain of politics, industry, television channels, and a pulpit that invites them to do so. In one way, people in blue states have their cake and eat it too, while many in red states have neither. Paradoxically, politicians on the right appeal to this sense of victimhood, even when policies such as those of former governor Jindal exacerbate the problem.

In the meantime, left and right need one another, just as the blue coastal and inland cities need red state energy and rich community. The rural Midwest and South need the cosmopolitan outreach to a diverse wider world. As sociologist Richard Florida notes, "Blue state knowledge economies run on red state energy. Red state energy economies, in their turn, depend on dense coastal cities and metro areas, not just as markets and sources of migrants, but for the technology and talent they supply."

In my travels, I was humbled by the complexity and height of the empathy wall. But with their teasing, good-hearted acceptance of a stranger from Berkeley, the people I met in Louisiana showed me that, in human terms, the wall can easily come down. And issue by issue, there is possibility for practical cooperation. Left and right in Congress now agree on the goal of reducing the prison population. Young conservatives are far more likely than their elders to care about the environment. The last time I saw Mike Schaff, he surprised me with another crossover issue. "Big money escalates our differences. Let's get it out of politics—both sides!"

Now seated back at my desk in California, with the names of my new friends in my address book and with hopes of continued contact, I gaze out my study window. Gray clouds are rising in the far distance to the north—the Richmond Chevron oil refinery on the east shore of the San Francisco Bay. I'm reminded that the issues raised by Bayou d'Inde are not so far away. The 1969 Union Oil spill in the waters outside Santa Barbara, California, was, at the time, the largest in the United States, and there are others elsewhere. Blue states are cleaner than red states, but the challenge is nationwide—and growing. For after decades of improvement, since 2009 rates of air, water, and land pollution have been rising again across the nation. The focus in this book on the keyhole issue—environmental pollution—is a keen reminder of the great importance to us all of what, beyond deep stories and politics, is at stake.

―――――

If I were to write a letter to a friend on the liberal left, I would say:

Why not get to know some people outside your political bubble? Set aside Ayn Rand; she's their guru, but you won't find people personally

233

as selfish as her words would lead you to expect. You'll probably meet some very fine people who will teach you volumes about strong community, grit, and resilience.

You may assume that powerful right-wing organizers—pursuing their financial interests—"hook" right-wing grassroots adherents by appealing to the *bad angels* of their nature—their greed, selfishness, racial intolerance, homophobia, and desire to get out of paying taxes that go to the unfortunate. As I saw at the Trump rally in New Orleans, some of that appeal goes on. But that appeal obscures another—to the right wing's *good angels*—their patience in waiting in line in scary economic times, their capacity for loyalty, sacrifice, and endurance—qualities of the deep story self.

Consider the possibility that in their situation, you might end up closer to their perspective.

If I were to write a letter to my Louisiana friends on the right, I might say:

Many progressive liberals aren't satisfied with the nation's political choices any more than you are. And many see themselves in some parts of your deep story. As one sixty-year-old white, female, San Francisco–based elementary school teacher put it, "I'm a liberal but, hey, I can sympathize with that part about waiting in line." I know the goals you have in mind—vital community life, full employment, the dignity of labor, freedom—but will the policies you embrace achieve those goals? You want good jobs and income, of course. You may not want to hear this, but in income and jobs, historically the Democrats have done better than the Republicans. In *Bulls, Bears, and the Ballot Box*, for example, Bob Deitrick and Lew Goldfarb note that over the last eighty years, on eleven of twelve indicators, the economy has fared better under Democratic presidents than under Republicans. (See Appendix C.) Still, differences between the parties are otherwise far from clear; Bill Clinton, a Democrat, ushered in an era of deregulation, generally favored by the right, while Richard Nixon, a Republican, initiated environmental regulations now generally favored by the left.

And Louisianans, take a look at Norway. It's a small, capitalist democracy with about the same population as Louisiana, five million people. It has a long coast and its people, like you, look to the water, boats, and fishing. Like you, Norway has oil. One difference between Louisiana and Norway, however, is their philosophy of governance and concept of freedom. Norwegians expect—and get—a great amount from their elected officials. Norway has the world's largest sovereign wealth fund—$800 billion—and the vast majority of Norwegians live upper-middle-class lives. They enjoy the very high scores in health, education, and overall well-being that come with such affluence— they enjoy freedom from need. We Americans have our own culture, but at our best we're good at drawing on good ideas from around the world. In the long run, we may be able to liberate ourselves from oil itself, but in the meantime, as an alternative to the Bobby Jindal path, it's worth a look at what could be done to "liberate" Louisiana from its paradox.

As you get to know them, you'll find progressives have their own deep story, one parallel to yours, one they feel you may misunderstand. In it, people stand around a large public square inside of which are creative science museums for kids, public art and theater programs, libraries, schools—a state-of-the-art public infrastructure available for use by all. They are fiercely proud of it. Some of them built it. Outsiders can join those standing around the square, since a lot of people who are insiders now were outsiders in the past; incorporation and acceptance of difference feel like American values represented in the Statue of Liberty. But in the liberal deep story, an alarming event occurs; marauders invade the public square, recklessly dismantle it, and selfishly steal away bricks and concrete chunks from the public buildings at its center. Seeing insult added to injury, those guarding the public square watch helplessly as those who've dismantled it construct private

McMansions with the same bricks and pieces of concrete, privatizing the public realm. That's the gist of the liberal deep story, and the right can't understand the deep pride liberals take in their creatively designed, hard-won public sphere as a powerful integrative force in American life. Ironically, you may have more in common with the left than you imagine, for *many on the left feel like strangers in their own land too.*

––––––––

Given our different deep stories, left and right are focused on different conflicts and the respective ideas of unfairness linked to them. The left looks to the private sector, the 1 percent who are in the over-class, and the 99 percent among whom are an emerging under-class. This is the flashpoint for liberals. The right looks to the public sector as a service desk for a growing class of idle "takers." Robert Reich has argued that a more essential point of conflict is in yet a third location—between main street capitalism and global capitalism, between competitive and monopoly capitalism. "The major fault line in American politics," Reich predicts, "will shift from Democrat versus Republican to anti-establishment versus establishment." The line will divide those who "see the game as rigged and those who don't."

Ironically, both sides of the political divide are struggling to address the same new and frightening face of global capitalism. In an age of extreme automation and globalization, how can the 90 percent for whom income is stagnant or falling respond? For the Tea Party, the answer is to circle the wagons around family and church, and to get on bended knee to multinational companies to lure them to you from wherever they are. This is the strategy Southern governors have used to lure textile firms from New England or car manufacturers from New Jersey and California, offering lower wages, anti-union legislation, low corporate taxes, and big financial incentives. For the liberal left, the best approach is to nurture new business through a world-class public infrastructure and excellent schools. An example is what many describe as the epicenter of a new industrial age: Silicon Valley—with Google, Twitter, Apple, and Facebook—and its environs, as well as the electric car and solar industries. The reds might be the Louisiana model, and to some degree, the blues are the California one.

Interestingly, *both* respond to the new challenge of global capitalism with a call for activist government, but activist about different things. When Bobby Jindal gave $1.6 billion of Louisiana taxpayer money as "incentives" to private corporations, he was being a government activist. Liberal politicians calling to restore our crumbling infrastructure are being a different kind of activist. And there are ideas beyond either party yet to be born.

I walk down Berkeley's Shattuck Avenue past Café Gratitude, a vegan restaurant (since closed) that once a month charged whatever customers wish to pay. I dropped in once a long while ago and wasn't thrilled with the maple coconut bacon, but felt charmed with the idea of the place. Now, I catch myself wondering: would Janice Areno see it as hippy-dippy or as a business with a touch of church? And what about those green, black, and gray recycling bins by my garage? Would Donny McCorquodale see them as regulatory "cement" or as a smart idea? Sharon Galicia, the single mother who had taken me with her as she sold medical insurance to plant workers, was planning to run for local office in the Republican Party, but her fifteen-year-old son was a fan of Democratic presidential candidate Bernie Sanders. She was giving her two children a childhood she had never received, taking them to California, Iceland, Finland, Sweden, Denmark, the UK, and Russia and inviting them to consider many universities, including U.C. Berkeley. I invited her to stay and to show her son around Berkeley—who knows what he would think? Our deep stories differ, of course, anchored as they are in biography, class, culture, and region. But I feel great admiration for the people I've met on the other side of the empathy wall. And while my vote will surely differ from theirs, I wish them well.

Farewells

With their canoe long upturned by the banks of Bayou d'Inde, near the dead cypress tree stumps that stood vigil over their ordeal, Harold and Annette

Areno opened the door to their friend, Mike Tritico. It was October 2014. They had long missed the evening racket of the frogs, the sound of jumping fish, and a sense of trust in their land and water. Mike sat with them in their living room and solemnly delivered bad news: their lawsuit over the harmful pollution of the waters had been thrown out. The Arenos had never been compensated for illness or lost value to their property, not to mention the mental anguish of living with a larger cultural amnesia about their plight. With Mike Tritico's help, Harold and twenty-one others—including Lee Sherman—had filed a class-action lawsuit in 1996 against a number of companies, including Pittsburgh Plate Glass. Now, after eighteen years, it had been dismissed for "lack of evidence." Nothing, the court said, connected pollution to deliberate harm to humans. So the Arenos were left as prisoners of their lost paradise, rememberers.

Meanwhile, like the lawsuit, talk of cleaning up Bayou d'Inde had dragged on lackadaisically for decades. At last, in February 2015 a cleanup crew had been stirred into action. The contaminated sediment from the bottom of seven hundred acres of the bayou was to be dredged and pumped into an open containment pool. Along the bottom of the bayou, workers would lay down a reinforced concrete mat and place six inches of clean sediment on top of it. "They say it really doesn't have to be a perfectly sealed clean layer," one local official remarked about the cleanup. "As long as you reduce the chemical concentrations on the surface, you're okay." But Mike Tritico saw potential danger. "What's going to happen to the large uncovered pool the toxics have been removed to? Tropical Storm Bill in June 2015 almost raised its level so high it overflowed," he told me.

On the other side of the Arenos' home, a South Korean firm has contracted with Axiall—the former Pittsburgh Plate Glass—to build a large ethane cracker and monoethylene glycol plant. At a small, public gathering of residents to air their views of the new plant Harold said, "To y'all, this is progress." But whether it is or not "depends on which side of the fence you're on." Noise from the plant was so loud one night that he rose from bed to read the Bible until 2:30 A.M., when it finally died down. In my last phone conversation with Annette, she explained that at certain times on certain days, odors from the plant keep them from stepping outside.

One day when I was thinking and writing about him, Lee Sherman, the man who held up the "I'M THE ONE WHO DUMPED IT" sign, telephoned me. Now eighty-three, Lee had been tuning up his racing cars. Leaning along one wall of his garage is that stack of thirty plastic lawn signs Lee plans to plant in local lawns for the EPA-cutting Tea Party candidate, John Fleming. "It's a little harder now I'm crippled up, but I get myself sitting down with my screwdriver and hammer," Lee reminds me. "The signs stay pretty good."

In Longville, Mike Tritico and Donny McCorquodale had been visiting Brother Cappy and Sister Fay's and arguing about Donald Trump, I heard. Mike was against, Donny was for. Cappy and Fay's cousin, Brother Michael, in training to become a minister, was considering setting up a Pentecostal church in the Marina neighborhood of San Francisco. "There are a lot of single people there, without family," Michael said. "I think I could do some good."

Madonna Massey, the lively gospel singer who took Rush Limbaugh as her "brave heart," was shocked to discover that her teenage daughter, Chapel, had downloaded "Anaconda" on her iPad—a video of the highly popular, black, scantily clad diva, Nicki Minaj doing buttock-mobilizing "twerking." When Chapel returned from school, Madonna spanked her, banished her iPad, unhinged her bedroom door, and stored it in the garage for a month. "Minaj is at the top of Billboard Top 100. *Look* at the culture we've got to protect our kids from," Madonna told me the last time I saw her.

Jackie Tabor, who had said, "Sunday is my favorite day," flew her family to Israel to see the Holy Land. "We were the youngest couple on the trip," she recounted. She has also opened a gym called "On a Roll," featuring stationary bicycling, energetic music, and healthy vegetable drinks, in downtown Lake Charles. Jackie was back to being her mother's girl, the organizer, the leader. In one promo video, some thirty people were featured cycling to rhythmic music, facing a vista of lush green countryside on a giant TV screen.

At the end of my last visit to Janice Areno, we passed her great array of colorful elephants, and as we headed out the door together, Janice adjusted the thermostat so the air conditioning would go off. "See," she said with an impish grin, "I'm a *green* person!"

At the last meeting of the Republican Women of Southwest Louisiana, a Benelli Super Black Eagle II shotgun was raffled off. Proceeds were to be used to promote "Pillows for the Troops, college scholarships, and assistance to military families." A tense split had opened between those who would vote for Donald Trump gleefully and those who would do so reluctantly. (A few didn't know what to do.)

The lifelong red-blue friends, Sally Cappel and Shirley Slack, now live in different towns—Sally in Lake Charles, Shirley in Opelousas. They talk two or three times a week by phone, and avoid mention of Donald Trump or Bernie Sanders. Sally is deeply upset about "the GMO monster Monsanto." Shirley frets about skyrocketing national debt. They recently flew together to Cleveland to see Shirley's daughter perform as a professional ballerina in the Ohio Ballet.

As for the friends living around Lake Charles, the last time I visited with them, most were still driving back and forth across the "spooky" I-10 bridge between Lake Charles and Westlake, but most did not link their distrust of the bridge to the EDC spill.

Former Bayou Corne residents had dispersed in every direction, some to Mississippi and Texas. The community of Bayou Corne was deserted—nearly. Twice a refugee from industrial accidents—one a 2003 methane leak from Dow Chemical, and one the sinkhole caused by the Texas Brine drill—an auto mechanic lives with his wife in a trailer on the ruined grounds of his old home near the sinkhole. Two couples relocated to the sprawling suburbs of Baton Rouge, over a hundred miles to the north. "We hate the area; we're just here to be near our son," one retired emergency response worker declared while her husband, a retired twelve-wheeler truck driver, nodded in agreement. Another refugee couple, now living hours away from former neighbors, spoke lovingly of good times past. Nick, a retired postal worker, shared a large color photo of himself, smiling in a white suit, cummerbund, and straw hat, among a dozen colorfully costumed neighbors—clown, Indian, cowboy, king, and queen, drinks held high, celebrating Mardi Gras in Bayou Corne before the disaster. "I used to collect driftwood along the shore of Bayou Corne, for my wife to paint and sell." He pointed to pieces of painted driftwood, "But we can't do that now."

The last time I visited Mike Schaff's abandoned home on Crawfish Stew Street in Belle Rose with him, the rose bush was dead, a few shingles had dropped from the roof, and there were signs of an attempted break-in. Thirty-eight feral cats (now called the Cajun Kitties of Bayou Corne) were wandering about. Mike and his wife had moved from their ruined home near the sinkhole into a beautiful, large fixer-upper on a canal flowing into Lake Verret. Some mailboxes along his street were shaped like open-mouthed fish. His new home was not far from where his father had long ago pulled him along as a three-year-old boy in a small plastic tub as he checked his crawfish nets. Mike was back on the water.

He had jacked up the living room floor, redone the bedroom molding, put in a new deck, and set up his airplane-building kit in the garage for later. A recent tornado had ripped the American flag from the pole extending from his garage, but it hadn't harmed the Confederate flag hanging from the porch of his next-door neighbor.

Mike's new home lay near the entrance to the spillway of the magnificent Atchafalaya Basin, an 800,000-acre National Wildlife Refuge—the largest bottomland hardwood swamp in the country—overseen, in part, by the Louisiana Department of Wildlife and Fisheries. Mike took me in his flat boat into this extraordinary basin to fish for perch. He pointed out a bald eagle on the bare branch of a tall cypress, a soaring white egret, a long-legged spoonbill watching for fish.

But, he explained, "I've gone from the frying pan to the fire. They are disposing of millions of gallons of fracking waste—the industry calls it produced water—right here in the basin. It can contain methanol, chloride, sulphates, radium. And they're importing it from Pennsylvania and other fracking sites to go into an injection well near here. Salt can corrode the casing of those wells, and it's not far from our aquifer." In 2015, the Texas state legislature effectively forbade any local bans of fracking and waste disposal—rendering them unenforceable.

I asked Mike who he was planning to back for U.S. president. His first choice was Tea Party favorite, Texas senator Ted Cruz, who had received $15 million in super PAC contribution from fracking billionaires Farris and Dan Wilks, calls fracking a "providential blessing," and adamantly opposes bans on it. Cruz has also called for gutting clean water protection, limiting citizens' access to the courts, and exempting power plants from having to comply with air standards. Like Mike, he didn't believe in man's role in climate change, and he called for cuts in research on its effects. Indeed, in the 2015 voting scores kept by the National League of Conservation Voters across twenty-five environmental issues, Ted Cruz won a score of 0 out of a possible 100 points. His lifetime score was 5. Still, Mike had to balance his powerful dislike of the federal government against his desire to protect the great majesty of the Atchafalaya Basin and prevent future waves of environmental refugees. He didn't want to vote for the menshevik or the bolshevik. So that left Ted Cruz. And if Cruz didn't win the Republican nomination? I asked. "I'll vote for Donald Trump."

On my last visit to Harold and Annette Areno at Bayou d'Inde, Harold told me he couldn't be sure, but these days maybe the water was looking a bit clearer. Then he kindly walked me across his driveway and opened my car door. I got in and opened the window on the driver's side. Now in his mid-eighties, Harold looked out at his beloved bayou, where once-majestic cypress had held out their moss shawls as if sashaying up the bayou and beyond. I recalled the photographs he'd shown me of them. Then Harold leaned on the window, and told me slowly: "I don't know when I'll see you next. Only the Angel Gabriel knows when each of our times come. But when it does, and gravity leaves our feet, and we rise up, I know I'll see you up there. And they say there are beautiful trees in Heaven."

Afterword to the Paperback Edition

The hardcover edition of this book was published in early September 2016. Two months later, something happened that the vast majority of America's pollsters, journalists, and politicians did not anticipate: Donald Trump was elected president of the United States. Over the next year I made three trips back to Louisiana to see how the people I'd come to know over the previous half decade were feeling. They were ecstatic. All those I profiled in the book and most of their kin, friends, and fellow parishioners had voted for Trump. "Mornings I have to pinch myself," Mike Schaff wrote in an e-mail a few months after the election, "to make sure it really happened."

When I visited Lake Charles in September 2017, an excited crowd of several hundred, grasping balloons and waving flags, gathered between parked pickups and a long band of orange safety tape to glimpse a presidential wave from the back window of a black limousine. President Trump was briefly stopping in Lake Charles to thank helpers on his way back from visiting victims of the devastating 2017 Houston floods. "He isn't scheduled to appear publicly," a heavyset woman told me, "but I thought there'd be a chance; he's one for surprises." High school students with life-size cutouts of Trump clicked photos of one another, and middle-aged members of the crowd, about a third African American, murmured as two rows of motorcycle escorts solemnly approached. "Honestly, I wanted Obama for a third term," one black woman explained out of the side of her mouth. "I just wanted to *see* the president."

In contrast, the mood in postelection Berkeley, California, was gloomy. Worried talk turned to Trump's impulsive leadership, his attacks on newspapers and on judges who didn't agree with him. How, folks in Berkeley asked, could the patriotic right overlook Russian meddling in an American election? How could the Christian right vote for a man who boasts of groping women? But in Louisiana, his joyous supporters were asking: how could liberals worry about Trump's sexual wandering and not remember Bill Clinton's? Why had the mainstream press turned against a man who promises to improve the national trade balance, halt illegal immigration, and restore good jobs and national pride?

Meanwhile, I myself wondered whether the politics of Louisiana might become the model Trump hoped to apply to the nation. Bobby Jindal, the Tea Party–style two-term Louisiana governor, had run on a slash-taxes and trust-all-to-the-market platform, leaving Louisiana the second-poorest state in the nation, facing the worst deficit in state history. The market price of oil had sunk and, in response, the energy and chemical company Sasol had canceled the bulk of its enormous planned expansion in Lake Charles. So some of that $1.6 billion "incentive" meant to lure Sasol to Lake Charles was being returned to the state, but some remained with Sasol to support its new ethane cracker. (That money supplied by taxpayers to the state was recycled by Sasol, so to speak, into part of its paychecks to new workers, who may have imagined their pay as purely derived from "the market" and not the "big, fat" government.) Meanwhile Trump had chosen Scott Angelle—a Louisiana official Mike Schaff blamed for the lax oversight that caused the Bayou Corne sinkhole and devastated his home and community—as the new director of the federal Bureau of Safety and Environmental Enforcement. And to head the EPA, Trump hired Scott Pruitt, a man who has since slashed its budget by a third while, in Louisiana at least, polluters often go unpunished. Both in 2012 and in 2013 the Axiall plant in Westlake exploded, in the latter incident spewing an enormous dark cloud containing hydrochloric acid, vinyl chloride monomer, and chlorine over the town and sending eighteen people to the emergency room. As of this date the state has issued no penalty. So, despite the glowing promises, was Trump's vision of great governance that of the Louisiana I describe in this book? I had my concerns.

About three-quarters of the e-mails and letters I received after the book appeared came from Trump opponents who were in various states of shock. Some despaired of developing empathy for the right; still others distrusted it—didn't I know this was a *war?*—a matter to which I'll return. Why don't conservatives reach out to *us*, a number of readers wrote, as much as we reach out to *them?* One man wrote, "Janice Areno feels she put herself through college. I did the same and was proud of it, but later I did the math, and my tuition didn't cover the *total* cost of my education; the *government* did."

About a quarter of responses came from conservatives, most of whom felt the book was a fair portrait. One man who described himself "very much to the right, perhaps the alt right" wrote, "I, along with so many other straight, white males are furious, and you articulated my/our pain better than I ever could." A few felt I had been condescending, but most thought the deep story described their reality and felt I was misguided to stand at one remove from it. In bold block letters, one man wrote, "TRUE," in pink marker on the page opposite the chapter on the deep story but told me he "nearly threw the book across the room" when he read in chapter 4 about permissive Louisiana gun laws. "My wife and I are both open-carry and I'm on the security committee at my church," he explained. His wife continued, "If I want to purchase a gun for a gift, I send my son to do it because the paperwork takes so much time." Other readers kindly offered minor corrections, which I've made to this paperback edition.

Many told me despairingly of encountering heated postelection impasses with loved ones. One liberal Lake Charles single mother, who has a master's degree in psychology and is a counselor in a drug rehabilitation clinic, was the loving daughter of parents fiercely loyal to Trump. Eyes averted, mouth squeezed tight, forcing cold laughter from the tearful center of her being, she said, "It's never been *this* bad. I'm very close to my parents, and sorry I don't live nearer to them. We visit twice a year and with Hurricane Harvey going through, my dad told me he had me 'covered by prayer' and I felt it. But after the election, I woke up and cried for an hour and a half. I *loved* Hillary and I need to protect my biracial son from Trump. I couldn't write or call my parents. I'm estranged from people I love in my church. Now I turn to clinic colleagues and school friends." Yet another man wrote, "My Texas relatives are just like the people you wrote about. They voted for Trump and we can't talk about it. I can't even go home. You sound more hopeful than I feel."

Even more than when I began my journey in 2011, the nation seemed split wide apart. So what had happened, I wanted to know, to the Louisianans in this book, and how had they come to feel about President Trump?

Sharon Galicia

On return visits to Louisiana since the election, I had dinner several times with Sharon Galicia, the young single mom and Tea Party advocate who had kindly taken me with her as she sold medical insurance to workers in plants on the outskirts of Lake Charles. Sharon recalled how she came to support Trump: "He wasn't my first choice. [Ted Cruz was.] At first I thought he was a joke. But when he talked about bringing good jobs back, building the wall against illegal immigrants, taking a businessman's eye to government, I changed to a 'yes.' "

Trump spoke to Sharon's sense that she was a stranger in her own land, a feeling echoed across the country by millions who voted for him. Those who told postelection pollsters that "things have changed so much that I often feel like a stranger in my own country" and that the "U.S. needs protecting against foreign influence" were three and a half times more likely to favor Trump than those who did not.

While in earlier conversations Sharon had said she was deeply concerned about the skyrocketing national debt, I heard nothing of that now. Foremost on her mind was the mainstream media, its opposition to Trump, its fake news. "A lot of us conservatives sometimes wish Trump would stop tweeting," she explained. "But we're also happy for social media because we feel we'd never get a president elected if we didn't have social media. You can't find a human being that's registered Republican who thinks the media gives Trump a fair shake. . . . To be honest Fox has gone in the opposite direction, but Fox hasn't gone pro-Trump as much as the mainstream media has turned against him." In other interviews, too, I noticed this shift in worry from debt to news.

Meanwhile, in a warm, lively, searching exchange, Sharon was expressing her views to her eighteen-year-old son, Bailey, who favored the Democratic primary contender Bernie Sanders. "Bailey's looking at colleges," Sharon told me one night over dinner in Lake Charles. "Would he be interested in looking at U.C. Berkeley?" I asked. Five months later, Sharon, Bailey, and his sister, Alyson, trudged up the front steps to our Berkeley home for a visit. My husband, Adam, and I showed them around the U.C. Berkeley campus and took the opportunity to arrange a right-meets-left "Living Room Conversation" as part of a project initiated by the mediation lawyer and co-founder of MoveOn.org, Joan Blades. Normally a small group of eight or ten, half Republican, half Democrat, gather first to describe their respective visions for America and then to see if they can find common ground on one specific issue of concern to both sides. Groups usually meet for six sessions—we had time for only one—and our talk about how to limit pollution left us without a clincher agreement but happy to have tried. Still, when sometime later a member of an Episcopal church in Massachusetts wrote asking me for contact with a congregation in Lake Charles, I asked Sharon if she could help. "Sure!" was the quick answer.

Mike Schaff

Mike had worked tirelessly fixing up his new house seven miles from the ruined homes of his former community around the Bayou Corne Sinkhole. But sometimes he stopped by the old place to harvest his satsuma oranges, and on his Facebook page he still listed Bayou Corne as "home." He loved boating through the labyrinthian waterways in the Atchafalaya Basin, wind in his face, but he was finding little time for that now, engrossed as he was in the care of his stepdaughter's two young sons.

Taking care of one of them, a newborn, full-time on weekdays, Mike had time to watch the news, mainly Fox, with some shopping around the "liberal" channels. "Some wonder why a person like myself who was directly affected by an environmental catastrophe would advocate getting rid of the EPA," he wrote on Facebook, explaining that, once again, he'd found an example of how the federal government betrays the taxpaying common man. He'd found an instance in Arkansas in which the federal EPA had given in to industry lawyers. The "*fricking* EPA scientists found that Georgia-Pacific had filed false pollution reports. Its [company] lawyers had sued and the *lame-assed EPA agreed.*" "Why waste countless hundreds of millions of our hard earned tax dollars," Mike fumed, "on a bunch of doughnut-bloated overpaid useless ass bureaucrats!"

So, fine, cut the EPA budget, Mike thought. But he had an alternative in mind: "I want scientists to determine the amount of toxins permissible to discharge into the environment, as they do now," he said. The feds could also use state-of-the-art monitors that report spills in real time, both to Washington and, through cell-phone apps, to fence-line residents. Then he wanted "a separate environmental enforcement agency which could temporarily shut down plants that didn't follow the rules" while getting rid of "all the excess and corrupt [federal] bureaucrats in between." He also wanted to abolish *state* environmental agencies that he saw as "in the hip pocket of industry and couldn't give a damn whether you or I developed cancer or our children are born with birth defects from the toxins that they allow to be spewed in our air and our water." When I subtracted his enormous— and understandable—distrust of Louisiana regulatory agencies, it seemed to me that Mike was advocating for an honest, well-functioning federal government.

The last time I visited him, I brought my son, David. The two were polar opposites in nearly every way. Mike was a Tea Party Republican, David a progressive Democrat. Mike voted Trump; David voted Clinton. Mike was born in the South, David in California with roots in the Northeast. Mike knew of no ancestors who fought for the South but honored those who had; David's great-great-grandfather was a Union soldier with the Seventeenth Maine. Mike was one of seven, David one of two. Mike's parents were a plumber and homemaker; David's parents were writers and professors. Mike worked in the private sector, David in the public. Mike had had a lifelong career in oil; David was a member of the California State Energy Commission, in charge of renewable energy. Mike had battled with a dysfunctional regulatory agency; David was a senior official in a large one that worked. The two had met once before and liked and respected each other. "See if you guys can agree on how to clean up our environment," I said. "I'll hold the tape recorder."

Out fishing in a late-afternoon mist, conversation between the two grew soft and slow. "We're running out of oil anyway," Mike told David, "so I'd love to rely on clean energy." They'd agreed that electricity from wind and solar had become about as cheap as that from fossil fuels, that the U.S. military was a leader in its use, and that California was on track to getting half its electricity from clean sources by 2030.

"California drills for oil like Louisiana does," David noted, "but with our better enforcement of regulations, it's cleaner."

"That's not *fair*," Mike answered.

"You're right!" David said. As with the Living Room Conversation with Sharon Galicia, big differences remained, but palpable common moral ground had grown larger. As the visit drew to an end, Mike declared, "I'd love to have solar on my roof, my boat, my motorcycle." As the two brought the boat to dock, David added, "And solar helps stop climate change too."

"Oh, *no* such thing," Mike countered. Then, adopting an avuncular tone, Mike said, "Look, David, if you want to sell solar panels to guys like me, tell them you can make them energy *independent*. Feeding clean energy back into the grid, you can make them free *entrepreneurs*. Just don't mention climate change."

Lee Sherman

Lee Sherman—who'd secretly dumped toxic waste into public waters and later showed angry fishermen the sign "I'M THE ONE WHO DUMPED IT IN THE BAYOU"—had kept in good touch with me by phone. ("You're in Berkeley near the Oakland shipyards. My dad worked in the Seattle shipyards.") Now eighty-three, he suffers from neuropathy in both legs. But that hadn't stopped him from riding in his motorized wheelchair, American flag waving from the back, bringing up the rear of a breast cancer awareness parade around a park in his hometown, DeRidder. "I let three little girls ride on it with me," he added cheerfully. In our calls, Lee shared stories of his past—his life as a 298-pound bodybuilder, as a Four Winds Cherokee dancer (he is part Native American), and as a daredevil child swimmer.

On a recent visit to Lake Charles, Lee gave me a hand-drawn map of the intricate Westlake industrial complex, including all the underground pipelines. Then he drove me by car around the area in what first seemed like confusing turns, stops, and loop-backs. Slowly I realized why; he was showing me aboveground what existed below: the mile-long pipeline that once leaked toxic ethylene dichloride—one of the largest chemical leaks in the country—softening the ground beneath that "spooky" I-10 bridge.

Almost more than anyone I knew, Lee *loved* President Trump. He watched Fox News "fourteen hours a day 'til I get sick of it and peek at CNN." He added, "The *New York Times* tells lies," although he admitted that he didn't read it. And the president, he felt, "has the right to his own opinion because it was protected by the First Amendment." Was he bothered by cuts to the EPA? I asked. "*Some.*"

On my last visit to Louisiana I drove to DeRidder to deliver a gift. Disturbed by the story of Lee's criminal release of toxic waste into public waters, but moved by his rescue of the bird that had been felled by the fumes "as if shot," a man sent me a poem he had composed about it. The bird had "clawed feet and dinosaur eyes." As Lee "places his mouth over her beak . . . her eyes disappear, appear, disappear and she makes a thin noise" until he "makes her breathe again." "I'm framing this poem," Lee told me as I left, "to hang on my living room wall."

Harold and Annette Areno

"Are you the Annette Areno in that book?" a lean, friendly man in his sixties had asked Annette when she opened the front door. The Arenos lived on the edge of Bayou d'Inde, long polluted by the toxic waste Lee secretly dumped on company orders.

"Yes, I am," Annette answered.

"Will you sign my book?"

"I didn't *write* the book," Annette clarified.

"I know, but I saw what y'all went through with the fish kills in this bayou," he said. Annette invited in a man named Ray Bowman. He was an exuberant Trump fan and retired plant operator who had, as president of the local union, represented fifteen hundred workers in six plants and whom I was later to meet at his horse farm in Ragley. "I was twenty-something, on temporary with Citgo, trying to get on permanent. My boss told me to go out in a boat and collect dead fish. They didn't tell us why but I knew."

Meanwhile, life had grown harder for the Arenos. On one side of their tidy home, white with blue shutters, lay the polluted bayou studded with lifeless cypress stumps. On the other side, across the road, Westlake Chemical was building an enormous ethane cracker plant, which would process ethane into ethylene. Through a thin barrier of trees, one could glimpse a vast clearing, piles of pipes and tanks. Although the Areno home was on a public road, a company flagman could halt traffic for hours. One did so when Lee Sherman and I drove in to visit the Arenos, though Lee whizzed defiantly past him. The Arenos had previously invited a nephew to lunch, but his car was turned back, his gumbo taken off the stove. Harold spoke with a company manager about rerouting the trucks, but to no avail.

One Sunday, I joined the Arenos for morning and evening services of the Lighthouse Tabernacle Pentecostal Church. Women in upswept hair and long floral dresses sang; wiggly children sat in patient maternal laps. Harold and Annette's devoted granddaughter, a Spanish teacher, sang in the choir. The minister warned darkly of secularists teaching *The Communist Manifesto* in schools; one had to beware of outside influences. But local community did for each other, he said. In response to the historic Houston flood, local parishioners had donated food, water, and clothing, all of which was transported by truck to a Pentecostal church in Houston that distributed aid to victims. "Blacks helping whites, whites helping blacks," the minister said proudly, parishioners murmuring approval.

Like others I talked to, Annette had criticisms of Trump ("I wish he'd think first and act second") but explained that Trump "wants to do very

good things, like build the wall, only the press and Congress won't let him."
The new construction jobs in town had attracted many Mexican workers,
they told me. "You see them in the shops, tortillas on the grocery shelves."
Echoing a comment I would hear often, she added, "The Mexicans are hard
workers; they could teach us a thing or two about work." Still, Harold, a
trained pipe fitter, speculated, "I think these companies hire unskilled Mexicans to do skilled work. The foremen train them, the company pays them
low wages, and the Mexicans send those home. We don't benefit."

Over lunch Annette reached across the table and asked, "Arlie, do you
read the Bible?" "I have read the Bible," I replied. "I think we're seeing
signs," she said, referring to the rapture. "First there was talk of moving
the capital of Israel from Tel Aviv to Jerusalem, then the floods, and maybe
nuclear war with North Korea. No one knows in advance. These could be
signs."

Janice Areno

Harold's niece Janice, the accountant with the collection of stuffed elephants on her office shelf, appeared at a dinner I hosted in Lake Charles,
just after the book came out, for those who'd helped me. She approached
with a mischievous grin and pulled open her jacket to reveal a bright red
jersey that read "ADORABLE DEPLORABLES"—a defiant counter to Hillary Clinton's description of half of Trump supporters as "a basket of deplorables." Months later, Janice sent me a duplicate jersey. (" I dare you to wear
this in *Berkeley*!" "No promises," I'd replied.)

Together with Lee, Janice was the staunchest of Trump fans. He spoke to
her impatience with the endless "line cutters" getting tax-supported handouts. If Trump was a bull in a china shop, there was a lot in that shop that
she didn't mind breaking; for example, she applauded cuts to the "overpad-
ded" EPA. "I've worked on the local planning board and know how FEMA
works. If we give a waiver to a homeowner who was supposed to raise his
barn fourteen feet, to avoid flood, and get flood insurance, and he's an inch
and a half off—and if we give him a pass, then FEMA takes it out on the

help or else says our parish [county] doesn't qualify for FEMA help. No, we're regulated to death." As for Trump's promised wall between the United States and Mexico, Janice wanted it extended to exclude way-too-liberal California, so if "Californians want to come into the U.S., they'll have to ask me." The South would remain; let California secede.

About a year after *Strangers in Their Own Land* appeared, thousands of torch-carrying white nationalists holding Confederate flags, and neo-Nazis giving the Hitler salute and shouting "Blood and soil!" and "Jews will not replace us!," held a "Unite the Right" gathering in Charlottesville, Virginia, to protest the planned removal of a statue of General Robert E. Lee. One participant drove his car into a group of counterdemonstrators, killing one woman and injuring many.

Some of the marchers were from old-guard groups like the Aryan Nation and the Ku Klux Klan (the former grand wizard David Duke among them) and some from the new alt-right and what one leader called "the new guard of white nationalism." The chief organizer, Jason Kessler, called the march a protest over the removal of Confederate symbols and "advocacy for white people." Richard Spencer, another prominent organizer, has called for a white "ethno-state" and "peaceful ethnic cleansing." President Trump publicly placed equal blame "on both sides" and later said he supported "very fine people on both sides." Former grand wizard of the KKK David Duke thanked President Trump for his support. A dark current of racism that has long run underneath the surface of American life was suddenly, nakedly, on view.

The public and the media had of course scrutinized the president's response; most noted (Fox News was a notable exception) that he had remained silent for forty-eight hours without condemning these groups by name—just the fourth time in 207 days of his presidency that Trump refrained for a full day from tweeting a message—a sign, many felt, of his reluctance to condemn them. In a *Washington Post* / ABC poll, in which people were asked, "Given what you know about it, do you approve or disapprove of Trump's response to these events [Charlottesville]?," only 28 percent approved: 6 percent of

Democrats and 62 percent of Republicans. They were asked a more pointed question as well: "In his comments on these events, do you think Trump has been putting neo-Nazis and white supremacists on equal standing with those who oppose them, or has he not being doing that?" Forty-two percent answered "yes" and 35 percent answered "no."

So were the torch-carrying white nationalists in Charlottesville rekindling a nationwide racism that had never disappeared? Yes, and not for the first time. The Ku Klux Klan was born just after the Civil War and flared up strongly in the 1920s, when its highest per capita membership was in Indiana and Oregon; half a century later, some of the fiercest white resistance to school desegregation took place in Boston.

And is white racism the overriding source of support for Donald Trump? Did it also underlie support for the Tea Party, as some have claimed? And do we all mean the same thing by the word "racism"? In this book I describe racism as a "belief in a natural hierarchy that places blacks at the bottom, and the tendency of whites to judge their own worth by distance from that bottom." Of the sixty people I interviewed, many tacitly agreed with this. Others believed, or seemed to want to believe, that there was no such hierarchy or way of judging worth, and that we live in a race-blind society. But a good number also believed that many fellow Americans do still live with the idea of such a hierarchy but that this is in no way natural or good.

When I brought up Charlottesville with my Louisiana informants, many wore troubled expressions. "Everyone should have stayed home," Annette Areno said, shaking her head. "I don't like violence." A number expressed equal horror at the left-affiliated "Antifa" (for anti-fascist). "They're like the KKK. They wear masks. They're violent. Why do they wear masks if they don't want to hurt people and not get caught?" Yet disavowing violence hardly set the matter to rest.

Most white Louisianans I spoke with were repelled by the torch-carrying KKK, and as Southern whites, they feared being tarred with the shame of it. "Because we're Southern, people think we're racist, but we're not!" one woman told me. Another posted an image of Uncle Sam turning indignantly to face a small Nazi emblem, "Not you again!" it read. At mention of the word "Nazi," Ray Bowman, the dead-fish collector who had knocked on the Arenos' door, told me when I visited him later, "Do you see that Nazi symbol on that dagger?" It was hanging on his living room wall, behind where I sat. "My uncle was a World War II GI who took that off a dead Nazi soldier. We *fought* the Nazis."

But—and here Ray and others felt stuck—they also had feelings for which they found no place in a liberal world. For one thing, they saw no special advantages to being white and were disturbed that some defined them as racists or white nationalists for feeling that way. In a September 2017 poll, 56 percent of all Americans agreed with the statement "White people benefit from advantages in society that black people do not have." But two-thirds of Republicans disagreed, including most featured in this book. (Among Democrats, 78 percent agreed whites had advantages.) Behind this partisan divide lies a strong difference in white exposure to sinking wages, unsteady work, and family disruption—paradoxically, blue-collar whites had closer encounters with some difficulties that make up the black experience.

Ray held two opinions that to him seamlessly cohered. On one hand, he condemned the Charlottesville KKK in no uncertain terms: "Those *idiots* with the flags—the American, Confederate, and Nazi flags all together— their whole white supremacist thing . . . How *stupid* can you get?" On the other hand, he also felt the white supremacists were giving the American *and* the Confederate flag "a bad rep," since the latter represented the honor he felt should be properly accorded young men who defended a Southern "homeland" against a Northern "invader." The homeland he imagined was very like that in which his own ancestors—poor white Kentucky farmers and horsemen—had grown up, and in which there were no slaves.

What I had imagined to be unitary and coherent, I discovered to be dis- aggregated into freestanding small narratives. Paradoxically, if the New York–born Trump seemed to hesitate to condemn the KKK, most of the Louisianans I spoke to did not hesitate a minute. "Oh, I wouldn't hesitate a minute to condemn the KKK," Mike Schaff told me. "The KKK are a dis- grace," Ray Bowman said, adding, "By the way, I'm from the *South*."

Yet as if an anticoagulant had been introduced into the American cultural bloodstream, smaller stories kept appearing, each suggesting an emotional tagline. There was the story of the Confederate flag as a matter of regional pride ("Don't shame us"). There was the story of "my ancestors were too poor to own slaves" ("Don't guilt-trip us"). There was the story of affirmative action whereby whites are victims ("Understand our resentment, desires, and needs"), and there was the story of moral strengths ("Black athletes who won't stand for the Pledge of Allegiance aren't as grateful to be American as we are. We are the real patriots; respect us for that"). To this was often added the more familiar premise that most blacks were not as hardworking or law-abiding as whites. What these subnarratives shared, I felt, was the absence of historical context. It was as if the people I came to know strongly disavowed any unitary premise that fit my initial definition of racism. But given that, they adopted smaller narratives that hung free, the one from the other: one man was incensed by black athletes who knelt for the pledge but had no special feelings for the Confederate flag. Another complained about a friend's son who was passed over for a place in college due to affirmative action but didn't embrace the "slavery isn't my responsibility" narrative. Disaggregated, such smaller narratives hung free, maybe to gather in some new way downstream. And to all this was the background presence of a powerful truth—life had been hard for them and it could get a lot worse.

The Louisianans I knew also thought *liberals* were way too race conscious, and that race consciousness was itself a form of racism. "Liberals are always identifying people by race," one said. "Or they're saying, 'You're a racist. I'm not a racist.'" Another said, "Look, I'm white. Why should I have to go around saying 'I'm not a racist.' I'm not racist but I am white, okay?" Ray explained further that he didn't want to be defined by that whiteness either: "I'd like you to define me by my interests and abilities and not by my race." But it was the liberals, he felt, who were always bringing up race. "When I worked at Citgo," Ray recounted, "an affirmative action officer called us in for a meeting and showed us a pie chart that reflected company goals. About half of new jobs should go to women, a quarter to African Americans, and twenty-five percent to white men. "That means my son has a lousy shot at getting a job like mine at Citgo. What's he supposed to do?" He added, "I don't think I'm a racist for saying this."

It doesn't make Ray Bowman a "racist" to care about his son's opportunities at the plant, I think, and to fear the pie chart. At the same time, the chart links race and gender with competition with white men over a small wedge of the economic pie when more powerful forces are reducing the size of that wedge itself, as I'll explain. When I returned from Louisiana and walked around the north Berkeley Hills, I began to wonder how Ray might respond to the hand-painted "Black Lives Matter" signs tucked into window frames or nailed to front doors. But since the dot-com revolution, the price of houses had risen and if you hadn't bought a place early on and didn't have a rent-controlled apartment or earn a Silicon Valley salary, it would be impossible to afford a place nowadays, which meant that nearly all the neighbors who believed in racial integration found themselves living in a largely white and Asian neighborhood. Nearly all were also highly educated and so—because of their social class—protected from the emotional draw of the deep story. Tragically and powerfully dividing many white Trump voters from Clinton or Sanders supporters were many things, among them family lore, history books, church sermons, and regional culture, but looming large, I believe, is everyone's luck of the draw—social class.

The Louisianans in this book differed from one another over the statue of Robert E. Lee. Some defended it as valuable "history." Others, like Brother Cappy, who'd presided over Sunday dinner debates between Mike Tritico and Donny McCorquodale, Vidalia onion at hand, said, "I think they should put Lee's statue in a museum where it won't offend anyone." I proposed the idea of a friend and sociology colleague, Troy Duster, of *two* statues—one of General Lee, and a matching statue of the African American abolitionist Frederick Douglass. Many, like Mike Schaff, responded with interest: "Well, why not?" Ray Bowman replied, "I don't have a problem with that." Another was dubious: "If you give in on this statue, they'll go for the next and the next. You'll never satisfy them." Considering the idea with extreme caution, Janice Areno concluded, "Well, if *they pay* for the second statue."

In Louisiana, as across the nation, the issue of race goes deep and looms large. But even among the Southern whites I came to know, economic anxieties exacerbated—and sometimes ran deeper than—purely racial ones. And cultural issues had explosive power, pro-life views primary among them. Pro-family views and a general distress at a perceived devaluation of Christianity, views shared with many blacks, also ran strong. Indeed, I was struck by the fact that in one sphere of life central to both whites and blacks in Louisiana—religion—there was a surprising degree of integration, unforced by any law. In the two largest churches whose services I attended, about one-fifth of the parishioners were African American.

Along with blacks and immigrants, women were also "line cutters," although in men's minds, women tended to divide into separate mental categories: daughters ("Be anything you want"), wives or partners ("Earn a lot but don't outshine me"), and potential rivals at work ("No pie charts, please"). Before becoming the main organizer of the Charlottesville march, the alt-right leader Jason Kessler had become enraged because a *female* job applicant whom he felt to be less qualified was given a job he sought. Trump's "good people on both sides" comment and long silence about Charlottesville, and his fury at black athletes, focus public attention on blacks and offer new leeway for extremist groups. But other things were on the minds of the people I interviewed as well. Harold and Annette Areno felt like strangers in their own land because Mexican immigrants had come to town. Others feared Muslims building local mosques that would teach sharia law. In other regions, white rural-area dwellers hotly resented white "elite" city dwellers. And Trump's election did not hinge on a new appeal to extreme racist groups. The same proportion of whites voted for Mitt Romney in 2012 as voted for Trump in 2016.

I glimpsed this complex mix of issues in the messages I received in response to *Strangers*. One young Southern man wrote, "I live in Gretna, fifteen miles outside a small one stoplight town of 2,500 in rural Virginia. I've lived here for all 23 years of my life save for the four years I spent at U of Virginia. . . . Half a mile deep in the woods behind my house is an abandoned grave of a nineteen-year-old Confederate Private. I found it one day when I was hunting. I was 19 myself at the time and standing there with a rifle in my hand I had to reckon with that. What was really the difference between me and him in that very moment except for the time in which fate placed us?" He went on to describe signs of the economic decline that surrounded him: "The furniture plant where my grandfather worked has closed down, the textile mill where my grandmother worked has been bulldozed down, the jobs outsourced overseas." He was trying to make sense of his changing world and ended by asking whether I thought he should apply to graduate school in the Sociology Department at U.C. Berkeley and perhaps whether he'd find good company there.

An older woman wrote from her farmhouse in Fairview, Kansas, "The number of dairies around here has dropped dramatically over the years. The larger dairies employ a couple of high school boys to work morning and evening; the boys go to work at 3:00 AM and after work, they stop at Cassey's for biscuits and gravy and bring them to school to eat before the tardy bell rings at 8:00 AM." In *The Politics of Resentment*, a book based on talks with people in coffee shops and diners in small-town and rural Wisconsin, Katherine Cramer describes people with strong feelings about "being looked down on" by the "big-city elites in Madison." A student—"the first in my family to go to college"—wrote from western Pennsylvania, where her father and uncles run a scrap-metal yard, operate a dirt track for car racing, and receive checks for natural gas extracted from their land: "the reason I don't have college debt." She explained that their childhoods were seared by a fear of poverty while hers was not, and this election sparked strong differences between them. So race, class, national identity, religion, region, views of gender and sexual orientation—all these joined to reinforce a sense that, outside of Louisiana, too, a precious way of life, like the nation itself, was being left behind.

Of course, the right has grown stronger outside the United States as well. In countries as varied as England, Austria, France, Hungary, Poland, Russia, India, Indonesia, Japan, even Denmark and Sweden, the politics of the right has grown. Leaders in each country differ in the losses they speak to—of farms, factories, the prevalence of a language or faith—and they also differ in what or whom to blame, though often it's immigrants. In different ways, they express a feeling of being strangers in their own land.

In the deep story, as felt by those I profile in this book, the weary worker waiting in line for the American Dream sees the federal government giving special help to people he perceives as line cutters. Some who benefit are citizens (blacks, women, public sector workers), and others are not (immigrants, refugees, recipients of American foreign aid). We can well understand the worn patience of the one waiting in line, because in truth for most middle- and lower-income Americans, the line has indeed stalled or moved back.

But what has *caused* this stall? Have blacks leapt ahead of whites in education and income? To judge by our daily exposure to images of African Americans as television news anchors, film stars, football and basketball stars, one could easily gain the impression that for a group that's only 13 percent of the population, blacks have enjoyed spectacular success, leaving whites behind, and one might assume that things like Ray Bowman's affirmative action pie chart were the cause.

But images can mislead. For over the last thirty years, *average* blacks have not gained relative to average whites in education, jobs, or wealth. Shockingly, in 2015, black freshmen were more underrepresented at the nation's top one hundred universities than they were in 1980. In 2015, 15 percent of American eighteen-year-olds were black, but at elite colleges only 6 percent of (noninternational) freshmen were black. The gap in household income has also remained about the same today as it was thirty years ago—with black households earning roughly 55 percent of that earned in white households. The 2008 financial crash also hit African Americans much harder than it hit whites. In 2004, the median wealth of white households was eleven times higher than that of blacks; in 2009 it was nineteen times higher.

In addition, of course, the history of the United States has been the history of whites cutting ahead of blacks, first of all through slavery, and later through Jim Crow laws and then through New Deal legislation and the post–World War II GI Bill, which offered help to millions of Americans with the exception of those in farm and domestic work, occupations in which blacks were overrepresented. And racial discrimination continues today. A classic 2003 study by sociologist Devah Pager compared black and white job applicants with identical job qualifications, some with and some without prison records. Blacks with no prison records, Pager discovered, received fewer callbacks (14 percent) than whites with prison records (17 percent). Meanwhile, 34 percent of whites with no prison record received callbacks.

In contrast to blacks, women have reduced the education and income gaps between themselves and men. They now earn slightly more bachelor's degrees than men do and have made moderate strides in income, shifting from 62 percent of what a man earned per hour in 1980 to 83 percent in 2016. Part of this reduced gap is due to women's higher wages, and some is due to a decline in male wages—itself largely due to a decline in the male-dominant manufacturing sector.

So if, relatively speaking, black wages have not risen, and if despite educational gains women's wages have yet to reach parity, and if between 2009 and 2014 more Mexicans left the United States than entered it, and if in a state like Louisiana there are relatively few anyway—just who *is* cutting in line?

For the most part, the real line cutters are not people one can blame or politicians can thunder against. That's because they're not people. They're robots. Nothing is changing the face of American industry faster than automation, and nowhere is that change more stark than in the cornerstone of Louisiana's industrial wealth, oil. According to a 2017 Bloomberg report, "Robots Are Taking Over Oil Rigs," Nabors Industries, the world's largest onshore driller, expects to cut the average number of workers at each oil well site from twenty to five. "To me, it's not just about automating the rig, it's about automating everything upstream of the rig," says Ahmed Hashmi, head of upstream technology for BP. Focusing on tasks and skills involved in seventy occupations, in 2013, scholars in the Department of Engineering Science at Oxford University made rough estimates of the "automatability" of each one. In oil the current vulnerability to automation is as follows:

Chemical engineers—less than 1 percent
Petroleum engineers—16 percent
Chemical technicians—57 percent
Petroleum pump system operators—71 percent
Derrick operators—80 percent
Chemical plant and system operators—85 percent
Petroleum technicians—91 percent

What's happening on oil rigs is happening to American workplaces everywhere. No sooner has Uber begun to edge out taxis than self-driving cars are expected to displace Uber drivers. Self-driving trucks are in the testing stages. Toll takers are being replaced by auto-recognition devices; grocery checkout clerks are being replaced by automated checkout systems, airline reservation clerks by automated check-in machines. And this is only the beginning. According to a McKinsey Global Institute study of two thousand work activities across eight hundred occupations, "half of today's work activities could be automated by 2055." To be sure, as old jobs go out, some new jobs appear. Still, automation as well as the squeeze big business mergers put on small business, as Robert Reich explains in *Saving Capitalism*, are very much at play.

In manufacturing, studies show, the main cause of job loss is automation. But job loss isn't the whole story. If a male worker is displaced from a well-paid job as a factory technician, he may find a new job, but it may be in the service sector—working as a home health aide or stocking shelves. Robots aren't simply displacing white men; they are bumping them down into lower-paid jobs that women and blacks have traditionally done.

Robots are profitable to business, of course, since they increase productivity and profits that don't need to be shared with workers. Andrew Puzder, former CEO of the fast-food restaurants Carl's Jr. and Hardee's, and Donald Trump's first choice for secretary of labor, explained in an interview with *Business Insider*, robots are "always polite, they always upsell, they never take a vacation, they never show up late, there's never a slip-and-fall, or an age, sex or race discrimination case." And so for millions of people, the line inching toward the American Dream has gotten slower and longer.

If automation is the big, hidden line cutter, why is it missing from our understanding of middle- and working-class resentment and from the deep story into which that resentment crystalizes? For one thing, we are invited to celebrate robots as a sign of progress, growth, greatness. They are technological marvels. They cut errors. They improve production. But whatever our politics, this leaves us at an emotional dead-end, for how can we get mad at wordless, raceless, genderless, home-made American robots cutting in line, one by one by one?

About a year after *Strangers in Their Own Land* first appeared, it was assigned as summer reading to all the entering freshmen at the Ogden Honors College of Louisiana State University in Baton Rouge, the flagship campus of the state's university system. The two dear friends—one left, one right—who'd generously helped me begin this project were both LSU graduates. I was invited to speak to these students during their first week of school. Although I had made a dozen or so trips to Louisiana to ask questions, this time I knew I would be called on for answers.

What made our encounter particularly poignant to me is that many young readers had come from the communities I had written about. The fathers had worked hard in the petrochemical plants along Cancer Alley and were conservative Republican Trump voters, while many of their bright, inquiring children were asking big questions. These students were in the very thick of all I'd struggled to understand. What could I say?

I decided to tell them how I would hope to respond to *Strangers in Their Own Land* if I were an eighteen-year-old Louisianan sitting in their seat that day. If I were interested in government, I told them, I'd want to know why U.S. surveys reflect a declining faith in government, and I'd want to check out the "best-practice" states around the world and to figure out what they're doing right. Why does Norway, another oil state, with roughly the same size population as Louisiana, have the world's largest sovereign wealth fund, $800 billion, while Louisiana, also rich in oil, remains our nation's second-poorest state and is facing its worst budget deficit?

If I were heading for a career in business, I said, I'd want to dig into the question of the relationship between industrial growth and clean environment. Must it be a trade-off? I'd investigate job prospects in clean energy and ask why West Virginia now has three times as many jobs in solar as in coal. If I were I interested in robots and jobs, I'd want to learn more about Germany, whose manufacturing sector is highly automated while maintaining high employment.

If I were interested in cleaning up the environment, I would want to research the effect of the 30 percent cuts now being enacted in the Environmental Protection Agency. Some websites that offered public access to environmental information in 2016 have now been discontinued. Will the very rates of exposure to hazardous waste (RSEI rates) used in the research I report in Appendix B remain available to the public?

If I were interested in psychology, I suggested, I would investigate why many of the oil workers I talked to reject the scientific evidence for climate change, while most CEOs of the very oil companies they work for—BP, Chevron, Shell, ConocoPhillips, Citgo, for example—affirm, in official speeches and on company websites, their companies' acknowledgment and acceptance of climate science?

If I was drawn to law, I might apply for a clerkship with the Louisiana judge who halted a state permit to drill into the bottom of Lake Peigneur. In 1980, a Texaco drilling accident sucked down two drilling platforms, eleven barges, four flatbed trucks, and a sixty-five-acre botanical garden. But in 2016, as I describe, the state issued a permit to AGL Resources, the nation's largest distributor of natural gas, to drill many more wells in the floor of that beleaguered lake. One judge stopped it. How did he do that? Why? Will he be overruled?

When I speak to audiences elsewhere in the country, I use different examples, but the spirit of what I say is the same. I suggest we address our present-day political impasse through four pillars of activism. The first is to affirm in every possible way our precious and potentially fragile system of democracy: its checks and balances, its independent judiciary, its free press. The second is to recognize that if the Democratic Party is to pose a real, viable, attractive alternative to Donald Trump, it must address the grievances, the life experiences, the sense of losing ground, of people like those in this book.

Third, those of us who identify as liberals are foolish to overlook the opportunity to get to know people who grew up in geographic regions, classes, or religious groups different from our own, and doubly foolish to thoughtlessly disparage them. My time in Louisiana made me acutely aware of the way movies and television shows sometimes ridicule the figure of the Southern redneck. I feel as uncomfortable about that now as I do about signs of racism.

Finally, to build the fourth pillar of activism I would reach across our painful partisan divide to initiate talks about race, robots, government, and more. Democrats might be surprised to discover that they are more isolated in their own political bubbles than Republicans are in theirs. According to a 2017 Pew poll, nearly half—47 percent—of Clinton supporters had no close friends who were Trump supporters, while only 31 percent of Trump supporters had no close friends who backed Clinton.

To complicate matters, after the election a few liberal pundits such as Frank Rich have come out squarely against talk across partisan lines. "Democrats need to stop trying to feel everyone's pain, and hold on to their own anger." To avoid ending up in a "softened state of unilateral disarmament," he advises, "hold on to the anger." I believe this is misguided; Rich confuses talk with surrender and empathy with weakness. Millions of voters opted for Barack Obama in 2012 and for Donald Trump in 2016. According to a Fox News poll, a quarter of Trump voters held a positive view of Bernie Sanders, and from 6 to 12 percent of Sanders fans later voted for President Trump. Some minds are open, and even in those that first seemed firmly shut, I discovered potential crossover topics—getting money out of politics, rebuilding our infrastructure, avoiding nuclear war, reducing nonviolent prison populations, limiting violent video games for children, expanding renewable energy, even compromising on town square statues.

More than seventy grassroots groups have risen across the country and I've personally participated in one of them, Living Room Conversations (https://livingroomconversations.org). On the website of the Bridge Alliance, one can find other cross-partisan groups with names such as Common Good, Better Angels, American Public Square, and AllSides. As of October 2017, the Bridge Alliance had three million supporters.

In the past, we had ways of mixing up Americans who differ by class, race, and region—lines along which we now often vote. More than four decades back, the compulsory draft offered that mix for men, and labor unions provided that for many workers, while public schools offered it to many children. Today we need to find new ways to get acquainted across our differences. A national service program could place young Americans of every race, region, and religion in a yearlong service project somewhere far from home. We could set up a nationwide high school domestic exchange program—high school seniors from the South could spend a month with families of students in the North, and the North could, in this way, go South. Coasts could go inland, the inland head to the coasts. In Gretna, Virginia; Fairview, Kansas; and Ragley, Louisiana, students could prepare by learning active listening and epistemology—how we know what we know—as well as history and civics. Students could lay solar panels on school roofs, build parks, plant gardens. Maybe I'm just dreaming. But in this dream, as students wash dishes, hammer nails, and plant seeds, they also take on the questions that so bitterly divide us. Are we drifting away from democracy? Who or what is cutting in line? How do we fairly distribute a chance at the American Dream? How can we build care for others into the very concept of it? Of course, by itself, the simple act of crossing the partisan divide will not resolve our crisis. But it could help us begin to slowly rebuild a nation in which no American—right or left—need ever feel like a stranger in our own land.

Arlie Russell Hochschild
December 2017

Acknowledgments

I owe so many thanks.

My first big thanks go to Sally Cappel. One Sunday in Berkeley when my former graduate student, Manuel Vallee, and his wife, Alise Cappel, were visiting, Manuel asked what I was researching. When I replied, "the political divide in America—I think I should get out of Berkeley, maybe go south," Alise said immediately, "My mother is a progressive, her lifelong friend is Tea Party, and you should visit *them!*" It wasn't long before an invitation arrived from Sally Cappel to visit Lake Charles, Louisiana, and my adventure began. The Cappel home became my home away from home as I began interviews around Lake Charles and elsewhere around the state on what became ten expeditions between 2011 and 2016. It was in Sally and Fred's cozy kitchen, the walls covered with vibrant oil paintings, an overflowing basket collection, a sign hung in the window that said "EAT," aromas from a pot on the large iron stove, that I first placed my tape recorder on the table and conducted four focus groups. (Appendix A describes my full research design.) Sally's Tea Party friend Shirley Slack also invited me to stay with her in Opelousas, where we browsed through her Louisiana State University yearbook and family photos, visited her church, the nursing home where her mother had stayed, and her granddaughter's school, and walked through her family graveyard. Her husband, Booty, drove us in his truck past tree-shrouded oil pumping rigs to his favorite fishing spot. This book could not have been written without Sally and Shirley and their families.

My heartfelt thanks to the Tea Party enthusiasts who allowed me into their lives. You gave me your trust, your time, and your insight, and you extended your famous Southern hospitality. Most of all, you shared with me the hope that something good could come of this. You probably won't agree with all I say in this book, but I hope you feel I've been true to your experience and perspective.

Many thanks to Susan Reed, who kindly put me in touch with a wide range of experts. I'm grateful to Peggy Frankland, author of the very fine *Women Pioneers of the Louisiana Environmental Movement*, about early kitchen-sink environmental activists, and who, along with Mike Tritico, kindly read an early draft of the manuscript. Thanks to Paul Ringo in Singer, Louisiana, for sharing his knowledge of the industrial pollution of Louisiana's rivers, especially the Sabine River. Thanks to Jimmy and Marilyn Cox, who shared their close knowledge of Louisiana state politics and their generous hospitality. Jimmy also helped me research "man camps." Thanks to Dan Schaad and Sherry Jones Miller of Aunt Ruby's Bed and Breakfast, where I stayed in Lake Charles, another home away from home. In Baton Rouge, a big thanks to Willie Fontenot, a former Louisiana assistant district attorney who, with his wife Mary, kindly hosted my son and me, and proved an extraordinary guide through Louisiana's environmental history.

I dedicate this book to six inspiring environmentalists: Willie Fontenot, Wilma Subra, Marylee Orr, Mike Tritico, Clara Baudoin, and General Russel Honoré. Thank you for all you do.

Through the images and text of their astonishing book *Petrochemical America*, Richard Misrach and Kate Orff opened my eyes—a solemnly received gift. An image from that book appears on the cover of this book.

Special thanks to Ron and Linda Alfieri. Ron made a creative and generous offer—I should watch a program he chose (Fox News's Bill O'Reilly) and he would watch one I chose (MSNBC's Rachel Maddow), and we would each take notes and later compare impressions. We did, and along the way we became good friends. Thanks also to Mari Harris Alfieri.

Other Louisianans of many political stripes greatly deepened my understanding of the right, including Wendy Aguilar, Michele Armstrong, William Baggett, John Barry, the late David Conner, Eric Cormier, Laura Cox, Janice and Bob Crador, Debra Gillory, Michael Hall, former U.S. congressman from Louisiana "Buddy" Leach, Daniel Lévesque, Father Henry Manusco, Reverend Keith Matthews, Robert McCall, Ann Polak, Deborah Ramirez, Stacey Ryan, Rachael and Eddie Windham, Carolyn Woosley, and Beth Zilbert.

Back in Berkeley, I had the help of two highly gifted research assistants. In the project's first year, Sarah Garrett scoured the literature—in sociology, psychology, political science, and history—that bore on political views. Later, Rebecca Elliott honed in on the history of industry and its impact on the environment. Both could zoom around datasets drawn from scientific and governmental sources as if on magic skates. Rebecca, now a professor at the London School of Economics, conducted the painstaking research behind Appendixes B and C and performed a highly complex analysis interrelating data from a national survey (the National Opinion Research Center's General Social Survey) with information on risk of exposure to hazardous waste (from the Environmental Protection Agency's Risk-Screening Environmental Indicators). Thanks to Bonnie Kwan, who heroically transcribed over four thousand pages of interviews, proofread much of the manuscript, and cheered me along. Also many thanks to Tyler Leeds, whose research for the afterword shows care and thought.

I'm also very grateful for the early editorial help of the highly gifted Connie Hale, who set a high standard and greatly helped me shape the narrative. Many thanks to my draft-reading friends, to Barbara Ehrenreich, who greatly inspires and ever encourages me, and who shook me back to "my Berkeley self," and to Ann Swidler, who pushed me to empathize more. A long while ago Ann was my student and I mentored her, but she has turned the tables on me and has—over many breakfasts at Saul's—very lovingly mentored me. So many thanks, Ann. Thanks also to Allison Pugh, dear friend and editor extraordinaire, who has a great gift for putting her finger on exactly the right hidden point. Thanks to Mike and Flo Hout for a very helpful read and to Mike for expertly shepherding Rebecca and me through the General Social Survey analysis mentioned above, and a great thanks to Troy Duster and Larry Rosenthal for help at every stage of this project. Many thanks to Harriet Barlow, whose deep concern about this political moment is an inspiration to many, and to Deirdre English for her continuing support and "wow" insights, and to Wayne Herkness, who advised me on details of the BP oil spill. Thanks to Chuck Collins for help understanding which public policies help big business and which help small businesses, and to Ruth Collier and Elizabeth Farnsworth for helpful conversation. I'm grateful to Gustav Wickstrom for his helpful critical feedback on an early prospectus and to Larry Rosenthal and Martin Paley for comments on an early draft. Huge thanks to Joan Cole, who remained an angel of encouragement throughout. When I most feared becoming a workaholic drudge to all my friends, Joan warmly you-hooed inside the emotional tunnel one digs in completing such projects with her loving, near daily, "So how's it going?"

My deepest gratitude goes to my longtime literary agent, Georges Borchardt, for his enormous support, his largeness of vision, and his unfailing sense of humor. Thanks also to two fantastic editors at The New Press, Ellen Adler and Jed Bickman, for wise and incisive edits. My special gratitude to Ellen for her equanimity under pressure and to Jed for sidebar theory chats; it was pure pleasure working with them both. And to Emily Albarillo for her good-humored and superb oversight of the production of the book.

More than I can say, I'm grateful for my family. My son David joined me at an environmental rally on the steps of the Louisiana state house in Baton Rouge, first spotted Mike Schaff (whom I profile in this book) at the podium, scoured a draft of the book, and offered great encouragement. Many thanks to my son Gabriel for wise meditations on politics and the human spirit, and to my nephew Ben Russell, who joined me on visits to Port Arthur, Texas, and Longville, Singer, and Lake Charles, Louisiana, and spent a day with me visiting a man living in a trailer without electricity or running water on land zoned "heavy industrial" for new development by Sasol. Many thanks to my daughter-in-law Cynthia Li, herself a gifted writer, who read a draft of the book and helped me see the text through her wondrously insightful eyes.

Finally, Adam. He twice set up at Aunt Ruby's, his own manuscript in tow. He visited with some of my new friends, attended church, explored bookstores, and caught beads thrown from a Lake Charles Mardi Gras float. He also red-penned multiple drafts, cooked, listened, wondered, lightened, encouraged, held, and shared with me the experience of writing this book as he has shared much else in the fifty years of our marriage. He is the light of my life and I so thank him for being that.

Appendix A:
The Research

This book is based on a kind of research sociologists describe as "exploratory" and "hypothesis generating." The goal of it is not to see how common or rare something is, or where one does and doesn't find it, or to study how the something comes and goes through time—although I draw on the research of others who address such questions. My goal has been to discover what that something actually is. I've long been fascinated by the emotional draw of right-wing politics; that's my "something." It took getting close and that determined my choice of method.

As with my other books based on this method—*The Second Shift: Working Families and the Revolution at Home*; *The Time Bind: When Home Becomes Work and Work Becomes Home*; *The Managed Heart: The Commercialization of Human Feeling*—I adapted my approach to the subject at hand. Decisions about sample selection, interviewing method, participant-observation profile selection, statistical analysis—all were the best ways I could think of to get close to the "something."

My first step was to conduct four focus groups, two of Tea Party supporters and two of Democrats, all composed of middle-class white women from Lake Charles, Louisiana. I then did follow-up interviews with nearly all of the conservative women and sometimes, in a method social scientists call "snowball sampling," with their husbands, parents, and neighbors. A member of one of the right-wing focus groups invited me to join the monthly luncheons of Republican Women of Southwest Louisiana, and this gave me the opportunity to talk to those around the luncheon table and do follow-up interviews. One was with the Pentecostal minister's wife whom you meet in chapter 8. She, in turn, introduced me to many members of her church, invited me to a church social, and opened a window into that community.

Following another path, I followed two rival congressional candidates on their campaign trails. The differences between their positions seemed very small to my Berkeley eyes but loomed large to many in Louisiana. At every campaign event, I tried to talk to the person next to me, who sometimes introduced me to still others. At a union hall meet-and-greet for a Tea Party candidate in Rayne, for example, a kind man took it upon himself to introduce me around a large picnic table to mainly retired white male workers: "Y'all, this lady is from California, and she's writing a book."

A Lake Charles–born environmental activist, Mike Tritico, who appears throughout this book, had many deeply conservative Tea Party, anti-environmentalist friends with whom he kept in close touch. I asked him if I could tag along as he visited with them. It was in this way that I came to attend a number of Sunday after-church luncheons at the home of Brother Cappy and Sister Fay Brantley (chapter 12) and to listen in on some of Mike's arguments with Donny McCorquodale.

Recognizing the importance of their debate for this book, I began attending public rallies on the environment. It was at such a rally that I met two people—Mike Schaff, a Tea Party advocate, and General Russel Honoré. To learn more about Honoré's capacity to talk effectively to those normally hostile to the environmentalist outlook, I followed him around for a day, listening to him speak to both businessmen and victims of extreme pollution. He also took me on a tour of the strip of oil and petrochemical plants along the Mississippi between Baton Rouge and New Orleans, known as Cancer Alley, which I describe in chapter 4.

Altogether, I talked with sixty people and accumulated over four thousand pages of transcribed interviews. Forty of these were people who embraced the principles of the Tea Party. An additional twenty helped me understand the core group; they included scientists, academics, two former members of the Louisiana legislature, ministers, a newspaper reporter, a librarian and volunteer River Watcher, two professors, a former director of the Louisiana

Department of Environmental Quality, a former assistant attorney general of Louisiana, an environmental chemist, a marine biologist, and a mayor. Eight of this latter group were black. I spent a day, for instance, with a black, male, disabled plant operator living in a trailer surrounded by land rezoned as "heavy industrial" and owned by Sasol, a large petrochemical company. His water and electricity had been cut off, and the mailman would no longer deliver his mail, but at the time I saw him, he was determined never to leave his home.

When I met my interviewees, I gave them my consent form, set up my tape recorder, and offered to turn it off any time they asked. A number of times they did, and those discussions are either reported in a way that completely separates the event from the person who told me of it, or not reported at all.

From among my forty core interviews, I chose six to profile as they most clearly and richly exemplified patterns of thinking and feeling that I'd noticed in many others among the forty. With these six people, I also did what sociologists call participant observation—visiting places of birth, churches, and burial plots, sharing meals, driving places together, attending events, and more.

Of the core group, roughly half were women and half were men. All were white and between the ages of forty and eighty-five. Their occupations placed them in the middle, lower-middle, and working class. Roughly one-third worked or had worked for oil directly (e.g., as pipefitters) or indirectly (e.g., as suppliers) and two-thirds were in lines of work unrelated to oil— teachers, secretaries, a flight attendant, and a trailer park owner, for example. Interestingly, attitudes across these groups varied very little.

Back in Berkeley, with the great help of two research assistants, both PhD candidates in the U.C. Berkeley Sociology Department, I set about studying Gallup, General Social Survey, and Pew opinion polls. I paid special attention to the degree to which my respondents seemed to reflect, exaggerate, or buck national patterns.

Midway through this research, I returned to the General Social Survey with an important new question. What was the link, I became curious to know, between an American's description of him or herself as a "strong Republican" or "strong Democrat," attitudes about regulating pollution, and actual exposure to it. For that research and finding, see Appendix B.

Finally, I explored Louisiana. I visited Angola Prison, the largest maximum security prison in the United States, and chatted with a trusty, a lifer in for murder. I attended a reenactment of a Civil War militia skirmish and talked with the reenactors. I attended the Junior Miss Black Pride Contest and interviewed the father of the winner, a petrochemical plant worker. I listened to the tour guide at the Oak Alley Plantation ("the slaves showed industry and skill"). I looked through bookstores and libraries, and walked all over Lake Charles, noticing mostly whites in the day, blacks in the evening at the public plaza by the edge of the lake. I studied tourist brochures and wedding photographs staged in plantation settings. I ate lunch at a restaurant with a white homeless man, a Republican. I even danced with a stranger at an all-day-dancing café in Breaux Bridge, where my liberal and Tea Party twosome, Sally Cappel and Shirley Slack, had mischievously taken me, to catch the Cajun spirit of *laissez les bon temps rouler.*

It helped, I think, that I was white, female, gray-haired, and writing a book about a divide that also troubled those I came to know. But what most eased my way was their great personal warmth and famous Southern hospitality, for which I remain deeply grateful.

Appendix B:
Politics and Pollution: National Discoveries from ToxMap

I had imagined, before I came, that the more polluted the place in which people live, the more alarmed they would be by that pollution and the more in favor of cleaning it up. Instead I found Louisiana to be highly polluted, and the people I talked with to be generally opposed to any more environmental regulation and, indeed, regulations in general. So was Louisiana an oddball state in this regard, or not?

According to previous research, the more polluted a state is, the more likely it is to vote red (chapter 5). So far from being an oddball state, what was true for Louisiana was true nationwide. But what went on *within* each red state? Was it, as journalist Alec MacGillis claimed in the *New York Times*, that within red states the people facing poverty, poor schools, and broken families didn't show up in political polls because they didn't vote at all and meanwhile, others living in the same state, two class levels higher, did vote as Republican? If we apply MacGillis's logic, we might expect that the people who live near polluting industry wish the polluters were regulated but don't bother to vote while Republicans, who are richer and live in cleaner places, don't think there's a problem and so reject the idea of regulating polluting industry. Maybe.

But a second possibility is more puzzling: did *the same person* both face pollution *and* vote against regulating polluters? Rebecca Elliott and I set about finding out by combining two key sets of data. One was from the General Social Survey (GSS). Run by the National Opinion Research Center at the University of Chicago, the General Social Survey is widely regarded by social scientists as one of the best datasets on social trends in the country. The survey asks people to rate their response, on a scale from "strongly agree" to "strongly disagree," to such statements as "people worry too much about progress harming the environment," "Industrial air pollution is dangerous to the environment," "The U.S. does enough to protect the environment," and "Some people think that the government in Washington is trying to do too many things that should be left to individuals and private business." We received permission from the National Opinion Research Center to analyze three thousand anonymous answers to these questions in the survey for 2010.

The second source of information was the Toxics Release Inventory of the Environmental Protection Agency. The Toxics Release Inventory (TRI) calculates various measures of exposure to toxic chemical releases and waste disposal. Based on reports from industrial and federal facilities, the most comprehensive of TRI measures are called the Risk-Screening Environmental Indicators (RSEI). For any particular zip code in the country, it gives us a measure of inhabitants' exposure based on three things—the *volume* of chemical releases, the *degree* of toxicity of those chemicals, and the *size* of the exposed population. We used risk-screening information for the matching year, 2010.

Then we interrelated information on political choice and attitudes about the environment on one hand with the actual risk of toxic releases in the county in which a person lives, on the other hand. With the help of Dr. Jon Stiles, director of U.C. Berkeley's Data Lab, and consulting with Professor Mike Hout of the Sociology Department at New York University, we used "bridging software" to do this.

Using regression analysis, we tested whether the riskiness of where one lives (RSEI score) "predicts" one's answer to various environment-related questions (from the GSS). We also reversed the analytical arrow to see if various sociodemographic and political variables predict the riskiness of the places in which a person lives. We also examined the relationship between riskiness associated with one's place of residence and one's political orientations generally.

The most interesting findings are these: as the relative riskiness of the county a person lived in *increased*, the more likely that person was to agree with the statement "People *worry too much* about human progress harming the environment." So the higher the exposure to environmental pollution, the less worried the individual was about it—and the more likely that person was to define him- or herself as a "strong Republican."

Those who identified themselves as male, high income, conservative, Republican, Christian, and "strongly religious" were also likely to believe that air and water pollution were not a danger. Further, the higher the risk within a person's county, the more likely a person was to agree with the statement that "the U.S. is doing more than enough to protect the environment." Again, curiously, the higher a person's exposure to pollution, given their residence, the *more* likely the individual was to think the United States is, in general, *overreacting* to the issue.

This is a paradox, but not one born of ignorance. For the greater the risk of exposure to pollution, the more individuals are likely to answer "agree" to the statement "Industrial air pollution is dangerous to the environment." The better off and more educated among them also expressed the idea that humankind can improve the environment. They disagreed that "it is too difficult to do anything about the environment."

In the end, red states are more polluted than blue states. And whether an individual does or doesn't vote, conservative and Republican individuals tend to brush aside the environment as an issue, and to suffer the consequences by living with higher rates of pollution. The Louisiana story is an extreme example of the politics-and-environment paradox seen across the nation.

Appendix C:
Fact-Checking Common Impressions

Often I felt that my new friends and I lived not only in different regions but in different truths. I would leave an interview wondering myself what the facts really were. So below I offer statements that I frequently heard, as well as the facts, as researched by Rebecca Elliott, based on the most recently available data, the sources of which are found in the endnotes.

"The government spends a lot of money on safety net programs."

About 10 percent of the federal budget in 2015 was aimed at keeping some 38 million low- and moderate-income working families out of poverty. Such funding includes unemployment insurance and Supplemental Security Income for the elderly or disabled poor. It also includes SNAP (food stamps), school meals, low-income housing assistance, child care assistance, help paying home energy bills, and aid for abused and neglected children. In 2014, the poverty rate was 15 percent; without safety net programs, experts estimate the rate would have risen to 27 percent.

"Welfare rolls are up, and people on welfare don't work."

Since President Bill Clinton declared "the end of welfare as we know it" in 1996, Aid for Families with Dependent Children (AFDC) ended and Temporary Assistance for Needy Families (TANF, with work requirements and time limits) began. TANF—assistance to the nation's poorest families with children—is now 20 percent below its 1996 levels in thirty-five states and the District of Columbia. But since the Great Recession of 2008, the number of Americans who receive food stamps (Supplemental Nutrition Assistance Program, SNAP) has risen above 1995 levels, although that number peaked in 2013 and has fallen steeply since then. Medicaid expenditures have also risen but, according to a Kaiser Family Foundation study, they are projected to fall to 1999 levels by 2016.

Most government aid recipients are children or the elderly. Of Medicaid recipients in 2013, for example, 51 percent were children under age eighteen and 5 percent were senior citizens over age sixty-five. As for those between the ages of eighteen and sixty-four on all forms of means-tested aid—i.e., "welfare"—based on 2010–2012 data, most work. Of Medicaid or Children's Health Insurance Program recipients—by far the largest recipient list— 61 percent work. Thirty-six percent of food stamp recipients and 32 percent of TANF families work. All Earned Income Tax Credit recipients work, but recipients work at jobs that are poorly paid and for which full-time work is unavailable. To turn it around, in 2013, among fast-food workers, 52 percent relied on some form of welfare to supplement low wages paid for full-time work. Among childcare workers, 46 percent relied on welfare, and among homecare workers, 48 percent did so. In such instances, public taxpayers can be said to make up for low wages offered by some companies—a form, some argue, of "corporate welfare."

"People on welfare depend entirely on money from us taxpayers to live."

For the poorest 20 percent of Americans, only 37 percent of their total income in 2011 came from the government; the rest was payment for work.

"Everyone who's poor gets a handout."

Not all poor people get government help. According to the U.S. Census Bureau's Survey of Income and Program Participation for 2012 (latest available), among families in poverty, 26.2 percent did not participate in any of the major means-tested benefit programs (i.e., Medicaid, SNAP, TANF/ GA, Housing Assistance, or SSI). States also differ, one from the other. In Vermont there are seventy-eight TANF recipients for every hundred poor persons. In Louisiana, the ratio is four TANF recipients to every one hundred poor people. And, more than one may imagine, the government is helping those at the top. By one estimate, half of all tax benefits go to the richest 20 percent of Americans.

"Black women have a lot more children than white women."

In the United States in recent years, the fertility rates for white and black women have almost converged. In 2013, the total fertility rate for black women was 1.88 children over the course of a lifetime; for white women it was 1.75.

"A lot of people—maybe 40 percent—work for the federal and state government."

According to the Bureau of Labor Statistics, at the end of 2014, 1.9 percent of the 143 million American non-farm workers were employed in the civilian sector of the federal government. An additional 1 percent were in the enlisted military. About 3.5 percent of workers work for state government, including school and hospital workers. In addition, 9.8 percent of workers—including public school teachers—work for local government. In 2014, 826,848 people—or 0.58 percent of all Americans—served in the military reserves. So adding together all military and civilian workers at the federal, state, and local levels, in 2014, less than 17 percent of Americans worked for the government.

"Public sector workers are way overpaid."

Using the Annual Social and Economic Supplement of the Current Population Survey for 2006 and 2007, and comparing public with private sector workers of similar education, experience, sex, race, ethnicity, marital status, full-time/part-time status, number of hours worked, and other variables, researchers reported that *private sector* workers earn 12 percent *more* than their public sector counterparts.

Women with advanced degrees earn 21 percent less than comparable men in the private sector but only 12 percent less in the public sector. So while women are underpaid in both sectors, they are less underpaid in the public sector. The same thing is true for blacks: at every level of education, blacks in the public sector earn less than whites—but not *as much* less as they do in the private sector. In the public sector they earn 2 percent less than whites; in the private sector, 13 percent less.

However, when we add salaries, benefits, and pensions, public sector workers more than catch up. For example, according to a 2017 study by the Congressional Budget Office, federal employees earned relatively more, a gap driven in large part by better benefits. The less educated the worker, the wider the private–public sector gap, again because private sector workers are less likely to receive pensions, have shorter job tenure, and so benefit less from promotion-related raises. Pay scales vary by municipality and state and again, the federal government employs only about 1.5 percent of the U.S. workforce.

"The more environmental regulations you have, the fewer jobs."

Nearly all the Tea Party sympathizers I interviewed referred to a trade-off between jobs and environmental protection. The tougher the environmental regulations, the logic goes, the higher the costs to firms, who pass that cost on by raising the price of their goods, thereby reducing sales and employment.

But does that either-or logic check out? Actually, it does not. A 1993 study that compared states' ratings on strictness of environmental protection with indicators of economic health (overall growth, employment growth, construction growth) over twenty years found that stronger environmental standards have not limited the relative pace of economic growth. In a 2001 study of new air-quality regulations for manufacturing plants in the Los Angeles area, researchers reported no evidence that local air-quality regulation, among the strictest in the nation, substantially reduced employment. A 2002 study also analyzed the impact of environmental regulations on four industries that generate significant pollution—and might therefore be expected to suffer losses from the effects of environmental regulation. In two of the four industries researchers studied (plastics and petroleum), the net employment impact of the environmental regulations was small but positive, while in the other two industries (pulp and paper, and iron and steel) there was no statistically significant impact. Finally, a 2008 study found that investments in environmental protection create some jobs and displace others, but that the net effect on employment is positive. In fact, environmental protection is itself a major sales-generating, job-creating industry. In a comparison of Florida, Michigan, Minnesota, North Carolina, Ohio, and Wisconsin, two researchers reported that stricter environmental policies did not inhibit job growth.

Do excessive demands imposed by environmental regulatory agencies lead to massive layoffs? According to the Mass Layoff Statistics kept by the Bureau of Labor Statistics, 0.1 percent of all layoffs were "environment and safety-related" from 1987 to 1990. The most recent data, from 2012, covering 6,500 private, non-farm layoff events, show that forty-five events, or 0.69 percent of the total layoffs, were "disaster or safety" related, including events attributed to "hazardous work environment" or "natural disaster." Only eighteen events, or 0.28 percent of the total, were attributed to "government regulations/intervention."

"Economic incentives and more relaxed regulations are needed to attract oil and gas business that could and would go elsewhere."

In 2004, researchers investigated the effects of local fiscal policy on the location decisions of 3,763 establishments that began operations in Maine between 1993 and 1995, and found that businesses favor municipalities that spend high amounts on public goods and services, even when these expenditures are financed by an increase in local taxes. This suggests that a local fiscal policy of reduced government spending to balance a tax cut may attract fewer new businesses than a policy featuring additional spending and higher taxes. There is also recent evidence that suggests, whether or not they "work" to attract business, governments that rely on incentives may face negative outcomes. A 2010 study, based on an analysis of national surveys of 700 to 1,000 local governments from 1994, 1999, and 2004 that tracked the use of business incentives over time, found that governments that rely most heavily on incentives may face more intergovernmental competition, stagnating or declining economies, and lower tax bases. For such governments, business incentives may contribute to a cycle of destructive competition.

"State subsidies to industry help increase the number of jobs."

An eight-part 2014 investigative special report in *The Advocate*, Louisiana's largest daily newspaper, was entitled "Giving Away Louisiana." If Louisiana gives away roughly $1.1 billion per year in taxpayer money to corporations as "incentives," the team of journalists wanted to know, are citizens getting their money's worth back in jobs? Their answer was "no."

The Louisiana taxpayer can pay enormous amounts for each job industry brings in. As Gordon Russell writes, "When Valero announced an expansion of its Norco operations, creating 43 new jobs, Louisiana promised to cover $10,000,000 of the cost, or nearly a quarter of a million dollars per job." When jobs do come to Louisiana, it's also not clear that they are in response to subsidies. In 2013, Louisiana paid $240,000,000 in tax exemptions to fracking companies, but Russell notes, "There is little evidence the tax break stimulates drilling . . ." Drilling goes up and down with the availability and price of oil and gas, he says, not with changing amounts of government subsidies. State subsidies to corporations have also been growing faster than the Louisiana state economy.

Good Jobs First, a watchdog group that researches the link between government subsidies to corporations and jobs, notes that the fifty states it has surveyed vary in their degree of disclosure. But with that disclaimer, it reports that, on a per-capita basis, Louisiana gives away more taxpayer money than any other state in the nation.

"Oil stimulates the rest of the economy."

Does the money oil generates stay in Louisiana, or does it end up leaving the state in the form of executive pay and returns to out-of-state shareholders? To answer this question, we compared Louisiana's gross state product (GSP) to its total personal income (TPI). The more money that "leaks" out of the state, the larger the difference between GSP and TPI. In other words, if the sum of all personal income is higher than the GSP, it must be going somewhere else because it doesn't add to the gross state product. Based on Bureau of Economic Analysis data, adjusted to 2012 dollars, we provide a measure of "leakage" as a percent of income from 1997 to 2012. For most years, leakage out of Louisiana is between 20 and 35 percent. (Leakage also varied from year to year; low in 2003 and high in 2005, for example.) Local businesses tend not to leak their profits away to other states, while large, multinational businesses with operations and headquarters elsewhere do.

"The economy always does better under a Republican president."

For the years 1949–2009, unemployment has been lower and gross domestic product has been higher under Democratic presidents. Political scientist Larry Bartels has also shown that inequality has increased greatly under Republican presidents and decreased slightly under Democrats. Recently, economists at Princeton confirmed that the U.S. economy has grown faster under Democratic presidents, who have also produced more jobs, lowered the unemployment rate, generated higher corporate profits and investments, and seen higher stock market returns. They attribute this, however, to the timing of oil shocks and when major technologies debuted that had positive effects on the economy (e.g., the Internet under Clinton)—in other words, some of the correlation is due to factors outside a president's control. Republican presidents have also added far more to federal debt levels than Democrats have, as a percent of GDP; since 1945, Reagan has added the most, with an almost 60 percent increase in federal debt to GDP. Presidents Truman, Kennedy, Johnson, Carter, and Clinton all managed to reduce debt as a percentage of GDP.

Endnotes

These notes guide the reader to the sources from which I drew information presented in the text. To check a source, note the page number in the text and locate the matching number on the left hand side of the page in the endnotes. Corresponding to the endnote page number, you will see an italicized phrase or sentence matching that in the text. Following the phrase is the reference—to a book or article to be found in print or online. Some notes include further information or analysis, and further reading is suggested in the bibliography.

1: Traveling to the Heart

5 *to cross the empathy wall* Progressives and Tea Party advocates have different tacit "empathy rules," as I call them. People of the right tend to empathize with the rich; those of the left, with the poor worker (Donald Trump and Bernie Sanders being favorites). During the summer of 2015, I found the Facebook pages of my right-wing interviewees to be filled with positive stories of white police officers, and those of my Bay Area friends to be discussing the Black Lives Matter movement. Each side has its own empathy map. See "Empathy Maps" in my book, *So How's the Family? and Other Essays* (Berkeley and Los Angeles: University of California Press, 2012 [1983]).

6 *33 percent of Democrats and 40 percent of Republicans answered "yes"* Shanto Iyengar and Sean Westwood, "Fear and Loathing Across Party Lines: New Evidence on Group Polarization," *American Journal of Political Science* 59, no. 3 (2014): 45; Shanto Iyengar, Gaurav Sood, and Yphtach Lelkes, "Affect, Not Ideology: A Social Identity Perspective on Polarization," *Public Opinion Quarterly* 76, no. 3: 405–31.

6 partyism, *as some call it, now beats race* Cass R. Sunstein, "'Partyism' Now Trumps Racism," *BloombergView*, September 22, 2014, http://www.bloom bergview.com/articles/2014-09-22/partyism-now-trumps-racism; Jonathan Chait, "Confessions of a 'Partyist': Yes, I Judge Your Politics," *New York Magazine*, October 30, 2014, http://nymag.com/daily/intelligencer/2014/10 /im-a-partyist-and-yes-i-judge-your-politics.html. One reason for the split is that as Democrats and Republicans become more internally consistent, those with non-straight-ticket viewpoints have become Independents.

6 *to live near others who share their views* Bill Bishop and Robert G. Cushing, *The Big Sort: Why the Clustering of Like-Minded America Is Tearing Us Apart* (New York: Houghton Mifflin Company, 2008).

6 *According to a 2014 Pew study* Charles Babington, "A Polarized America Lives as It Votes," Pew Research Center, summer 2014, http://magazine.pewtrusts .org/en/archive/summer-2014/a-polarized-america-lives-as-it-votes.

7 *some 20 percent of Americans* Christopher S. Parker and Matt Barreto, *Change They Can't Believe In: The Tea Party and Reactionary Politics in America* (Princeton, NJ: Princeton University Press, 2013), 14. Surveys find between 18 and 30 percent of Americans sympathize with the Tea Party. Steve Coll, "Dangerous Gamesmanship," *New Yorker*, April 27, 2015.

7 *politics is the single biggest factor determining views on climate change* "Not All Republicans Think Alike About Global Warming," Yale Project on Climate Change Communication, http://environment.yale.edu/climate-com munication/article/not-all-republicans-think-alike-about-global-warm ing. Also see "Three out of Four Believe Climate Change Is Occurring: Views of Key Energy Issues Are Shaped by Partisan Politics," *University of Texas News*, October 20, 2015, http://news.utexas.edu/2015/10/20/views -of-key-energy-issues-are-shaped-by-partisan-politics; Sheril Kirshenbaum, "Political Ideology Continues to Be the Single Greatest Determinant of Americans' Views on Climate Change," http://news.utexas.edu/2015/10/20 /views-of-key-energy-issues-are-shaped-by-partisan-politics.

7 *"strengthening the unemployment insurance system"* Amanda Terkel, "GOP Platform in Years Past Supported Equal Rights, Higher Wages, Funding for the Arts," *Huffington Post*, September 24, 2012, http://www.huffingtonpost .com/2012/09/04/gop-platform_n_1852733.html; Christina Wolbrecht, *The Politics of Women's Rights: Parties, Positions, and Change* (Princeton, NJ: Princeton University Press, 2000).

7 *Under Dwight Eisenhower, top earners were taxed at 91 percent* Joshua Gillin, "Income Tax Rates Were 90 Percent Under Eisenhower, Sanders Says," *PolitiFact*, November 15, 2015, http://www.politifact.com/truth -o-meter/statements/2015/nov/15/bernie-s/income-tax-rates-were-90 -percent-under-eisenhower-.

7 *fifty-eight House Republicans voted to abolish the Internal Revenue Service* "South Dakota House: Abolish U.S. Department of Education," Tea Party.org, January 29, 2015, http://www.teaparty.org/south-dakota-house -abolish-u-s-dept-education-80153; Pete Kasperowicz, "Who Wants to Abolish the IRS? So Far, 58 House Republicans," *The Blaze* (accessed

August 16, 2015), http://www.theblaze.com/blog/2015/01/07/who-wants
-to-abolish-the-irs-so-far-58-house-republicans.

7 *Some Republican congressional candidates call for abolishing all public schools*
Nick Bauman, "Tea Party Frontrunner: Abolish Public Schools," *Mother
Jones*, October 13, 2010.

8 *This would include forests, wildlife refuges, and wilderness areas* Will Rogers,
"Our Land, Up for Grabs," *New York Times*, Editorial, April 2, 2015 (accessed August 16, 2015), http://www.nytimes.com/2015/04/02/opinion/our
-land-up-for-grabs.html.

8 *called for the end of the Environmental Protection Agency* Jaime Fuller,
"Environmental Policy Is Partisan. It Wasn't Always." *Washington Post*,
June 2, 2014. https://www.washingtonpost.com/news/the-fix/wp/2014/06
/02/support-for-the-clean-air-act-has-changed-a-lot-since-1970.

8 *a majority of Americans turned away from it* Clem Brooks and Jeff Manza,
"A Broken Public? Americans' Responses to the Great Recession," *American
Sociological Review* 78, no. 5 (2013): 727–48.

8 *is the same as that between the United States and Nicaragua* The average
U.S. life expectancy is 78.9, and Nicaragua's is 74. The nine states with
the lowest life expectancies, all red, range from 75.0 (Mississippi) to 76.3
(Tennessee). The states with the highest life expectancies, all blue, range
from 80.3 (New Jersey) to 81.3 (Hawaii). World Health Organization,
Global Health Observatory Data Repository [*2013 data*] (accessed August 12,
2015), http://apps.who.int/gho/data/node.main.688. Also see Social Science Research Council, *The Measure of America: HD Index and Supplemental Indicators by State*, 2013–2014 Dataset (Brooklyn, NY: Measure
of America, 2014); Annie E. Casey Foundation, *2009 Kids Count Data
Book: State Profiles of Child Well-Being*, http://www.aecf.org/resources
/the-2009-kids-count-data-book. Also see Gallup-Healthways, "State of
American Well-Being," 2014, which ranks Louisiana 40th in overall well-
being.

9 *in overall health ranked last* United Health Foundation, *America's Health
Rankings, 2015 Annual Report*, 8, http://www.americashealthrankings.org.

9 *whites in Louisiana are worse off* Social Science Research Council, *The Measure of America: American Human Development Report 2008–2009* (Brooklyn, NY: Measure of America, 2009).

9 *$2,400 is given by the federal government* After Mississippi, Louisiana is the
state most dependent on federal dollars. David Freddoso, "State Government Dependence on Federal Funding Growing at Alarming Rate," *State

Budget Solutions, April 14, 2015, http://www.statebudgetsolutions.org/pub
lications/detail/state-government-dependence-on-federal-funding-growing
-at-alarming-rate.

10 *try to scale the empathy wall* Katherine Kramer Walsh, "Putting Inequality
in Its Place: Rural Consciousness and the Power of Perspective," *American
Political Science Review* 106, no. 3 (2012): 517–32.

10 *"Who Turned My Blue State Red?"* Alec MacGillis, "Who Turned My Blue
State Red?," *New York Times*, November 20, 2015.

11–12 *among college-educated whites, the increase was higher still* Larry Bartels, "What's the Matter with *What's the Matter with Kansas?*" *Quarterly
Journal of Political Science* 1 (2006): 211. In the nation as a whole, between
1972 and 2014 more whites were calling themselves Independent. But of
white American voters who identified with either party between these years,
Democrats plummeted from 41 percent to 24, and Republicans inched from
24 percent to 27. In the South, Democrats fell lower and Republicans rose
higher. If we focus on how people *identify* themselves, not on how they *vote*,
the numbers point in the same direction. According to the General Social
Survey, from 1972 to 2014, among Southern whites, Republicans rose from
19 percent (in 1972) to 34 percent (in 2014). In the country as a whole, they
rose from 24 percent (in 1972) to 27 percent (in 2014).

Florida, Georgia, South and North Carolina, and Virginia have also produced more than their share of 2015 presidential aspirants—Ted Cruz and
Rick Perry (both from Texas), Jeb Bush and Marco Rubio (both from Florida), Lindsay Graham (South Carolina), Mike Huckabee (Arkansas), and
Bobby Jindal (Louisiana).

12 *the share of whites identifying as Democrats* Tom W. Smith, Peter Mars-
den, Michael Hout, and Jibum Kim, *General Social Surveys*, 1972–2014
(machine-readable data file), sponsored by National Science Foundation,
NORC ed, Chicago: NORC at the University of Chicago [producer]; Storrs,
CT: The Roper Center for Public Opinion Research, University of Connecticut [distributor], 2015.

12 *I would need to get to know the white South* Among whites with a high school
degree or less, 36 percent voted Republican, 26 percent Democrat; among
whites with a bachelor's degree, it was about the same. Only among post-
graduate whites did the ratio favor the Democratic Party. A.D. Floser, "A Closer
Look at the Parties in 2012," Pew Research Center, August 23, 2012, http://
www.people-press.org/2012/08/23/a-closer-look-at-the-parties-in-2012.

12 *it was 14 percent—a smaller proportion than in the South as a whole* Henry
Wolff, "Race and the 2012 Election," *American Renaissance*, November 9,

2012, http://www.amren.com/features/2012/11/race-and-the-2012-election. In 2012, only one state, Mississippi, had a smaller proportion of white voters for Obama—10 percent.

12 *half of Louisianans support the Tea Party* According to a Clarus poll of 602 likely Louisiana voters, 46 percent supported the Tea Party. Associated Press, "Obama Approval Ratings Low in Louisiana," *New Orleans City Business*, October 13, 2011, http://neworleanscitybusiness.com/blog/2011/10/13 /obama-approval-ratings-low-in-louisiana.

12 *the highest proportion of state representatives in the U.S. House of Representative's Tea Party Caucus* The two candidates were among seven—now reduced to six—members of the U.S. House of Representatives from Louisiana, three of whom—John Fleming, Steve Scalise, and Jeff Landry—were members of the House Tea Party Caucus in 2014.

13 *to create an "astro-turf grassroots following"* Isaac William Martin, *Rich People's Movements: Grassroots Campaigns to Untax the One Percent* (New York: Oxford University Press, 2013).

13 *populist anti-government rage was orchestrated by corporate strategy* Taki Oldham, *The Billionaires' Tea Party*, https://www.youtube.com/watch?v=-z BOQL5lZuU.

13 *The* New Yorker *staff writer Jane Mayer* Jane Mayer, *Dark Money: The Hidden History of the Billionaires Behind the Rise of the Radical Right* (New York: Random House, 2016). According to the Center for Responsive Politics, in the 2014 election the oil and gas industry gave 87 percent of its political contributions—and coal companies, 96 percent—to Republican candidates. Alternative energy went 56 percent for Democrats. Paul Krugman, "Enemies of the Sun," *New York Times*, Op-Ed, October 5, 2015. Also see Miriam Diemer, "Energy and Natural Resources: Industry Influence in the Climate Change Debate," OpenSecrets.org, last updated January 29, 2015, https://www.opensecrets.org/news/issues/energy.

13 *to direct $889,000,000 to help right-wing candidates and causes in 2016 alone* Fredreka Schouten, "Koch Brothers Set $889 Million Budget for 2016," *USA Today*, January 27, 2015, http://www.usatoday.com/story/news /politics/2015/01/26/koch-brothers-network-announces-889-million-budget -for-next-two-years/22363809. In *Invisible Hands*, Kim Phillips-Fein traces contributions from David and Charles Koch and Rupert Murdoch to the Tea Party. See Kim Phillips-Fein, *Invisible Hands: The Businessmen's Crusade Against the New Deal* (New York: W.W. Norton & Company, 2007).

13 *"from idea creation to policy development to education to grassroots organizations to lobbying to litigation to political action"* Jane Mayer, "Covert

Operations," *New Yorker*, August 30, 2010. Also see Kenneth P. Vogel, *Big Money: 2.5 Billion Dollars, One Suspicious Vehicle, and a Pimp—on the Trail of the Ultra-Rich Hijacking American Politics* (New York: Public Affairs/Perseus Group, 2014); Daniel Schulman, *Sons of Wichita: How the Koch Brothers Became America's Most Powerful and Private Dynasty* (New York: Grand Central Publishing, 2015).

13 *$138 million to Republican candidates and $20 million to Democrats* Nicholas Confessore, Sarah Cohen, and Karen Yourish, "Buying Power," *New York Times*, October 10, 2015. Of course rich donors give to Democratic causes too, but, according to a *Forbes* survey of the fifty richest families, twenty-eight donate mainly to Republicans and only seven mainly to Democrats. Katia Savchuck, "Are America's Richest Families Republican or Democrat?" *Forbes*, July 9, 2014.

14 *"wealth is more concentrated than ever before in our lifetimes"* Thomas Frank, *What's the Matter with Kansas? How Conservatives Won the Heart of America* (New York: Metropolitan Press, 2004), 7.

15 *linked as that is to the defeat, 150 years ago, of the South by the North* Colin Woodard, *American Nations: A History of the Eleven Rival Regional Cultures of North America* (New York: Penguin Books, 2011).

15 *Resistance to federal taxation, the historian Robin Einhorn notes, also originated in the South* Robin L. Einhorn, *American Taxation, American Slavery* (Chicago: University of Chicago Press, 2008).

15 *white, middle to low income, older, married, Christian* Brian Montopoli, "Tea Party Supporters: Who They Are and What They Believe," CBS News, December 14, 2012, CBS/*New York Times* poll of 1,580 respondents.

15 *the Great Recession of 2008 and government efforts to forestall it, the presidency of Barack Obama, and Fox News* In an excellent and early overview of the Tea Party, Theda Skocpol and Vanessa Williamson (*The Tea Party and the Remaking of Republican Conservatism* [New York: Oxford University Press, 2012]) speak of making an "empathetic leap" (47), though the character of their interviews and their number is not stated. Their central focus is on the relationship between a mobilized grassroots group and the larger lay of the political land. They also focus on the confluence of factors that brought the Tea Party into being—the appearance of President Barack Obama, Fox News, and the financial scare of 2008. Other scholars have focused on the historical roots of the movement, as well as its being a reaction to the Occupy Wall Street movement. See Lawrence Rosenthal and Christine Trost (eds.), *Steep: The Precipitous Rise of the Tea Party* (Berkeley: University of California Press, 2012).

15 *a full understanding of emotion in politics* In *The Tea Party and the Remaking of Republican Conservatism*, Theda Skocpol and Vanessa Williamson persuasively argue that since President Obama became president, America has seen a new confluence of three long-standing conservative trends. Older, white, middle-class conservatives felt unrepresented by Obama and sought an alternative to him. They combined forces with free-market advocacy groups—primarily Americans for Prosperity and FreedomWorks—and Fox News, they argue, spread their word. In *Steep: The Precipitous Rise of the Tea Party*, Lawrence Rosenthal and Christine Trost (eds.) put the movement in a wider historical perspective as well.

16 *what I call a "deep story"* I was inspired by *Metaphors We Live By*, by U.C. Berkeley linguists George Lakoff and Mark Johnson (Chicago: University of Chicago Press, 2003). Metaphors, they argue, shape how we think and act. They also shape how we feel, I think. If the government is "big brother"— bossy, overbearing, intimidating—then it inspires fear and resentment. If the state is a giant "nanny," then we are made to feel like big babies, and so we feel unwelcome shame. Metaphors are not a form of extra decoration on ordinary speech; as the authors rightly point out, they are embedded in ordinary speech and so continually guide our feeling. For Lakoff and Johnson, metaphors come to us as proposals for how to see life, one by one, each static. In chapter 9 of this book, I extended a metaphor of waiting in line into a story, then I checked back with my right-wing friends to see if they felt as if it was true—and they did.

16 *Three percent were foreign-born* A third of those I interviewed were the progeny of Cajun settlers whose French Catholic ancestors had fled France in the 1600s and settled in Acadia, a colony of New France in what is today Nova Scotia, Canada. Over time, they became prosperous farmers and traders. Then, in the 1740s the British required them to pledge allegiance and pay taxes to the British king. This they refused to do, initiating the Grand Dérangement—the tragic Great Expulsion of 1755—described in William Wadsworth Longfellow's poem "Evangeline: The Tale of Acadia." The British burned homes and forcibly loaded Acadians onto ships to be offloaded at various stops along the American coast. Half died of cold and smallpox.

Once in Louisiana, Cajuns (from the French, *les Cadiens* or *les Acadiens*) faced a second, more gradual expulsion. After the Louisiana Purchase of 1803, other, more prosperous groups, including the Creoles (who descended from French, Spanish, and African colonial settlers), pushed them westward, off the prime farmland of the Mississippi levees. According to one historian, besides wanting the land, many sugar planters wanted the Cajuns to leave the vicinity so that slaves would not see the Cajun example of freedom and self-support. While a few Cajuns themselves became slave owners, as did some freed blacks, along the plantation-studded Mississippi River most Acadians were pushed to southwest Louisiana (where they raised cattle and grew rice, corn, and cotton), and south to the swamps in which they fished. On issues of Tea Party politics, Cajuns differed little from the non-Cajuns I talked with.

20 *student clubs included College Republicans and Young Americans for Liberty but not College Democrats* On December 7, 2015, I searched under College Student Life, "Special Interests," http://www.southwestern.edu /offices/studentactivities.

20 *are named after Confederate officials of the Civil War* Beauregard Parish is named after a Confederate general who helped design the Confederate battle flag; Jefferson Davis Parish is named after the president of the Confederacy. Allen Parish is named for a former Confederate States Army General, Henry Watkins Allen. For monuments, see "Louisiana Confederate Monuments and Markers," http://www.scvtaylorcamp.com/monu ments.html.

20 *a cross was burned* Associated Press, "Cross Burning Defendant Speaks Out," KPLC-TV, December 12, 2001, http://www.kplctv.com/story/317803 /cross-burning-defendant-speaks-out.

21 *Lake Charles had become ground zero for the production of American petrochemicals* Rachael Cernansky, "Natural Gas Boom Brings Major Growth for U.S. Chemical Plants," *Environment 360*, January 29, 2015 (accessed August 16, 2015), http://e360.yale.edu/feature/natural_gas_boom_brings_major _growth_for_us_chemical_plants/2842.

21 *13,000 of these workers were from out of state, including Filipino pipefitters* By far the largest plant expansion was that of the South African petrochemical giant, Sasol. It was in the process of buying out members of a long-beleaguered black community of Mossville whose land it wanted for a planned expansion. I attended meetings of Mossville citizens and spent a day with a man living in a trailer surrounded by fields filled with heavy machinery moving about on land now zoned "heavy industrial." His water and electricity had been cut off and the mailman no longer delivered letters to his address. If I could understand why those who suffered the effects of widespread pollution opposed stricter regulation of pollution, or funds for cleaning it up, then perhaps I could understand the opposition to government help in fixing all the other big problems too.

2: "One Thing Good"

26 *the second highest incidence of cancer for men and the fifth highest male death rate from cancer in the nation* "Cancer Facts and Figures 2015," American Cancer Society, http://www.cancer.org/acs/groups/content/@editorial/documents/document/acspc-044552.pdf.

27 *whose extraordinary connection to Lee* For much of his life, Lee had handled dangerous chemicals that came into being where he worked and ended up somewhere else, only to come back to him indirectly. One of them, ethylene dichloride, was added to other chemicals to form Agent Orange. During the war in Vietnam, this was shipped, Lee said, in fifty-five-gallon drums on railcars to the Alameda Naval Air Station in California. From there, it was loaded onto airplanes and flown to Southeast Asia to be sprayed over the vast jungle. Before being married to Lee, his wife had been married to a flight engineer who repaired leaks in chemical drums during flight. Accidently exposed to Agent Orange, he died a miserable death. His widow married Lee. Through washing her first husband's uniforms, she too suffered from Agent Orange, as did her son, Lee explained. Agent Orange had come full circle.

31 *seafood advisory warning people to limit their consumption of local fish* Lee's toxic waste dumps were not the only cause of the fish kill. Paul Ringo, a Riverwatcher on the Sabine River, got industry officials to admit to other sources of toxic waste while questioning them at one town hall meeting. Ringo held up a sheet of paper authoritatively, he recalls, and spoke as if reading a number of facts. "We knew the fish were dead. And someone had given me a tip that a large EDC tank was empty. So I acted like a lawyer. 'Is there anything about that tank that's unusual?' Then one admitted 'some EDC spilled' but said he didn't know how much. So I asked, 'About how much?' 'We're not sure,' came the answer. 'How much does the vat normally hold?' The answer came in tens of thousands of gallons. 'So is that about how much EDC was lost and unaccounted for?' I faked it and it worked!" This led to a field trip during which officials admitted to other spills that had occurred over a period of time.

32 *1,000 crawfish farmers and the 800 commercial fishermen who catch wild crawfish* The Louisiana Seafood Marketing and Promotion Board, "By the Numbers: Louisiana's Ecology," accessed April 8, 2015, http://www.louisianaseafood.com/ecology.

32 *and the Clean Water Act (1972)* On January 1, 1970, in his first official statement of the year, President Nixon said, "The 1970s absolutely must be the years when America pays its debt to the past by reclaiming the purity of its air, its waters and its living environment. It is literally now or never."

Jonathan Schell, *The Time of Illusion* (New York: Vintage Books, 1975), 74. (This positive step coincided, tragically, with the stealth invasion of Laos.)

32 *"front-porch"—or "kitchen-sink"—politics of the 1970s and 1980s* Jim Schwab, *Front Porch Politics: The Forgotten Heyday of American Activism in the 1970s and 1980s* (New York: Farrar Strauss, 2013).

3: The Rememberers

39 *It is 1950* A word on nomenclature: a *bayou* is a swampy river, and a *swamp* is a forested wetland. A *marsh* is a grassy wetland or wet prairie.

42 *French speakers were discouraged from attending* Sean Cockerham, "Louisiana French: L'heritage at Risk," *Seattle Times*, July 6, 2012. In 1921, the Louisiana Constitution forbade the use of any language other than English in public schools.

44 *Nowadays there's talk of cleaning it up, but I don't know how they can* As early as 1971, according to the files of the Louisiana Stream Control Commission, an agency predecessor of the Louisiana Department of Environmental Quality, mercury contamination of 1.5 parts per million was found in blue crab at a seafood processing facility on Calcasieu Lake. Interview, Willie Fontenot, 2014.

45 *a chlorinated hydrocarbon manufacturing facility* It binds together various building-block molecules. The company purchases its first building-block molecule (hydrocarbon ethylene) from another company. Then it pumps in brine (a second building-block molecule) to form sodium hydroxide, or caustic soda, which it can then sell. The company also bonds chlorine with hydrocarbons—from which various configurations emerge, such as EDC, perchloroethylene, and vinyl chloride. Waste from this processing lay in the "heavy bottoms" tar Lee Sherman dumped in the canal that connected with Bayou d'Inde.

46 *one of the largest chemical spills in North America* James Ridgeway, "Environmental Espionage: Inside a Chemical Company's Louisiana Spy Op," *Mother Jones*, May 20, 2008, http://www.motherjones.com/environment/2008/05/environmental-espionage-inside-chemical-companys-louisiana-spy-op.

46 *largest new industrial facility expansion in the United States* Chris Pedersen, "Sasol Clears Major Hurdle to Build America's First GTP Plant," OilPrice.com, September 4, 2014, http://oilprice.com/Energy/Natural-Gas/Sasol-Clears-Major-Hurdle-to-Build-Americas-First-GTL-Plant.html. Also Wilma Subra, e-mail correspondence, February 20, 2014, attachment: Sasol Permit.

46 *and of the Great Paradox* Also see "Hazardous, Toxic and Radioactive Waste Reconnaissance Report (HTRW) Calcasieu River and Pass," Louisiana

Dredged Material Management Plan, U.S. Army Corps of Engineers, New Orleans District, Prepared by Gulf Engineers and Consultants, Appendix G, maps.

47 *on grounds of faith and family values* Interview with Kevin Phillips, in *New York Times*, 1970. James Boyd, "Nixon's Southern Strategy: 'It's All in the Charts,'" *New York Times*, May 17, 1970, http://www.nytimes.com/packages /html/books/phillips-southern.pdf. Also see "Governor Bobby Jindal Says Americans Want a 'Hostile Takeover' of Washington," TeaParty.org, September 16, 2014, http://www.teaparty.org/gov-bobby-jindal-says-americans -want-hostile-takeover-washington-55848.

47 *among them nurses, nurse's aides, medical technicians, public school teachers* In 2007, 350 Filipino teachers were brought in by Universal Placement International to teach in public schools under the H-1B Guest Worker program. But they were forced to pay an initial $16,000 fee. Most had to borrow the money and were charged monthly interest. UPI took away their passports and visas until they repaid the loan. The contracts were later ruled illegal, and the agency officials were jailed for human trafficking. Claire Gordon, "Filipino Workers Kept as Slaves in Louisiana, Lawsuit Charges," *AOL Jobs*, November 15, 2011, http://jobs.aol.com/article /2011/11/15/filipino-workers-kept-as-slaves-in-louisiana-according-to -lawsu/20106284; "Lawsuit: Filipino Teachers Defrauded in International Labor Trafficking Scheme," LA.AFT.org, http://la.aft.org/news/lawsuit -filipino-teachers-defrauded-international-labor-trafficking-scheme.

48 *won a score of 0 on the League of Conservation Voters scorecard* "David Vitter on Environment," On the Issues (a website that describes congressional bills and candidate's votes across a range of issues), http://www.ontheissues.org /Domestic/David_Vitter_Environment.htm.

49 *for the affluent, a journey to the Swiss Alps* Svetlana Boym, *The Future of Nostalgia* (New York: Basic Books, 2001). Also see Svetlana Boym, "Nostalgia and Its Discontents," *Hedgehog Review* (Summer 2007): 13, http://www .iasc-culture.org/eNews/2007_10/9.2CBoym.pdf.

50 *new jobs, new money, and new products* E.E. Evans-Pritchard, *The Nuer: A Description of the Modes of Livelihood and Political Institutions of a Nilotic People* (Oxford, UK: Clarendon Press, 1940); Laura Ann Stoler, "Imperial Debris: Reflections on Ruins and Ruination," *Cultural Anthropology* 23, no. 2 (2008): 191–219; Laura Ann Stoler, "Colonial Aphasia: Race and Disabled Histories in France," *Public Culture* 23, no. 1 (2011): 121–56.

51 *They put fun into memory* http://www.bayousandbyways.com/festivals2.htm.

52 *Dominant within that system were men* Evans-Pritchard, *The Nuer*, 199–200.

53 *They've already waited long enough and nearly despair of politics* Just as people of faith spoke of the environment in religious terms, industry spokesmen could too. After the 2013 Axiall explosion, the CEO described it evasively to the company's stockholders as a "Force Majeure"—an act of God or a force out of human hands. Pavel Pavlov, "US' Axiall Declares Force Majeure on VCM from PHH Monomers Plant," *Platts*, December 23, 2013, http://www .platts.com/latest-news/petrochemicals/houston/us-axiall-declares-force -majeure-on-vcm-from-21990566.

54 *a man I have already met—Lee Sherman* Javier Auyero and Debora Alejandra Swistun, *Flammable: Environmental Suffering in an Argentine Shantytown* (Oxford: Oxford University Press, 2009), 128–29. Residents spent a great deal of time waiting; time was "oriented to and by others."

4: The Candidates

57 *curious what differences between the two men would emerge* WWL-TV Staff, "Poll: Obama Loses Support in La.; Perry, Romney, Cain Close on GOP Side," WWL-TV, October 13, 2011, http://www.wwltv.com/story/news/pol itics/2014/08/29/14408560. WWL-TV polled 602 likely Louisiana voters.

57 *and voted for the Keystone pipeline* Ibid.

57 *"If it ain't good for y'all, I ain't voting for it"* Scott Lewis, "Boustany and Landry Fight over Obamacare, Medicare, Negative Campaigns and Oilfield Jobs [Audio]," Cajun Radio, October 31, 2012, http://cajunradio.com/boustany -and-landry-fight-over-obamacare-medicare-negative-campaigns-and-oil field-jobs-audio/?trackback=tsmclip.

59 *the EPA listed eight as "impaired" and the ninth as "unassessed"* A January 24, 2015, search for Lafayette, LA, using the EPA's "MyEnvironment" tool yielded these findings. See http://www.epa.gov/myenvironment.

59 *eighty-nine with "formal enforcement actions in the last five years"* This data comes from the EPA's ECHO database, which tracks compliance with various environmental regulations. We accessed it using the EPA's Enforcement Compliance and History Online tool, which yielded these findings. (We searched September 29, 2015, for Lafayette Parish, Louisiana.) See https:// echo.epa.gov.

59 *many of whom were Tea Party members* Stacy Mitchell and Fred Clements, "How Washington Punishes Small Business," *Wall Street Journal*, May 7, 2015. Many Tea Party candidates from Louisiana—including Charles Boustany, John Fleming, Steve Scalise, and Bill Cassidy—voted "Aye" in the 114th Congress on HR 37, a House bill that rolled back Dodd-Frank restrictions on Wall Street companies. This bill had the counterintuitive

title of the "Promoting Job Creation and Reducing Small Business Burdens Act," but in fact, Mitchell and Clements argue, it strengthens big business, placing it in a better position to marginalize small business.

60 *Representative Landry did the same* See League of Conservation Voters, *Public Health Basis of the Clean Air Act, House Roll Call Vote 395* (Washington, D.C.: League of Conservation Voters, 2012), http://scorecard.lcv.org/roll -call-vote/2012-395-public-health-basis-clean-air-act. Sixteen Republican senators had voted in 2011 to abolish the EPA in a bill co-sponsored by Louisiana senator David Vitter.

60 *Boustany and Landry had earned a lifetime score of 6 out of a total possible 100* Brad Johnson, "Senate Republicans Introduce Bill to Abolish the EPA," *Think Progress,* May 6, 2011, http://thinkprogress.org/politics/2011/05/06/164077 /senate-republicans-introduce-bill-to-abolish-the-epa.

60 *Neither candidate said a word* In 2012, Louisiana produced 31.14 pounds of toxic releases (on- and off-site, to air/water/land, all industries) per person (i.e., 143,289,289 pounds TRI divided by 4.602 million people in 2012). By comparison, the United States as a whole produced 11.57 pounds of toxic releases per capita in 2012. Only five states produced more per capita. Alaska produced 1,198.6 pounds per capita. Montana produced 58.9 pounds per capita. Nevada produced 103.6 pounds per capita. North Dakota produced 49.3 pounds per capita. Utah produced 67.2 pounds per capita. The state's own Center for Environmental Health (part of the Department of Health and Hospitals) states on its website: "Louisiana ranks among the top states in the nation in per capita production of hazardous wastes and in the amount of chemicals released into its water, air, and soil."

63 *"There's hardly a public dock along it"* The Mississippi drains about 40 percent of the continental United States and provides drinking water to eighteen million people. But leaky pipes, spills, chemical dumps, and agricultural runoff along the thirteen parishes that depend on the Mississippi for drinking water have polluted it. The drinking water in one parish was found to contain seventy-five toxins, including carbon tetrachloride, DDT, and atrazine. Richard Misrach and Kate Orff, *Petrochemical America* (New York: Aperture Foundation, 2012), 143.

63 *The site offers a "Cajun Pride Swamp Tour"* "Gonzales," LouisianaTravel.com (the official state tourism site), http://www.louisianatravel.com/cities/gonzales.

63 *Gonzales seems to be a one-town ongoing party* In Norco, Louisiana, along the Mississippi, beautiful, white, billowy clouds are nicknamed "Norco cumulus" because they contain volatile hydrocarbons. Misrach and Orff, *Petrochemical America,* 4.

63 *top 3 percent of U.S. counties in reported toxic releases, according to the EPA*
See the EPA's Toxics Release Inventory (TRI) Explorer. According to the
EPA TRI, Calcasieu Parish—home to Westlake, Lake Charles, and Bayou
d'Inde—ranked in the top 2 percent of polluted counties in the nation in
2013, the latest data available (ranking 34th out of 2,428 reporting counties). In 1990, Calcasieu was ranked 24th in TRI emissions of 2,315 reporting U.S. counties (so almost in the top 1 percent of counties nationwide).
Environmental Protection Agency, *TRI Explorer [Data file]*, *1990 and 2013*
(Washington, D.C.: Environmental Protection Agency, 2015), http://iaspub
.epa.gov/triexplorer/tri_release.chemical. Information about toxic releases is
based on what facilities in certain regulated industries report, not on independent monitors—a practice Congress established in 1986 when it set up
the Emergency Planning and Community Right to Know Act.

64 *"because they've got stricter regulations than we do"* In 2000, Robert D.
Bullard found that nearly 60 percent of the nation's hazardous-waste landfill capacity was in five Southern states (Alabama, Louisiana, Oklahoma,
South Carolina, and Texas) and that four landfills in minority zip code
areas represented 63 percent of the South's total hazardous-waste capacity,
although blacks made up only about 20 percent of the South's total population. See Robert D. Bullard, *Dumping in Dixie: Race, Class, and Environmental Quality* (New York: Westview Press, 2000). According to the
Right to Know database, in 2011 (latest available) Louisiana ranked third of
all states in how much hazardous waste it manages (waste it receives from
elsewhere). This does not include ten of the fourteen kinds of wastes from
petroleum. Right to Know Network, *Biennial Reporting System Quantities
by State for 2011: Waste Received and Managed* (Washington, D.C.: Center
for Effective Government, 2015), http://www.rtknet.org/db/brs/tables.php
?tabtype=t3&year=2011&subtype=a&sorttype=rcv.

64 *worrisome studies had occasionally appeared in the press* Abrahm Lustgarten, "Injection Wells: The Poison Beneath Us," *ProPublica*, June 21, 2012,
https://www.propublica.org/article/injection-wells-the-poison-beneath-us.

64 *25,000 miles of underwater pipelines connect offshore drilling platforms to onshore refineries in Louisiana and Texas* Ken Silverstein, "Dirty South: Letter
from Baton Rouge," *Harpers*, November 2013, 45–56.

65 *"the worst environmental disaster America has ever faced"* "Remarks by the
President to the Nation on the BP Oil Spill," White House Press Release,
June 15, 2010, https://www.whitehouse.gov/the-press-office/remarks-presi
dent-nation-bp-oil-spill.

65 *Crab traps were soiled* Mark Hertsgaard, "What BP Doesn't Want You to Know About the Gulf Spill," *Newsweek*, April 22, 2013. The manual provided by Nalco, the producer of Corexit 9527 and Corexit 9500, the dispersants BP sprayed over the water, describes the effects of excessive exposure to it (nausea, vomiting, injury to the kidney or liver). BP did not distribute manuals or inform cleanup workers of potential hazards or provide them with safety training and protective gear, according to interviews with dozens of cleanup workers. They were given body suits and gloves but no respirators or air monitors. The Corexit was sprayed from a plane onto workers in boats and on shore, and workers were told the toxic dispersant was "as safe as dishwasher soap." Kate Sheppard, "BP's Bad Breakup: How Toxic Is Corexit?" *Mother Jones*, September/October 2010; http://www.motherjones.com/environment/2010/09/bp-ocean-dispersant-corexit. Also see "Deep Water: The Gulf Oil Disaster and the Future of Offshore Drilling," Report to the President, National Commission on the BP Deepwater Horizon Oil Spill and Offshore Drilling, January 2011, https://www.gpo.gov/fdsys/pkg/GPO-OILCOMMISSION/pdf/GPO-OILCOMMISSION.pdf; Hertsgaard, "What BP Doesn't Want You to Know About the Gulf Spill."

65 *other marine mammals, including whales, washed ashore* Scientists estimate that the mortality of marine mammals in the wild was sixteen to fifty times higher than that in the collected count. Rob Williams, Shane Gero, Lars Bejder, John Calambokidis, Scott D. Krauss, David Lusseau, Andrew J. Read, and Jooke Robbins, "Underestimating the Damage: Interpreting Cetacean Carcass Recoveries in the Context of the Deepwater Horizon/BP Incident," *Conservation Letters* 4, no. 3 (2011): 228–33; Natural Resources Defense Council, "The BP Oil Disaster at One Year" (Washington, D.C.: Natural Resources Defense Council, 2011).

65 *showed distorted body shapes, hearts, and eyes* Michael Wines, "Fish Embryos Exposed to Oil from BP Spill Develop Deformities, a Study Finds," *New York Times*, March 25, 2014.

65 *Vessels of Opportunity program* Joseph Goodman, "Gulf Oil Spill Threatens Louisiana Native Americans' Way of Life," *Miami Herald*, June 1, 2010.

65 *some developed skin lesions, blurred vision, breathing difficulties, and headaches* Antonia Juhasz, "Investigation: Two Years After the BP Spill, a Hidden Health Crisis Festers," *The Nation*, April 18, 2012, http://www.thenation.com/article/investigation-two-years-after-bp-spill-hidden-health-crisis-festers.

65 *so no one knew if they would work* BP engineers had violated standard operating procedures, skipping four of the five precautionary steps routinely

followed and relying solely, and fatally, on one last step. In a highly unusual move, Exxon officials publicly declared that the accident should never have happened.

66 *Half opposed it, and only a third favored it* Lawrence C. Hamilton, Thomas G. Safford, and Jessica D. Ulrich, "In the Wake of the Spill: Environmental Views Along the Gulf Coast," *Social Science Quarterly* 93, no. 4 (2012), 1053–64. Residents surveyed were nearly all Republicans, and in one of the two parishes surveyed 17 percent of all workers—and in the second 26 percent—worked for oil and gas companies. Others worked in service jobs in the area. Residents of Florida who were, ironically, less hurt by the spill were more in favor of the moratorium. Nationwide, only a third of those polled in a Bloomberg survey supported the ban. Kim Chipman, "Americans in 73% Majority Oppose Ban on Deepwater Oil Drilling," *Bloomberg*, July 14, 2010, http://www.bloomberg.com/news/articles/2010-07-14/ameri cans-in-73-majority-oppose-ban-on-deepwater-drilling-after-oil-spill.

66 *"The spill makes us sad, but the moratorium makes us mad"* Oliver A. Houck, "The Reckoning: Oil and Gas Development in the Louisiana Coastal Zone," *Tulane Environmental Law Journal* 28, no. 2 (2015), 185–296.

66 *they were managing strong feelings of anxiety, fear, and anger* In *The Managed Heart: Commercialization of Human Feeling* (Berkeley: University of California Press, 1983), I use the term "emotional labor" for the paid work of trying to feel or appearing to feel the required feelings for the job, and applied it to such paid service jobs as flight attendant, care worker, nurse, and salesperson. I used the term "emotion work" for the same emotion management we do for free at home, or anywhere else outside of paid work.

67 *Louisiana is one of the most permissive states in the nation* The state does not regulate "on-premises hours" (i.e., last call) for establishments that serve alcohol (though parishes can establish their own). *Louisiana Law Regarding the Unlawful Sale, Purchase and Possession of Alcoholic Beverages*, Louisiana R.S.14:93.10–14.

67 *supported, naturally, by an alcohol lobbying group* Michael Mizell-Nelson, "Nurturing the Drive-Through Daiquiri," *Louisiana Cultural Vistas*, March 12, 2015.

67 *Louisiana also has a "Stand Your Ground" law, permitting a frightened homeowner to shoot first* See "Louisiana State Profile" on the National Rifle Association's website (accessed July 31, 2015), https://www.nraila.org/gun-laws /state-gun-laws/louisiana. In a 2013 scorecard prepared by the Law Center to Prevent Gun Violence and the Brady Campaign, Louisiana ranked 40th

for its gun laws and received an "F." See Law Center to Prevent Gun Violence and the Brady Campaign, *2013 State Scorecard: Why Gun Laws Matter* (San Francisco: Law Center to Prevent Gun Violence, 2013), http://www .bradycampaign.org/sites/default/files/SCGLM-Final10-spreads-points.pdf.

68 *double the national average* "State Firearm Death Rates, Ranked by Rate, 2011," Violence Policy Center: Research, Investigation, Analysis & Advocacy for a Safer America, http://www.vpc.org/fact-sheets/state-firearm-death-rates -ranked-by-rate-2011. According to the report, which uses data from the federal Centers for Disease Control and Prevention's National Center for Injury Control and Prevention, Louisiana had a gun death rate of 18.91 deaths per 100,000 people in 2011, compared to the national firearm death rate of 10.38 deaths per 100,000 people.

68 *restrictions on clinics offering the procedure* Adam Liptak, "Supreme Court Blocks Louisiana Abortion Law," *New York Times*, March 4, 2016, http:// www.nytimes.com/2016/03/05/us/politics/supreme-court-blocks-louisiana -abortion-law.html.

68 *The parish imposed a $50 fine for a first offense and $100 for a second* "Baggy Pants Law Will Fine Offenders in Louisiana Parish," *Huffington Post*, April 14, 2013 (accessed November 3, 2015), http://www.huffingtonpost .com/2013/04/14/baggy-pants-law-fine-louisiana_n_3080851.html.

68 *wear "something reflective" and visible from all directions on an outer garment when walking after dark* Sarah Childress, "Has the Justice Department Found a New Town That Preys on Its Poor?" *Frontline*, April 27, 2015, http://www.pbs.org/wgbh/pages/frontline/criminal-justice/has-the-justice -department-found-a-new-town-that-preys-on-its-poor.

69 *more than Russia or Cuba* Institute for Criminal Policy Research, *World Prison Brief*, http://www.prisonstudies.org/highest-to-lowest/prison_popula tion_rate.

70 *calling everyone who knows somebody at the plant* Mishaps usually occur, she explained, during scheduled release (a legally permitted gas or liquid emission) or during a "turnaround" (a period during which workers bring a unit down, clean it or switch production to a new product, then bring it back online).

70 *the second in thirteen months* One explosion occurred December 24, 2012, according to the *Pittsburgh Business Times*. Malia Spencer, "Fire Damages PPG Industries Plant in Louisiana," December 27, 2012, http://www.biz journals.com/pittsburgh/news/2012/12/27/plant-fire-causes-force-majeure -for-ppg.html. A second occurred December 20, 2013. Associated Press, "Number of Injured from Axiall Chemical Plant Fire in Westlake Rises to

18," *Times-Picayune*, December 25, 2013, http://www.nola.com/environ
ment/index.ssf/2013/12/number_of_injured_from_axiall.html.

5: The "Least Resistant Personality"

74 *15 percent of all jobs in the state* Loren C. Scott, *The Energy Sector: Still
a Giant Economic Engine for the Louisiana Economy—an Update*, Louisiana Mid-Continent Oil and Gas Association and Grow Louisiana Coalition
report, 2014, http://www.growlouisianacoalition.com/blog/wp-content/up
loads/2014/07/Loren-Scott-Study.pdf. The energy sector "supports" 287,008
jobs, bringing the total estimate to 15 percent.

    According to the U.S. Census Bureau, of the 1,535,407 employed people
in Louisiana, 9,637 worked in "oil and gas extraction," 20,823 worked in
"chemical manufacturing," 12,163 in "petroleum and coal products manufacturing," and 2,734 in "plastics and rubber products manufacturing." See
Loren C. Scott, *The Energy Sector: A Giant Economic Engine for the Louisiana Economy*, Baton Rouge: Mid-Continent Oil and Gas Association (accessed June 18, 2015), http://www.scribd.com/doc/233387193/The-Energy
-Sector-A-Giant-Economic-Engine-for-the-Louisiana-Economy.

74 *pipeline transportation in 2014* The number of oil workers could be lower
still. According to the 2014 U.S. Bureau of Labor Statistics estimates, not
seasonally adjusted, total "Oil & Gas" jobs made up 3.32 percent of all Louisiana workers. This number included oil and gas extraction, support activities for mining, petroleum and coal products manufacturing, and pipeline
transportation. Bureau of Labor Statistics, "Quarterly Census of Employment and Wages [December 2014 estimates]" (accessed June 18, 2015),
http://data.bls.gov/cgi-bin/dsrv?en.

74 *be filled, the report said, by workers from outside southwest Louisiana* Sasol
funded the Southwest Louisiana Regional Impact Study, with a team that
included private sector consultants as well as academics from McNeese
State University. The study was released in October 2014. CSRS, *Southwest Louisiana Regional Impact Study, 2014*, 1, 3, http://www.gogroupswla
.com/Content/Uploads/gogroupswla.com/files/SWLA%20Regional%20
Impact%20Study_Final.pdf. Of the new hires, 13,000 out of 18,000 are
expected to be recruited from outside southwest Louisiana. As the report
notes, "SWLA (Southwest Louisiana) does not have enough people to supply the required additional workforce. Projections suggest that over 13,000
jobs will need to be filled by people migrating to SWLA" (3).

74 *Filipino workers have worked for over a decade on oil platforms in the Gulf*
CSRS, ibid. Often the presence of Filipino workers in Louisiana comes to

light via news of accidents on oil rigs. Jennifer A. Dlouhy, "Dangers Face Immigrant Contract Workforce in Gulf," *FuelFix*, November 3, 2013, http://fuelfix.com/blog/2013/11/03/dangers-face-immigrant-contractor-work force-in-gulf. The local television station also ran a story about an injured Filipino worker injured on a Gulf oil rig. Associate Press, "Gulf Platform Owner Sued Over Deadly 2012 Blast," KPLC-TV, http://www.kplctv.com /story/23832004/gulf-platform-owner-sued-over-deadly-2012-blast.

75 *tours through plantation manor homes, catching fish, and farming* Curt Eysink, *Louisiana Workforce Information Review, 2010*, Statewide Report, https://www.doleta.gov/performance/results/AnnualReports/2010_eco nomic_reports/la_economic_report_py2010_workforce.pdf

75 *down from 42 percent in 1982* Ballotpedia, "Louisiana State Budget and Finances," 2013, https://ballotpedia.org/Louisiana_state_budget_and_finances. Also see "Bureau of Economic Analysis [Regional Datafile]": Louisiana, 2013 (Washington, D.C.: Bureau of Economic Analysis), retrieved September 22, 2015.

75 *state revenue from such companies fell from $703 million in 2008 to $290 million in 2012* The total effective tax rate (based on all state and local taxes, including income tax, franchise tax, sales tax, and property tax) is less than 1 percent. "Today, the Tax Foundation ranks Louisiana No. 1 in the U.S. in overall tax competitiveness for new manufacturing operations, both those that rely heavily on labor investment and those that rely more heavily on capital investment. In addition, Louisiana ranks No. 1 in the U.S. in overall tax competitiveness for both new and mature research-and-development facilities." See "New Tax Foundation Ranking Indicates Dramatic Improvement in Louisiana's Business Tax Competitiveness," Louisiana Economic Development (accessed January 5, 2014), http://www.opportunitylouisiana. com/index.cfm/newsroom/detail/175. See Gordon Russell, "Giving Away Louisiana: An Overview," *The Advocate*, Special Reports, November 26, 2014, http://blogs.theadvocate.com/specialreports/2014/11/26/giving-away -louisiana/.

75 *the state received over $1 billion in 2008 but less than $886 million in 2012* "Governing, the State and Localities," Governing.com (accessed Sept 21, 2015), http://www.governing.com/gov-data/state-tax-revenue-data.html.

75 *offers "the lowest business taxes in the entire country for new manufacturing projects"* Louisiana Economic Development, "Louisiana: At the Epicenter of the U.S. Industrial Rebirth," 2012, http://www.opportunitylouisiana.com /index.cfm/newsroom/detail/265.

75 *between 2010 and 2013, performed no audits at all* Institute for Southern

Studies, "Looting Louisiana: How the Jindal Administration Is Helping Big Oil Rip Off a Cash-Strapped State," http://www.southernstudies
.org/2015/05/looting-louisiana-how-the-jindal-administration-is.html.
The report cites the Louisiana Department of Revenue, "Tax Exemption
Budget, 2011–2012" and "Tax Exemption Budget 2014–2015." Also see
Chico Harlan, "Battered by Drop in Oil Prices and Jindal's Fiscal Policies, Louisiana Falls into Budget Crisis," *Washington Post*, March 4, 2016,
https://www.washingtonpost.com/news/wonk/wp/2016/03/04/the-debili
tating-economic-disaster-louisianas-governor-left-behind.

76 *oil wages don't trickle down; they leak out* Paul H. Templet, "Defending the
Public Domain: Pollution, Subsidies and Poverty," PERI Working Paper
No. 12 (January 2001), http://ssrn.com/abstract=333280 or http://dx.doi
.org/10.2139/ssrn.333280.

76 *"rather where they live, in Greenwich, Connecticut, say, or Mill Valley, California"* Templet offered a hypothetical example. Exxon extracts a billion
dollars' worth of oil from Louisiana, but pays only half a billion in wages to
suppliers/contractors and workers and to taxes in Louisiana. The other half
a billion dollars flows to Exxon headquarters for distribution to management
and to dividends for shareholders of Exxon stock, usually located in other
states. This is why, he explained, in the 1990s, about a third of Louisiana's
annual wealth generated (GSP) flowed to other states. E-mail communication, November 5, 2015.

77 *the sum of the value of all goods and services produced by the state* P.H.
Templet, "Grazing the Commons; Externalities, Subsidies and Economic
Development," *Ecological Economics* 12 (February 1995): 141–59; P.H. Tem-
plet, "Defending the Public Domain, Pollution, Subsidies and Poverty," in
Natural Assets: Democratizing Environmental Ownership, edited by James K.
Boyce and Barry G. Shelley (Washington, D.C.: Island Press, 2003).

77 *In 1979, 19 percent of Louisianans lived below the poverty line; in 2014, it
was 18 percent* One reason oil doesn't alleviate poverty is that the oil sector
does not actually feed the non-oil sector of the Louisiana economy; the two
sectors rise and fall differently. Between 2003 and 2013, for example, jobs
in oil held steady, but the state's total employment fluctuated strongly—with
peaks in 2004 and 2007 and troughs in 2003 and 2005–2006.

77 *Nissan from California to Tennessee* Caroline Hanley and Michael T. Douglass, "High Road, Low Road or Off Road: Economic Development Strategies
in the American States," *Economic Development Quarterly* 28:3 (2014): 1–10.

77 *the Democratic, California model* Oil dominated in Louisiana and Texas. But
are there similar links to economic strategy elsewhere in the United States?

Tobacco is big in the southeast, where industry has long opposed excise taxes on cigarettes. Amanda Fallin, Rachel Grana, and Stanton A. Glantz, "'To Quarterback Behind the Scenes, Third-Party Efforts': The Tobacco Industry and the Tea Party," *Tobacco Control*, February 8, 2013, http://tobacco control.bmj.com/content/early/2013/02/07/tobaccocontrol-2012-050815. The Tea Party governor of Maine, Paul LePage, is backed by the logging industry and passed legislation to weaken lumber certification. While the company-sponsored certification system uses the term "sustainable" (as in the term Sustainable Forestry Initiative), it approves clear-cutting up to the size of ninety football fields. See Jackie Wei, "Governor LePage Undermines Maine's Green-Building Economy, Sets Back Sustainable Forestry," NRDC .org, December 12, 2011, https://www.nrdc.org/media/2011/111212. Were Tea Party state legislators in southern California mindful of agribusiness's interest in the "over-regulation" of pesticides? Heath Brown, *The Tea Party Divided: The Hidden Diversity of a Maturing Movement* (New York: Praeger, 2015), 78.

78 *A 2016 survey of the world's major economies* Catherine L. Mann, "Environment and Trade: Do Stricter Environmental Policies Hurt Expert Competitiveness?" Organisation for Economic Co-operation and Development, http://www.oecd.org/economy/greeneco/do-stricter-environmental-policies -hurt-export-competitiveness.htm. Also see Silvia Albrizio, Enrico Botta, Tomasz Kozluk, and Vera Zipperer, "Do Environmental Policies Matter for Productivity Growth? Insights from New Cross-County Measures of Environmental Policies," Working Paper Number 1176, December 3, 2014, http://www.oecd-ilibrary.org/economics/do-environmental-policies-matter -for-productivity-growth_5jxrjncjrcxp-en.

78 *I wondered why my Tea Party friends weren't hearing about it* Stephen M. Meyer, "Environmentalism and Economic Prosperity: Testing the Environmental Impact Hypothesis," MIT Project on Environmental Politics and Policy (1992); Stephen M. Meyer, "Environmentalism and Economic Prosperity: An Update," MIT Project on Environmental Politics and Policy (1993); Stephen M. Meyer, "Endangered Species Listings and State Economic Performance," MIT Project on Environmental Politics and Policy (1995); John R.E. Bliese, *The Great "Environment Versus Economy" Myth* (New York: Brownstone Policy Institute, 1999); Roger H. Bezdek, Robert M. Wendling, and Paula DiPerna, "Environmental Protection, the Economy, and Jobs: National and Regional Analyses," *Journal of Environmental Management* 86, no. 1 (2008): 63–79.

78 *Shell Oil Company supports the National Fish and Wildlife Foundation*

Barbara Koeppel, "Cancer Alley, Louisiana," *The Nation*, November 8, 1999, 16–24.

79 *live in cleaner environments* Arthur O'Connor, "Political Polarization and Environmental Inequality: A Pilot Study of Pollution Release Amounts and Practices in 'Red' Versus 'Blue' States," *International Environmental Review* 13, no. 4: 308–22. The seven remaining states (for fifty states plus the District of Columbia) are swing or "purple" states, with no strong or consistent margin of victory for a given political party in their voting records: Nevada, West Virginia, Arkansas, Colorado, Florida, Missouri, and Ohio. Using the EPA's 2010 Toxics Release Inventory (or TRI) for these states, he correlated pollution rates with the voting histories of various states in the union.

80 *The poorer the state, research found, the less regulated it was likely to be* In "Managing Community Acceptance of Major Industrial Projects," Ronald Luke—who served on the Texas Health and Human Services Council under Republican governor Rick Perry, and as director of the Texas Association of Business—reports that the wealthier the state, the greater the regulation of hazardous waste. He also notes, "the siting of major facilities in most areas of the country is predominantly a political question." Ronald Luke, "Managing Community Acceptance of Major Industrial Projects," *Coastal Zone Management Journal* 7 (1980): 292; James Lester, James Franke, Ann Bowman, and Kenneth Kramer, "Hazardous Wastes, Politics, and Public Policy: A Comparative State Analysis," *Western Political Quarterly* 36 (1983): 255–85.

80 *define communities that would not resist "locally undesirable land use"* Cerrell Associates, Inc., *Political Difficulties Facing Waste-to-Energy Conversion Plant Siting* (Los Angeles, CA: Cerrell Associates, 1984).

6: Industry: "The Buckle in America's Energy Belt"

85 *$84 billion spread over sixty-six industrial projects in southwest Louisiana over the next five years* Michael Kurth, "On the Brink of the Boom," *Lagniappe*, May 6, 2014, http://www.bestofswla.com/2014/05/06/brink-boom (*Lagniappe* is a local publication, publishing mostly business news). In 2013, along with Texas and Pennsylvania, Louisiana accounted for over 64 percent of the $145 billion in capital investments in the United States, according to the *2014 US Investment Monitor*, prepared by Ernst & Young LLP. A third of that investment came from abroad, and over half of foreign investment came from the chemical manufacturing sector, driven by the prospect of cheap natural gas (eleven out of the twenty biggest capital investments). The two very largest investments in Lake Charles were in expansions of pre-existing

export terminals for liquefied natural gas (LNG)—one in Port Arthur, one in Lake Charles. See Ernst & Young LLP, *2014 US Investment Monitor: Tracking Mobile Capital Investments During 2013* (accessed August 4, 2015), http://www.ey.com/Publication/vwLUAssets/EY-the-us-investment-monitor /$FILE/EY-the-us-investment-monitor.pdf.

85 *"new cities of fertilizer plants, boron manufacturers, methanol terminals, polymer plants, ammonia factories and paper-finishing facilities"* Dennis K. Berman, "Are You Underestimating America's Fracking Boom?" *Wall Street Journal*, May 27, 2014.

86 *It conveyed the idea of power, importance, and prosperity* The ethane cracker— soon to become the largest one in the United States—was designed to pipe in cheap natural gas, separate its parts under very high heat, and produce a cleaner-than-normal diesel fuel. The gas-to-liquid plant would also start with natural gas, add oxygen to create syngas, and refine that into paraffin, which is used in such things as candles and lipstick.

88 *and the Philippines to fill service industry and construction jobs* Eric Cornier, "Construction Boom: Labor Shortage Among Area Concerns," *American Press*, February 10, 2013.

89 *But in a sodden rice field in 1901* Oil was first spotted as bubbles in a sodden rice field in Jennings in 1901. Wildcat prospectors, then bigger companies, probed farther into the earth and farther out to sea. Then the petrochemical companies set up nearby, processed the oil, and produced various feed stocks, which they then shipped to companies that made things from it.

89 *then in the 1940s, along the outer continental shelf* Ruth Seydlitz and Shirley Laska, "Social and Economic Impacts of Petroleum 'Boom and Bust' Cycles," prepared by the Environmental Social Science Research Institute, University of New Orleans, OCS Study MMS 94-0016, U.S. Dept. of the Interior, Minerals Mgmt. Service, Gulf of Mexico OCS Regional Office (New Orleans, LA, 1993).

90 *a shiny new buckle in the nation's energy belt* A 2012 analysis by the American Chemistry Council reported that low-cost natural gas could directly generate a $121 billion increase in U.S. output from oil and petrochemical industries, resulting in yet more investment and construction. "Lake Charles: A Case Study: With Massive New Industrial Investments and up to 25,000 New Workers Headed to Town, the Landscape of Lake Charles Is Changing Dramatically," *Business Report*, September 25, 2014, https://www .businessreport.com/article/lake-charles-a-case-study-with-massive-new -industrial-investments-and-up-to-25000-new-workers-headed-to-town -the-landscape-of-lake-charles-is-changing-dramatically.

90 *a five-year growth rate for 2014–2018 of 4.7 percent* Louisiana Economic Development, "Louisiana: At the Epicenter of the U.S. Industrial Rebirth" (accessed January 4, 2014), http://www.opportunitylouisiana.com/index.cfm/newsroom/detail/265.

As of 2013, the Louisiana Chemical Association listed sixty-three companies operating in over a hundred sites across Louisiana. The Louisiana coast looks out on the Gulf of Mexico continental shelf, the largest oil-producing region in the United States, and the state owns more underwater footage than Texas or Mexico. It also boasts the world's only offshore super port—letting supertankers unload crude oil via pipeline to on- and near-shore terminals (80 percent of the Gulf of Mexico offshore wells are in Louisiana waters).

90 *which usually* imported *oil from Mexico and Venezuela, were reconfigured to* export *it* Kurth, "On the Brink of the Boom," 13.

90 *make ink pigment that wouldn't show through the back side of a newspaper* "We salute PPG on its decision to locate the new pigment plant here and want to assure the firm that all citizens of the area are grateful," an editorial in the *American Press* read in 1966, hailing PPG's announcement to expand its pigment production plant in Lake Charles. This is, the author said, "another step in a great future. . . . The magnitude of petro-chemical investments in Calcasieu Parish almost staggers the imagination. There can be no question that the Lake Charles area is indeed fortunate to have had such tremendous growth over the past 10 years in the two fields of petrochemical development. But even more important is the realization that greater things are yet to come." *The American Press*, June 22, 1966 (archive).

91 *four-and-a-half-hour public hearing regarding the Sasol expansion* Berman, "Are You Underestimating."

91 *This it would use, pollute, and dump back in the Calcasieu River* The thirteen million gallons was to be added to the five million gallons already permitted.

91 *10,000,000 tons of new greenhouse gases* Frank DiCesare, "All Water, Air Permits for Sasol Approved," *American Press*, June 2, 2014.

91 *"today's not a good day to be outside"* Justin Phillips, "Calcasieu, Cameron Areas 'on Bubble' with EPA for Air Quality," *American Press*, July 11, 2014, http://www.americanpress.com/news/local/Air-quality. The big money, the many workers, the euphoria—these centered on natural gas that was *cheaper than oil.* If the price of natural gas rose and that of oil fell too much, the entire bubble could burst. In 2007, oil cost seven times as much as natural gas on the world market. In 2014, oil cost about twenty-four times as much as natural gas. Sasol needs the price of oil to stay at least sixteen times higher. For the petrochemical companies, natural gas was the main ingredient to

what they produced, and if they could buy it cheap and sell what they made for more, they could make a profit. But who could predict the relative price of oil and natural gas? "They must know what they're doing," one man told me confidently. Berman, "Are You Underestimating." Also see Kurth, "On the Brink of the Boom."

91 *it could triple the amount of feedstock needed to make plastic* As Sandra Steingraber observes in *Living Downstream: A Scientist's Personal Investigation of Cancer and the Environment*, evidence is accumulating that should give us pause about health effects and pique interest in the green Chamber of Commerce. Sandra Steingraber, *Living Downstream: A Scientist's Personal Investigation of Cancer and the Environment* (New York: Vintage, 1998).

92 *that lifted the poor and added to the common good* Clem Brooks and Jeff Manza, "A Broken Public? Americans' Responses to the Great Recession," *American Sociological Review* 78, no. 5 (2013): 727–48.

93 *Blacks turn to black neighbors without them* Nancy DiTomaso develops this thesis in *The American Non-Dilemma: Racial Inequality Without Racism* (New York: Russell Sage Foundation, 2013). Also see Deirdre Roysler, *Race and the Invisible Hand: How White Networks Exclude Black Men from Blue Collar Jobs* (Berkeley: University of California Press, 2003). Also see Appendix C.

93 *"Good idea," Hardey says* This came in the form of outright payments, tax write-offs, and publicly funded services.

93 *Louisiana was a poor state* Richard Thompson, "Giving Away Louisiana: Industrial Tax Incentives," *The Advocate*, December 11, 2014, http://blogs.theadvocate.com/specialreports/2014/12/03/giving-away-louisiana-industrial-tax-incentives.

95 *advised them not to put their hands in local water if they had open wounds* The advisory reads: "The germs, bacteria and parasites in the State's natural waterways, such as rivers, lakes, marshes and the Gulf of Mexico can make you sick and sometimes may be fatal. Some microorganisms occur naturally, and others come from human and animal waste. These materials can enter water from sewage overflows, polluted storm water runoff, sewage treatment plant malfunctions, urban and rural runoff after rainfall, boating wastes, malfunctioning individual sewage treatment systems and agricultural runoff."

"Most people can swim and enjoy the water without any problems or concerns," said State Health Officer Dr. Jimmy Guidry. "But contaminates can find their way into all waterways, so there is always a slight level of risk for infections." The advisory continues, "Dr. Guidry also says it's not a good idea to ingest the water or swim if you have cuts or open wounds." Louisiana Department of Health and Hospitals, "Health Department Advises 'Take Precautions While Swimming,'" May 21, 2014, http://new.dhh.louisiana.gov /index.cfm/communication/viewcampaign/896?uid=gE&nowrap=1.

95 *The possibility of recruiting the best minds in the nation ground to a quick halt* In late 2015, Governor Jindal was proposing another $533 million in cuts. Kaitlin Mulhere, "In the Face of Colossal Cuts," *Inside Higher Ed*, April 27, 2015, https://www.insidehighered.com/news/2015/04/27/anxiety-over-mas sive-proposed-cuts-louisianas-colleges-felt-across-state.

95 *"explore options and ramifications of ending the Desegregation Order"* See CSRS, *Southwest Louisiana Regional Impact Study* (accessed August 4, 2015), 121, http://www.gogroupswla.com/Content/Uploads/gogroupswla.com/files /SWLA%20Regional%20Impact%20Study_Final.pdf. The U.S. Department of Justice has listed twenty-five un-desegregated schools on its Civil Rights Division's "Open Desegregation Cast List." And it has held up a school voucher program in an attempt to force desegregation—locking children into failing schools, critics charge. Since *Brown v. Board of Education* in 1954, desegregation of public schools has been legally mandatory. But today schools remain very separate and unequal. More than two million black students attend schools where 90 percent of the student body is made up of minority students. According to a Center for American Progress report, such schools spend a full $733 less per student per year than schools with 90 percent or more white students. Across all schools, a 10 percentage point increase in students of color at a school is associated with an average decrease in per-pupil spending of $75. Ary Spatig-Amerikaner, *Unequal Education: Federal Loophole Enables Lower Spending on Students of Color* (Washington, D.C.: Center for American Progress, 2012), https://www .americanprogress.org/wp-content/uploads/2012/08/UnequalEduation.pdf.

95 *Sasol, 10 percent* Heather Regan-White, "Westlake City Council Reaches Agreement with Sasol on Expansion Costs," *Sulphur Daily News*, November 25, 2015, http://www.sulphurdailynews.com/article/20151125/NEWS/151 129875.

96 *the largest chemical leak in American history* Condea Vista is a subsidiary of a German petrochemical company called RWE-DEA.

96 *"But Condea Vista management told them their illnesses derived from other causes"* Interviews with Robert McCall, May 29, 2015, and William B. Baggett, June 5, 2015, both of Baggett McCall, Injury Attorneys, Lake Charles.

7: The State: Governing the Market 4,000 Feet Below

100 *then remembered it had been broken for months* Deborah Dupre, "State Blames One Company for Gassy Sinkhole, Orders More Seismic Monitors," Examiner.com, October 12, 2012, http://www.examiner.com/article/state -blames-one-company-for-gassy-sinkhole-orders-more-seismic-monitors.

100 *when it began to shake* Xerxes A. Wilson, "Mysterious Tremors Raise Questions," DailyComet.com, October 4, 2012 (accessed November 19, 2015), http://www.dailycomet.com/article/20121004/ARTICLES/121009798. According to the U.S. Geological Survey (http://earthquake.usgs.gov/earth quakes/states/louisiana/history.php), the last local earthquake, which "rattled windows," was around Baton Rouge in 1958.

100 *the workers were rescued in time* Christina Ng, "Louisiana Boat Disappears into Sinkhole, Workers Rescued," ABC News, August 16, 2012, http:// abcnews.go.com/US/louisiana-sinkhole-engulfs-boat-workers-rescued/story ?id=17021557.

101 *unseen and fairly common in the Gulf* In a process known as injection mining, it sank a series of wells deep inside the dome, flushing them out with high-pressure streams of freshwater and pumping the resulting saltwater to the surface. From there, the brine was piped and trucked to refineries along the Mississippi River, where it was broken down into sodium hydroxide and chlorine for use in manufacturing everything from paper to medical supplies. Other brine-miners sell this super-salt to frackers, who add it to chemicals and water to force natural gas from shale rock.

101 *one wall of the cavern crumpled* Charles Q. Choi, "Gas-Charged Earthquakes Linked to Mysterious Louisiana Sinkhole," *Live Science*, http://www .livescience.com/46692-louisiana-sinkhole-explained.html.

102 *126 salt domes in Louisiana* Vicki Wolf, "Salt Dome Instability Caused by Bayou Corne Sinkhole Tragedy and Others," *Clean* (Citizen's League for Environmental Action Now, based in Houston, Texas), http://www.clean houston.org/misc/salt_dome.htm.

102 *Dow and Union Carbide* Other companies, too, own spaces and rent them out to those who want to store chemicals, some toxic, some not—OxyChem, Acadian, and Crosstex Energy Services, for example.

102 *the very idea of regulation has fallen into very low esteem* Jeffery D. Beckman and Alex K. Williamson, "Salt-Dome Locations in the Gulf Coastal Plain, South-Central United States," U.S. Geological Survey, Water-Resources Investigations Report 90-4060, 1990, http://pubs.usgs.gov/wri/1990/4060 /report.pdf. There are 624 salt domes in the Gulf of Mexico, south-central

United States, and adjacent continental shelf, many of them offshore from Louisiana, with names such as "Good Hope."

103 *done absolutely nothing helpful to this community* Robert Mann, "Residents of Bayou Corne Ask, Where Are You, Bobby Jindal?" December 16, 2012, http://bobmannblog.com/2012/12/16/residents-of-bayou-corne-ask-where-are-you-bobby-jindal.

103 *one disgruntled resident tells me—to address the gathering* Sheila V. Kumar, "Jindal Meets with Bayou Corne Residents, Promises to Fight Texas Brine for Fair Buyouts," *Times-Picayune*, March 19, 2013, http://www.nola.com/politics/index.ssf/2013/03/jindal_to_visit_assumption_par_1.html. On May 21, 2013, he made another visit.

104 *Had the governor seen the sinkhole?* Ibid.

106 *The sociability of Bayou Corne brought him out of himself* One 2007 study found that strong families, church attendance, and a belief that individuals, not government, offer the best solutions to social ills are all associated with giving to charity. Households headed by conservatives, the study also found, give 30 percent more to charity than do households headed by liberals. Conservatives give blood more often and are more likely to volunteer. *The Chronicle of Philanthropy* analyzed IRS data and found that the seventeen most generous states, as measured by *share* of income donated to charity, voted in 2012 for Republican nominee Mitt Romney. Arthur C. Brooks, *Who Really Cares: The Surprising Truth About Compassionate Conservatism* (New York: Basic Books, 2007).

Two MIT political scientists refuted this study, showing that conservatives are richer than liberals and tend to direct their giving to their own churches. See Michele F. Margolis and Michael W. Sances, "Who Really Gives? Partisanship and Charitable Giving in the United States," Working paper, Social Science Research Network (2013): 1–17, http://papers.ssrn.com/sol3/papers.cfm?abstract_id=2148033; "How States Compare and How They Voted in the 2012 Election," *Chronicle of Philanthropy*, updated January 13, 2015 (accessed August 5, 2015), https://philanthropy.com/article/How-States-CompareHow/152501.

107 *drilling too close to the cavern's edge* David J. Mitchell, "Texas Brine Shifts Blame to Occidental Petroleum, Others for Causing Bayou Corne Sinkhole," *The Advocate*, July 9, 2015, http://theadvocate.com/news/ascension/12870889-123/texas-brine-shifts-blame-to.

107 *"with the force of more than 100 H-bombs"* Deborah Dupre, "Sinkhole: H-Bomb Explosion Equivalent in Bayou Corne Possible," Examiner.com,

August 12, 2012, http://www.examiner.com/article/sinkhole-h-bomb-explo
sion-equivalent-bayou-corne-possible.

108 *"I feel like I've been betrayed by the Louisiana Department of Natural Resources"*
Melissa Gray, "Louisiana Probes Cause of Massive Bayou Sinkhole," CNN,
August 10, 2012, http://www.cnn.com/2012/08/09/us/louisiana-bayou-sink
hole.

109 *it had neglected to levy penalties or, if they were levied, to collect them* Office
of the Inspector General, *Audit Report: EPA Region 6 Needs to Improve
Oversight of Louisiana's Environmental Programs* (Washington, D.C.: Environmental Protection Agency, 2003), http://www.epa.gov/oig/reports/2003
/2003-p-0005.pdf. The report was issued in response to petitions from Louisiana citizens groups, received from October 2001 to March 2002, that
requested the EPA withdraw three programs from the state: the National
Pollutant Discharge Elimination System (NPDES) water program; the Resource Conservation and Recovery Act (RCRA) hazardous waste program;
and the Title V air permit program. The petitions asserted that Louisiana
was not properly implementing these programs, which the EPA had autho-
rized them to carry out.

109 *"unable to fully assure the public that Louisiana was operating programs in a
way that effectively protects human health and the environment"* Ibid., 1. The
report also faulted the head of EPA's Region 6 for its poor oversight of Louisiana. The inspector general could not assure, the report said, that Louisiana was protecting the environment because Region 6 leadership: "(1) did
not develop and clearly communicate a vision and measurable goals for its
oversight of the State or emphasize the importance of consistently conducting oversight, (2) did not hold Louisiana accountable for meeting goals and
commitments, and (3) did not ensure that data of poor quality was corrected
so that it could be relied upon to make sound decisions. As a result, the
working relationship between the Region and Louisiana was not cohesive."
Also see Office of the Inspector General, *EPA Must Improve Oversight of
State Enforcement* (Washington, D.C.: Environmental Protection Agency,
2011), http://www.epa.gov/oig/reports/2012/20111209-12-P-0113.pdf.

109 *"a culture in which the state agency is expected to protect industry"* Office
of the Inspector General, *EPA Must Improve,* 16. Upset by a high level of
disease in their community, residents appealed to sources outside the state
government to document the presence of dioxin in their blood, and high
rates were detected by a Louisiana chemist, Dr. Wilma Subra.

109–110 *"given back" about $13 million to oil and gas companies that it should*

have retained in taxes Julia O'Donoghue, "Louisiana Failed to Collect Millions in Oil and Gas Taxes," *Times-Picayune*, December 2, 2013, http://www
.nola.com/politics/index.ssf/2013/12/louisiana_oil_and_gas_taxes.html. In
2009 and 2010, the Department of Revenue's automated system sent out
notices for $11.9 million worth of unaccounted for taxes. The program was
shut down in September 2010 because of complaints that it was sending erroneous notices. Without the program in place, the Department of Revenue
had been relying on audits, which track far fewer companies, to catch those
who had not paid severance taxes. The state's legislative auditor said, "We
don't know. We don't know what the true [amount of money lost] is."

110 *Of these, only sixty—or .07 percent—were denied* LDEQ posts bulletins of
environmental permits received and has a "Check Permit Status" feature on
their website, which has 89,787 records for individual permits. The earliest
permit in the database is from 1967; the newest is from December 2013.
Some permits apply for a few years, others are decades long. The database
only has a few entries for the 1970s, and relatively fewer entries in the 1980s
and 1990s than for later—no explanation for this was given.

110 *detection levels were sometimes set high in the one and low in the other* In one
2013 study of dioxin levels in Mossville, the black township near the Arenos'
home in Bayou d'Inde now being displaced by Sasol, state scientists compared dioxin rates there (where a high rate was expected) with a comparison
group in another highly industrial area, Lafayette. Then the scientists declared that dioxins in one highly industrialized place (Mossville) were "no
higher than the comparison group" (Lafayette). Strangely, "detection levels"
were set high in Mossville (so that instruments didn't register trouble until
levels were high) and low in the area it was compared to. Given this, measures were not comparable. Sometimes the findings were simply recorded as
"not available." Meanwhile, an independent 2008 study by Dr. Wilma Subra,
a well-known chemist, reported dioxin levels in the blood of Mossville residents three times higher than in the nation as a whole. Wilma Subra, *Results of the Health Survey of Mossville Residents and Chemicals and Industrial
Sources of Chemicals Associated with Mossville Residents Medical Symptoms
and Conditions* (New Iberia, LA: Subra Company, 2008). A Spanish study
found nearness to the source of waste to be strongly correlated to tumors
of the pleura, stomach, liver, kidney, and other organs; the study took place
between 1997 and 2006. See Javier Garcia-Perez, et al., "Cancer Mortality
in Towns in the Vicinity of Incinerators and Installations for the Recovery or
Disposal of Hazardous Waste," *Environment International* 51 (2013): 31–44.
A similar study of childhood cancers in Great Britain associated childhood

cancers with prenatal or early postnatal exposures to oil-based combustion gases. E.G. Knox, "Oil Combustion and Childhood Cancers," *Journal of Epidemiology and Community Health* 59, no. 9 (2005): 755–60. Claims of a *causal* relationship between nearness to industry and illness are usually hard to prove and are not accepted in court.

110 *but not dangerous for "children six and under"* Louisiana Department of Health and Hospitals for the Agency for Toxic Substances and Disease Registry, *Health Consultation: Calcasieu Estuary Sediment Sample Evaluation, Calcasieu Parish, Louisiana, EPA Facility ID: LA0002368173* (Baton Rouge, LA: Office of Public Health, 2005).

110 *"Analyses reported as non-detects were analyzed using method detection limits that were higher than the comparison values used as screening tools"* Louisiana Department of Health and Hospitals for the Agency for Toxic Substances and Disease Registry, *Public Health Assessment, Initial/Public Comment Release, Review of Data from the 2010 EPA Mossville Site Investigation* (Baton Rouge, LA: Office of Public Health, 2013).

110 *the report was written by one set of state officials for another* The protocol was prepared by the Louisiana Department of Health and Hospitals, which collaborated with the Louisiana Department of Environmental Quality, the Louisiana Department of Agriculture and Forestry, and the Louisiana Department of Wildlife and Fisheries.

110 *Discard "juices which contain the fat . . . to further reduce exposure"* Louisiana Department of Health and Hospitals, Louisiana Department of Environmental Quality, Louisiana Department of Agriculture and Forestry, and Louisiana Department of Wildlife and Fisheries, *Protocol for Issuing Public Health Advisories for Chemical Contaminants in Recreationally Caught Fish and Shellfish* (Baton Rouge, LA: Office of Public Health, 2012), 24, http://www.dhh.louisiana.gov/assets/oph/Center-EH/envepi/fishadvisory/Documents/LA_Fish_Protocol_FINAL_Feb_2012_updated_links.pdf.

114 *our distance from necessity tends to confer honor* In *The Theory of the Leisure Class*, Thorstein Veblen (New York: Macmillan, 1899) noted that honor, as human beings construct and imagine it, is based on their degree of detachment from economic need and usefulness. So thin women were admired the closer they came to starvation, and thus showed they didn't fear it. In the realm of higher learning, Veblen argued, the more abstruse or useless the topic, the more honorific. The horse was thought more beautiful than the cow because the horse was useless and the cow was not. Perhaps each region, class, and racial group has its own expression of this principle.

8: The Pulpit and the Press: "The Topic Doesn't Come Up"

118 *has 82 churches—one for every 1,423 residents* See search results for "Lake Charles, LA" and "Berkeley, CA" on Churchfinder.com (accessed August 6, 2015), http://www.churchfinder.com.

119 *"I hope that we recognize our economic successes as a blessing from above"* "Bertrand Excited About Future of Southwest Louisiana," *American Press,* January 27, 2015, B4.

120 *Abraham's Tent, a local food pantry and soup kitchen* The soup kitchen itself is largely supported by church donations. A group called 635 Campus Ministries at McNeese State University puts on fundraisers for the organization. "Abraham's Tent Opens New Facility to Feed the Hungry," *Jambalaya News,* December 22, 2014, http://lakecharles.com/2014/12/abrahams-tent -opens-new-facility-feed-hungry.

122 *named as the poorest town in America* Jack E. White, "The Poorest Place in America," *Time,* August 15, 1994.

123 *"hunting . . . fishing in and around Louisiana, frogging"* See "Meet the Staff," First Pentecostal Church, Lake Charles (accessed August 28, 2014), http:// firstpentecostalchurchlc.org/about-us/meet-the-staff.

123 *I found no mention of activities concerned with the polluted environment* The church websites included those for Living Way, First Pentecostal Church of Lake Charles, Eastwood Pentecostal, Apostolic Temple, First Pentecostal Church of Westlake, Grace Harbor Lighthouse, First Baptist Church, Victory Baptist Church, South City Christian Church, and Trinity Baptist Church. None of the church websites mentioned ministry work related to environmental issues.

123 *leading organization of the religious right with a political voice* "Evangelical" churches differ from other Protestant churches in that they are grounded in the literal word of the Bible, especially the New Testament. Since the 1990s, evangelical leaders Pat Robertson, Jerry Falwell, Ralph Reed, and, more recently, David Lane have helped crystallize opinion on issues such as immigration, the right to abortion, and marriage equality through such organizations as the Moral Majority, Christian Coalition, Focus on the Family, Faith and Freedom Coalition, and the American Family Association.

123 *score of 10 percent or lower on the environmental scorecard of the League of Conservation Voters* A study by Glenn Scherer found that in 2003, 40 percent of the U.S. Congress—45 senators and 186 members of the House of Representatives—earned 80–100 percent approval ratings from the nation's three most influential Christian right advocacy groups: the Christian Coalition, the Eagle Forum, and the Family Resource Council. And many

in that 40 percent averaged very low scores (10 percent or less) on conservation measures from the League of Conservation Voters. See Glenn Scherer, "Christian-Right Views Are Swaying Politicians and Threatening the Environment," Grist.org, October 28, 2004, http://grist.org/article/scherer-christian.

124 *supported by various corporations, including ExxonMobil* Bill Moyers, "Welcome to Doomsday," *New York Review of Books*, March 24, 2005.

124 *calling for care of the environment—"creation care"* In a 2008 national survey of religious groups, the Bliss Center for Applied Politics at the University of Akron asked people if they agreed or disagreed with the following strongly worded statement: "Strict rules to protect the environment are necessary even if they cost jobs or result in higher prices." The least support came from traditional evangelical Protestants, among whom only 40 percent agreed. The most support came from "liberal faiths" (72 percent). John C. Green, *The Fifth National Survey of Religion and Politics* (Akron, OH: The Ray C. Bliss Center for Applied Politics at the University of Akron, 2008), http://www.uakron.edu/bliss/research/archives/2008/Blissreligionreport.pdf.

125 *many share these beliefs with Madonna* Some 50 million Americans, mostly evangelical, believe in the rapture. Belief in the rapture became widely popular in the United States in the 1970s with the publication of Hal Lindsey's *The Late Great Planet Earth*, and later through Jerry Jenkins and Tim La-Haye's series of twelve novels called Left Behind, which sold 62 million copies. See Scherer, "Christian-Right Views."

125 *the Second Coming "probably" or "definitely" will happen by the year 2050* Andrew Kohut, Scott Keeter, Carroll Doherty, Michael Dimock, Michael Remez, Robert Suls, Shawn Neidorf, Leah Christian, Jocelyn Kiley, Alec Tyson, and Jacob Pushter, "Life in 2050: Amazing Science, Familiar Threats: Public Sees a Future Full of Promise and Peril," news release, Pew Center for the People and the Press, June 22, 2010.

125 *alcohol, drugs, and even suicide* Gina Kolata, "Death Rate Rising for Middle Aged White Americans, Study Finds," *New York Times*, November 2, 2015. The rate was highest for high school–educated forty-five- to fifty-five-year-olds.

126 *shortened by three years—and truly, it seems, by despair* Sabrina Tavernise, "Life Spans Shrink for Least Educated Whites in U.S." *New York Times*, September 20, 2012.

127 *"green energy tyranny"* Fox News commentary by George Russell, December 19, 2011, "Exclusive: EPA Ponders Expanded Regulatory Power in Name of 'Sustainable Development,'" http://www.foxnews.com/poli

tics/2011/12/19/epa-ponders-expanded-regulatory-power-in-name-sustain
able-development.

127 *"[the EPA] could be part of the apparat of the Soviet Union"* "Lou Dobbs on
the EPA: 'As It's Being Run Now, It Could Be Part of the Apparatchik of
the Soviet Union,'" MediaMatters, June 6, 2011, http://mediamatters.org
/video/2011/06/06/lou-dobbs-on-the-epa-as-its-being-run-now-it-co/180331.

127–128 *compared the rise in EPA air quality standards to an "enemy attack" on
America* Todd Thurman, "Charles Krauthammer Destroys Global Warming
Myths in 89 Seconds," *Daily Signal*, February 18, 2014, http://blog.heritage
.org/2014/02/18/charles-krauthammer-destroys-global-warming-myths-89
-seconds.

128 *its oratory was inflammatory* A study by media watchdog MediaMatters analyzed the video archives of Fox News in May 2014 for references to the Environmental Protection Agency; they found seven citations of a Chamber of
Commerce study critiquing the EPA's 2014 proposed climate standards and
one citation of the National Resource Defense Council's study finding that
stricter standards would save money on household energy bills and create
jobs in clean energy industries. It also claimed that "every member of Congress who Fox News quoted or interviewed about the carbon standards also
received money from oil and gas, mining industries, or electric utilities in the
2014 election cycle," with the three biggest recipients being Senator Mitch
McConnell (R-KY), Representative Shelley Moore Capito (R-WV), and
Senator James Inhofe (R-OK). See Laura Santhanam, "Report: Fox News
Enlists Fossil Fuel Industry to Smear EPA Carbon Pollution Standards,"
MediaMatters, June 6, 2014, http://mediamatters.org/research/2014/06/06
/report-fox-news-enlists-fossil-fuel-industry-to/199622.

128 *lifted focus away from such a child's needs* See Candace Clark, *Misery and
Company: Sympathy in Everyday Life* (Chicago: University of Chicago Press,
1998).

130 *the company had hired spies to infiltrate RESTORE* James Ridgeway, "Environmental Espionage: Inside a Chemical Company's Louisiana Spy Op."

130 *a Maryland-based security firm* Ibid. Headquartered in Easton, Maryland,
BBI—or Beckett Brown International, as it was then called (the owners
since changed the name to S2i)—also served other clients (Halliburton,
Monsanto, the National Rifle Association), billing records revealed. Materials accessed through a lawsuit also showed that BBI mentioned other "possible sites" for its work—Center for Food Safety, U.S. Public Interest Research
Group, and Environment and Justice, an organization begun by Lois Gills,
who exposed the toxic waste thrown in New York's notorious Love Canal.

130 *What was that* Ibid. It emerged during the lawsuit that the company also "destroyed documents showing the full extent of the spill and the company's part in it."

130 *in a series that began with "Condea Vista Hired Spies"* Theresa Schmidt, "Condea Vista Hired Spies," KPLCTV, May 29, 2008, http://www.kplctv.com/story/8399515/condea-vista-hired-spies; Theresa Schmidt, "Spy Targets Call for Action," KPLCTV, May 30, 2008, http://www.kplctv.com/story/8404443/spy-targets-call-for-action; Theresa Schmidt, "Motion Filed to Force Disclosure of Spy Details," KPLCTV, June 4, 2008, http://www.kplctv.com/story/8433538/motion-filed-to-force-disclosure-of-spy-details; Theresa Schmidt, "Attorneys Seek Disclosure of Spy Operation," KPLCTV, December 3, 2008, http://www.kplctv.com/story/9366858/attorneys-seek-disclosure-of-spy-operation.

130 *which mentioned the 2008 exposé in passing* A Lexis-Nexis search for articles on this from 1980 to the present uncovered no coverage of the event other than the Ridgeway piece in *Mother Jones*.

9: The Deep Story

135 *I don't believe we understand anyone's politics, right or left, without it* The deep story crystalizes pre-existing feeling. It provides what T.S. Eliot calls an "objective correlative," which he describes as "a chain of events which shall be the formula (for a) particular emotion . . . such that when the external facts, which must terminate in sensory experience, are given, the emotion is immediately evoked." T.S. Eliot, *The Sacred Wood* (London: Methuen, 1920), 100. Metaphors are ways of organizing the situations that feed "emotional formulas." See Lakoff and Johnson, *Metaphors We Live By*. A metaphor is not imposed by reality, but seems, to the individual, to *fit* reality. Politics, I argue, gathers itself around a deep story—a metaphor in motion. I add the idea that the deep story implies a special corresponding self, which, once established, we guard by managing our emotions. I also add the idea that every deep story implies an area of amnesia, non-story, non-self. See also *The Managed Heart: Commercialization of Human Feeling*, 44.

136 *white, older, Christian, and predominantly male, some with college degrees, some not* David R. Gibson, "Doing Time in Space: Line Joining Rules and Resulting Morphologies," *Sociological Forum* 23, no. 2 (June 2008): 207–33.

139–140 *which celebrates so many black people, women, and immigrants* This is in accord with the analysis of Dr. Larry Rosenthal, Director of the Center for Right Wing Studies, Institute for the Study of Social Issues, U.C. Berkeley. See http://www.fljs.org/sites/www.fljs.org/files/publications/Rosenthal.pdf.

141 *"they have less income and less net wealth than people their age ten years before"* Phillip Longman, "Wealth and Generations," *Washington Monthly*, June/July/August 2015, 3, http://www.washingtonmonthly.com/magazine /junejulyaugust_2015/features/wealth_and_generations055898.php.

141 *share of men ages twenty-five to fifty-four no longer in the workforce has tripled* Ibid.

141 *Oneself, of course* See Allison Pugh, *The Tumbleweed Society: Working and Caring in an Age of Insecurity* (London: Oxford University Press, 2015).

143 *the repeated term "millionaire" floated around conversations like a ghost* As his wages drastically fell, Bill saw consumer aspirations around the nation rise to those of the 1 percent. In *The Overspent American*, the economist Juliet Schor notes that when asked to describe the "good life," 19 percent of Americans mentioned a "vacation home" in 1975; 35 percent mentioned it in 1991. A swimming pool? 14 percent in 1975, 29 percent in 1991. A lot of money? 38 percent in 1975, 55 percent in 1991. A job that pays much more than average? 45 percent in 1975, 60 percent in 1991. Juliet Schor, *The Overspent American: Why We Want What We Don't Need* (New York: Harper Perennial, 1999), 16.

144 *"Working class whites are now regularly portrayed as moronic, while blacks are often hyper-articulate, street smart . . . and rich"* Barbara Ehrenreich, "Dead, White, and Blue: The Great Die-Off of America's Blue Collar Whites," Tom Dispatch.com, December 1, 2015, http://www.tomdispatch.com/post/176075 /tomgram.

145 *to say 'under God'* In 1954, President Eisenhower signed a law that called for inserting the phrase "under God" into the pledge of allegiance. The phrase has been the target of lawsuits over the years, including one that was dismissed by the 9th Circuit Court of Appeals in 2010. The plaintiffs objected to the phrase, claiming it was an instance of religious messaging by public schools. The court ruled "under God" was not an endorsement of religion, noting the pledge has long been optional. In 1943, the Supreme Court ruled schools could not force children to recite the pledge. While in office, President Obama rejected a petition to remove "under God" from the pledge, though a right-wing Internet hoax claimed the president banned the pledge. "Pledge of Allegiance Fast Facts," CNN, April 24, 2017), http://www.cnn .com/2013/09/04/us/pledge-of-allegiance-fast-facts; Rachel Weiner, "White House Rejects 'Death Star' Petition," *Washington Post*, January 12, 2013; Caroline Wallace, "Obama Did Not Ban the Pledge," FactCheck.org, September 2, 2016, http://www.factcheck.org/2016/09/obama-did-not-ban-the-pledge.

145 *spontaneous mention of the idea of annoyance at others cutting in line* Nils

Kumkar, "A Socio-Analysis of Discontent: Protests Against the Politics of Crisis in the U.S. and Germany: An Empirical Comparison," PhD thesis, Department of Sociology, University of Leipzig (unpublished; e-mail communication, November 30, 2015).

146 *attitudes toward blacks, immigrants, public sector workers, and others* Skocpol and Williamson, *The Tea Party and the Remaking of Republican Conservatism.*

146 *the state's largest minority* Public Religion Research Institute's American Values Atlas, Louisiana, http://ava.publicreligion.org/#religious/2015/States/religion/m/US-LA.

148 *equal pay for equal work* Melissa Deckman, "A Gender Gap in the Tea Party?" paper prepared for the Midwest Political Science Association Meetings, April 11–14, 2013 (unpublished paper).

149 *haves and have-nots* The 90–10 distribution figure describes the situation if the federal government were out of the picture—i.e., pre-tax, and pre-distribution of funds through such programs as unemployment insurance, food stamps, and Medicaid. From 1980 to 2012, the U.S. GDP soared while the bottom 90 percent of Americans received no benefit from this growth. During this time, the top 10 percent averaged $260,488 a year and the bottom 90 percent, $31,659. No one I met earned anything like $260,489 a year. The income *threshold* to the top 10 percent was $118,140 in 2014 (or $115,938 in 2012). And those combining the incomes of both spouses—whatever the education of either—enjoyed incomes that were that high or higher.

150 *more profits to top executives and stockholders, and less to workers* Robert Reich, *Saving Capitalism: For the Many, Not the Few* (New York: Knopf, 2015); John Ehrenreich, *Third Wave Capitalism: How Money, Power, and the Pursuit of Self-Interest Have Imperiled the American Dream* (Ithaca and London: ILR Press, an Imprint of Cornell University Press, forthcoming 2016); Thomas Piketty and Emmanuel Saez, *2007 Average Incomes, U.S. 1980–2012* (in real 2014 dollars). Also see Thomas Piketty, *Capital in the Twenty-First Century* (Boston: Harvard University Press, 2014). Thomas Piketty and his French-American colleague, Emmanuel Saez, base this distribution on income individuals hold in the absence of government activity—so it's what people have if they neither pay taxes nor receive government distributions (e.g., Social Security, unemployment insurance, food stamps, Medicaid, or earned income tax credits). Also see Jacob S. Hacker and Paul Pierson, *Winner-Take-All Politics* (New York: Simon & Schuster, 2010). Within the United States, it has always been hard to make an extreme leap; an American child born in 1971 to parents in the bottom fifth of the income ladder has only an 8 percent chance of reaching the top

fifth—the romanticized rags-to-riches rise. To assess intergenerational mobility, researchers analyzed the tax returns of forty million thirty-year-old Americans and their parents' tax returns of twenty years earlier. Raj Chetty, Nathaniel Hendren, Patrick Kline, Emmanuel Saez, Nicholas Turner, "Is the United States Still a Land of Opportunity? Recent Trends in Intergenerational Mobility," NBER Working Paper 19844, http://www.nber.org/pa pers/w19844. Also see Raj Chetty, Nathaniel Hendren, Patrick Kline, and Emmanuel Saez, "Where Is the Land of Opportunity? The Geography of Intergenerational Mobility in the United States," *The Quarterly Journal of Economics* (2014): 1–71. Social mobility is very influenced by location for low-income young people, though not for their upper-income counterparts. See David Leonhardt, "In Climbing Income Ladder, Location Matters," *New York Times*, July 22, 2013, http://www.nytimes.com/2013/07/22/busi ness/in-climbing-income-ladder-location-matters.html?.

10: The Team Player: Loyalty Above All

159 *"but there's a positive side to the war"* Janice favored the invasion of Iraq and believed Saddam Hussein harbored weapons of mass destruction and had contact with Al Qaeda before the United States invaded Iraq.

162 *"that's the consensus in liberal Hollywood"* Chaz is now a transgender man, not gay.

163 *Industry had brought four toxic waste landfills to Sulphur, one only a block from her present home* Louisiana Department of Environmental Quality, "Solid Waste Landfill Report," (accessed August 7, 2015), http://www.deq .louisiana.gov/portal/DIVISIONS/WastePermits/SolidWastePermits/Solid WasteLandfillReport.aspx.

166 *did a person with that kind of self end up thinking "anything goes"?* For a helpful analysis of types of individualism, see Ann Swidler, "Cultural Constructions of Modern Individualism," paper delivered at Meeting of American Sociological Association, August 23, 1992.

12: The Cowboy: Stoicism

183 *handled electrical wires atop telephone poles—dangerous jobs* For his part, as a three-year-old child, Mike Tritico was a daredevil like Donny but was quickly cured of it. One of his earliest memories is being saved by a grandfather, Pappa Bill, from a foolish childhood flight into a fireplace at Christmas. "I thought I could fly like Superman," Tritico recounted, "and took off across the living room and into the fireplace, stuck my hands in the coals, was about to take a breath when my grandfather jerked me out by the shirt

[and] said, 'There are dangers we need to be saved from.'" In his adult life, Tritico has himself become a protector. His mother, highly intelligent but emotionally volatile, had led Mike to keep a protective eye on his siblings. Dangers are about; one has to keep watch.

184 *had begun to have trouble breathing and had sued* James Ridgeway, "Environmental Espionage: Inside a Chemical Company's Louisiana Spy Op."

188 *"Oh, that's probably Donny"* John Guldroz, "LSU Professor Discusses Climate Change, Erosion," *American Press*, June 28, 2013.

188 *since the woman in question should have learned her lesson* As in many such conversations, the race of the woman with too many children on welfare was left ambiguous. For the actual fertility rates of white and black mothers, see Appendix C.

188 *"Do you worry about exposure to these dangerous chemicals?"* John Baugher and J. Timmons Roberts, "Perceptions and Worry About Hazards at Work: Unions, Contract Maintenance, and Job Control in the U.S. Petrochemical Industry," *Industrial Relations* 38, no. 4 (1999): 522–41.

189 *workers worried less, and managers worried more* Less than 10 percent of clerical workers—nearly all of whom were women—said they were "often or always" exposed to dangerous chemicals, but 35 percent said they worried about that exposure (ibid., 531). So Donny resembled the hourly crafts-worker. Mike Tritico resembled the professional manager and clerical worker. In addition, union members were three times as likely to worry about safety as were non-union members, perhaps due to their greater safety training, and were likely to say the plant lacked sufficient safety regulations (28 percent union versus 10 percent non-union). Donny resembled the non-union worker; Tritico was similar to his union counterpart. Plants generally hire contract workers to help with their turnaround maintenance system, during which time workers are under great pressure to get the plant up and running again. Dangers increase during this time. Six out of ten workers felt the plant was less safe during such times. Core workers felt safer than contract workers and worried less about fires. Core workers were more secure (only 6 percent had experienced job layoffs in the preceding year, compared to 51 percent of contract workers). Insecurity increased fear. And contract workers were nearly twice as likely not to exercise their right to refuse unsafe work.

189 *minorities did so more than whites* As the authors note, "even when controlling for income, education and several other important factors, it became clear that the unusual—unworried—group was not the women, but white men" (ibid., 523).

189 *white males stood out from all other groups as being less likely to see risk* Matthew Desmond, *On the Fireline: Living and Dying with Wildland Firefighters* (Chicago: University of Chicago Press, 2007).

13: The Rebel: A Team Loyalist with a New Cause

194 *give victims the replacement value of lost homes within 180 days of an accident* Senate Bill 209 did not call for a halt to salt-dome drilling but rather amended the requirements for obtaining a permit to do so. It added the requirement to reimburse the state for the costs of disaster response, and reimbursement to property owners for the fair market value of their property. The bill was tabled.

194 *Mike Schaff wrote the secretary of the Louisiana Department of Environmental Quality to object* He addressed his letter to Ms. Peggy Hatch and it concerned Permit Number LA0126917 and Activity Number PER20140001, Texas Brine, LLC, 201.

195 *"I pray one day I'll be able to speak with no tears, just anger"* Mike Schaff, e-mail message to author, June 8, 2015.

197 *Mike called for the more reliable "Feds" to double-check* The Louisiana State Department of Environmental Quality claimed its meters had picked up no traces of gas and that air and water were "completely safe." But Mike wrote to officials that he smelled "very strong odors of crude and/or diesel wafting through the area. . . . It would calm fears," he wrote, "if we had back up from the feds to verify this. . . . We ask you to see if the EPA can send a representative to review the water quality and air quality" (personal communication).

199 *"where roseate spoonbills nest every spring"* "Iberia Parish, Louisiana," Tour Louisiana travel directory website (accessed August 7, 2015), http://www .tourlouisiana.com/content.cfm?id=15.

199 *in a massive new project in Lake Peigneur* Jefferson Island Storage and Hub (formerly AGL Resources) merged with energy giant Nocor Oil & Gas to become the largest natural gas distributor in the United States. It wants to expand its use of salt caverns to store gas. See AGL Resources, *2011 Annual Report* (accessed August 7, 2015), http://www.aglresources.com/about /docs/AGL_AR_2011/2011AnnualReport.pdf. Shareholder return in 2011 was 24 percent. Also see Yolanda Martinez, "Environmentalists Allege Constitutional Violation in Permitting Gas Storages Salt Dome Construction in Lake Peigneur," *Louisiana Record*, July 24, 2013.

199 *all inside the salt dome underlying Lake Peigneur* In 2013, a public hearing on one of the three remaining state permits was set. Atlanta-based AGL

Resources was proposing to scour out two new salt caverns for natural gas storage at its Jefferson Island Storage and Hub Facility, expanding on the two storage caverns that have been there since the 1990s and more than doubling storage capacity. AGL needed two other state permits for the project—one to scour out caverns in the salt dome and another to use the scoured caverns for natural gas storage. AGL's proposed expansion had been on hold since 2006, when then-governor Kathleen Blanco called for an extensive environmental study of the project. AGL filed a lawsuit against the state, and the case ended with a settlement in 2009 that called for additional safeguards, but not the environmental review that residents in the area had demanded. After the settlement, the permitting process started anew.

199 *"Thank God they decided the salt dome wasn't okay to store nuclear waste!"* In August 2012, *The Advocate* published an investigation into Department of Natural Resources records and found that Texas Brine had been allowed to inject radioactive disposal material into a cavern in the Napoleonville salt dome in 1995. See "Dome Issues Kept Quiet," *The Advocate*, August 12, 2012.

199 *The bill did not pass* "Good Morning, Senator Long," the letter read. "I am not a highly paid lobbyist for the energy industry, nor am I a 'tree-hugger.' In fact, my livelihood and that of many in this area has relied on that industry. . . . It's sad that members of my very own community face a bleak and uncertain future due to the unstable and poorly regulated mining of the salt dome beneath our feet. Hopefully, with this bill's passage, the residents surrounding the Jefferson Island dome won't face similar consequences." It was signed: Mike and Becky Schaff, Bayou Corne residents and Friends of Lake Peigneur.

200 *an average football field every hour* Coastal Wetlands Planning, Protection and Restoration Act (CWPPRA), "Frequently Asked Questions," https://la coast.gov/new/About/FAQs.aspx.

200 *de-listing coastal postal addresses* John Snell, "As More of Coastal Louisiana Is Lost, Official Map Makers Erase Names," WorldNow, April 21, 2014, http://apmobile.worldnow.com/story/24807691/as-more-of-coastal-louisiana -is-lost-mapmakers-erase-names.

200 *The church in Grand Bayou stands on stilts; a small cemetery is accessible only by boat* John Snell, "Despite Land Loss, Native American Community Clings to Life Along the Mississippi River," WorldNow, March 4, 2015, http://apmobile.worldnow.com/story/26559685/despite-land-loss-native -american-community-clings-to-life-along-the-mississippi-river; Amy Wold, "Washed Away," *The Advocate*, http://theadvocate.com/home/5782941-125 /washed-away.

200 *the first "climate refugees"* Coral Davenport and Campbell Robertson, "Resettling the First American 'Climate Refugees,'" *New York Times*, May 3, 2016.

202 *it wasn't worth believing in or paying taxes to* Shortly after I visited the Bayou Corne Sinkhole in 2014, Mike sent me an e-mail, with the subject line "Sinkhole of Another Sort" and a link to an article in the *Washington Post* about six hundred employees in Boyers, Pennsylvania, who process the paper-based retirement records of government workers by hand. The office is located in an abandoned salt mine to make room for storage. "See the waste?" he wrote. David Fahrenthold, "Deep Underground Federal Employees Process Paperwork by Hand in a Long Outdated Inefficient System," *Washington Post*, March 22, 2014.

14: The Fires of History: The 1860s and the 1960s

207 *as the historian Richard Hofstadter has noted* Richard Hofstadter, *The Age of Reform* (New York: Vintage, 1955), 4; see Richard Hofstadter, *Anti-Intellectualism in American Life* (New York: Vintage Books, 1966); Jill Lepore, *The Whites of Their Eyes: The Tea Party's Revolution and the Battle over American History* (Princeton, NJ: Princeton University Press, 2010).

208 *In his classic* The Mind of the South, *W.J. Cash says* W.J. Cash, *The Mind of the South* (New York: Vintage Books, 1991).

208 *"a potential planter or mill baron himself"* Ibid., 39, 217. Cash describes a "wide, diffuse gratefulness pouring out upon the cotton-mill baron; upon the old captains, upon all the captains and preachers of Progress, upon the ruling class as a whole for having embraced the doctrine and brought these things [economic progress of the 1890s] . . . as the instrument of salvation both for the South as such and for themselves" (ibid., 215).

208 *and poor whites took them as such* "However cynical his deeds may seem," Cash writes, the rich white planter "almost invariably thought of himself as a great public patron and came to his clients with the manner and the conviction of conferring inestimable benefits. . . . Hadn't he made it possible for you to grow cotton? Did not he enable you to keep on in that pursuit year after year? And if in the end he sold you out, would you, stout individualist, have done otherwise in his place? Wasn't he kind about it? Didn't he often see to it that you got a good place as tenant, either on his own acres or elsewhere?" Fearing slave revolts, rich planters offered favors and appealed to a common racial identity and made their poor neighbors feel like honorary planters. As Cash explains, rich whites "came to the use of white tenants only through the operation of race loyalty and the old paternalism. They felt . . . not the slightest responsibility for what had happened to the

dispossessed [poor white] . . . but here they were . . . under our planter eyes. Men we have known all our days, laughed with, hunted with and in many a case, fought side by side with" (ibid., 166).

208 *much more wealth to envy above, and far more misery to gasp at below* To be sure, the South had a small number of black slaveowners and white indentured servants, but overwhelmingly blacks were the victims, their fate the most feared. There were 3,959 lynchings in the South, 540 in Louisiana and 4 in Calcasieu Parish, but no monuments to commemorate the victims, some in the records for "being the father of the rapist" or "hiding under the bed" or "voodoo." But a school curriculum that discussed this history seemed to most of those I got to know a matter quite distinct from "racism." The highest number of lynchings in the South took place in the 1890s—as many as twenty-six in 1890. Two took place in 1928. Mostly black men, mostly for murder or rape, all males but for one female for attempted murder, two for murder and insurrection. Two white males were killed because they "angered Klan," one in Bossier County for "living with white woman," one "peeping Tom," and two simply as "brother of murder(er)." And another, in Calcasieu, "defending rapist." In Mississippi, some reasons given were "father of murderer," "frightened woman," "outraged young girl," "reproved white youth," "race prejudice," and "indolence." See the records kept by Project HAL: Historical American Lynching Data Collection Project, University of North Carolina–Wilmington, http://people.uncw.edu/hinese /HAL/HAL%20Web%20Page.htm. In a study of counties with the most lynchings between 1877 and 1950, four of the top five were in Louisiana (in Caddo, Lafourche, Ouachita, and Tensas Parishes). This number was fewer than in Mississippi and more than in Virginia. (The very highest numbers took place in Arkansas, Mississippi, and Georgia.)

208 *much room for the forgotten behind* Cash, *The Mind of the South*, 22. Often plantations were funded, and sometimes owned, by northern banks.

208–209 *"sagging rail fences . . . and crazy barns which yet bulged with corn"* Ibid.

209 *"armed with plentiful capital and solid battalions of slaves"* Ibid.

209 *"to all the marginal lands of the South"* Ibid., 23.

209 *"cornpone and the flesh of razorback hogs"* Ibid.

209 *left to live on what they themselves could produce* Ibid.

210 *"What oil and gas did is replace the agricultural with an oil 'plantation culture'"* Oliver A. Houck, "Save Ourselves: The Environmental Case That Changed Louisiana," *Louisiana Law Review* 72 (2012): 409–37.

211 *they should get me in a different costume to talk about that* Massive federal investments were made in the South during the period between the 1860s

and the 1960s, as Michael Hout has pointed out to me. See Claude Fischer and Michael Hout, *Century of Difference: How America Changed in the Last One Hundred Years* (New York: Russell Sage Foundation, 2008). Also see Ira Katznelson, *When Affirmative Action Was White: An Untold History of Racial Inequality in Twentieth-Century America* (New York: Norton Publishing Co., 2006).

212 *flame up years later as the Tea Party* See Chip Berlet, "Reframing Populist Resentment in the Tea Party Movement," in *Steep: The Precipitous Rise of the Tea Party*, edited by Lawrence Rosenthal and Christine Trost (Berkeley: University of California Press, 2012), 47–66. Lawrence Rosenthal has also stressed the importance of reactions to the resistance to the Vietnam War.

212 *June of 1964: Freedom Summer* Two organizations—CORE (the Chicago-based Congress for Racial Equality) and SNCC (Student Non-Violent Coordinating Committee)—together organized students.

213 *challenged the all-white regular delegation* Doug McAdam, *Freedom Summer* (Oxford: Oxford University Press, 1990).

214 *received any money from the federal government* In 1964, Title VII was added to the Civil Rights Act, stating that it was illegal to discriminate against women, and in 1972, Title IX banned discrimination in education.

214 *the critic Todd Gitlin, a former 1960s activist, lamented* Todd Gitlin, *The Twilight of Common Dreams: Why America Is Wracked by Culture Wars* (New York: Metropolitan Press, 1995), 124–25.

214 *fairness seemed to stop before it got to him* In 2015, the one thousand student activity groups of the University of California, Berkeley, reflected the student culture of its 37,000 students. Some student groups were based on professional interests (for example, the Society for Landscape Architecture). Others were focused on social causes (for example, the Campus Green Initiative, Amnesty International, the Anti-Trafficking Coalition). Still others were based on religion (the Acts 2 Fellowship) or recreation (the Berkeley Ballroom Dancers), or a group puts two themes together (the Christ-Centered Dance Group). Still others were based on personal challenge—for example, Body Peace, students addressing the challenge of eating disorders. In the spirit of identity politics, other groups were defined purely by ethnicity—the Asian and Pacific Islander Women's Circle, Cal Queer and Asian, the Albanian Association, the American Indian Studies Association. Or race and gender identification were mixed with a professional or recreational interest: the American Medical Women's Association at Berkeley, the Armenian Law Student Association, the Black Engineering and Science Student Association. Louisiana State University in Baton Rouge, from which many

of my informants had graduated, had, with its nearly 31,000 students, 375 recognized student groups. The groups reflected a busy sorority and fraternity life tacitly divided by gender, of course, and a few other groups, such as Minorities in Agriculture and Natural Resources, or the Minority Women's Movement, reflected ethnic status as a basis of membership.

215 *it was your sector, the free market, that was letting you down* Citizens for Tax Justice, "Corporate Taxpayers and Corporate Tax Dodgers, 2008–2010," November 2011, http://ctj.org/ctjreports/2011/11/corporate_taxpayers_cor porate_tax_dodgers_2008-2010.php. Most American companies also pay lower taxes in the U.S. than on their foreign operations.

15: Strangers No Longer: The Power of Promise

221 *the rally at the Lakefront Airport in New Orleans* According to *Wall Street Journal* commentator Gerald Seib, Trump is the "inheritor" of the Tea Party without fitting squarely into any of the conservative strands of thought it combines. Gerald Seib, "How Trump's Army Is Transforming the GOP," *Wall Street Journal*, February 23, 2016.

225 *"I'll press charges"* CNN Politics, "Trump Ends Wild Day on Campaign Trail by Calling for Protesters' Arrests," March 13, 2016, http://www.cnn.com /2016/03/12/politics/donald-trump-protests. Also see "Next Time We See Him, We Might Have to Kill Him: Trump Fan on Punching Black Protester," RT.com, March 11, 2016, https://www.rt.com/usa/335188-trump -protester-punched-arrest.

225 *"I would have gone bum, bum, bum"* Donald J. Trump, rally in Kansas City, Missouri, March 12, 2016, https://www.youtube.com/watch?v=owSn8IY QUks.

225 *"We're going to get rid of it in almost every form"* Coral Davenport, "E.P.A. Faces More Tasks, Louder Critics, and a Shrinking Budget," *New York Times*, March 19, 2016.

225 *"We're not silent anymore"* "Donald Trump Forcefully Removes Protesters from Louisiana Rally," Mic.com, March 5, 2016, http://mic.com/articles /137129/donald-trump-forcefully-removes-protesters-from-louisiana-rally.

225 *They gather to affirm their unity* Emile Durkheim, *The Elementary Forms of Religious Life* (New York: The Free Press, 1965 [1915]), 432; also page 417 on rites as a form of dramatic art and page 446 on scapegoating. Also see René Gerard, *The Scapegoat* (Baltimore: Johns Hopkins University, 1986).

228 *the reason for this shield of talk was to protect her elation* The need to believe is poignantly and insightfully described by Leon Festinger, Henry W.

Riechen, and Stanley Schachter in *When Prophecy Fails* (London: Pinter and Martin, 2008 [1956]).

16: "They Say There Are Beautiful Trees"

231 *their names on waiting lists with thousands of others* Chico Harlan, "Battered by Drop in Oil Prices and Jindal's Fiscal Policies, Louisiana Falls into Budget Crisis," *Washington Post*, March 4, 2016, https://www.washingtonpost.com/news/wonk/wp/2016/03/04/the-debilitating-economic-disaster-louisianas-governor-left-behind. Also see Campbell Robertson, "In Louisiana, the Poor Lack Legal Defense," *New York Times*, March 20, 2016.

233 *"but for the technology and talent they supply"* Richard Florida, "Is Life Better in America's Red States?" *New York Times Sunday Review*, January 3, 2015.

233 *Young conservatives are far more likely than their elders to care about the environment* Amanda Little, "Will Conservatives Finally Embrace Clean Energy?" *New Yorker*, October 29, 2015.

233 *1969 Union Oil spill in the waters outside Santa Barbara, California* Dan Fagin, *Toms River: A Story of Science and Salvation* (New York: Bantam Books, 2013).

233 *since 2009 rates of air, water, and land pollution have been rising again across the nation* Despite earlier progress, pollution trends in the nation as a whole have recently begun to rise. Toxic waste disposal in water has risen since 1988. Disposal in land has risen since 2009, and disposal in air and water has also gone up since 2009. County, state, and national trends for air, land, and water have mostly gone up in recent years. For the United States as a whole, total air emissions were 318,928,965.52 pounds in 2009 and 327,579,947 in 2012. As for water, in 2008, emissions were 12,165,940 pounds a year, and in 2012, 12,551,178. For injection wells, the figure in 2005 was 95,110,426 pounds deposited in the earth; in 2012 it was 96,246,373. For landfills, the figure was 74,721,866 pounds, but by 2013 it had risen to 78,374,459 pounds. Data from the Environmental Protection Agency's Toxics Release Inventory website can be found at http://www2.epa.gov/toxics-release-inventory-tri-program.

235 *Norwegians live upper-middle-class lives* In 2014, Louisiana corporate income taxes yielded $481,212,000 in revenue, and severance taxes brought in $862,150,000. According to information from the Louisiana Legislative Auditor and the state Department of Revenue, however, Louisiana lost $2.4 billion because companies were offered large exemptions between 2000 and 2014 on oil severance taxes. Indeed, for three years it was hard to tell whether the oil companies paid anything to the state, since the job of

auditing oil company payments was handed over to the Office of Mineral Resources, which has close ties with industry and which, between 2010 and 2013, performed no audits at all. U.S. Census Bureau, "State Government Tax Collections: 2014," Table STC005 (accessed December 11, 2015), http://factfinder.census.gov/bkmk/table/1.0/en/STC/2014/STC005. Institute for Southern Studies, "Looting Louisiana: How the Jindal Administration Is Helping Big Oil Rip Off a Cash-Strapped State," http://www .southernstudies.org/2015/05/looting-louisiana-how-the-jindal-administra tion-is.html. The report cites the Louisiana Department of Revenue's "Tax Exemption Budget, 2011–2012" and "Tax Exemption Budget 2014–2015."

235 *overall well-being that come with such affluence—they enjoy freedom from need* Paradoxically, it is partly Norway's culture of *ownership* as well its belief in sharing the proceeds from oil with the citizenry that have led to its great wealth. The assistant director of the Norwegian Ministry of Oil and Energy, Mette Agerup, explained that Norway operated on the premise that "the oil company was the helper in harnessing the country's natural resources, but that the oil ultimately *belongs to* the nation." Kevin Grandia, "If Canada Is 'Oil Rich' Why Are We So in Debt?" DESMOGCANADA, March 5, 2013, http://www.desmog.ca/2013/02/28/if-canada-oil-rich-why-are-we-so-debt.

236 *divide those who "see the game as rigged and those who don't"* Reich, *Saving Capitalism*, 188.

237 *The reds might be the Louisiana model, and to some degree, the blues are the California one* Caroline Hanley and Michael T. Douglass, "High Road, Low Road or Off Road: Economic Development Strategies in the American States," *Economic Development Quarterly* (2014): 1–10.

237 *there are ideas beyond either party yet to be born* See Thomas Frank *Listen Liberal, or What Ever Happened to the Party of the People?* (New York: Metropolitan Press, 2016), and Joe Bageant, *Deer Hunting with Jesus: Dispatches from America's Class War* (New York: Crown Books, 2007).

238 *So the Arenos were left as prisoners of their lost paradise, rememberers* The suit was filed April 2, 1996, and dismissed in 2014. *Harold Areno, et al. v. the Chemical Manufacturers Association, et al.*, 14th Judicial District Court, Calcasieu Parish, Louisiana. Harold Areno was one of twenty-two plaintiffs in the class-action petition for damages against PPG, Axiall, Citgo, Occidental Chemical, and Westlake Polymers, among others. As Mike Tritico explained in an e-mail, "with the failure of ATSDR (Agency for Toxic Substances and Disease Registry) to confirm any significant chlorinated hydrocarbon problem in the area, the plaintiffs' attorneys had no way to prove any damages," Mike Tritico, e-mail to the author, July 27, 2015.

238 *a cleanup crew had been stirred into action* Frank DiCesare, "Bayou d'Inde Cleanup to Begin This Month," *American Press*, February 16, 2015.

238 *place six inches of clean sediment on top of it* The idea of cleaning up Bayou d'Inde died under the local authority of the Louisiana Department of Environmental Quality, where PPG "took the leadership." Right nearby, curiously, Bayou Verdine, a small tributary of the Calcasieu River, which, like Bayou d'Inde, flows through both residential and industrial areas, had been in the 1980s equally contaminated, and is now clean. That contamination had not been left to the companies themselves but to federal agencies—the National Oceanic and Atmospheric Administration and the U.S. Fish and Wildlife Service.

238 *"As long as you reduce the chemical concentrations on the surface, you're okay"* William Fontenot, e-mail to the author, December 16, 2013.

242 *the Texas state legislature effectively forbade any local bans of fracking and waste disposal* Mose Buchele, "After HB 40, What's Next for Local Drilling Rules in Texas?" StateImpact, July 2, 2015, https://stateimpact.npr.org/texas/2015/07/02/after-hb-40-whats-next-for-local-drilling-bans-in-texas/.

242 *adamantly opposed bans on it* Zaid Jilani, "Fracking Industry Billionaires Give Record $15 Million to Ted Cruz's Super PAC," Alternet, July 25, 2015, http://www.alternet.org/election-2016/fracking-industry-billionaires-give-record-15-million-ted-cruzs-super-pac.

Afterword

244 *its enormous planned expansion in Lake Charles* Ted Griggs, "Low Oil Prices Claim Sasol's Proposed $15 Billion Gas-to-Liquids Plant Near Lake Charles," *The Advocate*, November 23, 2017, http://www.theadvocate.com/baton_rouge/news/business/article_3c940178-d051-11e7-8493-07a7ef24d003.html.

244 *Trump had chosen Scott Angelle* Richard Thompson, "Louisiana Political Veteran Scott Angelle to Head Federal Offshore Drilling Oversight Agency," *The Advocate*, May 22, 2017, http://www.theadvocate.com/baton_rouge/news/business/article_911560b2-3efb-11e7-9b89-03c7953e6b78.html.

244 *the Axiall plant in Westlake exploded* Associated Press, "Number of Injured from Axiall Chemical Pant Fire in Westlake Rises to 18," *Times-Picayune*, December 25, 2013, http://www.nola.com/environment/index.ssf/2013/12/number_of_injured_from_axiall.html.

246 *"I often feel like a stranger in my own country"* Daniel Cox, Rachel Lienesch, and Robert P. Jones, "Beyond Economics: Fears of Cultural Displacement

Pushed the White Working Class to Trump," *The Atlantic* and Public Religion Research Institute, May 9, 2017, https://www.prri.org/research/white -working-class-attitudes-economy-trade-immigration-election-donald -trump.

253 *Some of the marchers were from old-guard groups* Fox News, "Charlottesville and a ' New Generation of White Supremacists,' " August 17, 2017, http:// www.foxnews.com/us/2017/08/17/charlottesville-and-new-generation -white-supremacists.html.

253 *President Trump publicly placed equal blame* Graham Lanktree, "Donald Trump's Charlottesville Response Will Continue to Haunt Him, Says Watergate Veteran," *Newsweek*, August 21, 2017, http://www.newsweek.com/why -donald-trumps-charlottesville-response-will-continue-haunt-him-652670.

253 *he had remained silent for forty-eight hours* Dan Merica, "Trump Calls KKK, Neo-Nazis, White Supremacists 'Repugnant,' " CNN, August 14, 2017, http://www.cnn.com/2017/08/14/politics/trump-condemns-charlottesville -attackers/index.html.

253 *"do you approve or disapprove of Trump's response"* Scott Clement and David Nakamura, "Poll Shows Clear Disapproval of How Trump Responded to Charlottesville Violence," *Washington Post*, August 21, 2017, https://www .washingtonpost.com/politics/poll-shows-strong-disapproval-of-how-trump -responded-to-charlottesville-violence/2017/08/21/4e5c585c-868b-11e7-a9 4f-3139abce39f5_story.html?utm_term=.3ee5ffac299a.

254 *is white racism the overriding source of support* Eric D. Knowles, Brian S. Lowery, Elizabeth P. Shulman, and Rebecca L. Schaumberg, "Race, Ideology, and the Tea Party: A Longitudinal Study," *PLoS ONE* 8, no. 6 (2013): e67110, http://journals.plos.org/plosone/article?id=10.1371/journal .pone.0067110; "NPR Covers Robb Willer's Research on Racial Prejudice and the Tea Party," Stanford University, July 15, 2016, https://sociology .stanford.edu/news/npr-covers-robb-willers-research-racial-prejudice-and -tea-party.

255 *"White people benefit from advantages in society that black people do not have"* Baxter Oliphant, "Views About Whether Whites Benefit from Societal Advantages Split Sharply Along Racial and Partisan Lines," Pew Research Center, September 28, 2017, http://www.pewresearch.org/fact -tank/2017/09/28/views-about-whether-whites-benefit-from-societal-advan tages-split-sharply-along-racial-and-partisan-lines.

258 *Jason Kessler had become enraged* This American Life, "White Haze," WBEZ, September 22, 2017, https://www.thisamericanlife.org/radio-archives/epis ode/626/white-haze.

260 *black freshmen were more underrepresented* Jeremy Ashkenas, Haeyoun Park, and Adam Pearce, "Even with Affirmative Action, Blacks and Hispanics Are More Underrepresented at Top Colleges Than 35 Years Ago," *New York Times*, August 24, 2017, https://www.nytimes.com/interactive/2017/08/24/us/affirmative-action.html.

260 *The gap in household income has also remained* Paul F. Campos, "White Economic Privilege Is Alive and Well," *New York Times*, July 29, 2017, https://www.nytimes.com/2017/07/29/opinion/sunday/black-income-white-privilege.html?_r=0.

260 *The 2008 financial crash* Mallie Jane Kim, "Pew: Recession Hurts Hispanics, Blacks More Than Whites," *U.S. News & World Report*, July 26, 2011, https://www.usnews.com/news/articles/2011/07/26/pew-recession-hurt-hispanics-blacks-more-than-whites.

261 *black and white job applicants with identical job qualifications* To round out the picture, blacks with a criminal record had a 5 percent callback rate. Devah Pager, "The Mark of a Criminal Record," *American Journal of Sociology* (2003): 937–975.

261 *women have reduced the education and income gaps* Elise Gould, Jessica Schieder, and Kathleen Geier, "What Is the Gender Pay Gap and Is It Real?" Economic Policy Institute, October 20, 2016, http://www.epi.org/publication/what-is-the-gender-pay-gap-and-is-it-real. Also see Kevin Miller, "The Simple Truth About the Gender Pay Gap," American Association of University Women, Fall 2017, https://www.aauw.org/research/the-simple-truth-about-the-gender-pay-gap.

261 *They now earn slightly more bachelor's degrees* Camille L. Ryan and Kurt Bauman, "Educational Attainment in the United States: 2015," U.S. Census Bureau, March 2016, https://www.census.gov/content/dam/Census/library/publications/2016/demo/p20-578.pdf.

261 *more Mexicans left the United States than entered it* For information about the falling immigrant population, the study commonly cited is from the Pew Research Center. According to the report, from 2009 to 2014, there was a net loss of 140,000 Mexicans in the United States, including legal and illegal immigration. Ana Gonzalez-Barrera, "More Mexicans Leaving Than Coming to the U.S.," Pew Research Center, November 19, 2015, http://www.pewhispanic.org/2015/11/19/more-mexicans-leaving-than-coming-to-the-u-s.

261 *According to a 2017 Bloomberg report* David Wethe, "Robots Are Taking Over Oil Rigs," Bloomberg, January 24, 2017, https://www.bloomberg.com/news/articles/2017-01-24/robots-are-taking-over-oil-rigs-as-roughnecks-become-expendable.

261 *"To me, it's not just about automating the rig"* Ibid.

261 *rough estimates of the "automatability" of each one* Carl Frey and Michael Osborne, "The Future of Employment: How Susceptible Are Jobs to Computerisation?" (Oxford Martin School Working Paper, University of Oxford, September 2013), http://www.oxfordmartin.ox.ac.uk/publications /view/1314.

261 *the current vulnerability to automation* Many thanks to Jeff Gordon, graduate student, Sociology Department, U.C. Berkeley.

262 *"half of today's work activities could be automated"* McKinsey Global Institute, "A Future that Works: Automation, Employment and Productivity," January 2017, https://www.mckinsey.com/~/media/McKinsey/Global%20 Themes/Digital%20Disruption/Harnessing%20automation%20for%20 a%20future%20that%20works/MGI-A-future-that-works_Executive-summary.ashx; Michael Chui, James Manyika, and Mehdi Miremadi, "Where Machines Could Replace Humans—and Where They Can't (Yet)," *McKinsey Quarterly*, July 2016, https://www.mckinsey.com/business-functions /digital-mckinsey/our-insights/where-machines-could-replace-humans-and -where-they-cant-yet. The most authoritative recent source on the effects of robots on jobs is Daron Acemoglu and Pascual Restrepo, "Robots and Jobs: Evidence from U.S. Labor" (Working Paper 23285, National Bureau of Economic Research, March 2017), http://www.nber.org/papers/w23285.

262 *automation as well as the squeeze big business mergers put on small business* Robert Reich, *Saving Capitalism: For the Many, Not the Few* (New York: Alfred A. Knopf, 2015).

262 *the main cause of job loss is automation* Aimee Picchi, "The Robot Revolution Will Take 5 Million Jobs from Humans," CBS News, January 18, 2016, https://www.cbsnews.com/news/the-robot-revolution-will-take-5-million-jobs-from-humans.

262 *Robots are profitable to business* Ryan Derousseau, "Why Do American CEOs Make Twice as Much as German CEOs?" *Fortune*, November 4, 2014, http://fortune.com/2014/11/04/why-do-american-ceos-make -twice-as-much-as-german-ceos.

262 *robots are "always polite"* Kate Taylor, "Trump's Pick for Labor Secretary May Have Saved a Fast-Food Chain—but Workers Question if He's Right for the Job," *Business Insider*, January 21, 2017, http://www.businessinsider.com /puzders-business-methods-raise-questions-2017-1.

264 *Some websites that offered public access* Chris Mooney and Juliette Eilperin, "EPA Website Removes Climate Science Site from Public View After Two Decades," *Washington Post*, April 29, 2017, https://www.washingtonpost

.com/news/energy-environment/wp/2017/04/28/epa-website-removes-cli
mate-science-site-from-public-view-after-two-decades.

264 *their companies' acknowledgment and acceptance of climate science* On its
website, British Petroleum notes that the company "believes that climate
change is an important long-term issue that justifies global action." Conoco-
Phillips CEO Ryan Lance said at a shareholder meeting, "As a company
we recognize the impact that humans are having on the environment and
that CO2 is having an impact on what's happening in the climate." Chevron's website reads, "We recognize and share the concerns of governments
and the public about climate change. There is a widespread view that the
increase in atmospheric greenhouse gases (GHGs) is a contributor to climate change, with adverse effects on the environment." ExxonMobil's Ken
Cohen, a public relations employee, has said, "We know enough based on
the research and science that the risk is real and appropriate steps should
be taken to address that risk." "The risk of climate change is clear and the
risk warrants action," William Colton, a vice president at ExxonMobil,
said. Similar declarations came from Shell Oil in 2013. Shell's chief political analyst said a temperature increase of 2 degrees Celsius is like "the
flu," leading to heat waves, sea-level rise, and 10 to 20 percent less arable
land. "But the worst effects are beyond that limit, when you start to see
feedback loops," he warned. "I think it would be foolish to dispute the science [of climate change]." "Shell . . . decided to join more than 70 other
companies, including Adidas and Unilever, by signing onto a non-binding
document known as the 'Trillion Tonne Communiqué.' . . . In signing the
communiqué, Shell endorsed the idea of limiting cumulative greenhouse
gas emissions to less than 1 trillion tonnes of carbon since the start of the
industrial era, as recommended by the U.N. Intergovernmental Panel on
Climate Change (IPCC)." See "Oil Company Positions on the Reality and
Risk of Climate Change," University of Wisconsin-Oshkosh, Department
of Environmental Studies, http://www.uwosh.edu/es/climate-change/oil
-company-positions-on-the-reality-and-risk-of-climate-change.

265 *they are more isolated in their own political bubbles than Republicans
are in theirs* Aaron Blake, "Nearly Half of Liberals Don't Even Like
to Be Around Trump Supporters," *Washington Post,* July 20, 2017,
https://www.washingtonpost.com/news/the-fix/wp/2017/07/20/half-of-lib
erals-cant-even-stand-to-be-around-trump-supporters.

265 *squarely against talk across partisan lines* Frank Rich, "No Sympathy for
the Hillbilly," *New York,* March 19, 2017, http://nymag.com/daily/intelli
gencer/2017/03/frank-rich-no-sympathy-for-the-hillbilly.html.

265 *from 6 to 12 percent of Sanders fans later voted for President Trump* Danielle Kurtzleben, "Here's How Many Bernie Sanders Supporters Ultimately Voted for Trump," NPR, August 24, 2017, http://www.npr.org/2017/08/24/545812242/1-in-10-sanders-primary-voters-ended-up-supporting-trump-survey-finds.

265 *I discovered potential crossover topics* Nate Cohn, "The Obama-Trump Voters Are Real. Here's What They Think," *New York Times*, August 15, 2017, https://www.nytimes.com/2017/08/15/upshot/the-obama-trump-voters-are-real-heres-what-they-think.html.

265 *More than seventy grassroots groups have risen across the country* See the Bridge Alliance website, http://www.bridgealliance.us.

Appendix B: Politics and Pollution: National Discoveries from ToxMap

277 *and meanwhile, others living in the same state, two class levels higher, did vote as Republican* Alex MacGillis, "Who Turned My Blue State Red," *New York Times*, November 20, 2015.

278 *TRI measures are called the Risk-Screening Environmental Indicators (RSEI)* So the RSEI omits some sources of pollution—from car exhaust, for example.

279 *and one's political orientations generally* Initially we tried to relate attitudes (from GSS) to exposure levels (from RSEI) based on zip codes. But some zip codes lacked information from RSEI. That is, RSEI offered information for some zip codes but reported no information for others. So we based our analysis on RSEI measures of exposure in counties (a larger area) instead of zip codes (a smaller one).

Appendix C: Fact-Checking Common Impressions

281 *"government spends a lot of money on safety net programs* Center on Budget and Policy Priorities, "Policy Basics: Where Do Our Federal Tax Dollars Go?," March 4, 2016, https://www.cbpp.org/research/federal-budget/policy-basics-where-do-our-federal-tax-dollars-go.

281 *in thirty-five states and the District of Columbia* Ife Floyd and Liz Schott, "TANF Cash Benefits Have Fallen by More Than 20 Percent in Most States and Continue to Erode," Center on Budget and Policy Priorities (last updated October 15, 2015), http://www.cbpp.org/research/family-income-support/tanf-cash-benefits-have-fallen-by-more-than-20-percent-in-most-states.

282 *fallen steeply since then* Center on Budget and Policy Priorities, "SNAP Costs and Caseloads Declining," February 10, 2016, http://www.cbpp.org/research/food-assistance/snap-costs-and-caseloads-declining. The data is based on USDA reports, the U.S. Census Bureau (resident population

estimates and projections), and Congressional Budget Office data, using a January 2016 baseline.

282 *projected to fall to 1999 levels by 2016* Robin Rudowitz, Laura Snyder, and Vernon K. Smith, "Medicaid Enrollment & Spending Growth: FY 2015 & 2016," Henry J. Kaiser Foundation, October 15, 2015, http://kff.org/medi caid/issue-brief/medicaid-enrollment-spending-growth-fy-2015-2016.

282 *based on 2010–2012 data, most work* Ibid.; Louis Jacobson, "Are There More Welfare Recipients in the U.S. Than Full-Time Workers?" PunditFact, January 28, 2015, http://www.politifact.com/punditfact/statements/2015 /jan/28/terry-jeffrey/are-there-more welfare-recipients-us-full-time-wor (based on Census and Bureau of Labor statistics).

282 *Medicaid or Children's Health Insurance Program recipients* Ken Jacobs, Ian Perry, and Jenifer MacGillvary, "The High Public Cost of Low Wages," April 13, 2015, under section entitled, "The High Cost of Low Wages," http://laborcenter.berkeley.edu/the-high-public-cost-of-low-wages.

282 *All Earned Income Tax Credit recipients work* Jason Furman, Betsey Stevenson, and Jim Stock, "The 2014 Economic Report of the President," March 10, 2014, https://www.whitehouse.gov/blog/2014/03/10/2014-economic -report-president.

282 *among homecare workers, 48 percent did so* Jacobs, Perry, and MacGillvary, "The High Public Cost of Low Wages." The Bureau of Labor Statistics produces a yearly "profile of the working poor." In 2013, the BLS found that 5.1 million families in the United States were living below the poverty level, despite having at least one member in the labor force for half the year or more. The "working-poor rate"—the ratio of the working poor to all individuals in the labor force for at least twenty-seven weeks—was 7.7 percent for families (which the BLS defines as a group of two or more people residing together who are related by birth, marriage, or adoption). The count of families used in their report includes only primary families. A primary family consists of the reference person (householder) and all people living in the household who are related to the reference person. Families are classified either as married-couple families or as those maintained by men or women without spouses present. Bureau of Labor Statistics, *A Profile of the Working Poor, 2013* (Washington, D.C.: U.S. Department of Labor, 2015), http://www.bls .gov/opub/reports/cps/a-profile-of-the-working-poor-2013.pdf.

For the racial composition of working-poor families, see Deborah Povich, Brandon Roberts, and Mark Mather, *Low-Income Working Families: The Racial/Ethnic Divide* (Working Poor Families Project and Population

Reference Bureau, 2015), http://www.workingpoorfamilies.org/wp-content/uploads/2015/03/WPFP-2015-Report_Racial-Ethnic-Divide.pdf.

282 *the rest was payment for work* According to the Congressional Budget Office, in 2011 (the latest available), households in the lowest quintile of income (adjusted for household size) received an average of $9,100 in government transfers (cash payments and in-kind benefits from social insurance and other government assistance programs from federal, state, and local governments); that amounts to about 37 percent of an average pre-tax income of $24,600. Congressional Budget Office, *The Distribution of Household Income and Federal Taxes, 2011* (Washington, D.C.: Congressional Budget Office, 2014), https://www.cbo.gov/publication/49440, 2.

282 *26.2 percent did not participate* Shelley K. Irving and Tracy A. Loveless, *Dynamics of Economic Well-Being: Participation in Government Programs, 2009–2012: Who Gets Assistance?* (Washington, D.C.: U.S. Census Bureau, 2015), http://www.census.gov/content/dam/Census/library/publications/2015/demo/p70-141.pdf.

282–283 *the ratio is four TANF recipients to every one hundred poor people* See Figure 2 of Ife Floyd, Ladonna Pavetti, and Liz Schott, "TANF Continues to Weaken as a Safety Net," Center on Budget and Policy Priorities, updated October 27, 2015, http://www.cbpp.org/research/family-income-support/tanf-continues-to-weaken-as-a-safety-net.

283 *for white women it was 1.75* David J. Drozd, *Trends in Fertility Rates by Race and Ethnicity for the U.S. and Nebraska: 1989 to 2013* (University of Nebraska at Omaha: Center for Public Affairs Research, 2015), http://www.unomaha.edu/college-of-public-affairs-and-community-service/center-for-public-affairs-research/news/fertility-rate-gap.php. In 2010, the averages were 2.0 children per black woman and 1.8 children per white woman; see Mark Mather, *Fact Sheet: The Decline in U.S. Fertility* (Washington, D.C.: Population Reference Bureau, 2012), http://www.prb.org/publications/datasheets/2012/world-population-data-sheet/fact-sheet-us-population.aspx; U.S. Census Bureau, *5-Year American Community Survey [2009–2013 data]* (Washington, D.C.: U.S. Census, 2013). According to the Census's American Community Survey data from 2013, for the United States as a whole, the birth rate per 1,000 women is 59 for non-Hispanic white women, 58 for black women. The rate for poor women (women ages fifteen to fifty who have some form of poverty status) is 56 per 1,000 women. In Louisiana, the birth rate for non-Hispanic white women is 53 per 1,000 women, and 61 for black women. For poor women, it is 58 per 1,000 women.

283 *were employed in the civilian sector* Bureau of Labor Statistics, *Current Employment Statistics [2014 data]* (Washington, D.C.: U.S. Department of Labor, 2014) (accessed September 2, 2014), http://stats.bls.gov/ces/#data.

283 *An additional 1 percent* Defense Manpower Data Center, *Personnel, Workforce Reports & Publications* (Washington, D.C.: U.S. Department of Defense, 2014) (accessed November 25, 2014), https://www.dmdc.osd.mil/appj/dwp/dwp_reports.jsp.

283 *In addition, 9.8 percent of workers—including public school teachers—work for local government* Bureau of Labor Statistics, *Current Employment Statistics [2014 data]*.

283 private sector *workers earn 12 percent* more *than their public sector counterparts* David Cooper, Mary Gable, and Algernon Austin, "The Public-Sector Jobs Crisis: Women and African Americans Hit Hardest by Job Losses in State and Local Governments," *Economic Policy Institute*, May 2, 2012, http://www.epi.org/publication/bp339-public-sector-jobs-crisis (see Keefe, 2010, cited in Cooper, Gable, and Austin).

284 *In the public sector they earn 2 percent less than whites; in the private sector, 13 percent less* Among black public sector workers, in two out of five categories of education, blacks earn less than comparable whites (high school degree and some college)—and that accounts for most black public sector workers. Publicly employed black high school dropouts and those with a BA or advanced degree earn slightly more than their white counterparts, but very few blacks fit those categories (see Cooper, Gable, and Austin, "The Public-Sector Jobs Crisis," Table 4).

284 *public sector workers more than catch up* Congressional Budget Office, *Comparing the Compensation of Federal and Private-Sector Employees, 2011 to 2015*, Washington, D.C.: Congressional Budget Office, 2017, https://www.cbo.gov/system/files/115th-congress-2017-2018/reports/52637-federalprivatepay.pdf; Jeffrey H. Keefe, "Debunking the Myth of the Over-Compensated Public Employee," Economic Policy Institute, September 15, 2010, http://www.epi.org/ publications/entry/debunking_the_myth_of_the_overcompensated_public_employee; Jason Richwine and Andrew G. Biggs, "Public-Sector Compensation: Correction the Economic Policy Institute, Again," March 31, 2011, http://www.heritage.org/jobs-and-labor/report/public-sector-compensation-correcting-the-economic-policy-institute-again.

284 *Actually, it does not* See the review of environmental regulation by Eban Goodstein, *Jobs and the Environment: The Myth of a National Trade-Off* (Washington, D.C.: Economic Policy Institute, 1994). Also see Michael Porter and C. Van der Linde, "Toward a New Conception of the

Environment-Competitiveness Relationship," *Journal of Economic Perspectives* 9, no. 4 (1995): 97–118. Porter and Van der Linde argue that properly designed environmental regulations could lead to so much innovation they could completely offset costs of compliance. For a recent review of the literature, see John Irons and Isaac Shapiro, *Regulation, Employment, and the Economy: Fears of Job Loss Are Overblown* (Washington, D.C.: Economic Policy Institute, 2011).

284 *stronger environmental standards have not limited the relative pace of economic growth* Stephen M. Meyer, "Environmentalism and Economic Prosperity: An Update," working paper, Department of Political Science, Massachusetts Institute of Technology (1993): 1–10. See also Stephen Meyer, "Endangered Species Listings and State Economic Performance," Project on Environmental Politics & Policy, Massachusetts Institute of Technology (March 1995); J.R. Bliese, *The Great "Environment Versus Economy" Myth* (New York: Brownstone Policy Institute, 1999).

284 *among the strictest in the nation, substantially reduced employment* Eli Berman and Linda T.M. Bui, "Environmental Regulation and Labor Demand: Evidence from the South Coast Air Basin," *Journal of Public Economics* 79 (2001): 265–95.

285 *there was no statistically significant impact* Richard D. Morgenstern, William A. Pizer, and Jhih-Shyang Shih, "Jobs Versus the Environment: An Industry-Level Perspective," *Journal of Environmental Economics and Management* 43 (2002): 412–36.

285 *stricter environmental policies did not inhibit job growth* Roger H. Bezdek, Robert M. Wendling, and Paula DiPerna, "Environmental Protection, the Economy, and Jobs: National and Regional Analyses," *Journal of Environmental Management* 86, no. 1 (2008): 63–79.

285 *According to the Mass Layoff Statistics* The U.S. Bureau of Labor Statistics asks employers to identify the primary cause of each layoff that idles more than fifty manufacturing workers. Bureau of Labor Statistics, *Mass Layoff Statistics [2012 data]* (Washington, D.C.: Department of Labor, 2012) (accessed March 13, 2014), http://www.bls.gov/mls.

285 *0.1 percent of all layoffs were "environment and safety-related" from 1987 to 1990* Paul Templet, "Integrating Resource Conservation and Economic Development, People First: Developing Sustainable Communities," working paper (March 1997), 1.

285 *were attributed to "government regulations/intervention"* See also Irons and Shapiro, *Regulation, Employment, and the Economy: Fears of Job Loss Are Overblown*.

285 *may attract fewer new businesses* Todd M. Gabe and Kathleen P. Bell, "Tradeoffs Between Local Taxes and Government Spending as Determinants of Business Location," *Journal of Regional Science* 44, no. 1 (2004): 21–41.

286 *business incentives may contribute to a cycle of destructive competition* Lingwen Zheng and Mildred Warner, "Business Incentive Use Among U.S. Local Governments: A Story of Accountability and Policy Learning," *Economic Development Quarterly* 24, no. 4 (2010): 325–336.

286 *eight-part 2014 investigative special report* Gordon Russell, "Giving Away Louisiana: An Overview," *The Advocate,* Special Reports, November 26, 2014, http://blogs.theadvocate.com/specialreports/2014/11/26/giving-away -louisiana.

287 *leakage out of Louisiana is between 20 and 35 percent* Bureau of Economic Analysis, *Personal Income and Gross Domestic Product by State [1997–2012 data]* (Washington, D.C.: Department of Commerce, 2012) (accessed March 13, 2014).

287 *gross domestic product has been higher under Democratic presidents* Michael Comiskey and Lawrence C. Marsh, "Presidents, Parties, and the Business Cycle, 1949–2009," *Presidential Studies Quarterly* 42, no. 1 (2012): 40–59.

287 *decreased slightly under Democrats* Larry Bartels, *Unequal Democracy: The Political Economy of the New Gilded Age* (Princeton, NJ: Princeton University Press, 2008).

287 *in other words, some of the correlation is due to factors outside a president's control* Alan S. Blinder and Mark W. Watson, "Presidents and the U.S. Economy: An Econometric Exploration," National Bureau of Economic Research, Working Paper No. 20334 (July 2014), http://www.nber.org/papers/w20324.

287 *Truman, Kennedy, Johnson, Carter, and Clinton all managed to reduce debt as a percentage of GDP* Steve Clemons, "GOP Presidents Have Been the Worst Contributors to the Federal Debt," *The Atlantic,* October 27, 2012, http:// www.theatlantic.com/politics/archive/2012/10/gop-presidents-have-been -the-worst-contributors-to-the-federal-debt/264193.

Bibliography

"Abraham's Tent Opens New Facility to Feed the Hungry." *Jambalaya News* (December 22, 2014). http://lakecharles.com/2014/12/abrahams-tent-opens -new-facility-feed-hungry.

AGL Resources. *2011 Annual Report* (accessed August 7, 2015). http://www.agl resources.com/about/docs/AGL_AR_2011/2011AnnualReport.pdf.

Albrizio, Silvia, Enrico Botta, Tomasz Kozluk, and Vera Zipperer. "Do Environmental Policies Matter for Productivity Growth? Insights from New Cross-County Measures of Environmental Policies." Working Paper Number 1176, December 3, 2014. http://www.oecd-ilibrary.org/economics/do -environmental-policies-matter-for-productivity-growth_5jxrjncjrcxp-en.

Annie E. Casey Foundation. *2009 Kids Count Data Book: State Profiles of Child Well-Being.* http://www.aecf.org/resources/the-2009-kids-count-data-book.

Associated Press. "Cross Burning Defendant Speaks Out." KPLC-TV (December 12, 2001). http://www.kplctv.com/story/317803/cross-burning-defen dant-speaks-out.

———. "Gulf Platform Owner Sued over Deadly 2012 Blast." KPLC-TV. http:// www.kplctv.com/story/23832004/gulf-platform-owner-sued-over-deadly -2012-blast.

———. "Number of Injured from Axiall Chemical Plant Fire in Westlake Rises to 18." *Times-Picayune* (December 25, 2013). http://www.nola.com/environ ment/index.ssf/2013/12/number_of_injured_from_axiall.html.

———. "Obama Approval Ratings Low in Louisiana." *New Orleans City Business* (October 13, 2011). http://neworleanscitybusiness.com/blog/2011/10/13 /obama-approval-ratings-low-in-louisiana.

Ashkenas, Jeremy, Haeyoun Park, and Adam Pearce. "Even with Affirmative Action, Blacks and Hispanics Are More Underrepresented at Top Colleges Than 35 Years Ago." *New York Times* (August 24, 2017).

Auyero, Javier, and Debora Alejandra Swistun. *Flammable: Environmental Suffering in an Argentine Shantytown.* Oxford: Oxford University Press, 2009.

Babington, Charles. "A Polarized America Lives as It Votes." Pew Research Center, summer 2014. http://magazine.pewtrusts.org/en/archive/summer-2014/a-polarized-america-lives-as-it-votes.

Bageant, Joe. *Deer Hunting with Jesus: Dispatches from America's Class War.* New York: Crown Books, 2007.

"Baggy Pants Law Will Fine Offenders in Louisiana Parish." *Huffington Post* (April 14, 2013; accessed November, 3, 2015). http://www.huffingtonpost.com/2013/04/14/baggy-pants-law-fine-louisiana_n_3080851.html.

Ballotpedia. "Louisiana State Budget and Finances." 2013. https://ballotpedia.org/Louisiana_state_budget_and_finances.

Bartels, Larry. *Unequal Democracy: The Political Economy of the New Gilded Age.* Princeton, NJ: Princeton University Press, 2008.

———. "What's the Matter with *What's the Matter with Kansas?*" *Quarterly Journal of Political Science* 1 (2006): 201–26.

Baugher, John, and J. Timmons Roberts. "Perceptions and Worry About Hazards at Work: Unions, Contract Maintenance, and Job Control in the U.S. Petrochemical Industry." *Industrial Relations* 38, no. 4 (1999): 522–41.

Bauman, Nick. "Tea Party Frontrunner: Abolish Public Schools." *Mother Jones* (October 13, 2010).

Beckman, Jeffery D., and Alex K. Williamson. "Salt-Dome Locations in the Gulf Coastal Plain, South-Central United States." U.S. Geological Survey, Water-Resources Investigations Report 90-4060, 1990. http://pubs.usgs.gov/wri/1990/4060/report.pdf.

Berlet, Chip. "Reframing Populist Resentment in the Tea Party Movement," in *Steep: The Precipitous Rise of the Tea Party*, edited by Lawrence Rosenthal and Christine Trost, 47–66. Berkeley: University of California Press, 2012.

Berman, Dennis K. "Are You Underestimating America's Fracking Boom?" *Wall Street Journal* (May 27, 2014).

Berman, Eli, and Linda T.M. Bui. "Environmental Regulation and Labor Demand: Evidence from the South Coast Air Basin." *Journal of Public Economics* 79 (2001): 265–95.

"Bertrand Excited About Future of Southwest Louisiana." *American Press* (January 27, 2015, B4).

Bezdek, Roger H., Robert M. Wendling, and Paula DiPerna. "Environmental Protection, the Economy, and Jobs: National and Regional Analyses." *Journal of Environmental Management* 86, no. 1 (2008): 63–79.

Bishop, Bill, and Robert G. Cushing. *The Big Sort: Why the Clustering of Like-Minded America Is Tearing Us Apart.* New York: Houghton Mifflin Company, 2008.

Blake, Aaron. "Nearly Half of Liberals Don't Even Like to Be Around Trump Supporters." *Washington Post* (July 20, 2017).

Bliese, John R.E. *The Great "Environment Versus Economy" Myth*. New York: Brownstone Policy Institute, 1999.

Blinder, Alan S., and Mark W. Watson, "Presidents and the U.S. Economy: An Econometric Exploration," National Bureau of Economic Research, Working Paper No. 20334 (July 2014). http://www.nber.org/papers/w20324.

Boyd, James. "Nixon's Southern Strategy: 'It's All in the Charts.'" *New York Times* (May 17, 1970). http://www.nytimes.com/packages/html/books/phillips -southern.pdf.

Boym, Svetlana. *The Future of Nostalgia*. New York: Basic Books, 2001.

———. "Nostalgia and Its Discontents." *Hedgehog Review* (Summer 2007): 13. http://www.iasc-culture.org/eNews/2007_10/9.2CBoym.pdf.

Brooks, Arthur C. *Who Really Cares: The Surprising Truth About Compassionate Conservatism*. New York: Basic Books, 2007.

Brooks, Clem, and Jeff Manza. "A Broken Public? Americans' Responses to the Great Recession." *American Sociological Review* 78, no. 5 (2013): 727–48.

Brown, Heath. *The Tea Party Divided: The Hidden Diversity of a Maturing Movement*. New York: Praeger, 2015.

Buchele, Mose. "After HB 40, What's Next for Local Drilling Rules in Texas?" StateImpact (July 2, 2015). https://stateimpact.npr.org/texas/2015/07/02 /after-hb-40-whats-next-for-local-drilling-bans-in-texas.

Bullard, Robert D. *Dumping in Dixie: Race, Class, and Environmental Quality*. New York: Westview Press, 2000.

Bureau of Economic Analysis. "Bureau of Economic Analysis [Regional Datafile]: Louisiana, 2013." Washington, D.C.: Bureau of Economic Analysis (retrieved September 22, 2015).

———. *Personal Income and Gross Domestic Product by State [1997–2012 data]*. Washington, D.C.: Department of Commerce, 2012 (accessed March 13, 2014).

Bureau of Labor Statistics. *Current Employment Statistics [2014 data]*. Washington, D.C.: U.S. Department of Labor, 2014 (accessed September 2, 2014). http://stats.bls.gov/ces/#data.

———. *Mass Layoff Statistics [2012 data]*. Washington, D.C.: Department of Labor, 2012 (accessed March 13, 2014). http://www.bls.gov/mls.

———. *A Profile of the Working Poor, 2013*. Washington, D.C.: U.S. Department of Labor, 2015. http://www.bls.gov/opub/reports/cps/a-profile-of-the-work ing-poor-2013.pdf.

————. "Quarterly Census of Employment and Wages [December 2014 estimates]" (accessed June 18, 2015). http://data.bls.gov/cgi-bin/dsrv?en.

Campos, Paul F. "White Economic Privilege Is Alive and Well." *New York Times* (July 29, 2017).

"Cancer Facts and Figures 2015." American Cancer Society. http://www.cancer .org/acs/groups/content/@editorial/documents/document/acspc-044552 .pdf.

Cash, W.J. *The Mind of the South*. New York: Vintage Books, 1991 (1941).

Center on Budget and Policy Priorities. "SNAP Costs and Caseloads Declining" (February 10, 2016). http://www.cbpp.org/research/food-assistance/snap -costs-and-caseloads-declining.

Cernansky, Rachael. "Natural Gas Boom Brings Major Growth for U.S. Chemical Plants." *Environment 360* (January 29, 2015; accessed August 16, 2015). http://e360.yale.edu/feature/natural_gas_boom_brings_major_growth_for _us_chemical_plants/2842.

Cerrell Associates, Inc. *Political Difficulties Facing Waste-to-Energy Conversion Plant Siting*. Los Angeles: Cerrell Associates, 1984.

Chait, Jonathan. "Confessions of a 'Partyist': Yes, I Judge Your Politics." *New York Magazine* (October 30, 2014). http://nymag.com/daily/intelligencer/2014/10 /im-a-partyist-and-yes-i-judge-your-politics.html.

Chetty, Raj, Nathaniel Hendren, Patrick Kline, and Emmanuel Saez. "Where Is the Land of Opportunity? The Geography of Intergenerational Mobility in the United States." *The Quarterly Journal of Economics* (2014): 1–71.

Chetty, Raj, Nathaniel Hendren, Patrick Kline, Emmanuel Saez, and Nicholas Turner. "Is the United States Still a Land of Opportunity? Recent Trends in Intergenerational Mobility." NBER Working Paper 19844 (January 2014). http://www.nber.org/papers/w19844.

Childress, Sarah. "Has the Justice Department Found a New Town That Preys on Its Poor?" *Frontline* (April 27, 2015). http://www.pbs.org/wgbh/pages /frontline/criminal-justice/has-the-justice-department-found-a-new-town -that-preys-on-its-poor.

Chipman, Kim. "Americans in 73% Majority Oppose Ban on Deepwater Oil Drilling." *Bloomberg* (July 14, 2010). http://www.bloomberg.com/news/arti cles/2010-07-14/americans-in-73-majority-oppose-ban-on-deepwater-drill ing-after-oil-spill.

Choi, Charles Q. "Gas-Charged Earthquakes Linked to Mysterious Louisiana Sinkhole." *Live Science*. http://www.livescience.com/46692-louisiana-sink hole-explained.html.

Citizens for Tax Justice. "Corporate Taxpayers and Corporate Tax Dodgers,

2008–2010." November 2011. http://ctj.org/ctjreports/2011/11/corporate _taxpayers_corporate_tax_dodgers_2008-2010.php.

Clark, Candace. *Misery and Company: Sympathy in Everyday Life.* Chicago: University of Chicago Press, 1998.

Clark, Stephen. "Gun Control Advocates Decry Louisiana's New Law Allowing Churchgoers to Pack Heat." Fox News (July 8, 2010). http://www.foxnews .com/politics/2010/07/08/gun-control-advocates-decry-louisianas-new-law -allowing-churchgoers-pack-heat.html.

Clemons, Steve. "GOP Presidents Have Been the Worst Contributors to the Federal Debt." *The Atlantic* (October 27, 2012). http://www.theatlantic.com /politics/archive/2012/10/gop-presidents-have-been-the-worst-contributors -to-the-federal-debt/264193.

Coastal Wetlands Planning, Protection and Restoration Act (CWPPRA). "Frequently Asked Questions." https://lacoast.gov/new/About/FAQs.aspx.

Cockerham, Sean. "Louisiana French: L'heritage at Risk." *Seattle Times* (July 6, 2012).

Cohn, Nate. "The Obama-Trump Voters Are Real. Here's What They Think." *New York Times* (August 15, 2017).

Cohn, Nate, and Toni Monkovic. "How Did Donald Trump Win Over So Many Obama Voters?" *New York Times* (November 14, 2016).

Coll, Steve. "Dangerous Gamesmanship." *New Yorker* (April 27, 2015).

Comiskey, Michael, and Lawrence C. Marsh. "Presidents, Parties, and the Business Cycle, 1949–2009." *Presidential Studies Quarterly* 42, no. 1 (2012): 40–59.

Confessore, Nicholas, Sarah Cohen, and Karen Yourish. "Buying Power." *New York Times* (October 10, 2015).

Congressional Budget Office. *The Distribution of Household Income and Federal Taxes, 2011.* Washington, D.C.: Congressional Budget Office, 2014. http:// www.cbo.gov/sites/default/files/cbofiles/attachments/49440-Distribution -of-Income-and-Taxes.pdf.

Cooper, David, Mary Gable, and Algernon Austin. "The Public-Sector Jobs Crisis: Women and African Americans Hit Hardest by Job Losses in State and Local Governments." *Economic Policy Institute* (May 2, 2012). http://www .epi.org/publication/bp339-public-sector-jobs-crisis.

Cornier, Eric. "Construction Boom: Labor Shortage Among Area Concerns." *American Press* (February 10, 2013).

CSRS. *Southwest Louisiana Regional Impact Study, 2014* (accessed August 4, 2015). http://www.gogroupswla.com/Content/Uploads/gogroupswla.com/files /SWLA%20Regional%20Impact%20Study_Final.pdf.

Davenport, Coral. "E.P.A. Faces More Tasks, Louder Critics, and a Shrinking Budget." *New York Times* (March 19, 2016).

Davenport, Coral, and Campbell Robertson. "Resettling the First American 'Climate Refugees.'" *New York Times* (May 3, 2016).

"David Vitter on Environment." On the Issues. http://www.ontheissues.org/Domestic/David_Vitter_Environment.htm.

Deckman, Melissa. "A Gender Gap in the Tea Party?" Paper prepared for the Midwest Political Science Association Meetings, April 11–14, 2013 (unpublished paper).

"Deep Water: The Gulf Oil Disaster and the Future of Offshore Drilling." Report to the President, National Commission on the BP Deepwater Horizon Oil Spill and Offshore Drilling (January, 2011). www.oilspillcommission.gov.

Defense Manpower Data Center. *Personnel, Workforce Reports & Publications*. Washington, D.C.: U.S. Department of Defense, 2014 (accessed November 25, 2014). https://www.dmdc.osd.mil/appj/dwp/dwp_reports.jsp.

Desmond, Matthew. *On the Fireline: Living and Dying with Wildland Firefighters*. Chicago: University of Chicago Press, 2007.

DiCesare, Frank. "All Water, Air Permits for Sasol Approved." *American Press* (June 2, 2014).

———. "Bayou d'Inde Cleanup to Begin This Month." *American Press* (February 16, 2015).

Diemer, Miriam. "Energy and Natural Resources: Industry Influence in the Climate Change Debate." OpenSecrets.org (updated January 29, 2015). https://www.opensecrets.org/news/issues/energy.

DiTomaso, Nancy. *The American Non-Dilemma: Racial Inequality Without Racism*. New York: Russell Sage Foundation, 2013.

Dlouhy, Jennifer A. "Dangers Face Immigrant Contract Workforce in Gulf." *FuelFix* (November 3, 2013). http://fuelfix.com/blog/2013/11/03/dangers-face-immigrant-contractor-workforce-in-gulf.

"Dome Issues Kept Quiet." *The Advocate* (August 12, 2012).

"Donald Trump Forcefully Removes Protesters from Louisiana Rally." Mic.com (March 5, 2016). http://mic.com/articles/137129/donald-trump-forcefully-removes-protesters-from-louisiana-rally.

Drozd, David J. *Trends in Fertility Rates by Race and Ethnicity for the U.S. and Nebraska: 1989 to 2013*. University of Nebraska at Omaha: Center for Public Affairs Research, 2015. http://www.unomaha.edu/college-of-public-affairs-and-community service/center-for-public-affairs-research/news/fertility-rate-gap.php.

Dupre, Deborah. "Sinkhole: H-Bomb Explosion Equivalent in Bayou Corne

Possible." Examiner.com (August 12, 2012). http://www.examiner.com/article/sinkhole-h-bomb-explosion-equivalent-bayou-corne-possible.

———. "State Blames One Company for Gassy Sinkhole, Orders More Seismic Monitors." Examiner.com (October 12, 2012). http://www.examiner.com/article/state-blames-one-company-for-gassy-sinkhole-orders-more-seismic-monitors.

Durkheim, Emile. *The Elementary Forms of Religious Life.* New York: The Free Press, 1965 (1915).

Ehrenreich, Barbara. "Dead, White, and Blue: The Great Die-Off of America's Blue Collar Whites." TomDispatch.com (December 1, 2015). http://www.tomdispatch.com/dialogs/print/?d=176075.

Ehrenreich, John. *Third Wave Capitalism: How Money, Power, and the Pursuit of Self-Interest Have Imperiled the American Dream.* Ithaca and London: ILR Press, an Imprint of Cornell University Press, forthcoming 2016.

Einhorn, Robin L. *American Taxation, American Slavery.* Chicago: University of Chicago Press, 2008.

Eliot, T.S. *The Sacred Wood.* London: Methuen, 1920.

Environmental Protection Agency. *TRI Explorer [Data file], 1990 and 2013.* Washington, D.C.: Environmental Protection Agency, 2015. http://iaspub.epa.gov/triexplorer/tri_release.chemical.

Ernst & Young LLP. *2014 US Investment Monitor: Tracking Mobile Capital Investments During 2013* (accessed August 4, 2015). http://www.ey.com/Publication/vwLUAssets/EY-the-us-investment-monitor/$FILE/EY-the-us-investment-monitor.pdf.

Evans-Pritchard, E.E. *The Nuer: A Description of the Modes of Livelihood and Political Institutions of a Nilotic People.* Oxford, UK: Clarendon Press, 1940.

Eysink, Curt. *Louisiana Workforce Information Review, 2010.* Statewide Report. https://www.doleta.gov/performance/results/AnnualReports/2010_economic_reports/la_economic_report_py2010_workforce.pdf.

Fagin, Dan. *Toms River: A Story of Science and Salvation.* New York: Bantam Books, 2013.

Fahrenthold, David. "Deep Underground Federal Employees Process Paperwork by Hand in a Long Outdated, Inefficient System." *Washington Post* (March 22, 2014).

Fallin, Amanda, Rachel Grana, and Stanton A. Glantz. "'To Quarterback Behind the Scenes, Third-Party Efforts': The Tobacco Industry and the Tea Party." *Tobacco Control* (February 8, 2013). http://tobaccocontrol.bmj.com/content/early/2013/02/07/tobaccocontrol-2012-050815.abstract.

Festinger, Leon, Henry W. Riecken, and Stanley Schachter. *When Prophecy*

Fails: A Social and Psychological Study of a Modern Group That Predicted the Destruction of the World. London: Pinter and Martin, 2008 (1956).

Fischer, Claude, and Michael Hout. *Century of Difference: How America Changed in the Last One Hundred Years.* New York: Russell Sage Foundation, 2008.

Florida, Richard. "Is Life Better in America's Red States?" *New York Times Sunday Review* (January 3, 2015).

Floser, A.D. "A Closer Look at the Parties in 2012." Pew Research Center (August 23, 2012). http://www.people-press.org/2012/08/23/a-closer-look-at-the-parties-in-2012.

Floyd, Ife, Ladonna Pavetti, and Liz Schott. "TANF Continues to Weaken as a Safety Net." Center on Budget and Policy Priorities (updated October 27, 2015). http://www.cbpp.org/research/family-income-support/tanf-continues-to-weaken-as-a-safety-net.

Floyd, Ife, and Liz Schott. "TANF Cash Benefits Have Fallen by More Than 20 Percent in Most States and Continue to Erode." Center on Budget and Policy Priorities (last updated October 15, 2015). http://www.cbpp.org/research/family-income-support/tanf-cash-benefits-have-fallen-by-more-than-20-percent-in-most-states.

Frank, Thomas. *Listen Liberal, or What Ever Happened to the Party of the People?* New York: Metropolitan Press, 2016.

———. *What's the Matter with Kansas? How Conservatives Won the Heart of America.* New York: Metropolitan Press, 2004.

Frankland, Peggy. *Women Pioneers of the Louisiana Environmental Movement.* Jackson: University Press of Mississippi, 2013.

Freddoso, David. "State Government Dependence on Federal Funding Growing at Alarming Rate." *State Budget Solutions* (April 14, 2015). http://www.statebudgetsolutions.org/publications/detail/state-government-dependence-on-federal-funding-growing-at-alarming-rate.

Frey, Carl, and Michael Osborne. "The Future of Employment: How Susceptible Are Jobs to Computerization." Oxford Martin School Working Paper (September 2013). http://www.oxfordmartin.ox.ac.uk/publications/view/1314.

Fuller, Jaime. "Environmental Policy Is Partisan. It Wasn't Always." *Washington Post* (June 2, 2014). https://www.washingtonpost.com/news/the-fix/wp/2014/06/02/support-for-the-clean-air-act-has-changed-a-lot-since-1970.

Furman, Jason, Betsey Stevenson, and Jim Stock. "The 2014 Economic Report of the President" (March 10, 2014). https://www.whitehouse.gov/blog/2014/03/10/2014-economic-report-president.

Gabe, Todd M., and Kathleen P. Bell. "Tradeoffs Between Local Taxes and

Government Spending as Determinants of Business Location." *Journal of Regional Science* 44, no. 1 (2004): 21–41.

Garcia-Perez, Javier, Pablo Fernandez-Navarro, Adela Castello, Maria Felicitas Lopez-Cima, Rebeca Ramis, Elena Boldo, and Gonzalo Lopez-Abente. "Cancer Mortality in Towns in the Vicinity of Incinerators and Installations for the Recovery or Disposal of Hazardous Waste." *Environment International* 51 (2013): 31–44.

Gerard, René. *The Scapegoat*. Baltimore: Johns Hopkins University, 1986.

Gibson, David R. "Doing Time in Space: Line Joining Rules and Resulting Morphologies." *Sociological Forum* 23, no. 2 (June 2008): 207–33.

Gillin, Joshua. "Income Tax Rates Were 90 Percent Under Eisenhower, Sanders Says." *PolitiFact* (November 15, 2015). http://www.politifact.com/truth-o -meter/statements/2015/nov/15/bernie-s/income-tax-rates-were-90-percent -under-eisenhower-.

Gitlin, Todd. *The Twilight of Common Dreams: Why America Is Wracked by Culture Wars*. New York: Metropolitan Press, 1995.

Goldstein, Dana. "When Affirmative Action Isn't Enough." *New York Times* (September 17, 2017).

"Gonzales." LouisianaTravel.com. http://www.louisianatravel.com/cities/gonzales.

Goodman, Joseph. "Gulf Oil Spill Threatens Louisiana Native Americans' Way of Life." *Miami Herald* (June 1, 2010).

Goodstein, Eban. *Jobs and the Environment: The Myth of a National Trade-Off*. Washington, D.C.: Economic Policy Institute, 1994.

Gordon, Claire. "Filipino Workers Kept as Slaves in Louisiana, Lawsuit Charges." *AOL Jobs* (November 15, 2011). http://jobs.aol.com/articles/2011/11/15/fili pino-workers-kept-as-slaves-in-louisiana-according-to-lawsu.

"Governing, the State and Localities." Governing.com. Source: U.S. Census Bureau (accessed September 21, 2015). http://www.governing.com/gov-data /state-tax-revenue-data.html.

"Governor Bobby Jindal Says Americans Want a 'Hostile Takeover' of Washington." TeaParty.org (September 16, 2014). http://www.teaparty.org/gov-bobby -jindal-says-americans-want-hostile-takeover-washington-55848.

Grandia, Kevin. "If Canada Is 'Oil Rich' Why Are We So in Debt?" DESMOG-CANADA (March 5, 2013). http://www.desmog.ca/2013/02/28/if-canada -oil-rich-why-are-we-so-debt.

Gray, Melissa. "Louisiana Probes Cause of Massive Bayou Sinkhole." CNN (August 10, 2012). http://www.cnn.com/2012/08/09/us/louisiana-bayou -sinkhole.

Green, John C. *The Fifth National Survey of Religion and Politics*. Akron, OH:

The Ray C. Bliss Center for Applied Politics at the University of Akron, 2008. http://www.uakron.edu/bliss/research/archives/2008/Blissreligionre port.pdf.

Guldroz, John. "LSU Professor Discusses Climate Change, Erosion." *American Press* (June 28, 2013).

Gulf Engineers and Consultants. "Hazardous, Toxic and Radioactive Waste Reconnaissance Report (HTRW) Calcasieu River and Pass." Louisiana Dredged Material Management Plan, U.S. Army Corps of Engineers, New Orleans District.

Hacker, Jacob S., and Paul Pierson. *Winner-Take-All Politics: How Washington Made the Rich Richer—and Turned Its Back on the Middle Class.* New York: Simon & Schuster, 2010.

Hamilton, Lawrence C., Thomas G. Safford, and Jessica D. Ulrich. "In the Wake of the Spill: Environmental Views Along the Gulf Coast." *Social Science Quarterly* 93, no. 4 (2012): 1053–64.

Hanley, Caroline, and Michael T. Douglass. "High Road, Low Road or Off Road: Economic Development Strategies in the American States." *Economic Development Quarterly* 28:3 (2014): 1–10.

Harlan, Chico. "Battered by Drop in Oil Prices and Jindal's Fiscal Policies, Louisiana Falls into Budget Crisis." *Washington Post* (March 4, 2016). https://www.washingtonpost.com/news/wonk/wp/2016/03/04/the-debilitating -economic-disaster-louisianas-governor-left-behind.

Hertsgaard, Mark. "What BP Doesn't Want You to Know About the Gulf Spill." *Newsweek* (April 22, 2013).

Hochschild, Arlie Russell. *The Managed Heart: Commercialization of Human Feeling.* Berkeley: University of California Press, 2012 (1983).

———. *The Outsourced Self: Intimate Life in Market Times.* New York: Metropolitan Press, 2012.

———. *The Second Shift: Working Families and the Revolution at Home.* New York: Penguin Books, 2012 (1989).

———. *So How's the Family? and Other Essays.* Berkeley and Los Angeles: University of California Press, 2013.

———. *The Time Bind: When Work Becomes Home and Home Becomes Work.* New York: Metropolitan Press, 2000 (1997).

Hofstadter, Richard. *The Age of Reform.* New York: Vintage, 1955.

———. *Anti-Intellectualism in American Life.* New York: Vintage Books, 1966.

Houck, Oliver A. "The Reckoning: Oil and Gas Development in the Louisiana Coastal Zone." *Tulane Environmental Law Journal* 28, no. 2 (2015): 185–296.

———. "Save Ourselves: The Environmental Case That Changed Louisiana." *Louisiana Law Review* 72 (2012): 409–37.

"How States Compare and How They Voted in the 2012 Election." *The Chronicle of Philanthropy* (updated January 13, 2015; accessed August 5, 2015). https://philanthropy.com/article/How-States-CompareHow/152501.

"Iberia Parish, Louisiana." Tour Louisiana (accessed August 7, 2015). http://www.tourlouisiana.com/content.cfm?id=15.

Institute for Criminal Policy Research. *World Prison Brief.* http://www.prisonstudies.org/highest-to-lowest/prison_population_rate.

Institute for Southern Studies. "Looting Louisiana: How the Jindal Administration Is Helping Big Oil Rip Off a Cash-Strapped State." http://www.southernstudies.org/2015/05/looting-louisiana-how-the-jindal-administration-is.html.

Irons, John, and Isaac Shapiro. *Regulation, Employment, and the Economy: Fears of Job Loss Are Overblown.* Washington, D.C.: Economic Policy Institute, 2011.

Irving, Shelley K., and Tracy A. Loveless. *Dynamics of Economic Well-Being: Participation in Government Programs, 2009–2012: Who Gets Assistance?* Washington, D.C.: U.S. Census Bureau, 2015. http://www.census.gov/content/dam/Census/library/publications/2015/demo/p70-141.pdf.

Iyengar, Shanto, Gaurav Sood, and Yphtach Lelkes. "Affect, Not Ideology: A Social Identity Perspective on Polarization." *Public Opinion Quarterly* 76, no. 3 (2012): 405–31.

Iyengar, Shanto, and Sean Westwood. "Fear and Loathing Across Party Lines: New Evidence on Group Polarization." *American Journal of Political Science* 59, no. 3 (2014): 45.

Jacobs, Ken, Ian Perry, and Jenifer MacGillvary. "The High Public Cost of Low Wages" (April 13, 2015). http://laborcenter.berkeley.edu/the-high-public-cost-of-low-wages.

Jacobson, Louis. "Are There More Welfare Recipients in the U.S. Than Full-Time Workers?" PunditFact (January 28, 2015). http://www.politifact.com/punditfact/statements/2015/jan/28/terry-jeffrey/are-there-more-welfare-recipients-us-full-time-wor.

Jilani, Zaid. "Fracking Industry Billionaires Give Record $15 Million to Ted Cruz's Super PAC." Alternet (July 25, 2015). http://www.alternet.org/election-2016/fracking-industry-billionaires-give-record-15-million-ted-cruzs-super-pac.

Johnson, Brad. "Senate Republicans Introduce Bill to Abolish the EPA." *Think Progress* (May 6, 2011). http://thinkprogress.org/politics/2011/05/06/164077/senate-republicans-introduce-bill-to-abolish-the-epa.

Juhasz, Antonia. "Investigation: Two Years After the BP Spill, a Hidden Health Crisis Festers." *The Nation* (April 18, 2012). https://www.thenation.com/ar ticle/investigation-two-years-after-bp-spill-hidden-health-crisis-festers.

Kasperowicz, Pete. "Who Wants to Abolish the IRS? So Far, 58 House Republicans." *The Blaze* (accessed August 16, 2015). http://www.theblaze.com /blog/2015/01/07/who-wants-to-abolish-the-irs-so-far-58-house-republicans.

Katznelson, Ira. *When Affirmative Action Was White: An Untold History of Racial Inequality in Twentieth-Century America.* New York: Norton Publishing Co., 2006.

Kenen, Joanne, and Jennifer Haberkorn. "Who Will Replace Price?" *Politico* (October 1, 2017). http://www.politico.com/story/2017/09/29/who-will-re place-tom-price-243317.

Kirshenbaum, Sheril. "Political Ideology Continues to Be the Single Greatest Determinant of Americans' Views on Climate Change." http://news.utexas.edu /2015/10/20/views-of-key-energy-issues-are-shaped-by-partisan-politics.

Knox, E.G. "Oil Combustion and Childhood Cancers." *Journal of Epidemiology and Community Health* 59, no. 9 (2005): 755–60.

Koeppel, Barbara. "Cancer Alley, Louisiana." *The Nation* (November 8, 1999), 16–24.

Kohut, Andrew, Scott Keeter, Carroll Doherty, Michael Dimock, Michael Remez, Robert Suls, Shawn Neidorf, Leah Christian, Jocelyn Kiley, Alec Tyson, and Jacob Pushter. "Life in 2050: Amazing Science, Familiar Threats: Public Sees a Future Full of Promise and Peril." News release, Pew Center for the People and the Press (June 22, 2010).

Kolata, Gina. "Death Rate Rising for Middle Aged White Americans, Study Finds." *New York Times* (November 2, 2015).

Koran, Laura. "Tillerson Signs Declaring Stressing Climate Change Threat." CNN (May 12, 2017). http://www.cnn.com/2017/05/12/politics/tillerson -climate-change-fairbanks-declaration/index.html.

Krugman, Paul. "Enemies of the Sun." Op-Ed. *New York Times* (October 5, 2015).

Kumar, Sheila V. "Jindal Meets with Bayou Corne Residents, Promises to Fight Texas Brine for Fair Buyouts." *Times-Picayune* (March 19, 2013). http://www .nola.com/politics/index.ssf/2013/03/jindal_to_visit_assumption_par_1.html.

Kumkar, Nils. "A Socio-Analysis of Discontent: Protests Against the Politics of Crisis in the U.S. and Germany: An Empirical Comparison." Unpublished PhD thesis, Department of Sociology, University of Leipzig (November 30, 2015).

Kurth, Michael. "On the Brink of the Boom." *Lagniappe* (May 6, 2014). http:// www.bestofswla.com/2014/05/06/brink-boom.

Kurtzleben, Danielle. "Here's How Many Bernie Sanders Supporters Ultimately Voted for Trump." NPR (August 24, 2017). http://www.npr.org /2017/08/24/545812242/1-in-10-sanders-primary-voters-ended-up-support ing-trump-survey-finds.

"Lake Charles: A Case Study: With Massive New Industrial Investments and up to 25,000 New Workers Headed to Town, the Landscape of Lake Charles Is Changing Dramatically." Business Report (September 25, 2014). https:// www.businessreport.com/article/lake-charles-a-case-study-with-massive -new-industrial-investments-and-up-to-25000-new-workers-headed-to -town-the-landscape-of-lake-charles-is-changing-dramatically.

Lakoff, George, and Mark Johnson. Metaphors We Live By. Chicago: University of Chicago Press, 2003.

Lauderdale, Benjamin. "Nearly All Voters Are Going to Support the Same Party Again (Again)." YouGov (November 3, 2016). https://today.yougov.com/news /2016/11/03/nearly-all-voters-are-going-support-same-party-aga.

Law Center to Prevent Gun Violence and the Brady Campaign. 2013 State Scorecard: Why Gun Laws Matter. San Francisco: Law Center to Prevent Gun Violence, 2013. http://www.bradycampaign.org/sites/default/files/SCGLM -Final10-spreads-points.pdf.

"Lawsuit: Filipino Teachers Defrauded in International Labor Trafficking Scheme." LA.AFT.org. http://la.aft.org/news/lawsuit-filipino-teachers-de frauded-international-labor-trafficking-scheme.

League of Conservation Voters. Public Health Basis of the Clean Air Act, House Roll Call Vote 395. Washington, D.C.: League of Conservation Voters, 2012. http:// scorecard.lcv.org/roll-call-vote/2012-395-public-health-basis-clean-air-act.

LaHaye, Tim, and Jerry B. Jenkins. Left Behind: A Novel of the Earth's Last Days. Carroll Stream, IL: Tyndale House Publishers, 2011.

Leonhardt, David. "In Climbing Income Ladder, Location Matters." New York Times (July 22, 2013). http://www.nytimes.com/2013/07/22/business/in -climbing-icome-ladder-location-matters.html.

Lepore, Jill. The Whites of Their Eyes: The Tea Party's Revolution and the Battle over American History. Princeton, NJ: Princeton University Press, 2010.

Lester, James, James Franke, Ann Bowman, and Kenneth Kramer. "Hazardous Wastes, Politics, and Public Policy: A Comparative State Analysis." Western Political Quarterly 36 (1983): 255–85.

Lewis, Scott. "Boustany and Landry Fight Over Obamacare, Medicare, Negative Campaigns and Oilfield Jobs [Audio]." Cajun Radio (October 31, 2012). http://cajunradio.com/boustany-and-landry-fight-over-obamacare-medicare -negative-campaigns-and-oilfield-jobs-audio/?trackback=tsmclip.

Little, Amanda. "Will Conservatives Finally Embrace Clean Energy? *New Yorker* (October 29, 2015).

Lindsey, Hal. *The Late Great Planet Earth*. Grand Rapids, MI: Zondervan, 1970.

Liptak, Adam. "Supreme Court Blocks Louisiana Abortion Law." *New York Times* (March 4, 2016). http://www.nytimes.com/2016/03/05/us/politics/supreme -court-blocks-louisiana-abortion-law.html.

Longman, Phillip. "Wealth and Generations." *Washington Monthly* (June/July/ August 2015). http://www.washingtonmonthly.com/magazine/junejulyau gust_2015/features/wealth_and_generations055898.php.

"Lou Dobbs on the EPA: 'As It's Being Run Now, It Could Be Part of the Appa- ratchik of the Soviet Union.'" MediaMatters (June 6, 2011). http://media matters.org/video/2011/06/06/lou-dobbs-on-the-epa-as-its-being-run-now -it-co/180331.

"Louisiana Department of Environmental Quality. "Solid Waste Landfill Re- port" (accessed August 7, 2015). http://www.deq.louisiana.gov/portal /DIVISIONS/WastePermits/SolidWastePermits/SolidWasteLandfillRe port.aspx.

Louisiana Department of Health and Hospitals, Louisiana Department of Envi- ronmental Quality, Louisiana Department of Agriculture and Forestry, and Louisiana Department of Wildlife and Fisheries. *Protocol for Issuing Public Health Advisories for Chemical Contaminants in Recreationally Caught Fish and Shellfish*. Baton Rouge, LA: Office of Public Health, 2012, 24. http:// www.dhh.louisiana.gov/assets/oph/Center-EH/envepi/fishadvisory/Docu ments/LA_Fish_Protocol_FINAL_Feb_2012_updated_links.pdf.

Louisiana Department of Health and Hospitals for the Agency for Toxic Sub- stances and Disease Registry. *Health Consultation: Calcasieu Estuary Sed- iment Sample Evaluation, Calcasieu Parish, Louisiana, EPA Facility ID: LA0002368173*. Baton Rouge, LA: Office of Public Health, 2005.

―――. *Public Health Assessment, Initial/Public Comment Release, Review of Data from the 2010 EPA Mossville Site Investigation*. Baton Rouge, LA: Of- fice of Public Health, 2013.

Louisiana Department of Health and Hospitals. "Health Department Advises 'Take Precautions When Swimming'" (May 21, 2014). http://new.dhh.louisiana .gov/index.cfm/communication/viewcampaign/896?uid=gE&nowrap=1.

Louisiana Economic Development. "Louisiana: At the Epicenter of the U.S. In- dustrial Rebirth" (accessed January 4, 2014). http://www.opportunitylouisi ana.com/index.cfm/newsroom/detail/265.

Louisiana Law Regarding the Unlawful Sale, Purchase and Possession of Alcoholic Beverages. Louisiana R.S.14:93.10–14.

Louisiana Seafood Marketing and Promotion Board. "By the Numbers: Louisiana's Ecology" (accessed April 8, 2015). http://www.louisianaseafood.com/ecology.

"Louisiana State Profile." *National Rifle Association* (November 12, 2014; accessed July 31, 2015). https://www.nraila.org/gun-laws/state-gun-laws/louisiana.

Luke, Ronald T. "Managing Community Acceptance of Major Industrial Projects." *Coastal Zone Management Journal* 7 (1980): 271–96.

Lustgarten, Abrahm. "Injection Wells: The Poison Beneath Us." *ProPublica* (June 21, 2012). https://www.propublica.org/article/injection-wells-the-poison-beneath-us.

MacGillis, Alec. "Who Turned My Blue State Red?" *New York Times* (November 20, 2015).

Mann, Catherine L. "Environment and Trade: Do Stricter Environmental Policies Hurt Expert Competitiveness?" Organisation for Economic Co-operation and Development. http://www.oecd.org/economy/greeneco/do-stricter-environmental-policies-hurt-export-competitiveness.htm.

Mann, Robert. "Residents of Bayou Corne Ask, Where Are You, Bobby Jindal?" December 16, 2012. http://bobmannblog.com/2012/12/16/residents-of-bayou-corne-ask-where-are-you-bobby-jindal.

Margolis, Michele F., and Michael W. Sances. "Who Really Gives? Partisanship and Charitable Giving in the United States." Working paper, Social Science Research Network (2013): 1–17. http://papers.ssrn.com/sol3/papers.cfm?abstract_id=2148033.

Martin, Isaac William. *Rich People's Movements: Grassroots Campaigns to Untax the One Percent.* New York: Oxford University Press, 2013.

Martinez, Yolanda. "Environmentalists Allege Constitutional Violation in Permitting Gas Storages Salt Dome Construction in Lake Peigneur." *Louisiana Record* (July 24, 2013).

Mather, Mark. *Fact Sheet: The Decline in U.S. Fertility.* Washington, D.C.: Population Reference Bureau, 2012. http://www.prb.org/publications/datasheets/2012/world-population-data-sheet/fact-sheet-us-population.aspx.

Mayer, Jane. "Covert Operations." *New Yorker* (August 30, 2010).

———. *Dark Money: The Hidden History of the Billionaires Behind the Rise of the Radical Right.* New York: Random House, 2016.

McAdam, Doug. *Freedom Summer.* Oxford: Oxford University Press, 1990.

McKinsey Global Institute. "A Future That Works: Automation, Employment and Productivity" (January 2017). https://www.mckinsey.com/business-functions/digital-mckinsey/our-insights/where-machines-could-replace-humans-and-where-they-cant-yet.

"Meet the Staff." First Pentecostal Church, Lake Charles (accessed August 28, 2014). http://firstpentecostalchurchlc.org/about-us/meet-the-staff.

Meyer, Stephen M. "Endangered Species Listings and State Economic Performance." MIT Project on Environmental Politics and Policy, 1995.

———. "Environmentalism and Economic Prosperity: An Update." MIT Project on Environmental Politics and Policy, 1993.

———. "Environmentalism and Economic Prosperity: Testing the Environmental Impact Hypothesis." MIT Project on Environmental Politics and Policy, 1992.

Meyers, Scottie Lee. "Biggest Job Killer in Manufacturing Industry? Automation." Wisconsin Public Radio (January 26, 2017). https://www.wpr.org/biggest -job-killer-manufacturing-industry-automation.

Misrach, Richard, and Kate Orff. *Petrochemical America.* New York: Aperture Foundation, 2012.

Mitchell, David J. "Texas Brine Shifts Blame to Occidental Petroleum, Others for Causing Bayou Corne Sinkhole." *The Advocate* (July 9, 2015). http://thead vocate.com/news/ascension/12870889-123/texas-brine-shifts-blame-to.

Mitchell, Stacy, and Fred Clements. "How Washington Punishes Small Business." *Wall Street Journal* (May 7, 2015).

Mizell-Nelson, Michael. "Nurturing the Drive-Through Daiquiri." *Louisiana Cultural Vistas* (March 12, 2015).

Montopoli, Brian. "Tea Party Supporters: Who They Are and What They Believe." CBS News (December 14, 2012).

Morgenstern, Richard D., William A. Pizer, and Jhih-Shyang Shih. "Jobs Versus the Environment: An Industry-Level Perspective." *Journal of Environmental Economics and Management* 43 (2002): 412–36.

Moyers, Bill. "Welcome to Doomsday." *New York Review of Books* (March 24, 2005).

Mulhere, Kaitlin. "In the Face of Colossal Cuts." *Inside Higher Ed* (April 27, 2015). https://www.insidehighered.com/news/2015/04/27/anxiety-over-massive -proposed-cuts-louisianas-colleges-felt-across-state.

Natural Resources Defense Council. "The BP Oil Disaster at One Year." Washington, D.C.: Natural Resources Defense Council, 2011.

"New Tax Foundation Ranking Indicates Dramatic Improvement in Louisiana's Business Tax Competitiveness." Louisiana Economic Development (February 29, 2012; accessed January 5, 2014). http://www.opportunitylouisiana .com/index.cfm/newsroom/detail/175.

"Next Time We See Him, We Might Have to Kill Him: Trump Fan on Punching

Black Protester." RT.com (March 11, 2016). https://www.rt.com/usa/335188
-trump-protester-punched-arrest.

Ng, Christina. "Louisiana Boat Disappears into Sinkhole, Workers Rescued."
ABC News (August 16, 2012). http://abcnews.go.com/US/louisiana-sink
hole-engulfs-boat-workers-rescued/story?id=17021557.

"Not All Republicans Think Alike About Global Warming." Yale Project on Climate Change Communication. http://environment.yale.edu/climate-com
munication/article/not-all-republicans-think-alike-about-global-warming.

O'Connor, Arthur. "Political Polarization and Environmental Inequality: A Pilot
Study of Pollution Release Amounts and Practices in 'Red' Versus 'Blue'
States." *International Environmental Review* 13, no. 4: 308–22.

O'Donoghue, Julia. "Louisiana Failed to Collect Millions in Oil and Gas Taxes."
Times-Picayune (December 2, 2013). http://www.nola.com/politics/index
.ssf/2013/12/louisiana_oil_and_gas_taxes.html.

Office of the Inspector General. *Audit Report: EPA Region 6 Needs to Improve
Oversight of Louisiana's Environmental Programs.* Washington, D.C.: Environmental Protection Agency, 2003. http://www.epa.gov/oig/reports/2003
/2003-p-0005.pdf.

———. *EPA Must Improve Oversight of State Enforcement.* Washington, D.C.: Environmental Protection Agency, 2011. http://www.epa.gov/oig/reports/2012
/20111209-12-P-0113.pdf.

Oldham, Taki. *The Billionaires' Tea Party.* https://www.youtube.com/watch?v=
-zBOQL5lZuU.

Pager, Devah. "The Mark of a Criminal Record." *American Journal of Sociology*
(2003): 937–975.

Parker, Christopher S., and Matt A. Barreto. *Change They Can't Believe In: The
Tea Party and Reactionary Politics in America.* Princeton, NJ: Princeton University Press, 2013.

Pavlov, Pavel. "US' Axiall Declares Force Majeure on VCM from PHH Monomers
Plant." *Platts* (December 23, 2013). http://www.platts.com/latest-news/pet
rochemicals/houston/us-axiall-declares-force-majeure-on-vcm-from-219
90566.

Pedersen, Chris. "Sasol Clears Major Hurdle to Build America's First GTP Plant."
Oilprice.com (September 4, 2014). http://oilprice.com/Energy/Natural
-Gas/Sasol-Clears-Major-Hurdle-to-Build-Americas-First-GTL-Plant.html.

Peterson, Erica. "Silicon Hollow: More Tech Jobs Coming to Eastern Kentucky." WFPL (March 15, 2017). http://wfpl.org/more-tech-jobs-coming-to
-eastern-kentucky.

Phillips, Justin. "Calcasieu, Cameron Areas 'on Bubble' with EPA for Air Quality." *American Press* (July 11, 2014). http://www.americanpress.com/news /local/Air-quality.

Phillips-Fein, Kim. *Invisible Hands: The Businessmen's Crusade Against the New Deal.* New York: W.W. Norton & Company, 2007.

Picchi, Aimee. "The Robot Revolution Will Take 5 Million Jobs from Humans." CBS News (January 18, 2016). https://www.cbsnews.com/news/the-robot -revolution-will-take-5-million-jobs-from-humans.

Piketty, Thomas. *Capital in the Twenty-First Century.* Boston: Harvard University Press, 2014.

Piketty, Thomas, and Emmanuel Saez. *2007 Average Incomes, U.S. 1980–2012* (in real 2014 dollars). The World Top Incomes Database. http://topincomes .g-mond.parisschoolofeconomics.edu.

Porter, Michael, and C. Van der Linde. "Toward a New Conception of the Environment–Competitiveness Relationship." *Journal of Economic Perspectives* 9, no. 4 (1995): 97–118.

Povich, Deborah, Brandon Roberts, and Mark Mather. *Low-Income Working Families: The Racial/Ethnic Divide.* Working Poor Families Project and Population Reference Bureau, 2015. http://www.workingpoorfamilies.org /wp-content/uploads/2015/03/WPFP-2015-Report_Racial-Ethnic-Divide .pdf.

"Project HAL: Historical American Lynching Data Collection Project." University of North Carolina–Wilmington. http://people.uncw.edu/hinese/HAL /HAL%20Web%20Page.htm.

Pugh, Allison. *The Tumbleweed Society: Working and Caring in an Age of Insecurity.* London: Oxford University Press, 2015.

Regan-White, Heather. "Westlake City Council Reaches Agreement with Sasol on Expansion Costs." *Sulphur Daily News* (November 25, 2015). http://www .sulphurdailynews.com/article/20151125/NEWS/151129875.

Reich, Robert B. *Saving Capitalism: For the Many, Not the Few.* New York: Knopf, 2015.

"Remarks by the President to the Nation on the BP Oil Spill." White House Press Release (June 15, 2010). https://www.whitehouse.gov/the-press-office/re marks-president-nation-bp-oil-spill.

Rich, Frank. "No Sympathy for the Hillbilly." *New York Magazine* (March 19, 2017). http://nymag.com/daily/intelligencer/2017/03/frank-rich-no-sympathy -for-the-hillbilly.html.

Ridgeway, James. "Environmental Espionage: Inside a Chemical Company's Louisiana Spy Op." *Mother Jones* (May 20, 2008). http://www.motherjones.com

/environment/2008/05/environmental-espionage-inside-chemical-compa
nys-louisiana-spy-op.

Right to Know Network. *Biennial Reporting System Quantities by State for 2011: Waste Received and Managed.* Washington, D.C.: Center for Effective Government, 2015. http://www.rtknet.org/db/brs/tables.php?tabtype=t3&year =2011&subtype=a&sorttype=rcv.

Robertson, Campbell. "In Louisiana, the Poor Lack Legal Defense." *New York Times* (March 20, 2016).

Rogers, Will. "Our Land, Up for Grabs." Editorial. *New York Times* (April 2, 2015; accessed August 16, 2015). http://www.nytimes.com/2015/04/02/opinion /our-land-up-for-grabs.html.

Rosenthal, Lawrence, and Christine Trost (eds.). *Steep: The Precipitous Rise of the Tea Party.* Berkeley: University of California Press, 2012.

Roysler, Deirdre. *Race and the Invisible Hand: How White Networks Exclude Black Men from Blue Collar Jobs.* Berkeley: University of California Press, 2003.

Rudowitz, Robin, Laura Snyder, and Vernon K. Smith. "Medicaid Enrollment & Spending Growth: FY 2015 & 2016." Henry J. Kaiser Foundation (October 15, 2015). http://kff.org/medicaid/issue-brief/medicaid-enrollment -spending-growth-fy-2015-2016.

Russell, George. "Exclusive: EPA Ponders Expanded Regulatory Power in Name of 'Sustainable Development.'" Fox News commentary (December 19, 2011). http://www.foxnews.com/politics/2011/12/19/epa-ponders-expanded -regulatory-power-in-name-sustainable-development.

Russell, Gordon. "Giving Away Louisiana: An Overview." *The Advocate,* Special Reports (November 26, 2014). http://blogs.theadvocate.com/special reports/2014/11/26/giving-away-louisiana.

Santhanam, Laura. "Report: Fox News Enlists Fossil Fuel Industry to Smear EPA Carbon Pollution Standards." MediaMatters (June 6, 2014). http:// mediamatters.org/research/2014/06/06/report-fox-news-enlists-fossil-fuel -industry-to/199622.

Savchuck, Katia. "Are America's Richest Families Republican or Democrat?" *Forbes* (July 9, 2014).

Schell, Jonathan. *The Time of Illusion.* New York: Vintage Books, 1975.

Scherer, Glenn. "Christian-Right Views Are Swaying Politicians and Threatening the Environment." Grist.org (October 28, 2004). http://grist.org/article /scherer-christian/.

Schleifstein, Mark. "Louisiana Politician Scott Angelle Chosen to Head Federal Offshore Oil Safety Agency." *Times-Picayune* (May 23, 2017). http://www.nola .com/politics/index.ssf/2017/05/scott_angelle_named_head_of_fe.html.

Schmidt, Theresa. "Condea Vista Hired Spies." KPLCTV (May 29, 2008). http://www.kplctv.com/story/8399515/condea-vista-hired-spies.

———. "Spy Targets Call for Action." KPLCTV (May 30, 2008). http://www.kplctv.com/story/8404443/spy-targets-call-for-action.

———. "Motion Filed to Force Disclosure of Spy Details." KPLCTV (June 4, 2008). http://www.kplctv.com/story/8433538/motion-filed-to-force-disclosure-of-spy-details.

———. "Attorneys Seek Disclosure of Spy Operation." KPLCTV (December 3, 2008). http://www.kplctv.com/story/9366858/attorneys-seek-disclosure-of-spy-operation.

Schor, Juliet. *The Overspent American: Why We Want What We Don't Need.* New York: Harper Perennial, 1999.

Schouten, Fredreka. "Koch Brothers Set $889 Million Budget for 2016." *USA Today* (January 27, 2015). http://www.usatoday.com/story/news/politics/2015/01/26/koch-brothers-network-announces-889-million-budget-for-next-two-years/22363809.

Schulman, Daniel. *Sons of Wichita: How the Koch Brothers Became America's Most Powerful and Private Dynasty.* New York: Grand Central Publishing, 2015.

Schwab, Jim. *Front Porch Politics: The Forgotten Heyday of American Activism in the 1970s and 1980s.* New York: Farrar Strauss, 2013.

Scott, Loren C. *The Energy Sector: A Giant Economic Engine for the Louisiana Economy.* Baton Rouge: Mid-Continent Oil and Gas Association, 2014. http://www.scribd.com/doc/233387193/The-Energy-Sector-A-Giant-Economic-Engine-for-the-Louisiana-Economy.

———. *The Energy Sector: Still a Giant Economic Engine for the Louisiana Economy—an Update.* Louisiana Mid-Continent Oil and Gas Association and Grow Louisiana Coalition report, 2014. http://www.growlouisianacoalition.com/blog/wp-content/uploads/2014/07/Loren-Scott-Study.pdf.

Seib, Gerald. "How Trump's Army Is Transforming the GOP." *Wall Street Journal* (February 23, 2016).

Seydlitz, Ruth, and Shirley Laska. "Social and Economic Impacts of Petroleum 'Boom and Bust' Cycles." Prepared by the Environmental Social Science Research Institute, University of New Orleans. OCS Study MMS 94-0016. U.S. Dept. of the Interior, Minerals Mgmt. Service, Gulf of Mexico OCS Regional Office. New Orleans, LA, 1993.

Shauk, Zain, "Oil CEO: Humans Are Involved with Climate Change." *Fuel Fix* (May 15, 2013). http://fuelfix.com/blog/2013/05/15/no-doubts-on-need-to-act-on-climate-change.

Sheppard, Kate. "BP's Bad Breakup: How Toxic Is Corexit?" *Mother Jones* (September/October 2010). http://www.motherjones.com/environment/2010/09/bp-ocean-dispersant-corexit.

Silverstein, Ken. "Dirty South: Letter from Baton Rouge." *Harpers* (November 2013), 45–56.

Skelley, Geoffrey. "Just How Many Obama 2012–Trump 2016 Voters Were There?" University of Virginia Center for Politics, Sabato's Crystal Ball (June 1, 2017). http://www.centerforpolitics.org/crystalball/articles/just-how-many-obama-2012-trump-2016-voters-were-there.

Skocpol, Theda, and Vanessa Williamson. *The Tea Party and the Remaking of Republican Conservatism.* New York: Oxford University Press, 2012.

Snell, John. "As More of Coastal Louisiana Is Lost, Official Map Makers Erase Names." WorldNow (April 21, 2014). http://apmobile.worldnow.com/story/24807691/as-more-of-coastal-louisiana-is-lost-mapmakers-erase-names.

———. "Despite Land Loss, Native American Community Clings to Life Along the Mississippi River." WorldNow (March 4, 2015). http://apmobile.worldnow.com/story/26559685/despite-land-loss-native-american-community-clings-to-life-along-the-mississippi-river.

Social Science Research Council. *The Measure of America: American Human Development Report 2008–2009.* Brooklyn, NY: Measure of America, 2009.

———. *The Measure of America: HD Index and Supplemental Indicators by State.* 2013–2014 Dataset. Brooklyn, NY: Measure of America, 2014.

"South Dakota House: Abolish U.S. Department of Education." TeaParty.org. (January 29, 2015; accessed August 16, 2015). http://www.teaparty.org/south-dakota-house-abolish-u-s-dept-education-80153.

Spatig-Amerikaner, Ary. *Unequal Education: Federal Loophole Enables Lower Spending on Students of Color.* Washington, D.C.: Center for American Progress, 2012. https://www.americanprogress.org/wp-content/uploads/2012/08/UnequalEduation.pdf.

Spencer, Malia. "Fire Damages PPG Industries Plant in Louisiana." *Pittsburgh Business Times* (December 27, 2012). http://www.bizjournals.com/pittsburgh/news/2012/12/27/plant-fire-causes-force-majeure-for-ppg.html.

Staff. "Where's Bobby Jindal Now? In Global Investments," *Greater Baton Rouge Business Report* (August 15, 2017). https://www.businessreport.com/article/jindal-takes-new-role-ares-management.

Steingraber, Sandra. *Living Downstream: A Scientist's Personal Investigation of Cancer and the Environment.* New York: Vintage, 1998.

Stoler, Ann Laura. "Colonial Aphasia: Race and Disabled Histories in France." *Public Culture* 23, no. 1 (2011): 121–56.

————. "Imperial Debris: Reflections on Ruins and Ruination." *Cultural Anthropology* 23, no. 2 (2008): 191–219.

Subra, Wilma. *Results of the Health Survey of Mossville Residents and Chemicals and Industrial Sources of Chemicals Associated with Mossville Residents Medical Symptoms and Conditions.* New Iberia, LA: Subra Company, 2008.

Sunstein, Cass R. "'Partyism' Now Trumps Racism." *BloombergView* (September 22, 2014). http://www.bloombergview.com/articles/2014-09-22/partyism-now-trumps-racism.

Swidler, Ann. "Cultural Constructions of Modern Individualism." Paper delivered at Meeting of American Sociological Association (August 23, 1992).

Tavernise, Sabrina. "Life Spans Shrink for Least Educated Whites in U.S." *New York Times* (September 20, 2012).

Taylor, Kate. "Trump's Pick for Labor Secretary May Have Saved a Fast-Food Chain—But Workers Question if He's Right for the Job." *Business Insider* (January 21, 2017). http://www.businessinsider.com/puzders-business-methods-raise-quesions-2017-1.

Templet, Paul H. "Defending the Public Domain, Pollution, Subsidies and Poverty," in *Natural Assets: Democratizing Environmental Ownership,* edited by James K. Boyce and Barry G. Shelley. Washington, D.C.: Island Press, 2003.

————. "Defending the Public Domain: Pollution, Subsidies and Poverty." PERI Working Paper No. 12 (January 2001). http://ssrn.com/abstract=333280 or http://dx.doi.org/10.2139/ssrn.333280.

————. "Grazing the Commons: Externalities, Subsidies and Economic Development." *Ecological Economics* 12 (February 1995): 141–59.

————. "Integrating Resource Conservation and Economic Development, People First: Developing Sustainable Communities." Working paper (March 1997).

Terkel, Amanda. "GOP Platform in Years Past Supported Equal Rights, Higher Wages, Funding for the Arts." *Huffington Post* (September 24, 2012). http://www.huffingtonpost.com/2012/09/04/gop-platform_n_1852733.html.

Thompson, Richard. "Giving Away Louisiana: Industrial Tax Incentives." *The Advocate* (December 11, 2014). http://blogs.theadvocate.com/specialreports/2014/12/03/giving-away-louisiana-industrial-tax-incentives.

"Three out of Four Believe Climate Change Is Occurring: Views of Key Energy Issues Are Shaped by Partisan Politics." *University of Texas News* (October 20, 2015). http://news.utexas.edu/2015/10/20/views-of-key-energy-issues-are-shaped-by-partisan-politics.

Thurman, Todd. "Charles Krauthammer Destroys Global Warming Myths in 89 Seconds." *Daily Signal* (February 18, 2014). http://blog.heritage.org/2014/02/18/charles-krauthammer-destroys-global-warming-myths-89-seconds.

"Trump Ends Wild Day on Campaign Trail by Calling for Protesters' Arrests." CNN Politics (March 13, 2016). http://www.cnn.com/2016/03/12/politics /donald-trump-protests.

United Health Foundation. *America's Health Rankings, 2015 Annual Report.* http://www.americashealthrankings.org.

U.S. Census Bureau. *5-Year American Community Survey* [*2009–2013 data*]. Washington, D.C.: U.S. Census, 2013 (accessed August 17, 2015). http:// factfinder.census.gov/faces/nav/jsf/pages/guided_search.xhtml.

———. "State Government Tax Collections: 2014." Table STC005 (accessed December 11, 2015). http://factfinder.census.gov/bkmk/table/1.0/en/STC /2014/STC005.

Veblen, Thorstein. *The Theory of the Leisure Class.* New York: Macmillan, 1899.

Vogel, Kenneth P. *Big Money: 2.5 Billion Dollars, One Suspicious Vehicle, and a Pimp—on the Trail of the Ultra-Rich Hijacking American Politics.* New York: Public Affairs/Perseus Group, 2014.

Walsh, Katherine Kramer. "Putting Inequality in Its Place: Rural Consciousness and the Power of Perspective." *American Political Science Review* 106, no. 3 (2012): 517–32.

Wei, Jackie. "Governor LePage Undermines Maine's Green-Building Economy, Sets Back Sustainable Forestry." NRDC.org (December 12, 2011). https:// www.nrdc.org/media/2011/111212.

Wethe, David. "Robots Are Taking Over Oil Rigs." *Bloomberg* (January 24, 2017). https://www.bloomberg.com/news/articles/2017-01-24/robots-are-taking -over-oil-rigs-as-roughnecks-become-expendable.

White, Jack E. "The Poorest Place in America." *Time* (August 15, 1994).

Williams, Rob, Shane Gero, Lars Bejder, John Calambokidis, Scott D. Krauss, David Lusseau, Andrew J. Read, and Jooke Robbins. "Underestimating the Damage: Interpreting Cetacean Carcass Recoveries in the Context of the Deepwater Horizon/BP Incident." *Conservation Letters* 4, no. 3 (2011): 228–33.

Wilson, Xerxes A. "Mysterious Tremors Raise Questions." DailyComet.com (October 4, 2012; accessed November 19, 2015). http://www.dailycomet.com /article/20121004/ARTICLES/121009798.

Wines, Michael. "Fish Embryos Exposed to Oil from BP Spill Develop Deformities, a Study Finds." *New York Times* (March 25, 2014).

Wolbrecht, Christina. *The Politics of Women's Rights: Parties, Positions, and Change.* Princeton, NJ: Princeton University Press, 2000.

Wold, Amy. "Washed Away." *The Advocate.* http://theadvocate.com/home/57829 41-125/washed-away.

Wolf, Vicki. "Salt Dome Instability Caused by Bayou Corne Sinkhole Tragedy and Others." *Clean* (Citizen's League for Environmental Action Now). http://www.cleanhouston.org/misc/salt_dome.htm.

Wolff, Henry. "Race and the 2012 Election." *American Renaissance* (November 9, 2012). http://www.amren.com/features/2012/11/race-and-the-2012-election.

Woodard, Colin. *American Nations: A History of the Eleven Rival Regional Cultures of North America.* New York: Penguin Books, 2011.

World Health Organization. *Global Health Observatory Data Repository* [*2013 data*] (accessed August 12, 2015). http://apps.who.int/gho/data/node.main.688.

WWL-TV Staff. "Poll: Obama Loses Support in La.; Perry, Romney, Cain Close on GOP Side." WWL-TV (October 13, 2011). http://www.wwltv.com/story /news/politics/2014/08/29/14408560.

Zheng, Lingwen, and Mildred Warner. "Business Incentive Use Among U.S. Local GBovernments: A Story of Accountability and Policy Learning." *Economic Development Quarterly* 24, no. 4 (2010): 325–336.

Index

Reading Group Guide

1. Early in the book, when introducing her important idea of "empathy walls," Arlie Russell Hochschild mentions that in 1960 fewer than 5 percent of Americans would have been disturbed if their child married a member of the opposite political party, while in 2010 over 30 percent would find it troubling. Clearly this speaks to our ever-increasing political divide. Have you yourself experienced or observed this phenomenon in your community? (p. 6)

2. Hochschild argues that our political split has widened because "the right has moved right—not because the left has moved left." Do you agree or disagree? Is her evidence persuasive? What are the implications for our democracy? (p. 7)

3. What does Hochschild consider "the Great Paradox" and why is Louisiana an extreme example? (p. 8)

4. Early on as well as later in the book, Hochschild mentions the friendship of Sally Cappel and Shirley Slack and says she believes "their friendship models what our country needs to forge: the capacity to connect across difference." Do you agree? Do you have friends from across the political divide? What challenges do these "across-the-divide" friendships present? (pp. 13, 240)

5. Discuss the story of Lee Sherman—how does he represent "the Great Paradox through a keyhole"? How is it possible for an environmentalist whistle blower to also be a member of the Tea Party? (p. 33)

6. When telling the story of Harold Areno, Hochschild quotes him as saying, "If you shoot an endangered brown pelican, they'll put you in jail. But if a company kills the brown pelican by poisoning the fish he eats? They let it go. I think they *overregulate* the *bottom* because it's *harder* to regulate the *top*." Hochschild mentions the brown pelican throughout the book—how does the pelican function as an important motif in the book? (pp. 52, 138, 212)

7. When spending time with the General, whom Hochschild calls an "empathy wall leaper," she writes that Louisiana residents prize the freedom to do certain things but resent the *freedom from* things like gun violence or toxic pollution, even when such restrictions might improve their lives. How does the General deal with what he calls this "psychological program"? (p. 71)

8. Hochschild provides overwhelming evidence that establishes a correlation between pollution and red states. She also discusses a report from the 1980s that helped identify communities that would not resist "locally undesirable land use." Do you think she's right to connect this profile of the "least resistant personality" with the General's idea of the "psychological program"? (p. 81, Appendix B)

9. In a moment of feeling stuck on her own side of the empathy wall, Hochschild asks Mike Schaff what the federal government has done that he feels grateful for. What do you make of his answer and the idea that the less you depend on the government, the higher your

status? Do you feel one's status is diminished by receiving government help of any sort? Do others you know feel this way—and why? Do you think people generally feel less gratitude to the government today than in the past? What are you grateful for from the government? (pp. 113–114)

10. Discuss the role of religion in the lives of the individuals Hochschild profiles in determining their political choices, priorities, and outlook. How does it contribute to the Great Paradox? What do you make of Hochschild's observation that the churches she visited "seemed to focus more on a person's moral strength to endure than on the will to change the circumstances that called on that strength"? (pp. 124, 179)

11. Hochschild says that Fox News exerts a powerful influence over her Tea Party friends—what is it about Fox that appeals to them and what do they find troubling about liberal commentators? Is all media biased? What media do you read, watch, or listen to, and do you think it is impartial? (p. 126)

12. In the chapter "The Deep Story," Hochschild presents the perspective of people she meets to understand and explain their point of view, focusing on feelings and emotions. Does this ring true to you? Hochschild says we all have a "deep story"—do you agree? What is yours? (p. 135)

13. In this same chapter, Hochschild suggests that blue-collar Americans have felt marginalized in a number of ways, including by the election of President Obama. How do you think these feelings culminated in the election of Trump? What role did racism possibly play in the election? Later, Hochschild attends a Trump rally—why does she call him an "emotions candidate"? (p. 140, 225)

14. How does Hochschild's idea of racism differ from Mike Schaff's? Which resonates more with you? (pp. 147)

15. Throughout the book, Hochschild discusses the Great Paradox mainly in terms of the environment. But she also notes that by embracing the free market—which favors big business—Tea Party members are often working against their own interests, since many of these members own or work for small businesses. Why does their deep story make it hard for them to see this? Must we choose between the free market and a healthy environment? (p. 150)

16. Hochschild presents Mike and Donny's argument about the I-10 bridge as dialogue—how does this capture the Great Paradox? If you could enter the conversation, what would you say to Mike and/or Donny? (p. 185)

17. What role does memory play in Hochschild's story of the people she meets with regard to the environmental disasters, the development of industry, and the way things used to be? Looking at Hochschild's visit with Mayor Hardey, how do industry and local government allow the potential disaster and pollution to re-occur in the name of business? What is it about the residents' deep story that allows them to be susceptible to "structural amnesia"? (pp. 51, 90, 198)

18. How does Hochschild explain Tea Party members' identification with Trump and the 1 percent? After reading *Strangers in Their Own Land*, are there ideas or stories that you can draw from the book that help you understand Trump's victory? (p. 217)

19. What does Hochschild mean by the "Northern strategy"—and how does it fit into the historical narrative she provides? She suggests that

the Southern legacy of secession has been applied to social class: it's not that the South is seceding from the North but that the rich are seceding from the poor. What do you make of this point? (p. 220)

20. By the end of the book, Hochschild expresses admiration for her new Tea Party friends, mentioning their capacity for loyalty, sacrifice, and endurance. Are there other notable traits you became aware of while reading the book? (p. 234)

21. Many of the people Hochschild meets are worried about jobs and blame government regulations for getting in the way of jobs. Yet the petrochemical companies in Louisiana are for the most part owned by foreign companies, so the money leaves the state and the jobs are often held by temporary workers from the Philippines or Mexico. How do you explain this disconnect?

22. Did the book make you feel hopeful about climbing the empathy wall and the possibility of bridging the political divide with people in your own community?

23. In Appendix C, Hochschild provides some startling research that contradicts more than a few commonly held perceptions. For example, 40 percent of people do not work for the federal and state government; the correct number is 1.9 percent. And it's not true that "the more environmental regulations we have, the fewer jobs." Why are the perceptions of some of the people Hochschild writes about so deeply at odds with the research and facts?

24. Hochschild argues that left and right focus on different areas of conflict or "flashpoints." Do you agree? (p. 236)

25. Hochschild says that our deep stories lead us to embrace certain aspects of reality and avoid others. What aspect of reality does the right tend to avoid? What about the left?

26. Hochschild argues that attached to the deep story of the right and left are different strategies for coping with the new trends in globalization, which are frightening to both sides. Which resonates more with you? Do you think different versions of the deep story apply to voters in rural areas or rust belt towns? (p. 236)

27. Some readers and critics have reported having been changed by the experience of reading *Strangers in Their Own Land*. Did the book change the way you see the world or think or feel?

Also Available from The New Press

The Climate Swerve: Reflections on Mind, Hope, and Survival
by Robert Jay Lifton

From "one of the world's foremost thinkers" (Bill Moyers), a profound, hopeful, and timely call for an emerging new collective consciousness to combat climate change

"A powerful and well-reasoned call to action."

—*Kirkus Reviews*

Cutting School: Privatization, Segregation, and the End of Public Education **by Noliwe Rooks**

A timely indictment of the corporate takeover of education and the privatization—and profitability—of separate and unequal schools, published at a critical time in the dismantling of public education in America

"Poignant and plainly stated, Rooks's thorough narrative of socioeconomics urges greater criticism and thoughtfulness about education reform in the 21st century."

—*Publishers Weekly* (starred)

The Hamlet Fire: A Tragic Story of Cheap Food, Cheap Government, and Cheap Lives **by Bryant Simon**

A "gifted writer" (*Chicago Tribune*) uses a long-forgotten factory fire in small-town North Carolina to show how cut-rate food and cheap labor have become the new American norm

"Captivating and brilliantly conceived . . . [*The Hamlet Fire*] will provide readers with insights into our current national politics."

—*The Washington Post*

Hypercapitalism: The Modern Economy, Its Values, and How to Change Them **by Larry Gonick and Tim Kasser**

From the bestselling cartoonist of *The Cartoon History of the Universe* comes an explosive takedown of capitalism

"Accompanied with breezily quirky cartooning that cleverly fuses art and hard information, Gonick's latest is another triumph: a new self-education classic for these troubled times."

—*Publishers Weekly*

Lower Ed: The Troubling Rise of For-Profit Colleges in the New Economy **by Tressie McMillan Cottom**

A former insider discloses the story behind for-profit schools to explain the exorbitant price tags, the questionable credentials, and the lose-lose options for Americans seeking a better life

"With great compassion and analytical rigor, McMillan Cottom questions the fundamental narrative of American education policy, that a postsecondary degree always guarantees a better life."

—*The New York Times Book Review*

Making It: Why Manufacturing Still Matters **by Louis Uchitelle**

From the longtime *New York Times* economics correspondent, a closely reported argument for the continuing importance of industry for American prosperity

"An elegant swan song for a lost era of U.S. manufacturing greatness. . . . Uchitelle convincingly debunks explanations that blame supposedly unskilled workers for their own plight."

—*Publishers Weekly*

Out of Sight: The Long and Disturbing Story of Corporations Outsourcing Catastrophe **by Erik Loomis**

In the tradition of Naomi Klein, a powerful new analysis of labor and environmental harm in the age of globalization by an award-winning scholar and public intellectual

"This captivating book offers many damning examples of corporate sociopathy while skillfully delving into the complex network of international trade agreements that facilitate it; at the same time, the book also charts a history of resistance and a path forward, away from catastrophe."

—*Choice*

Right Out of California: The 1930s and the Big Business Roots of Modern Conservatism by Kathryn S. Olmsted

A new history of modern American conservatism, uncovering its roots in the turbulent agricultural fields of depression-era California

"Olmsted's vivid, accomplished narrative really belongs to the historiography of the left . . . as her strong research shows, race and gender prejudice informed or deformed, almost the whole of American social and cultural life in the 1930s and was as common on the left as on the right."

—*The New York Times Book Review*

State of Resistance: What California's Dizzying Descent and Remarkable Resurgence Mean for America's Future by Manuel Pastor

A leading sociologist's brilliant and revelatory argument that the future of politics, work, immigration, and more may be found in California

"Teaching and research about civil society needs to focus not just on big names and famous leaders—but on the everyday people and daily practices that stitch together society and make change possible."

—Manuel Pastor

Teeth: The Story of Beauty, Inequality, and the Struggle for Oral Health in America by Mary Otto

From a veteran *Washington Post* journalist, the view from inside America's mouth—and what our teeth reveal about inequality today

"[Otto infuses] what could be a mundane topic with quirky history, heart-wrenching real-life stories, and prose that is . . . poetic . . . this harrowing book pulls at the heartstrings. It's a must-read for anyone who cares about public health policy."

—*Newsday*

Publishing in the Public Interest

Thank you for reading this book published by The New Press. The New Press is a nonprofit, public interest publisher. New Press books and authors play a crucial role in sparking conversations about the key political and social issues of our day.

We hope you enjoyed this book and that you will stay in touch with The New Press. Here are a few ways to stay up to date with our books, events, and the issues we cover:

- Sign up at www.thenewpress.com/subscribe to receive updates on New Press authors and issues and to be notified about local events
- Like us on Facebook: www.facebook.com/newpressbooks
- Follow us on Twitter: www.twitter.com/thenewpress

Please consider buying New Press books for yourself; for friends and family; or to donate to schools, libraries, community centers, prison libraries, and other organizations involved with the issues our authors write about.

The New Press is a 501(c)(3) nonprofit organization. You can also support our work with a tax-deductible gift by visiting www.thenewpress .com/donate.